Pitt Latin American Series

Pitt Latin American Series
James M. Malloy, Editor

RECENT TITLES

The Constitution of Tyranny: Regimes of Exception in Spanish America
Brian Loveman

Domestic and Foreign Finance in Modern Peru, 1850–1950: Financing Visions of Development
Alfonso W. Quiroz

Economic Management and Economic Development in Peru and Colombia
Rosemary Thorp

Education and Society in Latin America
Orlando Albornoz

Institutions, Parties, and Coalitions in Argentine Politics
Luigi Manzetti

Frondizi and the Politics of Developmentalism in Argentina, 1955–62
Celia Szusterman

Military Rule and Transition in Ecuador, 1972–92
Anita Isaacs

Peru and the International Monetary Fund
Thomas Scheetz

Peru under García: An Opportunity Lost
John Crabtree

Restructuring Domination: Industrialists and the State in Ecuador
Catherine M. Conaghan

Poverty and Peasantry in Peru's Southern Andes, 1963–90

R. F. Watters

University of Pittsburgh Press

Published in the USA by the University of Pittsburgh Press,
Pittsburgh, Pa. 15260

Published in Great Britain by
The Macmillan Press Ltd

Printed in Hong Kong

ISBN 0–8229–1182–5
LC 93–60584

To Bethlyn

‘Those who have seen our Andean solitudes will have seen those great masses of sad, ragged, and melancholy *campesinos* who carry the burdens of four hundred years of slavery on their shoulders.’

Haya de la Torre, quoted in Davies (1974): 102

Contents

List of Tables

List of Figures

List of Plates

Acknowledgements

Many people and institutions should be thanked for assisting the production of this book. The Food and Agriculture Organisation (FAO) of the United Nations, the Wenner Gren Foundation, the Ministry of Foreign Affairs in New Zealand and the Victoria University of Wellington all funded the initial study on fallow agricultural systems, and later on peasant studies in pasture improvement and rural development.

In Lima a number of scholars and friends provided interest and encouragement to the research: Carlos Aramburú, Alejandro Camino, Dr Adolfo Figueroa, Dr José Matos Mar, Dr Enrique Mayer and Dr Efrain Gonzalez de Olarte. I am also grateful for the assistance of Neil Johnson of the New Zealand Embassy.

When I first visited the Andes with my wife Bethlyn in 1964, we were fortunate to meet Sr Dante Huerta, a tourist guide who became a firm friend. His enthusiasm and deep interest in Inca culture was infectious. On most of my visits to Cuzco I have stayed at the Hostal el Solar, whose staff made me warmly welcome. I also thank my friend Pepe (Sr José Gonzalez Tisoc), the manager.

I am grateful to Jorge Flores Ochoa, Professor of Anthropology at San Antonio Abad Universidad, Cuzco, for his advice; he is a scholar with great experience of the high Andes. A deep and special debt is owed to Oscar Nuñez del Prado, formerly a professor and currently Director at the Instituto Nacional de Cultura, Cuzco, the agronomist Ing Diana Reinoso, and Steve Kling, originally a Peace Corps volunteer working with the Servicío Forestal.

Over many years my family have had to suffer from my lengthy preoccupation with and meandering pursuit of this demanding subject. I am grateful to Bethlyn and our three children, Jane, Carla and Andrew, for their forebearance and understanding.

Many people have assisted with preparation of the manuscript: Robin Mita, the late Jean Benfield, Rhyl Singleton, Ginette Sullivan and Anna Roberts.

The greatest debt of course is owed to the people of 'Chilca'. Special thanks are due to Rosindo Gudel, Edgar Vargas and

Santos Kehuarucho, to the late Balthazar Ravelo and his innovative son Jenaro Ravelo, to my friends Cesar and Susanne Vargas for their kind hospitality, and to Francisco Rayme, president of the community in 1979. My greatest debt of all is to the late Jacinto Teniente Leguía, a courageous and determined *comunero* whose life was one of unending struggle to defend the interests of the community.

R. F. WATTERS

List of Abbreviations

APRA	Alianza Popular Revolucionaria Americana (left-wing party founded by Haya de la Torre in 1924)
BFA	Banco de Fomento Agropecuario
CAEM	Centro de Altos Estudios Militares
CAP	Agrarian Production Co-operative
CENCIRA	Agrarian Reform National Training and Research Unit
CNA	National Agrarian Confederation
COMARCA	a commission set up to distribute expropriated lands in the Anta area
ENCI	Empresa Nacional de Comercialización de Insumos
EPSA	a body regulating certain agricultural inputs and products to ensure availability and price stability in urban areas
FAO	Food and Agriculture Organisation
FDCC	a provincial peasant organisation
FLN	Frente Liberación Nacional
FUCA	Frente Unico de Campesinos de Anta
IBRD	International Bank for Reconstruction and Development
IMF	International Monetary Fund
IU	Izquierda Unida (left-wing group of parties)
MRTA	Movimiento Revolucionarió Tupac Amaru
MSP	Medium-sized producer
NPK	Nitrogen Phosphate Potash
ONRA	Oficina Nacional de Reforma Agraria
PAC	Provisional Administrative Commission
PIARs	Integral Rural Development Plans
PRODERM	Peru–Netherlands agricultural project
SAIS	Social Interest Agricultural Societies
SINAMOS	Sistema Nacional de Apoya a la Movilización Social

Part I

Background

1 Introduction: The Problem and Method

The Indian problem in Peru, it has often been said, is in large measure also the Andean problem. Indeed, to think of the Quechua and Aymará Indians apart from their eroded earth, their ancient mountains and their windswept *altiplano* (high plateau) is like thinking of an island society separated from the sea, the centre and source of much of its culture. With their hard jutting cheekbones, eyes like quiet lakes, thick firm lips and large hooked noses, Indian faces seem to express, in their deep sorrow, resignation and futility, their history of conquest, extirpation and exploitation, and their unending struggle against the elements.

The very meaning of life itself in these communities seems to lie in the earth and in the annual garnering of corn, wheat and potatoes. Expressing these close ties with the earth, Quechua poetry and songs are rich with allusions to nature, plants, birds and animals as well as to medicine, magic and sorcery:

> I was born like a lily in the garden,
> So also was I raised.
> As my age came, I have grown up
> And, as I had to die,
> So likewise I dried up,
> And I died.

Against the magnificent rock-ribbed vastness of the Andes it is possible to romanticise the condition of the Indian. But such a Redfieldian picture by itself, stressing as it does harmony and stability, is incomplete and one-sided, and needs to be complemented by a 'Lewisian' approach that recognises also the other, darker side of Indian peasant life.[1] Many communities are rent by factionalism and disunity; and the chronic lack of land, accompanied by growing population pressure and accelerated erosion, together with the vagaries of a harsh and unpredictable nature, have led inevitably to poverty and hardship. Andean valleys can suddenly be lashed by hailstorms, or transformed to bleak winter by blizzards, while frosts and droughts are so destructive that in the Cuzco region the entire crop is lost one year in seven.

Peasant villages tend to be squalid compounds of miserable mud-floored, smoke-filled *adobe* houses (made of sun-dried bricks), where half-naked, pot-bellied, worm-infested children scramble on dung heaps, and scavenging pigs clean up human faeces. Added to this picture is the fact that in 1960 the life expectancy at birth in the Andes averaged only 36 years, and infant mortality was four times higher than in Western countries.[2]

There are also scourges of disease and malnutrition. Influenza and pneumonia cause 21 per cent of the deaths of children in Peru under five years old and gastritis and enteritis kill another 12 per cent. Although conditions had improved by 1980, Peru still had the fourth lowest average life expectancy among 20 Latin American countries.[3] In 1978–80, Peru was in the lowest group of Latin American countries for average daily calorie intake and below the Latin American average in total protein consumption.[4] Inferior nutrition and health are merely part of the sub-standard living conditions that are experienced daily by many Peruvians and especially by the Andean peasantry. This book will present many illustrations of these sub-human living conditions and attempt to explain the perpetuation of poverty.

POVERTY AND THE PEASANTRY

When we enquire 'Who are the poor?' or 'What are their characteristics?', we find immediately that a large proportion of the poor in Peru are identified as peasant (*campesino*) and especially as Indian (Quechua or Aymará) peasants. To understand their poverty and their toleration of it, we need to examine Peruvian peasant culture and the accommodations that Indian peasants have made to it over time. Peasantry is as much a *process* of adaptation as it is a social *structure*.

The forging of any culture represents the selective processes by which a society gradually works out survival techniques. For peasant cultures, these processes enable them to wrest a livelihood from the reluctant earth in a peculiarly harsh and changeable environment, and to adapt to different political and social conditions. Because of their lowly socio-economic position, and the incipient inequality of the societies in which they live, peasants tend to remain sunk in poverty and degradation.[5]

One of the main arguments of this book is that the Andean peasantry, despite possessing an intricate technology admirably adapted to winning a living from a mountainous terrain, is an archaic society that lacks the *capability*[6] in the wider environment of the modern world to overcome its problems and escape the fate of poverty. And while internal reasons also exist for this failure to develop the capability (see Chapters 6, 8 and 12), the most fundamental reasons arise from external factors, such as the political economy which has made the peasantry a poor underclass within the social pyramid of modern Peru (see Chapters 4, 11 and 17).

In adapting to and coping with hostile physical environments, the Indians of the Andes have forged their peasant culture as a system that has ensured subsistence and a measure of security, but at the same time they have paid a heavy price. The rigid traditionalism of the closed corporate communities and inflexible value system prevents healthy economic growth from within, leaving abandonment of the Indian culture, upward social mobility and flight to the cities as the main solutions to poverty (Chapters 6, 8, 14 and 16). While class and ethnicity are empirically separate factors, ceasing to be a peasant is thus virtually synonymous with ceasing to be Indian.

The concept of capability draws attention to whether the individual community or class possesses a sufficient *endowment* of resources such as land, stock, irrigation water, plough teams, fertiliser and capital. Many of the peasants described in the following pages are clearly poor because of their lack of endowment of such resources. Many are also poor because of their lack of *entitlement* to use such resources, or to gain access to them.

There are several kinds of entitlement: the patron (*patrón*)–client relationship between *haciendas* (large estates) and peasants provides peasants with *exchange entitlement*; the earning of subsistence or cash income by using one's own resources (or hiring resources from others) to produce goods is a type of *production entitlement*; *own labour entitlement* entitles one to goods earned with one's own labour power; *trade-based entitlement* is a right to goods obtained by trading goods that one owns; and *inheritance and transfer entitlement* extends ownership to one who is given or bequeathed property or goods.

Taken together, the concepts of *endowment*, *access* to different kinds of *entitlement*, *capability*, and relative changes in these over time assist in the study of the nature of poverty and pauperisation. So far, we have addressed the issue of poverty essentially in *economic* terms, and stressed its *absolute* elemental core. However, poverty in the Southern Andes tends to be as much *relative*, and to arise also from the *social* conditions of Indian peasants.

In such a highly class-structured society affected also by differences in ethnicity, the Indian *campesino* is generally considered to be the lowest, most inferior creature of all, with the exception of beggars and common thieves. This has a great deal of bearing on peasant poverty in general.

Poverty in the Andes is also revealed by social dynamics and the links and access which are provided by social ties. Some of the poorest, most pitiable households observed were those headed by widows, or ones which lacked able-bodied males. Especially poor were those who lacked relatives in the area (*wakcha*) who would normally be expected to help alleviate hunger or assist with access to land (see Chapter 8).

APPROACH: GOALS AND THEMES

The Southern Andes of Peru and neighbouring areas of Bolivia represent the largest concentration of monolingual speakers of indigenous languages in the Western hemisphere. Eight to ten million people are native speakers of Quechua and Aymará, and at least half of them speak little or no Spanish. The 5 500 000 peasants in Southern Peru who live overwhelmingly in closed corporate communities make up one of the poorest, most traditional and distinctive peasantries in Latin America.

This book began as a practical study of land use systems and an exploration of poverty and the development paths that would have to be followed if the Andean people were to break their shackles of poverty and achieve better lives. The description and analysis of the closed corporate peasantry of the Southern Andes of Peru, focusing mainly on one village community, is the primary purpose of this book.

A number of themes and purposes emerge: to identify and evaluate a number of major approaches to the peasantry; to locate the peasantry in its *environmental* and geographic milieu;

and to consider the *historical*, *economic*, *social* and *political* forces that have shaped it, constraining, warping, repressing or developing the peasant community. Moreover a pronounced *cultural* tradition is associated with all aspects of peasant life.

The framework for the study is provided by the powerful national and international forces that have buffeted Peru over the last 30 years, challenging the survival of the peasant subculture. The 27-year period of fieldwork, from the early 1960s to 1990, was a momentous time in the history of Peru, for it marked the most decisive challenge to the dominating *hacienda* system ever mounted, including the overthrow of the oppressors, the launching of an important nationalist revolution and the initiation of a massive agrarian reform throughout the countryside.

The 1960s and 1970s were also marked by the deeper penetration of capitalism, a greater role played by multinational corporations in Peru, the spread of consumerism and several important shifts in Peru's export-led economy including, in the 1970s and 1980s, a steady deterioration in her position in the world economy. At the same time over these three decades numerous attempts have been made to initiate economic development in the countryside and to modernise all sectors of the economy.

This study focuses on a *production* model of the peasantry.[7] The emphasis is on the resources available (or lacking) and the means of access to resources: the amount, quality and distribution of land; the tenure system; capital equipment; the availability of labour and the methods of mobilising labour; and access to credit, markets, new inputs (fertilisers, fungicides, insecticides, new seeds) and other innovations.

Closely related to the production model is the emphasis placed on the importance of *environmental factors*. Although the peasantry of the Andes has been the subject of a number of valuable studies,[8] few deal with the environment in a functional or contextual way.[9] Any study which hopes to deal with the round of life, or to understand the travail of the peasantry, must deal with life as the peasants *experience* it.

In my fieldwork, I concentrated on a community (Chilca) located in its particular ecological niche, and thus *local* factors and *local* forms of adaptation were emphasised. However, as well as this local context, links with the outside world were also of great importance. Those people who sold a few sacks of potatoes, maize or a cow to truckers or itinerant middlemen were immediately relating to outsiders, who usually wielded more power than the peasants and were in a position to enforce a low purchase price or to gain some other unfair advantage. In the field, it proved to be especially difficult to gather comprehensive data on such transactions because sales were often very rapid, or were made either in a nearby market town or in Cuzco. Inevitably, records of market transactions were based on word-of-mouth statements by informants after the event and were thus sometimes incomplete or inaccurate. However, in building up income and expenditure budgets for households, such marketing transactions were included because they indicate both the economic context of the peasantry and also the connections between the peasantry and the outside world.

Similarly many people who possessed only one or two *topos* (in the Cuzco region, a *topo* is 80 × 40m of land, a little less than 0.33ha) of poor land were compelled to gain access to one of the large *haciendas* that dominated the region, and in return for labour they were granted a small plot or two on an usufruct basis, or sometimes grazing rights for their cattle or sheep. The relations between the peasants and dominating landlord class (exchange entitlement) were obviously of crucial importance, and the ways in which the peasants were granted access (and paid for it) or were denied access, critically affected the peasantry. The overall social structure and class relationships were clearly significant.

Finally, two external linkages greatly affect peasant livelihoods. The links between kinsfolk in the cities and peasants expose them to urban markets, urban institutions and values, a better educational system and a totally different and more complex world. At the same time, the changing role of the government in the countryside and the increasing tendency, over recent decades, for the peasantry to appeal to government to intercede on its behalf in its struggle with the landed oligarchy made the national scene highly relevant to the study. And acting sometimes in alliance with government or underlying the inexplicable changes in prices that affected the marketing of peasant produce were such factors as foreign investment, world capitalist forces or multinational corporations. Persistent poverty, apparently rooted in purely *local*, archaic or inadequate conditions, cannot be wholly and satisfactorily explained at the local level.

We therefore explore, to some extent, the nature of particular structures and systems (like peasantry and capitalism), and their inter-relationship over time (for example, the *patrón*–client relationship before and after the agrarian reform).

FIELDWORK

This book attempts to document and describe peasant livelihoods by presenting two cross-sectional studies of a community visited intensively in 1964 and 1979, supplemented by four very brief visits in 1966, 1974, 1976 and 1990.[10] Fieldwork followed the standard geographic and anthropological methods of interviews, participant observation and microstudies.

Although hundreds of peasant villages in the Andes display a great diversity of characteristics and often dramatic differences, many basic similarities occur. I chose, after reconnaissance, a particular village that seemed to be broadly representative of an ecological zone, and which illustrated some significant stages in the overall development process.[11] The community of Chilca is an example of a relatively wealthy, moderately modernised village with clear potential for development since it possesses some gently sloping land of reasonable fertility, is located on a major road and has good linkage to the nearby city of Cuzco with its many opportunities for marketing, innovation and education.

The Anta region, in which Chilca lies, was one of the first regions in the Sierra to experience the sweeping agrarian reform initiated by the new Revolutionary Government after 1969. It became something of a national showcase for reform, and for this reason it is even more important.

ORGANISATION

Chapter 2 broadly reviews some of the literature on the nature of peasantry. An outline of Peru, the Southern Sierra, peasant communities and the unique ecology of the Andes is presented in Chapter 3. Chapter 4 describes some of the major features of the historical legacy, concentrating on the influence of major institutions of the Conquest and subsequent patterns of exploitation. Chapter 5 outlines the main features of the Peruvian economy and political system to show how the evolution of various kinds of export-led growth have, since the nineteenth century, failed to involve the peasants.

Following this description of the background in Part I, the primary focus in Part II is on the peasant community up to 1979. Chapters 6 and 8, which describe Chilca in 1964 and 1979, make up the core of the book. In Chapter 9, external economic relations experienced by peasant producers are described, along with the effects on the peasantry of unfavourable price trends.

Part III considers a number of outcomes, destinies or solutions to the problems afflicting the peasantry. The nature of the Peruvian Revolution and the degree of success that it achieved in redressing the condition of the peasantry are discussed in Chapter 10. In Chapter 11 changes in the agricultural sector over the last three decades are analysed. The scope of innovation within the village community and the role of peasant leaders is dealt with in Chapter 12, and the response of Chilca to the agrarian reform in Chapter 13. In Chapter 14 the solution of out-migration is considered, along with the associated process of 'cholofication' (change of status from peasant towards *mestizo*, or a more middle-class Spanish type). The revolutionary 'solution' to the peasant predicament is considered in Chapter 15, which describes various forms of mobilisation of the peasantry from historic times through the classic period of mobilisation in the 1960s, invasion of the new co-operatives in the 1970s to the current civil war with the Sendero Luminoso (Shining Path) guerrillas.

Part IV, on peasant destinies and outcomes, specifically examines the recent agencies for change in Southern Peru, and introduces material from the 1990 fieldwork. Chapter 16 discusses some of the main agencies of change that impinge upon and generally erode the strength of the peasantry, while Chapter 17 presents an overview of Peru in 1990. Chapter 18 gives an account of the 1990 fieldwork findings, especially in relation to change and outcomes.

Finally, Chapter 19 summarises the main findings on the nature of the peasantry in the Southern Sierra. A contextual 'Jack in the Box' model of the peasantry is presented and some comments are offered on likely future outcomes.

2 Approaches to the Peasantry

The umbrella term 'peasant' is much used and abused to describe the many rural societies which, until recently, comprised about half the population of the world. It has become common in recent years to argue about what 'peasantry' actually means, but in general the term has come to denote an underclass of small rural cultivators from whom a surplus has been extracted (rent in the form of free or cheap labour or product) to underwrite the living standards of a more powerful upper class and the needs of the state.[1]

The most fundamental point about peasantry is the structural relationship between it and the rest of society.[2] This relationship, and the prevailing economic forces that impinge upon the countryside, have stamped certain qualities on the peasants and largely determine the underdog position in which they continue to live. We need, however, to move beyond this broad structural relationship to consider more closely both peasant culture and peasant economy.

FIVE APPROACHES TO THE PEASANTRY

To do this, we shall critically employ five conceptual approaches to the study of the peasantry: (1) the ethnographic cultural tradition, (2) the Durkheimian tradition often allied to functionalist sociology, (3) the 'specific economy' approach, (4) the Marxist tradition of class analysis and the dependency approach, and (5) the ethnohistorical approach.

Despite the insights each approach reveals, the complexity of the topic requires a comprehensive, many-sided examination. As Redfield noted, peasantry is 'a whole that is both enclosed within other wholes and is also in some part permeated by them'.[3] The test of the degree of validity of each approach here is its adequacy in explaining the nature of peasantry in the Southern Andes.

The Ethnographic Cultural Tradition

This approach treats peasants as representatives of an archaic rural social order, the heirs of an earlier national tradition. Such societies, inherently conservative and traditional, are characterised by inertia and acculturate only slowly to Western and urban standards of rationality. Such an analysis often arises from developmentalists who focus on traditional obstacles to industrialisation and 'modernisation'.

A number of well-known studies of peasantry use this approach. Erasmus (1968) concluded that peasantry disappeared only because great changes occurred in infrastructure and technology, permitting a transition from a 'paleotechnic ecotype'[4] to a neotechnic (machine age) ecotype. In this transition process, the *encogido* personality syndrome (the timid and withdrawn personality of the 'passive peasant' who avoids persons of higher status except those who serve as culture or power brokers) becomes less common as a prominent type among rural lower classes; and the contrasting syndrome of the *entrón* personality becomes more common. The *entrón* person is aggressive, confident, achievement-oriented, extroverted and not opposed to making contacts with higher status individuals whose friendship will be to his advantage.

Another variant of this approach was offered by Foster (1965) as an explanation for the reluctance of peasants of Tzinzuntan, Western Mexico, actively to follow development-oriented strategies. In this corporate peasant community, the desirable things in life – whether land, money, livestock or women – existed only in finite quantities, and one could obtain the desired goods only at the expense of someone else. One person's gain is another's loss, and the person who appropriates more than his fair share of the 'limited good' is strongly criticised and condemned. This concept helps to explain the reluctance of peasants to innovate, to become achievement-oriented or to show more entrepreneurial spirit than their neighbours.[5]

Rogers's model of the 'sub-culture of peasantry',[6] derived from the work of various social scientists, also exhibits this approach. A sub-culture contains many elements of the broader culture of which it is a part, yet it is also characterised by other qualities that separate it from other sectors of the general culture. Peruvian peasants share many national characteristics with other

Peruvians, but as primarily subsistence farmers who have experienced poverty and exploitation over a long period, the Southern Andean people possess certain traits that make them members of a 'peasant culture' which transcends national boundaries.

The Durkheimian Tradition and Functionalist Sociology

Durkheim, Tonnies and Maine developed an approach that posited a division of societies into traditional and modern. Traditional societies are made up of social segments which are autonomous, closed, uniform, informal and cohesive. Modern ones, on the other hand, are seen as based upon a division of labour and necessary, 'organic' and formalised interaction of their units. Redfield (1956) refined this concept in his folk-urban continuum and Kroeber (1948) also developed the idea in his view of peasants as being rural, but belonging to 'part societies with part cultures'.[7] The merit of this approach was that it saw peasants in a wider context.

Redfield introduced his notion of the 'Great Tradition' and 'Little Tradition'. Peasants in any single village shared their local language and customs derived from perhaps centuries of common experience and co-residence (Little Tradition). At the same time, in Latin America they had been shaped by the major institutions of Hispanicisation: the Catholic church, Spanish language, forms of local government, the legal system and the *hacienda* system. Together these constituted the Great Tradition. Unlike the isolated tribal or 'folk society', peasants know of and are dependent upon more civilised people.

This approach stresses an increase in societal complexity and a multiplication of institutions as societies undergo change. It becomes functionally necessary for social structure to be reintegrated. Functionalist theories of change, with their various strengths and weaknesses, are employed.

The Specific Economy Approach

This approach views peasant social structure as being characterised by a specific type of economy, which is a kin-based small farm enterprise, highly autonomous and consumption-based. This in turn generates a typical peasant social structure and a peasant/non-peasant dualism at the national level.[8] The roots of this approach go back to Marx, but its main proponents are Chayanov (originally 1925, this edition 1966), and more recently the anthropologists Firth (1951) and M. Nash (1966), and the geographer Franklin (1969).

In economic anthropology, some scholars have adopted a 'substantivist' approach which rejects the claim of 'formalists' that the conceptual framework developed by modern economics can be used to study *any* form of economy. In contrast, they emphasise that the economies of non-Western peasant or tribal societies have to be studied in their own right and that processes such as production, distribution and exchange should be seen in the context of these particular societies and their peculiar institutions. As Firth has noted, a 'production relationship is often only one facet of a social relationship. . . . Economic relations can be understood only as a part of a scheme of social relations.'[9]

This is clearly true of the Andean peasantry: a number of scholars, such as Alberti and Mayer (1974) and Murra (1972) have shown how important the roles of reciprocity and redistribution are for understanding Andean peasant society over time and as it continues to function today. Reciprocity is of vital importance not only for understanding relations among peasants themselves,[10] but also between peasants and *mestizos*[11] and between peasants and their deities.[12]

Moreover, as the analysis of Gonzalez de Olarte (1984) shows clearly, the production and consumption behaviour of Andean peasants is explained partly by the semi-mercantile and non-capitalist character of communal production as well as the extreme poverty of the peasants. A 'communal economy' is characteristic of the peasantry, with the organisation of production and work being affected by a system of family interrelations that has a 'communal effect'. While economic benefits in production, income and well-being are gained that are higher than would accrue to peasant families that operated entirely individually, it is also true that the *comunidad* (community) as an organisation induces through its poverty a series of individual and collective behaviours and survival strategies (such as levelling devices) which reinforce tradition and the subsistence priorities of the family components. A logical consequence is the formation of restricted markets characterised by small volumes of merchandise traded.

Thus the specific economy approach is important in emphasising these features, for peasantry in the Andes is not only an economy that conforms to the *family* unit of production and consumption but also to decisions made by other families in the communities. The *family–comunero* (member of a community) economy differentiates it from peasant economy in general.

The Marxist Tradition and the Dependency Approach

This school of thought, which usually employs a two-class model of society, studies the peasantry in terms of power relationships. Peasants are viewed as the suppressed and exploited producers of pre-capitalist society, and contemporary peasantry appears as a leftover from an earlier social formation, with its members being powerless to climb out of their position since they remain at the bottom of the social pyramid.

In this approach the state is usually seen as representing and maintaining the position of the dominant class; state institutions fetter the majority of the masses, including the peasantry, in the historical development of the pre-capitalist and capitalist systems. Powerlessness and productivity are the two key aspects of peasantry under such a definition. The peasants are dominated by powerful outsiders or minorities and their agricultural surpluses are expropriated by the ruling class, leading to repeated attempts at peasant revolt. The process of expropriation leads to accumulation of capital and creation of new class structures, culminating, it is believed, in the disappearance of both the old rural aristocracy and the peasantry as such.[13]

In Peru the Marxist approach to the peasantry has been used to explain the exploitation of the Andean peasant by the local *hacendados* (estate owners), middlemen, government employees and the state bureaucracy. Many approaches in Peru and in Latin America draw on the seminal work of Wolf (1957 and 1966), which emphasises the structural position of the peasantry in relation to the rest of society rather than dwelling on peasant culture. Wolf's analysis is not characteristically Marxist, but in identifying and emphasising the importance of power relationships in peasant societies he has made a major contribution. The relationship between the *hacendado* and the peasants is not purely economic: the *patrón* is also a power broker who is expected to reciprocate with certain social obligations, from helping 'his people' avoid the draft to the armed services, to baptising their children. In the same way the economic surplus of peasants, whether in labour, produce or cash, is siphoned off by the local power structure in return for some small acts of reciprocity. Although peasants *are* quite aware of their dependency on the local power structure and the extreme asymmetrical nature of many such relationships, there is little they can do about it as they have few options available.

A variant of class domination and exploitation is the 'internal colonialism' thesis. This view suggests that relationships between regions such as the Andes and the dominant coastal region are similar to those between a colony and its metropolis. In Chapters 4 and 5 we argue that, to a degree, such a case can be sustained for the Southern Andes.

Another variant is the 'triangle without a base' approach.[14] The apex of each baseless triangle is the *patrón*. He is not only sovereign in the local area because of the power he wields over his subordinates (peasants or serfs), but he also represents the essential link with the outside world from which all information is likely to come that might be used by the subordinates towards their own emancipation.

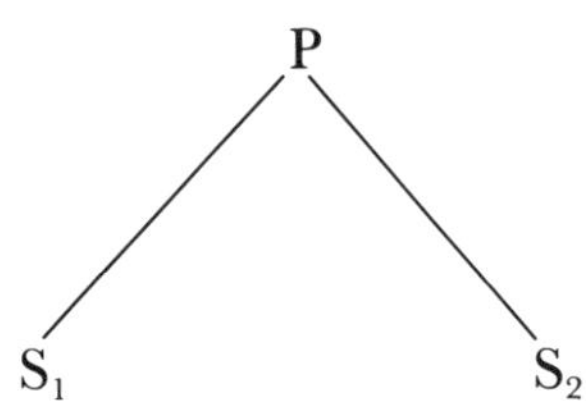

P = *Patrón*
S = Subordinate

In such a baseless triangle the subordinate peasants are isolated and atomised. It is only where the base of the triangle is closed by alliances (when the subordinate populations become aware of their conditions of subordination and common class) that they achieve the means to enable them either to challenge the power of the *patrón*, or to establish links with new, more beneficial *patrones*. We draw on some of these ideas in interpreting peasant mobilisation in Chapter 13.

The Ethnohistorical Approach

The rather simplistic and mechanistic nature of some of these conceptualisations is largely avoided by the fifth approach, which refuses to treat the peasant as a passive object but sees each rather as the repository of cherished qualities not extinguished by centuries of repression. An attempt to understand the peasant world through peasant eyes accepts, for example, the importance of traditional religion and ritual as a means of explaining, predicting and controlling the world: that is, as fulfilling the same role that science does in the West. Indeed, as Gow (1976) argues, the flame of peasant autonomy burns brightly in an inner life, in secret rituals, values and beliefs associated with Andean religion.

On the social level, myths explain the origins and identity of a people. For Peruvian peasants, they reveal their close identification with their ancestors, and particularly the Incas. The defeat of the Incas symbolised their own defeat; since then a long period of discrimination has continued up to this day.

It is on the cosmological level, however, that religion achieves its greatest explanatory power. Reciprocity, whether balanced or asymmetrical, is the mode for ordering the universe. While the ideal on the community level is balanced reciprocity, peasants accept that relationships with their deities, as with *mestizos*, are highly asymmetrical.

Andean religion and cosmology reflect an intimate attachment to nature, a view that nature is sacred, being the dwelling place of their ancestors, containing the vital life-force and serving as source for many of their myths and cults. Certain gods or cult heroes are directly associated with the peasants and the poor in general; some are associated with the eventual overthrow of the *mestizo* oppressors.

EVALUATION OF ALTERNATIVE APPROACHES TO THE PEASANTRY

All the above approaches have both a degree of validity and serious deficiencies. None is at all adequate on its own. The fieldworker becomes aware that the past is still heavily present in the Andes, and that the peasant tradition is still strong. In spite of the evident power and persuasiveness of the Marxist class and dependency approach in the Andes, for example, one cannot so easily dismiss culture and the shaping of human action by inherited or learnt patterns of behaviour.

When I began work in Chilca in 1964 I soon became aware of a robust tradition, clearly centuries old, surviving even here, near an important modern city. This folk tradition incorporated major elements forcibly implemented by the Spanish Conquistadores or their rapacious descendants, but it consisted too of ancient elements, some of pre-Inca origin, that have been conditioned and in some cases tempered in the furnace of social change.

The persistence of the peasant tradition needs to be documented (this book does so only to a small degree),[16] but at the same time the inadequacy of many elements of the old folk culture for present needs must be made clear. (We must not confuse respect for Andean Indians with the value-orientation, attitudes and forms of organisation that are necessary for them to achieve the development goals that they seek.)

The modern study by anthropologists of peasantry really began with the famous debate on the nature of peasantry that arose from the alternative interpretations of the Mexican village of Tepoztlán by Redfield and Lewis. In his earlier study Redfield drew a picture of a relatively homogeneous and well-integrated society, with a high level of general contentment, and a sober, individual restraint in deference to the collective utility. Although he later admitted the existence of maladjustment and conflict in peasant communities, in his work on peasant culture in 1956 Redfield returned to his original conception, characterising peasants everywhere by: 'an intense attachment to native soil; a reverent disposition toward habitat and ancestral ways; a restraint on individual self-seeking in favor of family and community; a certain suspiciousness, mixed with appreciation, of town life; a sober and earthy ethic'.[17]

In contrast to this 'consensus model', Oscar Lewis presented a 'conflict model' of the same community, stressing the ugly, coercive and disintegrative face of society. Lewis emphasised 'the poor quality of interpersonal relations', noticing the attributes of constraint, detachment, lack of affection, suspicion and distrust of others, malice, hidden and indirect hostility, absence of altruism, envy, and harsh and unrelenting gossip.[18]

Although it is widely agreed that Redfield gave inadequate emphasis to conflict and maladjustment and that Lewis's study was superior in that it was more comprehensive, it is wrong to dismiss Redfield's approach as purely a romantic, Rousseau-like conception of the peasantry. The debate underlines an important point, besides illustrating the great difficulty of social scientists in reaching objective truth about human societies. Lewis and Redfield are both right rather than wrong in their interpretations; each is portraying a different side of the same coin. While the two approaches are partly antagonistic they are also, to a degree, complementary and compatible. Redfield's view must, to some extent, be true since peasantries have survived and the strength of community has won out. Lewis's view emphasises the difficulties they faced inherently. In addition, given the impact of modern capitalism, urbanisation and the demands of the modern state, it is indeed remarkable that the corporate community still manages to hang together.

It is interesting to note that in 1964 the peasants of Chilca expressed their viewpoint of life in remarkably Redfieldian terms (see Chapter 6), rejecting the migration option as a solution to their problems. At the same time the consensus model, and belief in harmony, equilibrium or centripetal tendencies, were being challenged even then by forces of conflict, maladjustment and centrifugal tendencies that threatened disintegration. This latter model appeared to dominate over the former in interpreting the character of the community in 1979. Yet the fact that this model presents only part of the whole truth is attested in the continuing survival of both the peasantry and the closed corporate community.

The ethnographic cultural tradition approach, then, especially if combined with a positive ethnohistorical approach, can take us some way towards describing the nature of peasants, since both approaches emphasise the nature of peasantry from within and also place peasantry firmly in the context of the larger society and historical developments.

The need to view peasants in a broad setting and within their own context becomes obvious when we consider them in relation to the surrounding capitalist and market economy. More important than *what* peasants produce for the various exchange systems in which they are involved is *how* and to *whom* they dispose of what they produce. The structural relationship is of primary importance. And since the peasant is forced to sell in the market in order to buy what he cannot produce, the peasant economy transfers net value to the capitalist sector. The Marxist approach is important in this analysis.

In view of the fact that peasants have a lowly position in the marketplace, and that there is a frequent glut of the commodities they produce, they are hard put to obtain a price for their commodities that adequately reflects the amount of labour necessary for their production. Moreover, middlemen frequently purchase their commodities at a level close to, or below, the necessary labour time needed to produce them, and then resell to other purchasers at a considerably higher price, thus appropriating surplus value. Since standards of living are so low, the value of a peasant's labour power is low compared with other capitalistic classes in the nation which customarily enjoy higher standards of living. In Chapter 9 we will examine this dimension of peasant life, which helps to explain their pauperisation.

It is also important to place peasants in the wider social context of their contacts with various types of non-peasant: the ex-peasant *cholos* now working away from their home villages, the poor townsfolk, the various urban middle classes, the *hacendados*, the bureaucrats, the urban rich. Furthermore, considering peasants as a whole, as a sub-culture in relation to the rest of the culture, stresses an important dimension that is not adequately catered for merely by focusing on the occupation of peasants compared with non-peasants.

There are many ways of evaluating and analysing the social context of the peasantry. The internal colonialism approach examines the many different ways in which power is exercised over the subordinate population and surplus is extracted, while the baseless triangle model suggests how an isolated, subordinated peasantry can be atomised and fragmented since their only access to information that might enable them to interpret their conditions differently is through the local *patrón*, who monopolises power in the area.[19] However, these various formulations, despite their valuable insights, tend to be too neat, simplistic and mechanistic, and provide only limited understanding of the lives of peasants.

Dependency approaches are also appealing, for they have explanatory power in economic, social, political and ideological spheres and can be used at both macro and micro levels. The difficulty often occurs in achieving a credible integration of both macro- and micro-level approaches. Some such theorists, however, view almost all peasants as having a predominant personality trait of fatalism, exhibiting political lethargy and an inability to modify such a situation. And in spite of the importance of the Vicos project[20] for achieving an understanding of peasantry and initiating guided change, some of the analysis on that project showed little respect for peasant culture, but conformed faithfully to *mestizo* stereotypes of peasant behaviour, believing the manor serf suffered so seriously from fear that the local sub-culture barely worked out an effective escape from danger or insecurity.[21]

One can see daily in the streets of Cuzco examples of servile behaviour by Indians dealing with more powerful *mestizos*, but the peasant has had centuries of experience in 'impression management'. If their sub-culture were not viable, then how have the Indians managed to survive so long? Surely, if things were as bad as implied by some dependency theorists, peasants would all be paranoid and schizophrenic, if not extinct? But they are not, and the reason is that their society and culture are viable so long as contact with the *mestizo* world is confined to certain well-known kinds of transaction and is generally kept to a minimum.

Another major approach focuses on the articulation of modes of production. Earlier attempts to analyse Third World societies as dualistic, with a traditional subsistence system co-existing with a surrounding modern capitalistic system, have been superseded in recent years by structuralist and modes of production schools. These approaches are usually very formalistic, mechanistic and highly abstract. In their concern with structure and their attempt to explain social relationships as arising out of the inherent logic of capitalism, they ascribe little importance to history and the primary importance of human agents. The conscious role of individuals and groups in shaping their societies needs to be remembered, for the fluidity and subtleties of individuals and even classes can considerably affect the operation of impersonal forces.

Peasant society or culture must not be viewed as a monolithic structure or as a deadweight; rather the fifth and third approaches suggest that behind the peasant's reluctant, suspicious reaction to agricultural innovation lies either a very different and vibrant value-orientation, or the sensible conservatism of a practical countryman. Moreover, as this work shows, we must not treat peasantry as a homogeneous entity; the focus should be on heterogeneity. Within peasant society, despite a common *encogido* type of personality, there is scope for a range of personalities expressed in a range of behaviour patterns.

The Durkheimian tradition is valuable in reminding us that social change leads to an ongoing process of increasing specialisation of function along with greater secularisation and rationalisation of society. In a relatively traditional society, as Wolf has described, many people may be joined in 'coalitions' through sharing many interests such as kinship and friendship relations, the same social sanctions and the existence of symbols which reinforce and represent the other relations. These may be conceived of as separate strands that are tightly interwoven in a many-stranded coalition. Social change is a process of structural differentiation as new functions and roles replace old ones and become distinct from one another. But it is also an additive process, different qualitatively from the earlier functions, and not merely substituting for them. The new, more specialised functions will of course require new processes of integration so that society can assimilate the new changes and keep abreast of differentiation.

In explaining growing social complexity and the necessary reintegration of the social structure, recourse is invariably made to theories of functionalism. The value of a functionalist approach is that it attempts to understand the contribution of the part to the whole; it points to the possible interconnectedness of institutions. But the weaknesses and biases of functionalism lie in its stress on stability and social order and its glossing over of the dynamic forces of change. More seriously, functionalism is ahistorical, removing society from its historical context.

The specific economy approach, unlike most of the other approaches, addresses the essence of peasantry in analysing its distinctive consumption-based nature. In its most fundamental sense, the household is a social unit concerned with the survival and reproduction of the peasant family; yet it is also the consumption unit that strives to feed itself. As Marx recognised, the primary task is 'production for use' (consumption) and this must take precedence over 'production for exchange'. This basic inbuilt contradiction in goals of production that so often frustrates the efforts of developmentalists can be resolved only where the scale of production reaches the point that the family's basic needs are assured. Efforts can then be directed at diversifying production and specialising to some extent for market sale. Since the household is both the production and the consumption unit, the particular stage it is at in its demographic cycle will be expressed in both its pattern of needs and in its potential production capacity. Thus the ratio between the number of labour units possessed compared with the number of consumption units is likely to vary greatly over the years. The ratio between young and old, male and female, workers and dependants will be important and affect household motivation.

Consideration of such factors led the Russian economist Chayanov (1966) to conclude that peasants do not manage their farms to maximise profits. This is so because, first, the peasant farm is basically a family operation. Second, the intensity of family labour application is directly related to the ratio of consumers to workers in the family. Third, economic differentiation among peasants, particularly farm size, is more a measure of relative family size and composition than of differential economic success. Finally, the family labour farm could survive (and in some cases prevail) in competition with the commercial farm enterprises. Although Chayanov's third point on expansion of farm size with growing family size is not applicable to the Andes today because of acute population pressure, there is little doubt that Chayanov and other scholars of the 'specific economy' approach have made the greatest contribution to understanding the peasantry. To the extent that other approaches utilise capitalistic or Western concepts, they distort and misinterpret the peasant reality.

Work, or even productive activity, is very hard to define in a household. Where two or three children guard a few sheep or cattle on an unfenced hillside, it is a little artificial to assert that one would do, and the others are 'surplus labour'. Moreover, it may be almost impossible to distinguish idleness from leisure. In a peasant economy where young children imperceptibly enter the 'labour force' as they begin to mind younger siblings, gather dung or firewood for fuel or tend sheep, and older people gradually leave it, the identification of the economically active population and the measurement of full labour capacity are difficult exercises which require assigning a fraction of an 'adult labour unit' to each person in the household.[22] The extent of utilisation of resources and what constitutes a standard wage are rather difficult problems. Moreover, although a significant trend towards proletarianisation may be occurring among the peasantry of the Andes, much of the 'trend' may be illusory, representing a purely seasonal phenomenon in which peasants deliberately seek paid labouring work in relatively idle periods, although making sure they return to the village to perform the major agricultural tasks when required.

CONCLUSION

This review of approaches to peasantry suggests that peasant culture is complex and many-sided and that peasant economy is unique. Each of the five different approaches outlined provides some illumination in the search for understanding and explanation, but at the same time each tends to be myopic. With due regard for the overall structural circumstances in which the Indian peasantry is located (Chapter 11), we must not endow the individual peasant with superhuman powers and scope for free action. Neither should we so concentrate on the powerful systems and structures which surround the peasant world that we deny peasants any role in shaping and changing their lives (Chapter 13). And as Oscar Lewis (1967) advised, we must neither sentimentalise nor brutalise them. The task is difficult and the interpretation presented here makes no claim to succeed. It is necessary, however, to be explicit about one's assumptions and approaches and to attempt to avoid the likely pitfalls.

Although a variety of perspectives has been employed, the fieldwork experience has generally been decisive. The environmental and geographic context has been of extreme importance. In addition, considerable weight is placed on the overall political economy of Peru and how the country's evolution has generated, crystallised, hardened, modified or perpetuated a particular kind of peasantry in the Andes. Such an approach requires recognition of the various forces and structures implied by the concept of political economy. Erasmus's study[23] is regarded as salient here partly because of its comparative approach to studying peasant societies undergoing change, and partly because it is a valuable test of Wolf's important model[24] of the peasantry. My own work produced very similar conclusions. The approach must also analyse the 'depeasantising' process and consider what kind of 'post-peasant' rural societies are emerging. Since capitalistic tendencies are strong in Peru, as in many Latin American rural areas, it would be extremely doctrinaire to assert that any socialist model will be at all applicable for post-peasant societies in the immediate future.

3 The Setting: Nation, Ecology, Region and Community

NATION

Peru is a diverse country. Large in size (at 1 285 000sq.km, it is over twice the size of France), it has a population of only about 22 million people. It has been said, with a little exaggeration, that 'Peru is a beggar sitting on a bench of gold'. Certainly the country possesses a considerable array of valuable natural resources, but the excessively difficult terrain and great problems of exploitation and communication have hindered their development.

With less than 2 per cent of its land usable, Peru is much more poorly endowed than most countries; only Brazil in South America has a lower percentage.[1] Similarly, on a *per capitum* basis of 0.18ha of usable land, Peru is well below the continental average of 0.50ha.[2]

Most peasants in Peru live in the Andes or Sierra (see Table 3.1). There are three great natural regions in the country, the Sierra, the coast (*Costa*), and the rain forest (*selva* or *montaña*: see Figure 3.1).

The coast is the economic heart of Peru, although it comprises only 11 per cent of the national area. It is a narrow coastal desert, only 30–90km wide, which receives a mere 20–30mm of rainfall annually. But this arid coastal plain is traversed by 52 rivers that flow from the Sierra to the sea: 'green snakes on a drab desert'. These river valleys are veritable oases, allowing about 807 000ha to be irrigated. Truck farming of vegetables for the Lima-Callao metropolis and the earlier important export crops of cotton and sugar, together with maize and rice, dominate the crop area. High soil fertility on the alluvial piedmonts and the sub-tropical climate allow year-round cropping and some multiple cropping. The region is dominated by the great metropolitan conurbation of Lima-Callao (about 5 million people), and several intermediate cities.

Table 3.1 Peru: total rural population by ecological region, 1972

Region	*Altitude (feet)*	*Total population (thousands)*	*Total population per cent*	*Rural population (thousands)*	*Rural population per cent*	*Limit products**
1) *costa*	Less than 1 500	5 929	43.8	1 208	17.0	
2) *yunga*	1 500 to 6 000	926	6.9	725	10.2	sugar cane and some fruit
	(3 000 to 4 500)	(258)	(1.9)	(212)	(3.0)	
	(4 500 to 6 000)	(440)	(3.3)	(391)	(15.5)	
3) *quechua*	6 000 to 10 500	4 037	30.1	3 215	45.3	maize, wheat and other fruits
	(6 000 to 7 500)	(892)	(6.6)	(625)	(8.8)	
	(7 500 to 9 000)	(1 171)	(8.7)	(1 012)	(14.3)	
	(9 000 to 10 500)	(2 010)	(14.8)	(1 578)	(22.2)	
4) *suni*	10 500 to 12 000	1 325	9.8	110	15.5	Andean crops: tubers (*oca*, *olluco*, *mashua*), cereals (*quinoa* and legume) lupin
5)	12 000 to 13 500	192	1.4	124	1.7	very little agricultural activity (potatoes and barley), *auchenedae*[†]
6) *cordillera*	over 13 500	13	0.1	9	0.1	no agricultural activity
7) high Jungle	1 500 to 3 000	371	2.7	280	3.9	
8) low Jungle	Less than 1 500	709	5.3	444	6.3	
	Total	13 538	100.0	7 106	100.0	

*Products which cannot be produced in higher ecological levels.
[†]*Llama*, *alpaca*, and *vicuñas*.

Source: Alvarez (1984): Table 2.9 citing Figueroa (1981: 27), Table 1.4.

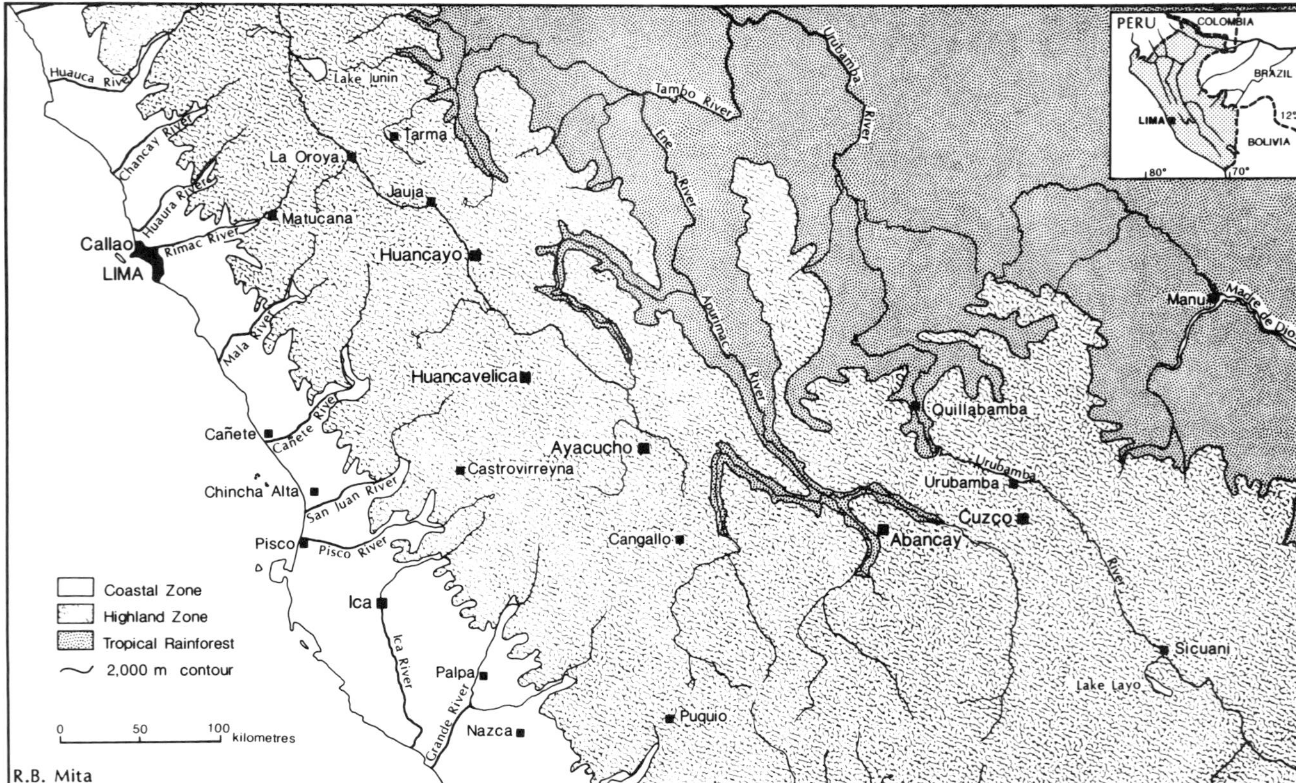

Figure 3.1 NATURAL REGIONS OF SOUTHERN PERU: COAST, SIERRA AND JUNGLE

On the other side of the great central Sierra, in the east of the country, the vast tropical rain forest or *selva* rolls away from the foothills of the Andes to the Brazilian frontier thousands of kilometres beyond. The *selva*, which basically comprises part of the great Amazonian Basin, is the largest of the three natural regions and makes up 58 per cent of the total area of the nation. Commonly it is divided into the 'high jungle' (*montaña alta*) or *ceja* ('eyebrow' of the jungle) and the 'low jungle' (*montaña baja*). The *ceja* lies between 1500m and 2000m in altitude and the 'low jungle' below 1500m.

Traditionally the *selva* has been occupied by only a very small population of Amerindian tribes, but since 1940 there has been a steady population influx of settlers, mostly from the overpopulated and impoverished Sierra. However, only about 13 per cent of the soils of the vast *selva* seem to have good agricultural potential and most of these have extremely poor access. Thus, only 0.8 per cent (605 000ha) of the *selva*'s area is cultivated, mainly for bananas, maize, rice and *yucca* (manioc). The contribution of the huge underdeveloped region to the nation's wealth has been very small. Recently, however, *coca* growing for the illicit cocaine trade has greatly expanded (see Chapter 15).

The Andes or Sierra is the third great natural region (see Figure 3.1). Until the last few decades, the Sierra was the heart of the nation, for most of the population had lived here since the Conquistadores had come from the high temperate tablelands of Spain. Here, too, most of the nation's resources could be found. It comprises 26 per cent of the total area of Peru. In 1950, almost 62 per cent of the nation's population lived in the Sierra, but this has declined steadily, and in 1981 about 31 per cent lived there.[3] The region produced at most about 25 per cent of the nation's wealth in 1980. In spite of the difficult ecology, the relatively high density of population in the fertile valleys, basins and on the *altiplano* has led to a greater proportion of the land area being cropped: 6.8 per cent (2 280 000ha).

THE ANDEAN ECOSYSTEM

Flying across the Sierra, an observer is filled with a sense of the awesome power of the Andes. This jumbled mass of *cordillera*, a gigantic towering massif of mountains that rises to 6550m,

Figure 3.2 SOUTHERN PERU, PROVINCES AND DEPARTMENTS

separated by deep valleys, is unquestionably one of the most difficult and inhospitable environments occupied by humans. Yet this region has been a major culture hearth of plant domestication and the centre of the remarkable Inca civilisation. Over many hundreds of years, people have evolved incredibly resilient and ingenious forms of land use admirably adapted to this mountain environment. Their achievements are a powerful testimony to human ingenuity and the rewards won through sound collaboration and organisation (see Plate 1). Regrettably, they are also a testimony to the appalling exploitation of human labour.

Since valleys and basins that lie next to gigantic mountain peaks have been cut down deeply to tropical levels, an immense variety of different micro climates, biotic communities and different cultural landscapes, representing a variety of human adaptations, can be found almost side by side in the Andes.

The most decisive climatic factors are altitude and exposure to orographic rainfall. It has been estimated that for the Andes as a whole, the mean annual temperature drops 0.5°C for each 100m of elevation. On the *altiplano*, at between 4500 and 5000m, the mean annual temperature falls rather more, 0.8°C per 100m.[4] There is also enormous diurnal variation: from peak afternoon temperatures of about 17°C, the temperature commonly falls below freezing at night, with a mean range of 20°C or more. Where cropping is possible, frost is the main natural hazard. Exposure to the wind on eastward facing slopes usually brings higher rainfall than on leeward slopes or in interior land-locked basins, which are also often affected by serious droughts. Precipitation may vary considerably between adjoining valleys, and variability from year to year is often great.

CULTURAL ADAPTATIONS TO THE ANDEAN ENVIRONMENT

A combination of archaeological and soil research in the 1950s and 1960s in Northern Chile and Peru has provided valuable insights into the transition from nomadic hunting groups to settled agricultural communities.[5]

It appears that this change was associated with the capture and domestication of young *llamas* or *alpacas*. At a time of growing aridity, people shunned the brackish waters of mountain lakes and the cold inhospitable *altiplano*. Atacameño people living at altitudes of 2100 to over 4000m began to congregate at the only ecological niches suitable as permanent dwelling places: *quebradas*, or gullies of richer alluvial soils fed by streams of sweet water. Here appeared the first groups of stone-walled dwellings, with walled 'patios' or small corrals for holding livestock, and the first crude terraces across valley bottoms. Domesticated *llamas* probably grazed on the more luxuriant vegetation found along the bottom of *quebradas*; cross-walls were built, probably to facilitate rounding up of animals. During flood time these would act as silt traps and with every flood the soil upstream of the walls would be deepened. It is possible that carrying fodder to livestock in the long dry season led to the concentration of edible seed-bearing plants; hollowed grinding stones suggest the people crushed seeds to obtain starch and protein foods. The trapped soil deposits would be the logical place in which to propagate food plants, and the availability of water which could easily be led to the crop without elaborate irrigation canals would ensure their survival through the long dry season.

Perhaps such a series of happy accidents led to the neolithic revolution in arid areas of the Southern Andes. The use of walls led to the development of lateral terraces, and the building of channels to carry the spring water to the lateral terrace soils led to the creation of efficient irrigation systems. The evolution of multiple terraces, rising tier upon tier along the valley side, would have to await the development of efficient types of canals, but these would be more in the nature of technical improvements possible once the initial idea of lateral terracing had been discovered.[6]

The adaptation of irrigation to high altitude farming permits the cultivation of a broader crop repertoire. In both Inca and modern times, irrigation was considered highly desirable wherever maize was grown,[7] but this crop is limited to specific climatic conditions. Much more vital to human occupancy in the Andes is the potato.

One wild species of potato has been found blooming at 5000m in an 18°C frost, and many cultivated varieties bear tubers regularly at 4200m. Many of the hardy, frost-resistant, bitter varieties will not grow below 2500m and will not propagate themselves without human help. Some Andean varieties of potato keep for seven to 12 months under *puna* (high altitude land) conditions which have a 'mummifying effect' on vegetables, *llama* meat and other tissues. The freeze-thaw dried *chuño* (for which many of the better high altitude varieties of potato are exclusively grown) will apparently keep for many years.[8]

Generally in Peru, then, agricultural methods are micro-adaptations, and combine agriculture with pastoral activities. Transhumance of *llamas*, *alpacas* and sheep is practised to take advantage of new shoots of bunch grass (*ichu*) and other *ch'inki* plants growing in *bofedales* or other moist areas. The pack animals – *llamas*, horses, donkeys – keep relatively free of hoof disease and parasites through exposure to hard, dry, rocky surfaces. The animals permit food, dung, wool and clothing to be moved between production zones. In the lower zone, between 3900 and 4200m, cultivation of land by the foot plough (*chaquitaclla*), when enriched by dung, enables grass to be planted in the furrows, and tubers between them. A fixed pattern of crop rotation has evolved. After fallowing for several years, a field is planted in tubers. The following year grains are sown and then the field is left in fallow for three to 12 years until the required level of nitrogen is restored.

Corrals, in which animals are herded for shelter at night, are good accumulators of dung. At one location, at 4250m, potatoes can be planted only in dung-enriched and sheltered corrals; elsewhere at 4050m the ancient tubers *olluco* and *oca* can grow in corrals.[9]

In lower, dry zones, where water retention is poor, the construction of *qochawiña* is an interesting adaptation. These irregularly shaped depressions, averaging between about 7 and 10m^2, are dug only 1–2cm deep with vertical edges; several of them can commonly be found in an area of a hectare or two. The *qochawiña* are usually dug at the end of the rainy season when they retain water longer than the soil adjacent to them. *Qochawiña* allow crops to withstand short dry spells during the rainy season and extend the period of water availability to plants by a week or two at the end of the rains. *Ch'inki* grows profusely within the *qochawiña* and appears in them early. In this manner *qochawiña* lengthen the period in which pasture is available to the herd animals in the lower zone.[10]

It is surprising to a Western observer to see furrows in parts of the Andes running vertically up slopes, rather than following the contour. In areas of heavy seasonal rainfall this allows fields to drain, whereas contour ploughing would hold water and lead to rotting tubers. Fields for crop planting are commonly sited on slopes rather than on valley bottoms which are more subject to frosts. Furrows serve to alter the microenvironment with each acting in effect as a narrow *qochawiña*. Furrows hold moisture longer than ridges, favouring the return of wild grasses. Cutting the ancient grains, *quinoa* and *cañihua*, does not destroy the furrows, so that planting grains after tubers rather than before ensures that a field enters the fallow period of its cycle with its furrows intact.

The temporal pattern of cultivation practised by Andean Indians is usually governed by the *laymi* system: a set of *laymi* or sections on the lands of a given community or *hacienda*. The *laymi* average between 50 and 250 ha in area. Each is divided into a number of smaller individually owned (or held, if communally owned) plots of land.

The same sequence of planting or fallowing is followed for all *laymi* sections in a system. During the fallow period *laymi* sections are used for grazing herd animals. Nitrogen deficiency makes fallowing necessary, and at this altitude, severe frosts and the lack of moisture slow biogeochemical processes so that a lengthy fallow period is necessary. In no instance is more than one-fifth to one-third of the land under cultivation at any one time. Long fallowing also eliminates certain pests as some nematode cysts cannot remain dormant in the soil for more than three or four years. The provision of dung by herd animals grazing on the fallow also accelerates the return of cultivation.

To gain a livelihood in their difficult terrain, therefore, Andean peasants resort to a wide range of traditional practices that have been skilfully fashioned over the ages. As they tap the resources of different ecological zones and simultaneously engage in both pastoralism and cropping, it is difficult often to distinguish between the two.

ECOLOGY AND PRODUCTION ZONES

Although the great variety of multiple altitudinal floors and associated micro climates and biotic communities (see Figure 3.3) has led to a bewildering array of historic human adaptations, in several parts of the Andes four major production zones may be identified.[11]

The highest production zone is above 3600 to 4000m (zone 1).

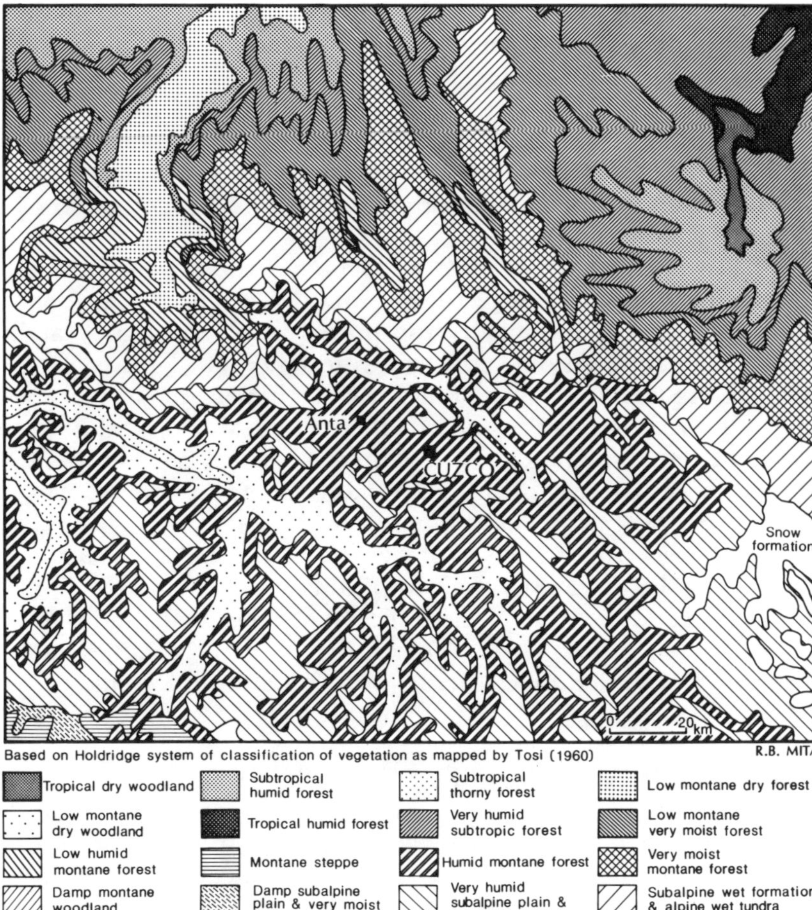

Figure 3.3 ECOLOGICAL ZONES OF CUZCO REGION

This is the harsh area of grassland termed the *puna* (a name that is also commonly extended to zone 2), a zone of pastoralism above the micro climates at which cropping is possible. Animals pastured here are *llamas* and *alpacas*, cattle, sheep and horses.

The *suni* (zone 2), 3300 to 4000m (often also termed *puna* in the south or *jalka* in the Central and Northern Sierra), supports the cultivation of tubers such as potatoes, *ocas*, *ollucos* and *mashuas* as well as wheat, barley and *quinoa*. This zone has traditionally been a major focus of subsistence activity throughout the Andes. Here many economies have evolved based to a considerable extent on the development and selection of a great variety of potato varieties (over 400 indigenously named cultivars have been recorded),[12] as well as the important production of freeze-thaw dried potatoes (*chuño* and *moraya*). In many zone 2 parts of the Andes, the area of land under cultivation and the man-days of labour expended are greater for potatoes than for all other crops combined.

The *quechua* (zone 3), 2400 to 3300m, is the primary cereal producing zone, lying beneath the tuber zone. Before the Conquest, maize was the major crop in this zone, and barley and wheat have since become important. In some communities, as in Chilca, these grains have at times become important cash crops, as well as being significant in subsistence. Maize is also important, remaining the most favoured Andean food, and *chicha* (maize beer) is ceremonially important. Broad beans and *tarwi* (lupin) are other crops of this zone.

The lowest zone, zone 4 or *yunga* (also termed *montaña* or *temple*), lies below 2400m. Sub-tropical crops such as *coca*, plantains, sweet potatoes, *yucca*, citrus fruits, peppers, chilli and sugar cane can be grown there. Tree fruits, green vegetables and squash (and in dry zones cactus fruit) are also important.

UTILISATION OF ALTITUDINAL ZONES

For some time observers have been fascinated by the patterns of 'vertical complementarity' that enabled Andean communities both to specialise in producing goods appropriate to each ecological niche and to exchange the surplus with higher and lower ecological zones. In recent years recognition of this ecological complementarity has spread, with identification of at least three patterns of Andean zonation[13] (see Figure 3.4).

Compressed Type

In regions characterised by a very steep environmental gradient, different crop zones are likely to be placed close to one another. Chilca, the village community described in this study, has a compressed pattern of zonation, with the *suni* zone of potato and tuber production lying a mere hour from the *quechua* zone where

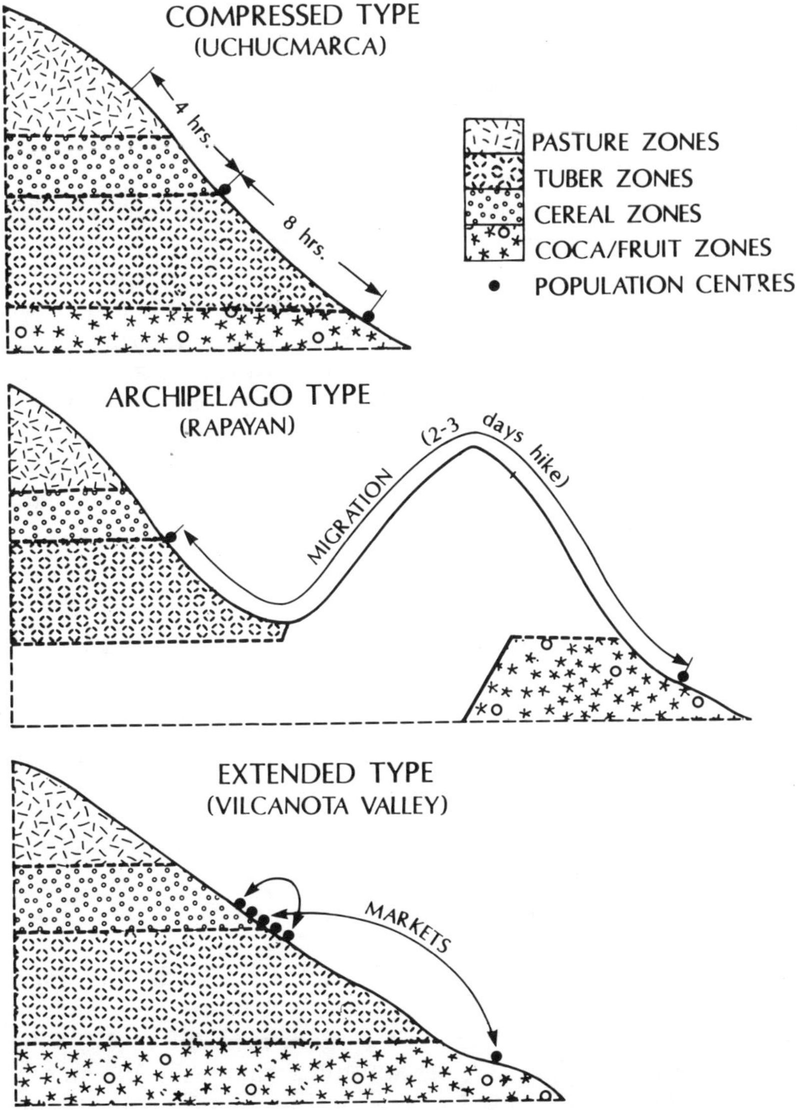

Drawn by R.B.Mita adapted from diagram by S. Vaughn in Brush (1977a)

Figure 3.4 TYPES OF ANDEAN ZONATION

irrigated maize dominates, with the intermediate barley or wheat *temporal* zone lying in between. Compressed types are, however, usually less closely spaced, and travelling between them may take one to three days.

Archipelago Type

The archipelago type identified by Murra (1967) remains a common pattern in some areas. The zones in this type are not contiguous but widely separated, requiring exploitation by lengthy migrations involving colonists. Murra's term 'archipelago' is an appropriate one, for in many cases control and exploitation of a distant zone involved sending colonists from one 'island' in the highlands to occupy another 'island' in the *montaña* amid different ethnic groups.

Contemporary examples of the archipelago type exist, with perhaps three to four migrations a year taking four to eight days each time.

Extended Type

A relatively gentle gradient, as in long valleys, produces a pattern of contiguous zones that is much more extended. Instead of population being clustered in nuclei, as between the *suni* and *quechua* zones, to permit direct exploitation, the population is spread more evenly throughout the valley. Instead of direct exploitation and constant movement, as in the first two types, the products of the different zones move through the system through exchange networks, which are often highly developed market systems.

One of the best examples of the extended type is the Vilcanota Valley (Urubamba) of Southern Peru, which was the centre of the Inca Empire with Cuzco, its capital, near the head of the valley. The valley is about 300km long, running from roughly 4300 to 1000m altitude. Impressive Inca temples and ruins testify to very heavy population density and intensive utilisation since before the Conquest. Today the valley has a very dense population, especially between Ollantaytambo (2790m) and Sicuani (3531m). Before 1968, the floor of the valley was dominated by *haciendas*, with peasant occupation often pushed up the steep valley sides (see Plate 2). The ecological complementarity in a region of gradual gradient has led to a high degree of specialisation and exchange between peasant communities.

ECOLOGY AND RESISTANCE TO CAPITALISM

The hypothesis of vertical complementarity suggests that Andean producers have had a largely self-sufficient economic base which has enabled them to remain resistant and largely impervious to the capitalist system. The exchange of surplus production from different zones has allowed communities to broaden and diversify their subsistence base. The Incan system in fact gave them ecological control, by which they gained the maximum surplus of agricultural or craft products through the vertical control of the ecological steps to which they themselves did not have direct access.[14] This sort of system still exists today.

Since Inca times there has often been a slow breakdown in central control over neighbouring ecological zones as subordinate populations sometimes managed to form horizontal ties with market centres.[15] In regions where market relations are reasonably promising, exchanging products for capitalist gain can liberate peasants from the central control that maintains subsistence through ecological differentiation. In modern times, this is most apparent in the Andes in the sub-tropical areas such as La Convención, where good coffee prices and warmer growing seasons encourage independent capitalistic enterprise.

Higher up the Andean slope, good prices for wool and *alpaca* fibre might at times have a similar effect, but in remote valleys and difficult environmental conditions the relatively complete, balanced and overarching nature of a subsistence system does indeed seem to provide considerable resistance to the inroads of capitalism. Since social relations based on exchange between the different zones have evolved, the whole system has developed a degree of cohesion. Given the ideology of peasants who definitely seek to retain their autonomy and identity in the modern world, if the forces of change remain weak, vertical complementarity can be a powerful factor in enabling peasants to preserve much of their traditional culture and to resist change.

However, this 'resistance to capitalism' should not be over-emphasised for, as we shall see, the situation is ambivalent. While peasants seek to preserve an ethos of independence and integrity for their community, capitalism has long since deeply penetrated the Andes in numerous ways: the products of mass production, the use of money and wage labour are all evident, and the need to supplement local production by engaging in wage labour, either locally or by undertaking circular migration, is very widespread.

REGION

The Andes are conventionally divided into three regions: Northern, Central and Southern Sierra. The last, named Mancha India, comprising the departments of Apurimac, Ayacucho, Huancavelica, Cuzco and Puno, has long been identified as the region of Peru in which poverty, inequality and underdevelopment are most starkly evident. A large proportion of the poorest quartile of Peru's population lives in Mancha India. This poorest quartile, which receives a mere 3 per cent of the nation's income, mostly comprises subsistence farmers (80 per cent); 63 per cent of them live in the Southern Sierra and another 13 per cent of the poorest group are non-farm wage earners of Sierra towns. Webb (1975) estimated an average income for 1961 of only US$280 a year in the Southern Sierra compared with $870 in Lima, the richest region. The spread of incomes was greater in the Southern Sierra, however, with 14 per cent of the population in the top quartile (over $540).[16] Moreover, this is the most characteristically Indian region of the country, for the 1961 census showed that 87 per cent of the population over 5 years old spoke Quechua or Aymará, and over half did not speak Spanish.

In the 1950s the large-scale regional plan for the development of Southern Peru[17] described and documented conditions in this bleak, denuded region. Although, with its high density of population, Southern Peru had nearly half of the cultivated lands of Peru, the region produced only a little over one-sixth of the total income from agriculture in the country. Eighty-one per cent of the economically active population was engaged in agriculture, yet only 38 per cent of gross regional income came from agriculture. Not only was agriculture unproductive but it was primarily subsistence-oriented; as much as 39 per cent of the total value of agricultural production was estimated to be consumed directly by the producers. Local production supplied 80 per cent of food consumed in the region. The small extent of commercialisation was reflected in the fact that only 22 per cent of the farmland was occupied by commercial crops (such as sugar, cotton, *coca*, fruits, vegetables and cocoa), although these crops produced 68 per cent of the total trade movement. Moreover, these crops are all grown on the lower sub-tropical flanks of the Andes, and do not come from the main region of the Sierra.

Underdevelopment and stagnation of agricultural output can be attributed largely to the scarcity of good land, traditional agricultural techniques and the fact that the social structure was oriented to a subsistence rather than a market economy. Other major causes of low productivity are unfavourable environmental conditions, excessively small farm size and fragmentation of holdings, lack of roads, inequitable land distribution between large and small landholders, poor technological levels and low nutritional levels.

The report declared there were about 390 000 small landholders in the Southern Sierra in 1958; most of these were Indians possessing family farms with an average of 0.9ha of cultivated land divided into three or as many as 25 tiny plots. It was estimated that the farm labour force was employed at only 20–45 per cent capacity, because of low efficiency and periods of enforced idleness with seasonal fluctuation. The report concluded that 'with the application of known techniques production on the Coast could be doubled and in the Sierra tripled'.[18]

This study of peasantry is based on case studies in Cuzco Department (see Figure 3.5). With a land area of 9 per cent of the national total, the department had in 1972 a population of 713 000 people, or 5.3 per cent of the total. The department was broadly characteristic of the Southern Sierra in many of its socio-economic or demographic features. Over 61 per cent of the labour force was employed in agriculture, herding and fishing. Eighty-five per cent of the farming units in 1961 were characteristic *minifundio* (fragmented, subsistence-based) peasant holdings, being less than 5 ha in size. Although some of the *latifundia*

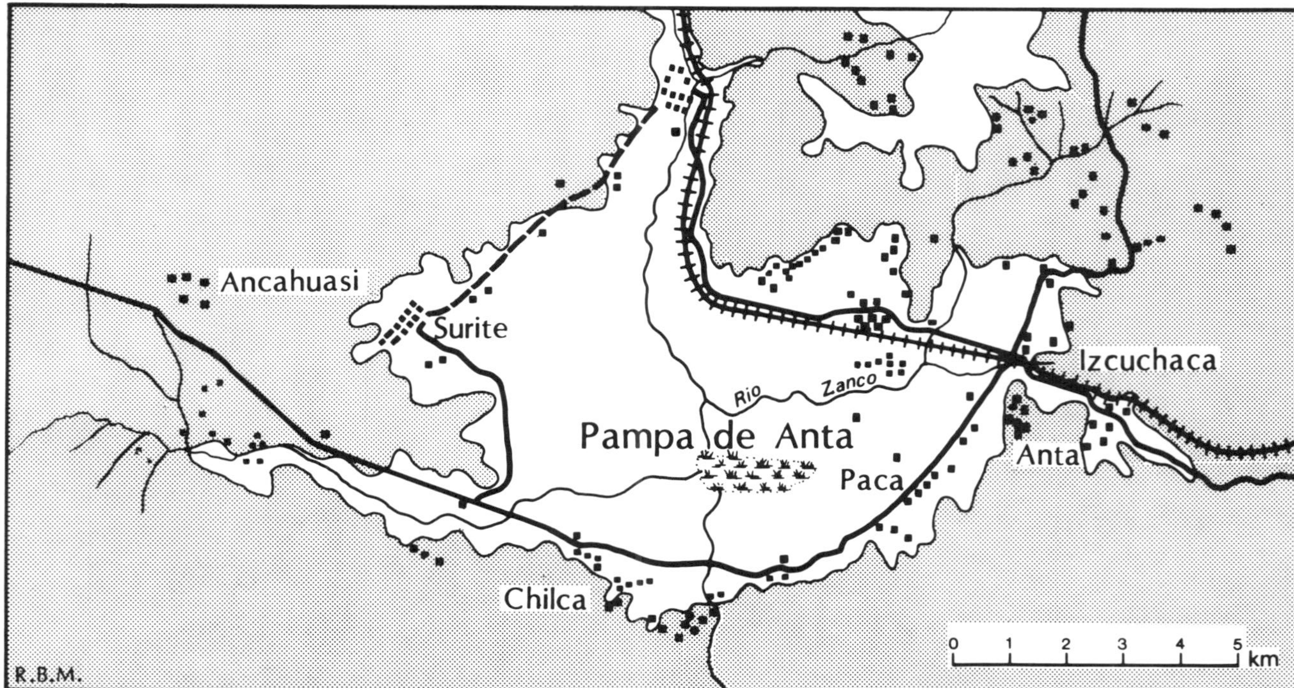

Figure 3.5 REGION OF FIELDWORK: PAMPA DE ANTA, CUZCO

(large farms) reached 65 000ha or more, most *haciendas* did not exceed 10 000ha and for the most part were between 3000 and 5000ha.[19]

In 1961, Cuzco ranked third among departments in the number of illiterates and only 39.5 per cent of the labour force could understand Spanish. In 1963, when one was required to be literate to have the franchise, only 2.9 per cent of the population could vote. The per capitum income of only 4392 *soles* in 1961 appears to have been well below the national average and below the regional average for the Southern Sierra. Within the region only Puno had a lower figure. Other social indicators suggest the poverty or backwardness of the department: in 1963 Cuzco owned only 0.7 per cent of all refrigerators and 2.7 per cent of all radios in Peru.[20] The modern tourist industry was one of the few signs of progress in this area of backward peasantry.

THE COMMUNITY: A PRODUCT OF HISTORY

The peasant community of the Andes can be seen as an historical repository and as a living manifestation of all the collective struggles of the Indians, of their corporate sentiments and the social ties that have bound them to their ancestral earth and to one another. It is important, as Wolf has emphasised,[21] to insist on this *historical* approach to the *comunidad* and to view it in the perspective of the economic and political forces that shape human actions, for the *comunidad* has been historically fashioned both as the structure that has enabled the peasant to be integrated into the nation and as a set of defence mechanisms that serve to protect his or her interests. Furthermore, in the Andes the nature of the community and of peasantry are closely linked and perhaps inextricably intertwined.

In an ideal scenario, the hopes of *indigenista* writers for the recognition of Quechua culture and human rights in a vigorous bi-cultural hybrid, uniting the best of the old Castilian heritage (and modern Euro-American elements) with revitalised Quechua and Aymará cultures,[22] are attractive and persuasive. But such a conception *is* purely ideal. It has been sought in vain for well over a century, with the forces of opposition repeatedly proving too powerful to be overcome. But even if the *indigenistas* triumph, it is far from clear that the creature they would have saved in the

Andean village community would be the same one they believed they were championing. For the perpetuation of the corporate community also means the perpetuation of a major type of peasantry and all the structures that sustain it. It means the perpetuation of poverty, sustained by its associated institutions and values.

Wolf's concept of the corporate community which underlies this study directs attention to the long, complex historical process by which the Spanish tried to resettle the conquered Indians and incorporate them in administrative, social and liturgical-religious ways, and yet create a convenient and available labour force to work their mines and great estates. Spasmodic attempts in the colonial period not only to create corporations but also to dissolve commercial guilds, ecclesiastical holdings, entailed estates and Indian communities, were followed by many nineteenth-century liberal government attempts to disestablish Indian corporate jurisdiction over land and introduce private ownership or open up community lands to the market or outside colonisation. Many such policies have left their mark, just as the stubborn efforts of the Indian communities to defend themselves and retain communal land ownership have both won a measure of success and have steeled them for the continuing long struggle with outside forces. There is no doubt that the communities (like peasantry itself) have demonstrated their survival value.

OPEN AND CLOSED CORPORATE PEASANT COMMUNITIES

I came to recognise the validity of the distinction made by Wolf (1955 and 1957) between 'open' and 'closed' corporate communities after working for five months in 1963 among several examples of each type of peasant community in the Venezuelan Andes and flanking lowlands, and in the Southern highlands of Mexico and neighbouring lowlands of Vera Cruz, Oaxaca and the Yucatan Peninsula.[23] Wolf distinguishes the 'closed corporate community' mainly found in the highlands from the 'open' peasant community which is widespread in the humid low highlands and tropical lowlands. The latter has evolved in response to the rising demand for cash crops which has accompanied the development of capitalism. It lacks a formalised corporate structure, land is usually owned privately, and individuals have greater scope for a wider range of economic activities and choices. Peasants sell cash crops which constitute probably between 50 and 75 per cent of their total production.

In contrast, production in the closed corporate community is dominated above all by the needs of subsistence. The community organisation reflects both its history of providing labour services for the landholding class and the political structure of the state which incorporated each sub-cultural group, defined its activity by law and imposed communal and individual burdens of forced labour and taxation.

Wolf identified 11 characteristics of the corporate peasant community. It (1) is invariably located on marginal land (since *mestizos* had occupied the best land), (2) utilises traditional technology and is (3) characteristically poor. The corporate structure of the community is retained by (4) community jurisdiction over the disposal of land. The system of power (5) in the community is often tied into the religious system and the politico-religious system as a whole tends to define the boundaries of the community and acts as a symbol of collective unity (see Plate 3). While class divisions exist within the community (6), levelling mechanisms minimise their divisiveness and reinforce solidarity. The lack of resources and the need to sustain the politico-religious system and its associated ceremonials force members of the community to undertake income-earning activities to supplement earnings from their marginal economy (7: see Plate 4). This may be day labour (*jornal*) on the *haciendas* or in the nearby towns, or involve some craft or occupational specialisation such as weaving or carpentry. A culturally recognised standard of consumption (8) consciously excludes cultural alternatives and rejects kinds of behaviour, norms or preferences which are seen as a threat to the community's integrity. Wolf calls this 'defensive ignorance' (9), a stance that has been analysed in depth by Isbell (1978). The community's need to maintain itself in a steady state, to decrease expenditures at a time of rising prices or falling incomes, often leads to (10) belt-tightening strategies of consuming less and a self-exploitation that Wolf termed a 'cult of poverty' and which I have described as a '*minifundio* mentality'.[24] Finally (11), the main unit of consumption and of labour obligations is the nuclear family, or peasant household.

In general we can say that a 'communal economy' exists

within and underpins the corporate peasant community when the organisation of production and work is affected by a system of inter-relations among families that have a 'communal effect': that is, a conjunction of economic benefits (productive, income and well-being) that are greater than would accrue to individual peasant families.

The closed corporate community, thus defined, clearly represents one of the most important types of peasantry in Latin America. With considerable qualification, the concept still proved useful when I returned for further fieldwork in Peru in 1979. But Wolf's approach has been criticised and he has recently admitted that his typology of the 1950s was overly schematic and somewhat naive. More research, which is now less dominated by Spanish sources or the top-down approach, has increased our appreciation of kinship or friendship networks linking people, and directed attention to territorial entities or kinship structures between the levels of household and community. More seriously, although internal conflicts were recognised in the 1950s, their nature was not well understood. Redistribution may increase the social solidarity of community members, but it can also reinforce inequality.[25] Although reciprocity may have great social value, as Dow (1977) has emphasised, redistribution not only converts wealth into prestige, but that prestige is itself also convertible into authority, which can be wielded by an elite to commit people and resources under their influence. Accumulating evidence suggests that internal struggles between Indian villagers within communities are a much more important factor than hitherto realised, while Gonzalez de Olarte (1984) has provided a rigorous analysis of the internal dynamics of the *comunero* economy.

Advances made in the study of ethnicity show that the old boundaries between 'Indian' and non-Indian which have never been static are less clear-cut, especially with recent greater social and geographical mobility. Despite the excesses of the dependency paradigm, newer approaches have at least heightened our awareness that the closed corporate communities functioned as a kind of 'internal colony' or labour reserve, whose exploitation underwrote at least in part the economic growth of the modern capitalist sector.

Clearly the distinction between closed corporate and open peasant communities is much less clear-cut than was formerly thought; rather, the traditional rural sector should be thought of as an open field within which the workings of macro-economic and political forces operate with varying degrees of intensity and are met by varying strategies of peasant resistance. The fieldwork evidence still suggests that the *relative* distinction between 'open' – becoming incorporated into national economic participation – and 'closed' – maintaining structures that slow the process of incorporation – remains important; they are best seen as poles linked by a continuum.

PERU'S PEASANT COMMUNITIES

In 1980, in addition to the more individualised peasantry ('open peasantry'), there were over 3230 recognised peasant communities in Peru with a population of approximately 2.8 million inhabitants, or over 650 000 families (67 per cent of total rural families or 30 per cent of all Peruvian families) whose labour force bordered on a million *campesinos*. The peasants of these 'corporate communities' utilised 8.6 million hectares, corresponding to 29 per cent of the cultivable lands and natural pastures. Living for the most part between 2000 and 4000m above sea level, each family possessed on average 3.9 cows, 12.1 sheep and 2.5 *llamas* or *alpacas*. According to J. M. Caballero (1981) and Alvarez (1984), they contribute only about 3–4 per cent of the internal domestic product at most, or between 2 and 4 per cent of national income (the estimates of Figueroa (1981) and Gonzalez de Olarte (1984) are slightly lower), which represents 27–28 per cent of the gross agro-livestock production. This shows their very low productivity since they represent more than 20 per cent of the national labour force.

The majority of the peasant communities are found in the Sierra and especially in the Southern Sierra, in regions distinguished by the semi-mercantile and non-capitalist character of communal production. The *comunidad* is almost exclusively a settlement associated with the Andes. In 1990, Cuzco Department contained 215 such communities,[26] all of them corporate landholding bodies with legal and jural status by virtue of a long series of laws.

While the communities are now changing quite rapidly and in fundamental ways, and corporate communities are failing to maintain closure, it would be a mistake to underestimate the strength of the corporate community and peasant belief in its way of life. For example, in 1977 a squatter settlement built on a steep hill of sand on the outskirts of Lima attempted to replicate the mother community in Huancavelica, which is located high in the Andes.[27] In the tropical heat of the coast, the living conditions were appalling: there was no running water and no proper drainage facilities, and people were horrifically crowded together. Dressed in their clothes from the cool Sierra, they greeted each other in Quechua as they walked up and down the sandy alleyways.

4 Historical Evolution of the Peasantry

Some of the salient features of Andean society existed long before the Inca conquest. The Andes were occupied by a dispersed population of many tribal groups and small states. Although they shared many elements of culture, they differed linguistically and politically.[1] There was a vast difference between the unelaborated cultures of some of the poor disorganised societies and some of the rich complex cultures of the coast.

THE INCAS

The 90-odd years of the Inca Empire resulted from a combination of military might, skilful diplomacy and conciliatory treatment of peoples who submitted to the imperialists from Cuzco.

The brilliant Inca civilisation is well known for its marvels of organisation and celebrated road and bridge building in very precipitous terrain so that a huge empire could be controlled from the centre. Apart from their extraordinary engineering, stonemasonry and other skills of material culture, the Incas perfected a system of communication and administration that rose above the challenge posed by the highland environment. A system of messengers covered about 50 leagues (240km) a day in relays, so that messages from Lima to Cuzco (670km) could be carried in 3 days.

Although the Inca civilisation was hierarchical and tyrannical, the emperor could be conciliatory to subject groups and adopt indirect rule; it was often wiser and less chaotic than many regimes which followed it. Quechua, the imperial language, began to supplant the myriad dialects spoken in the region. The Andean foot plough, still a major tool today, became the standard agricultural implement of the empire. State-sponsored irrigation and terracing projects expanded, bringing more land under cultivation. The technique of mortarless masonry became widespread. Inca domination gave a new orientation to Andean culture. Efficient administration levelled up cultural differences among subject peoples, and populations changed as colonists or *mitimaes* replaced newly conquered peoples. Gradually the life, languages, religions and institutions of the whole vast Inca Empire (stretching from Chile in the south to Ecuador in the north) were unified.

The basic social unit above the household was the *ayllu*, which probably pre-dates Inca times. Although opinions differ over the exact nature of the *ayllu*, it appears to have been a kin group that possessed a common territory (*marca*). *Ayllu* members were frequently blood relatives who believed that they were descended from a common ancestor, usually a mythical demigod.[2] There was little or no social stratification within the *ayllu* save for the *curaca*, or headman, often chosen by consensus. Soon, however, the *curacas* became hereditary rulers, many of them petty tyrants. As *curaca*, a man was excused tributary labour to the state and his own lands were worked for him.

Land within the *ayllu* community was divided into three: for the state, for the official state religion and for the *ayllu*. Where the surplus generated was not enough, the lineage lands of conquered tribes were incorporated into the state. Onerous agricultural and military *corvée* (forced labour) and public works were imposed.[3]

Alongside this state-imposed system of production and appropriation were universal pre-Inca systems of reciprocal help and obligations which the Incas were careful not to tamper with. These involved unirrigated subsistence systems of agriculture or group work based on reciprocity. So two systems of agriculture and land tenure existed, with that of the *ayllu* community functioning within the state's framework of economic, social and political controls.

Inca administrators' careful use and continuation of traditional reciprocity and group work to establish and extend their *corvée* labour system shows their skilful statecraft. The Inca imperial labour tax, called the *mita*, was also based on ancient traditions of *minka* (community work) and reciprocal labour. And the state was careful to furnish its obligations to the workers as part of a reciprocal system: just as a new house-owner would fete the builders, or a *curaca* the workers harvesting his fields, so the state would show its 'generosity' by providing food and *chicha*.

It is an argument of this book that Inca techniques of statecraft have played a major role in fashioning over time an acquiescent, at times servile, peasantry. If a conquered peasantry has no other option save revolt or death, then oppression may at least be much more palatable and in time even acceptable where the superordinate party, in a reciprocity system, assumes some responsibility of patronage for the subordinate population. The history of Peru is littered with examples of 'institutionalised generosity' which sheathes and to some extent mitigates marked exploitation of the poor by the powerful upper classes.[4] Reciprocity should not, however, be confused with appropriation and redistribution, which are different economic mechanisms or systems of distribution.

In spite of its efficiency as a system of reciprocity, appropriation and redistribution, the Inca Empire could not endure indefinitely. Large numbers of *mitimaes* had been removed from their ethnic communities, and class or even caste differences were widening and hardening. In the long run, the innovations created instability or threatened the self-sufficiency of the peasant community on whom, in the last resort, the whole hierarchical state structure depended.[5]

In sum, we can understand the wonder of the Spanish invaders who found a brilliant civilisation high in the Andes, with cultured people, cities and temples, irrigation and elites, warehouses, and an absence of poor or starving. But all of this was achieved at a price, and the ones who paid the price were largely the disenfranchised medley of tribal societies in the Andes who formed the first historically documented peasantry of Peru.

THE SPANISH CONQUEST: DESTRUCTURATION AND ACCULTURATION

The new 'conquest culture' introduced by the invading Spanish after 1530 is well known for its rapaciousness and ruthlessness. However, it is often overlooked that the Conquistadores learnt a great deal about the techniques of imperial administration and the mechanisms of extracting a 'surplus' from the Incas, just as the Incas had no doubt learnt from earlier cultures. Moreover, the Spanish were not slow to appreciate the value of legitimating culturally obligatory myths, such as the one that the Emperor was a good master and a guardian of the weak. Such a concept of *noblesse oblige* would prove to be useful to future post-conquest *hacendados* in ruling their large estates, for a 'kindly' *patrón* was much more likely to ensure obedience (or at least acquiescence).

The trauma of the Conquest and the profound changes that it initiated have been brilliantly summed up by Wachtel (1977). Two concepts play a key role in Wachtel's model of social change between 1530 and 1580: 'destructuration' and 'acculturation'. Destructuration refers to the snapping of the links which presumably made the different parts of the traditional social system into a meaningful whole. Traditional institutions and customs survived piecemeal after 1530, but the old structure disintegrated under the Spanish tyranny. Tribute survived, for example, but without the old system of state redistribution of which it had formed a part. Traditional religion survived, but became a clandestine cult, regarded as 'idolatry' by the Spanish missionaries who did all they could to uproot it.

Acculturation, on the other hand, describes the various reactions of the Indians to Spanish conquest. Acculturation of the Indians sometimes involved acceptance of the values of their conquerors, but often masked the persistence, conscious or unconscious, of traditional habits of thought.

Although it might appear (since much of the social structure remained) that the Spanish had merely replaced the Incas in a colonial state system, in reality that structure was a mere shell because the spirit that gave it life and meaning no longer existed. There was now a totally new system of domination and exploitation, and consequently a new social structure. A long continued process of destructuration and 'restructuration' ensued, marking the profound trauma experienced by the Indians, accompanied as it was by massive depopulation and the gradual evolution of the new institutions of conquest culture.

COLONIAL ECONOMY

In establishing a colonial economy, the Spanish (being ignorant of the native system) interfered with it directly when they shared out Indians among themselves and established colonies, peopled by *mitimaes*, which were detached from their original centres. Collapse of the old system of redistribution and population decline led to a reduction of arable land, the decay of many large terrace systems and lower yields. While the Indian population declined, the Spanish population grew as the mining economy boomed and the establishment of vast new estates aroused interest in food production for the urban centres and mining settlements. Arbitrary theft of land by the Spanish and redirection of water channels to their own land deprived some Indian communities of their essential means of production.

The tribute system of the Incas, based on reciprocity and redistribution, might have had harsh aspects but it was part of a meaningful socio-cultural system. The Indian peasants were now thrust outside any self-regulating system and became appendages to be used, with little recourse to constraining norms or to a legal structure.

The Spanish invaders were greedy for gold, for silver and for land. Their greed was justified in the name of 'civilisation' and the supposed desire to 'save' the Indians in the name of the Cross. Land was, however, useless to the Spaniards without labour to work it, and the institution of *encomienda* became their means to exploit it and to achieve the riches to which they aspired. An *encomienda* is generally described as a royal grant, in reward for meritorious service at arms, which entitles the *encomendero* (or grantee) to enjoy the tributes of Indians within a certain boundary, in return for protecting them and seeing to their religious welfare. An *encomienda* was not a grant of land, but it went beyond its initial terms to entitle the *encomendero* to use the Indians in mines or agricultural enterprises.[6]

The *encomienda* was the most powerful instrument used by the Spanish in the colonisation of the conquered Quechua. It signified the progressive dissolution of the Indian communities or their enforced dispersal to remote or less productive lands.[7]

Exploitation involved excessive exactions of tributary obligations and a marked increase in the amount of labour required. It also took the form of demanding without payment anything from sheep and poultry to fodder and firewood, and sometimes included the violation of Indian women not only by the *encomendero*, but also by his sons, brothers and even his *mayordomo* (foreman).[8]

The driving force in post-Conquest Peru was provided by the mercantile economy of the invaders. Whereas the Inca economy was self-sufficient, the Spanish economy was based on exports and imports. The Spanish greed for silver and gold knew no bounds and they squeezed the Indians to the limit; hopeless rebellion or escape to the hinterland appeared to be the only alternatives. *Encomienda* led to an immense increase in the number of *yanaconate*, or Indian vagrants, alienated from their communities. Clearly the rapid depopulation made the burden of tribute, *mita* or forced labour in the mines and other labour service much greater for those who survived.

New forms of tribute evolved in the direction of a tax system and the introduction of money and a market economy into the peasantry. The first tax assessments, drawn up in the 1550s, consisted of numerous food products, cloth, salt, *coca* and various manufactured articles. These often exacted from the Indians goods they did not have, for which they had to barter or travel long distances. Assessments were later simplified and silver became more important in tributes. From the various forms of tribute or tax all public works, religious instruction, monastic foundations, institutions of learning, hospitals and civil salaries were provided. Payment of tribute, along with the provision of *mita*, played a central position in individual Indian lives.

Horrendous depopulation was caused by ill-treatment, wars and epidemics – all external causes – but destructuration also signified a collapse of former rules of life, for the world no longer had meaning for the Indian. Drunkenness, forbidden by the Incas, now appears to have become common, and there was a great expansion in *coca* growing and addiction to *coca* chewing. *Coca* was indispensable for Indians working in the mines, enabling them to work almost without eating. Wachtel has suggested that there was a downward trend in the birth rate. While population estimates can only be tentative and crude, it has been suggested that an Inca Empire population of about 8 million in 1530 (before the Conquest) fell by about 80 per cent to about 1.3 million by 1590.[9]

CORREGIMIENTO AND *REDUCCIÓN*

Forty years after the Conquest it had become apparent that the mines and *encomiendas* were antithetical; they were both labour-intensive and the latter had the upper hand. The workforce for the silver mines was provided by the *encomiendas*, from the nascent estates or *haciendas*, or by the *yanaconas* or landless labourers. But work in the mines endangered the production of food and antagonised colonists engaged in agriculture or stock-raising. The solution was to be the *corregimiento*, an institution for the administration of Indians using individuals appointed by the Crown. At the same time as the extension of the *corregimiento*, the number of *encomiendas* was declining and much more land and tributary labour was passing to the Crown. In practice the financially burdened Crown also demanded a larger share of the tribute.

The new policy entailed the forced regrouping of the Indian population from their dispersed dwellings into over 1000 compact villages known as *reducciones* to facilitate their social control and manipulation by crown government. (In this century we have witnessed similar colonial policies in Algeria, Malaya and Vietnam.) The ostensible purpose of the *reducciones*, which were introduced in the 1570s and under which a million or more Indians were torn from their homes, was evangelisation, for as the viceroy Toledo himself sternly declared, 'it was not possible to indoctrinate each Indian without wresting them from their hiding places'.[10]

All Indians who had not previously been assigned to a Spanish administrator were to be placed in one of the controlled villages. Clearly, economic motivation tended to outweigh any ideological motivation, for the *reducción* provided tribute, a permanent labour force for the Crown and also led to the alienation of the Indians' lands. In order to discourage Indians thus 'reduced' from returning to their ancestral homes, Toledo ordered their houses to be burnt and anyone caught there to receive 1000 lashes.[11]

The Toledo regime established 614 *reducciones*. Within them, there was considerable exploitation of Indians by both Spanish and Indian administrative officers, as well as by the priests and religious orders. It soon became apparent that, far from introducing humane administration to the Indians, the *reducciones* and *corregidores* (people appointed to administer the *corregimiento*) were a worse evil than the situation they were intended to remedy. The salary of the *corregidor* was so small that office-bearers repeated the exactions formerly practised on the Indians by other government and religious officials. Indeed, the office of *corregidor* was to degenerate into probably the most odious, exploitative institution of the colonial period.[12]

Lands unwillingly vacated by Indians were disposed of through *composición*, an official process of land distribution which was introduced by the Spanish Crown in 1631. This policy was probably prompted by the existence of many defective land titles and the desire to bring in new fees to the royal treasury. The legalisation of many fraudulent land claims and illegal land sales brought much protest from Indians.

Two other new institutions were also imposed on the Indian tributaries: the *cabildo* and the *cofradía*. Out of the conjunction of *reducción*, *cabildo* and *cofradía*, much of the organisation of contemporary rural Peru was to evolve. The *cabildos*, town councils responsible for running the *reducción*, included one or two native *alcaldes* (mayors), four *regidores* (aldermen), an *aguacil* (policeman), and an *escribano* (clerk). The creation of these *cabildos*, modelled on Spanish municipalities, undoubtedly greatly weakened the power of the formerly influential and wealthy Indian elite, the *curacas*, who continued as leaders and spokesmen of their people.

The *cofradía*, or religious brotherhood, was an association of faithful devoted to the cult of a particular saint or the Virgin. These sodalities, characteristic of Spanish Catholicism during the sixteenth and seventeenth centuries, spread widely in Peru after 1650. Over time, civil and religious posts tended to increase in communities; gradually the modern prestige system based on *cargo* (sponsoring *fiestas* and holding political or religious office in a community) evolved from a fusion of the two institutions, *cabildo* and *cofradía*.

Although it is likely that these two Spanish institutions were established to be additional mechanisms of social control, the Indians soon learnt to live with them and indeed to adapt the system of municipal authorities to their own needs.

Indians in the late seventeenth century still suffered severely from paying tribute, being drafted for tributary labour and paying the costs incurred by engaging priests for baptisms, marriages, funerals and *fiestas*. Only three partial solutions existed: wage labour, sale of their lands, or flight to become despised *yanacona*. Wage labour on the growing number of *haciendas* or in the mines was but another form of exploitation, since wages were usually below the legal minimum.

The trauma of Conquest was followed by the shattering of native society, equivalent perhaps, in a social sense, to the largest modern earthquakes. The gigantic cataclysm was furthered by devastating depopulation, wholesale population transfers and the creation of homeless people. Even the entire balance of the economy, based on the complementary vertical ecology of the Andes (see Chapter 3), seemed to be in danger of collapse.

Psychologically the Indians did not totally submit to violence, for in the Taqui Onqoy millenarian movement of the 1560s a new cycle in the history of the world was predicted to begin. However, the movement was crushed by Toledo and when Tupac Amaru, the last Inca of Vilcabamba, was arrested and beheaded in the public square of Cuzco in 1572 before an enormous dismayed crowd, it seemed that the world had ended.[13] After economic, social and political destructuration, there occurred ideological destructuration.

However, human cultures are extraordinarily resilient, and even before destructuration had wrought its worst effects in the sixteenth and seventeenth centuries, restructuration had begun. A long process of reintegration also began, at economic, social, political and ideological levels. But the dominant form of restructuration adopted by the peasantry of the Southern Andes has been to forge, out of the furnace of repression, domination and exploitation, a toughened peasant culture that remains faithful to the old tradition of resisting the Spanish.

LAND USE

It was intended that the resources of the *reducciones* would provide the Indians with subsistence and also furnish a surplus for tribute. Pastoralism was considered undesirable as it would undermine efforts to control and acculturate the Indians in ordered arable villages; moreover, the Spanish initially wished to reserve commercial livestock production for themselves. The Indian was viewed primarily as a tiller of the soil, even though the zone was ecologically suited to pastoralism. Provision was made for arable cultivation in each *reducción*, with small garden plots around the dwellings.

The major crop fields, under communal ownership, lay outside the village in a radial pattern several kilometres wide. Slopes were divided into sections that were cultivated for two or three years, then left fallow for 3–10 years. Each section in turn was divided into longitudinal strips corresponding to the *ayllus* in a village. Each household in an *ayllu* farmed a plot in its strip.

Community control over land use was considered essential if a large nucleated village was to meet its subsistence requirements and the demands for tribute.

Viewed in perspective, the whole *reducción* policy is an interesting example of the imposition by the Spanish of a concept of clustered community, which was deemed to be the basis both for sociability and for civilisation, on the alien world of the Andes. In the Andes there is an incongruous would-be urban quality about the *pueblos* in which almost only peasants dwell; a Quixotic dream of an urbane and urban people seems to have been imposed abstractly on this difficult highland terrain. As would be expected, great dispersion has occurred; today less than 30 per cent of the population live in villages that originated as *reducciones*. Some settlements are more isolated than they have ever been since the Conquest and many will not survive. What *is* surprising is that the effects of *reducciones* have survived with such force for four centuries, in part due to the high birth rate, the strong attachment of peasants to their home area and to inertia. But it also suggests a considerable measure of success for Spanish colonial domination and the adaptation that the Indian peasants were forced to accept.

THE *HACIENDA* AND THE COMMUNITY

This book argues that while the peasant household is probably the most fundamental economic and social unit influencing peasant behaviour, a process of interaction between the *hacienda* system and the Indian communities has played a huge role in shaping the character of the peasantry. While three levels are involved – the global economy, the agricultural production unit and the individual rational actor – there is no doubt that at the local level the organisation of agrarian production by the great estates or *haciendas*, and by peasant households that are often linked to communities, are crucial. *Haciendas* and peasantry are alike in being complex, elastic and chameleon-like institutions that expand or contract in response to growth or regression of the world, national or regional economy.[14]

A *hacienda* is here defined as a rural property possessed by a dominating owner, using dependent labour, little capital and producing for a small-scale market. Under such a system the factors of production allow for the accumulation of capital, and also confer social prestige on the owner. It is often argued that the lack of capital and advanced technology result from dependence on regional markets which are incapable of generating sufficient demand to justify large investments. Control of the labour force of serf-like *peones* (workers) is maintained by using a variety of social and economic mechanisms, not least of which is the monopolisation of land.

It has often been debated whether the *hacienda* in Peru evolved from the *encomienda*. Lockhart (1969) has tried to emphasise the continuity between the two, a kind of convergence of interests. Keith (1971), however, has usefully distinguished between the *encomienda*, which is dependent on the traditional economy of its region and which therefore required survival of the indigenous society without radical change, and the *hacienda*, which became an institution with a labour force largely removed from its traditional social environment and permanently settled on land belonging to the estate. Once transitional practices (such as the labour draft of *mita* for the mines) had ceased, Keith argues that the *hacienda* had become quite distinct from and independent of the traditional indigenous economy of its region.[15] By the early seventeenth century the *encomienda* system was declining sharply, whereas *haciendas* associated with commercial agriculture were well established in much of the Andes. The further development of the *hacienda* system required the continued destruction of the indigenous communities and the transformation of its members into an agricultural proletariat.

EARLY REPUBLIC

In the late eighteenth century, peasant millenarian movements and the deterioration of the Indian position led to an investigation by the Spanish Crown. Efforts at modernisation and greater efficiency threatened almost every portion of the existing network of interests, and against this convulsive background a huge revolt led by José Gabriel Condorcanqui, who assumed the name Tupac Amaru II, was mounted. The revolt began as an Indian mass movement but lost support from the middle or higher Creole classes, and when it was finally put down after two years, about 100 000 people had died out of a population of 2 000 000.[16]

In the early nineteenth century, rebellion in Peru was threatened more by conservative elements who resented liberal colonial legislation. In 1821, the independence leader San Martín issued a decree abolishing Indian tribute and all forms of personal service, specifically the *mita* and the *encomienda*. Although San Martín sought to make the Indian a citizen of Peru, the legislation had little effect. Likewise Simon Bolivar, the liberator, tried to integrate the Indians into the nation by breaking up their *comunidad*, redistributing their land and converting them into yeoman farmers. His ideas had little relevance to the hierarchical and indigenous conditions of the Andes.

However, formal equality for the Indians and the ending of communal land ownership only deprived them of their former protection and opened the way to even greater exploitation and usurpation of their land. Although the oppressive colonial institutions of *corregimiento* and *encomienda* were gone, Indians were still the victims of inhuman systems of forced labour and conscription.

The period from about the 1820s to the middle of the nineteenth century was one of expansion of large estates. Communities were sometimes successful in defending their lands, and some local administrators sought to protect Indians. Indians displayed active resistance, a will to survive and apparently strengthened community solidarity, a basis for the modern closed corporate community attitudes (Wolf, 1957).

Fiscal crisis, political instability and variable acceptance of Western liberal ideas were reflected in the inconsistent attitudes towards Indian land tax. San Martín had terminated Indian tribute in 1820, but the Congress reinstated it in 1826 because it was an essential source of revenue.

The Peruvian Civil Code of 1852, which tied together some of the broken threads of liberalism that ran through the 1820s, defined the status of the Indian simply as a Peruvian citizen with the same legal rights as whites and *mestizos*. Immediately following its promulgation, however, the economically powerful latifundian oligarchies began to be formed in Peru. The 1852 code was a benchmark for the onset of a new phase of economic development in Peru. The Castilla administration launched the country on a programme of industrial and commercial expansion, based mainly upon lucrative exports of *guano* and the natural nitrates of the southern deserts. Booming conditions were symbolised in the launching of a vast programme of public works, including national railroads. For the first time since Independence, coastal agriculture began to flourish. Civil war and the shortage of labour following the abolition of slavery in 1855 had caused depressed conditions, but now new streams of investment capital began to flow into the coast. European markets were now desperately seeking new sources of cotton, and the American Civil War favoured rapid agricultural development in Peru.

Around 1870, the expansion of the coastal sugar industry motivated planters to search the Andes for workers. Under a forced labour draft known as *enganche*, agents of planters cajoled highland Indians into signing labour contracts which committed them to extensive work periods on coastal plantations. Meanwhile *haciendas* in the Sierra began their most dynamic phase of expansion in the late nineteenth century, fuelled by capitalist expansion on the coast, the beginnings of copper and lead mining, transport extensions and a steady increase in *alpaca* fibre exports from 1845 to 1875. New incentives arose for the acquisition of Indian lands.

The process of 'bonanza development',[17] however, was soon aborted by unforeseen difficulties, resulting from unsound decisions and a vulnerable form of political economy that had evolved with the capitalist expansion. A long, deep depression followed. Various factors contributed to national bankruptcy, but the 1879–83 War of the Pacific with Chile – basically an economic struggle over the rich nitrate fields of the Atacama and Tarapacá deserts – was a major cause. Just as a chain of fortunate events had produced an upward spiral leading to prosperity, now a series of related calamities spiralled the economy downward into ruin. The national economic surplus was quickly dissipated by the cost of waging the war. Then, defeated by Chile, Peru was forced to cede its own nitrate fields of Tarapacá. Finally, as Chile's nitrate exports increased, the price of *guano* on the world market collapsed. As foreign-held bonds which had supported the ambitious, overexpanded public works programme came due, they were defaulted. Furthermore, it was revealed that much of the currency issued by various Lima banks was completely without backing. The financial collapse was complete and there was no real system of national finance for a decade. It was not until the 1890s that the country began to show signs of recovery and renewed economic growth.

CONCLUSION

This chapter has shown that the social matrix of Peruvian society in rural areas has been thoroughly affected by a variety of colonial influences and pre-capitalist relationships. Just as the word *varayoq*, referring to lower rank Indian leaders, is appropriately half Spanish and half Quechua (the root *vara* denotes the wooden staff of office, and in Quechua *yoq* means bearer), the character of Andean communities is an amalgam of Andean and Hispanic institutions.[18] In Peru the penetration of capitalist relations of production came relatively late, dating only from the latter part of the nineteenth century. The expansion of capitalism offered possibilities of growth that were squandered by inept governments rather than being capitalised on in a manner which could have benefited not only the commercial and financial classes, *hacendados*, but also peasants engaged in *alpaca* and sheep rearing. Under nineteenth-century conditions it would, of course, have been quite unrealistic to hope that any kind of 'developmentalist state' might emerge; instead a highly hierarchical class structure existed in which a critically important alliance was forged between the landed elite of the highlands and the modernising and export-oriented bourgeoisie of the coast. As the *hacienda* system began a process of determined expansion and modernisation, the peasantry was inevitably squeezed further. The survival of pre-capitalist relationships in which the peasants were inextricably involved was convenient to the dominant classes, for it was they who could extract and monopolise the surplus in a system where economic and political factors were not easily separated.

5 Modern Peru, 1895–1968

ESTABLISHMENT OF THE PERUVIAN GROWTH MODEL

By the 1890s the prospects for Peru appeared to be bleak indeed. The country had lost a war and faced a national economic disaster. Within a few years it had shifted from being the wealthiest state in Spanish America in terms of government revenues to the second poorest.[1]

Yet the challenge of defeat and bankruptcy evoked a remarkable response. In the second half of the 1890s Peruvian and foreign capitalists built a very successful framework which promoted autonomous development. Against a background of Neopositivistic thinking which was optimistic about the future, stressing materialism, rationalism, modernisation and government intervention, President Piérola displayed administrative genius in organising the national reconstruction.

Four inter-related processes explain the success of this important period in Peru's history: local resources were intensively mobilised; a vigorous and expanding financial system was put in place; new export sectors were developed; and a rapid expansion occurred of urban, import-substituting manufacturing and utilities, accompanied by a decline in imports of consumer goods.[2] Exchange depreciation and accumulated investment from 1895 to 1900 led to reorganised, re-equipped export sectors by 1900 and increased profitability encouraged further heavy investment. Over two decades, the coast was transformed by massive capitalist development: for example, US and British direct investment rose from US$17 million in 1880 to $209 million in 1929.[3]

Great changes in social relations were inevitably induced by the economic revolution. The period was one of rapid population growth, the emergence of new social groups and of substantial urbanisation. Massive immigration of foreigners, including many Italians, Germans and Japanese, brought much needed skills, and many of the most influential entrepreneurs and capitalists emerged from this group. Small crop farmers and tenants evicted by the expansion of the new, large plantations often became labourers, mechanics and managers for the new enterprises. Increasing numbers of additional temporary labourers were obtained from the Sierra through the *enganche* system.[4]

The best hope of peasants and the Sierra regional economy lay in the adoption of a major staple, such as wool, which required only a few factor inputs. Under certain conditions, however, it could lead to pronounced long-term economic growth. If the returns were sufficiently attractive, they might lead to substantial investment, with important backward and forward linkages in the economy. Furthermore, investment in the infrastructure for one staple industry might prove to be complementary to another staple, encouraging its rapid growth.

Wool (including *alpaca* fibre) became an important commodity in the rise, and later fall, of Peruvian controlled export sectors. Although it contributed, at its peak, only about 10 per cent of the nation's export earnings, it did provide the means to draw the Southern Sierra into the international market in the mid-nineteenth century. Following completion of the Southern Railway extension to Sicuani in 1894 and to Cuzco in 1907, a rapid expansion of the wool trade occurred. From 1916 to 1930, wool accounted for 73 per cent of total exports through the southern port of Mollendo.

The wool industry reached its peak in 1910–19 but declined thereafter as per capitum income in the Sierra fell even further behind the national average. Recession plagued the regional economy during the 1920s and the expansion of the *haciendas* was slowed both by the stern resistance of peasant graziers and the declining incentive for large landowners to exclude tenants' flocks. Since the Second World War wool has never exceeded 3–6 per cent of national exports.[5]

The Peruvian growth model was unfortunately undercut and replaced by the domination of foreign capital, and Peruvians outside the coastal areas largely became passive participants, while the problem of how best to deal with newly mobilised elements of the population became the paramount political issue.

The characteristic Peruvian response to this situation was to resort to demagogic *caudillo* (leadership) policies, as President Billinghurst did in 1914 when he made populist appeals to the masses over the heads of the aristocratic oligarchy in favour of such demands as the eight-hour day. This violated an unwritten premise of the Aristocratic Republic, and the military responded to the elite's appeals by removing Billinghurst from office. Thus was established in modern Peru the precedent for military intervention which would be followed frequently thereafter.

THE *ONCENIO* OF LEGUÍA

These trends and their consequences reached both their apogee and logical conclusion in the 11-year dictatorship (*Oncenio*) of Augusto Leguía, which began in 1919.

Leguía possessed a keen mind, resolution, cunning and great pragmatic adaptability. He had been educated in Chile, spent years in London and became an extremely rich businessman with close links to American and British interests. His main goal was to transform Peru into a thoroughly modern, progressive and dynamic capitalist nation by making the country more advantageous for the operation of capitalism. He appealed to the restless, emergent middle and popular classes of Lima, and presented himself as the man of the hour, a would-be reformer and patriot, involved in the welfare of student, merchant and worker alike.

The real tragedy, however, was that Leguía's rule was entirely personalistic and arbitrary. In destroying the old parties, he left a potential vacuum so that government depended totally on the individual at the helm. He thus delivered a staggering blow to the political institutionalism that had evolved with some success between 1895 and 1919. In fostering a new, self-conscious and assertive middle sector, Leguía succeeded in building a countervailing force to the aristocracy. To the extent that some of the middle groups supported him and fed his vanity, they demonstrated their political immaturity, their conformist character and their susceptibility to purely populist policies.

Leguía was careful not to give away too much: the working classes were granted only enough in improved living conditions to remove their potential for instituting revolution. Moreover, the embourgeoisement of the middle groups in the last resort ensured their neutralisation. Although they were mostly excluded from the bountiful patronage handouts, the new groups of businessmen, bankers and landowners could enrich themselves from the growing economic pie.

Assured of the backing of the military, Leguía dissolved

Congress, did away with municipal elections, promulgated a new constitution – and perpetuated himself in office through electoral devices. His flair for the spectacular led him to carry through enormous legislative programmes and grandiose projects and to establish numerous agencies, most of which accomplished very little.

The 1920s were a period of rapid change and massive urbanisation. Lima's population rose by 68 per cent between 1920 and 1931, and the urban population of the nation almost doubled in the decade. The number of students increased from 195 000 to 313 000. Some 400 000 Peruvians were directly affected in their employment by the *Oncenio*.[6] Peru had become a very mobile society.

An almost unconditional surrender to foreign capital seemed to occur. Leguía expanded the government sector very rapidly and, with the international financial markets favouring loans to Latin America, the net increase in funded foreign debt was $105 million between 1920 and 1928.[7]

During this time much visual success was certainly achieved, such as the impressive rebuilding of Lima and the construction of roads into the interior, but the decrease in national autonomy over economic growth, the decline of industrialisation, the rise of food imports and the fact that export agricultural expansion in the 1920s was achieved at the expense of non-export agricultural production were all unfavourable trends.

The populist appeal of many of Leguía's policies and their fraudulent hypocritical results can be illustrated by his role in Indian affairs.[8] In the early 1920s socialists, communists and liberals were all arguing for integration of Indians into the national society, and turning their attention to Inca history, folklore and archaeology. Leguía joined the modish homage to the indigenous people and even styled himself Viracocha after a white Inca god. Ever ready to advance his career and hoping to cut the ground from under the feet of other reformers, he launched between 1919 and 1924 the most extensive programme of Indian legislation ever attempted in Peru.

Since 1918, a series of bloody uprisings had occurred when Indian peasants, responding to legal chicanery and violence on the part of expanding large landowners in the Sierra, tried to retrieve their communal lands. In an attempt to restore tranquillity, Leguía collaborated with congress in appointing the

Roca commission to investigate Indian complaints in the south. Erasmo Roca and José Antonio Encinas were genuinely concerned to protect and uplift Indian society and to act as pioneers of Indian land reform. The commission began an extensive investigation of land ownership titles in Puno and drafted for congress a comprehensive legislative code intended to implement Article 58 (which recognised the legal existence of Indian *comunidades* and provided for the protection and education of Indians) of the 1920 constitution. When many Indians presented their complaints, however, large *hacendados* became alarmed and successfully pressured Leguía to dissolve the commission.

Leguía succeeded in maintaining the delicate position of seeming to advance *indigenista* and liberal causes without alienating the Sierra landowners by pushing them too hard. The institutions he set up, such as the Bureau of Indian Affairs and the Guardianship of the Indian Race, appeared to be admirable state agencies which met liberal *indigenista* aims to protect and advance the Indians, but in reality they were little more than spectacular gestures from a distant Lima.

The whole period 1890–1930 marked the take-off of proletarianisation. Although the Sierra remained an isolated and archaic enclave, the home of an impoverished peasantry, it too had been deeply affected by the modernising processes that emanated from Lima and the coast. Indeed, it was a tragic paradox that, to the extent that the peasants were victorious in resisting the development or expansion of capitalistic *haciendas*, so they extinguished their prospects of participating in any broad process of modernisation. In defending their independence, the peasants condemned themselves to a future of isolation on the margins of progress, destined to be involved only as lowly, exploited, temporary workers.

POPULISM, APRA AND THE ENTRY OF THE MASSES

Before the end of the *Oncenio* and the onset of the world depression in 1929, the destructive dynamics of Peruvian politics and the economy had become more apparent.

The catalyst for the increasingly explosive character of sections of the working, student and lower-middle classes was provided by a young student, Victor Raul Haya de la Torre, a man who was to become one of the great revolutionary leaders of Latin America. An important influence in Haya's growing social awareness was the writing of Manuel Gonzalez Prada, the unrelenting critic of the oligarchy and diagnostician of exploitation in Peru and the thinking of José Carlos Mariátegui. Two other important influences were Haya's involvement in the eight-hour day movement and his visit to Cuzco in 1917, where he saw appalling levels of suffering.

The ideology of the early 1920s stressed the 'purity' of youth and urged them to assume the heroic mission of transforming the political and social fabric of Peru. Gonzalez Prada's phrase, 'the aged to the tomb and the youth to work', became the watchword of those who were to open the eyes of the masses and prepare them for the dawn of a new social order. The general strike in January 1919 for the eight-hour day, the first massive show of strength by organised labour in Peru's history, marked the beginnings of links between labour and students and also demonstrated the effectiveness of Haya as a leader. A further baptism of fire for Haya occurred when a crowd he led defeated Leguía's attempt to consecrate Peru to the Sacred Heart of Jesus. This victory of 23 May 1923 consolidated the bonds between students and workers, although Haya and other leaders were arrested and deported.

In 1924 the APRA (Alianza Popular Revolucionaria Americana) political movement was founded. It emphasised militant political activism rather than naive intellectual involvement.

Haya planned a revolution in Peru in 1930 but it was an army officer, Sánchez Cerro, who led a revolution which overthrew Leguía, and in 1931 Cerro beat Haya in the presidential election. APRA, still a nascent party, could not count on the support of all working-class people, and while it had broken with the Communist Party, this quarrel had hampered its progress.[9] Moreover, it was regarded as a party of *mestizos* based mainly on the north coast and, despite the enormous volume of writing on Indian affairs, its Indian programme (both then and later) was lacking in design and execution and so had little influence on the Indian community. The aristocratic classes saw APRA as a totally subversive party determined to tear down the Peruvian social, economic and political structures.

On the international scene, worsening terms of trade, tariff discrimination and increasing demands for the repayment of loans soured Peruvian relations with developed countries. Foreign investment increasingly came to be seen in the 1930s as an instrument of exploitation. Politics polarised as both extreme left-wing and Fascist groups emerged. As violence escalated and the middle- and upper-class alliance disintegrated, the military became ready to intervene at the behest of the aristocratic class 'in the interests of peace and stability'.

During the 1930s and 1940s APRA engaged in at least seven major attempts to overthrow the Peruvian Government by force, and party members were responsible for several assassinations of prominent figures. While the party hierarchy disavowed these violent acts,[10] many middle-class people rejected APRA as a whole; given the implacable hostility of the military, the party never achieved power during the period 1930–68.

THE DOMINANCE OF THE MILITARY

After the fall of Leguía in 1930, military officers held power in Peru in 1930–9, 1948–56, 1962–3 and 1968–80. What is the explanation for the military ruling for 31 of these 50 years?

Ever since 1913, when Billinghurst reduced the proportion of the budget allocated to the military from 27.8 to 21.6 per cent, any attempt to lower the proportion by more than about 2 per cent earned the ire of the armed forces. Such policies were seen as attempts to weaken their power, and contributed to military opposition to the government of the day. A stunning victory in a short war with Ecuador in 1941 over boundary disputes further enhanced military morale, elevating some generals to national eminence as 'national heroes' and 'supreme patriots'. Throughout the 1950s and 1960s, however, a section of mainly younger army officers just below the top level grew discontented with their traditional role of acting as a police force for the domestic elite or taking over government from time to time as the agent of the dominant class. A number of events radicalised their outlook, including the failure of the elite to deal with the problem of land tenure and foreign penetration of the economy. Moreover the vastly broadened scope of military training provided by the new Centro de Altos Estudios Militares (CAEM) widened the horizons of military officers and greatly increased their confidence in analysing the nature of Peruvian problems and prescribing appropriate solutions.

By the mid-1950s, in a period of strong American influence, with the democratic model appealing to the expanded working class and the frustrated masses, the old community of interest between the elite and the armed forces did not appear to be sufficient to maintain government and hold the masses at bay.[11] While the military regimes could sometimes present themselves as preservers of constitutional principles, of political ethics or as guardians of the nation, they could also tend towards the more usual Latin American stereotype. Moreover, the elite had discovered that the military, once in power, were not always predictable and could not always be manipulated.

NEW SOCIAL FORCES AND THEIR POLITICAL CONSEQUENCES

A 'terrible problem of social equilibrium' seemed to face Peru, and most countries of Latin America, by the mid-1950s. The choices were anarchy or tyranny. The widely respected but inept government of Bustamente had brought the country to a state of near anarchy in 1947–8. Under APRA influence, unions had extended and consolidated their control, winning various benefits for their members. Yet the government proved unable to cope with contending forces or to set any sense of direction for the country. Brigadier-General Manuel Odría's administration (1948–56) represented the other pole of tyranny. He not only banned APRA but also purged the unions, universities and armed forces of all suspected 'subversives'. Apristas (followers of APRA) were often hunted down and shot by government agents. The citizens, confronted with a choice between two equally unacceptable extremes, were condemned to impotence. In their hatred for violent solutions, the growing urban classes lurched from implicit support for oligarchy to demagogy, since there was no genuine middle ground.[12]

The rapid expansion of various urban classes and social groups in the 1940s and 1950s made society as a whole more complex, more divisive and more difficult to govern. Because capitalist expansion was overwhelmingly concentrated on the export sectors of the coast and in the cities, a massive influx of population naturally flowed into the towns. However, for a number of reasons most of these new urban migrants did not rapidly or wholly become proletarians. Data from the 1950s to the 1970s support this view.

In terms of political activity, it was difficult for political parties or trade unions to mobilise the atomised, shifting mass of workers, and it appears their degree of class consciousness remained low. Hence they remained susceptible to patron–client relationships and populist leadership of a 'democratic caesarist' type, and were especially concerned with instrumental ends, voting usually for the party which seemed most likely to respond to local grievances and to deliver jobs, housing and other services needed in the *barriadas* or slums.[13] Only APRA had any success in Lima's *barriadas* before 1968.

Towards the close of his term, the luxury-loving Odría had to contend with mounting problems. He was accustomed to closing his eyes to the corruption of his associates. Pedro Beltrán, an influential member of the coastal oligarchy, published a courageous demand for honesty in the next presidential elections. A huge uprising in Arequipa called for a return to democratic processes and the sacking of a hated minister whose programme of political repression had frequently degenerated into virtual terrorism. The fact that a right-wing autocrat like Odría was forced to accede to such pressures and even to enfranchise women (a change which more than doubled the size of the electorate in 1956) shows how volatile the political situation had become, and how pragmatic and even 'liberal' some of Odría's actions had to be.

The long-standing alliance between the upper classes and the military[14] virtually ended with the disputed 1956 elections[15] in which Belaúnde lost narrowly to Manuel Prado, who succeeded with APRA backing. The events of that year revealed the significance of new social groups which had now burst on to the political scene with unusual force. From the 1950s onwards, political participation spread throughout all regions of Peru and to almost all social levels, except to the most traditional Indian elements in remote areas.

Resolution of the 1956 crisis was achieved by the reconciliation of what had hitherto been irreconcilable: the final realisation that the tactics employed by the oligarchy up to date – coercion and political clientalism – were no longer, by themselves, adequate. A *convivencia* (co-existence) was worked out between APRA and the conservative Prado; this finally removed the revolutionary threat of the former but also lowered the standing of Prado in the eyes of the military. Old-style patron–client politics and paternalism had been extended by state paternalism under Odría but, most urgently, the exigencies of managing and co-opting the masses in the burgeoning squatter settlements called for the rapid extension of the state, and for it to become something of a welfare state.

The later years of the 1950s were marked by growing peasant mobilisation, land invasions and disputes with landlords (mainly over labour). The Prado administration was a low-key, moderate government which did little to influence the course of events. It was sustained by very favourable conditions of rapid economic growth and booming exports, yet the threat of widespread social revolution still hung over Peru, and the declining strength of the Sierra landowners, the stagnation of agriculture, the growing boldness of the peasantry, the growing flood of rural–urban migration, the insistent demands of the urban classes for employment, housing and other needs that would require massive redistribution, and the perceived need to embark on import-substituting industrialisation, all created problems and tensions.

THE ECONOMY IN THE 1960S

Peru entered the 1960s with the economy booming. Over the period from 1950 to 1967 the gross national product (GNP) rose, and imports, exports and productivity all grew. Gross investment, private and public, matched export growth at 7.0 per cent.[16] Yet beneath these impressive figures a number of significant changes were occurring which were to induce considerable unease. When we consider the composition of exports in this modern period, only one (copper) was a major export in 1930. Four new commodities – fish products, lead, zinc and iron – had contributed less than 7 per cent of total exports in 1930, yet by 1960 they had risen to 28 per cent and by 1970 to 46 per cent. By the mid-1960s, the economy had become so mineral-dependent that the large cutback of foreign and local firms on new investment and the absence of any new large mining projects produced a crisis in the export sector. At the same time the faltering of the other commodity in the pattern of bonanza development, fish products, exacerbated the growing crisis.

Over 15 years, the fishmeal industry showed that a highly valued staple could provide the motor for development and the basis for the achievement of a broader process of growth, narrowing the gap between the two sectors of the dual economy. It employed surplus unskilled labour from rural areas, it stimulated boat building, jute growing and a widespread coastal industry, and was predominantly owned and controlled by Peruvians, in contrast with the copper industry.[17] Unfortunately, however, the new staple was subject to an inflexible natural resource constraint: the maximum fish catch was limited by the natural reproductive capacity of anchovy. Maximum extraction could not exceed 8–9 million tons annually, but in some years production soared above 12 million tons.[18] Government attempts to impose official limits were ineffective, and so many new boats were built that a capacity to catch 30 million tons annually existed by 1970–1. The abundance of Peruvian fishmeal on the world market pushed down the price in the late 1960s, and in 1972 the long-feared ecological collapse occurred with disruption of the ocean currents. This virtually finished the industry.

The other significant development in the economy in the 1960s was rapid industrialisation. The widespread belief in Latin America that industrialisation was essential to expand employment and promote economic growth led several large export enterprises to move into large-scale industrial ventures by the late 1950s, with foreign firms inviting influential members of the elite to join the boards of their Peruvian subsidiaries. An Industrial Promotions Law, first drafted in Odría's term and finally passed in 1959, was exceptionally generous in its provisions, encouraging local resources, usually in alliance with foreign capital, to move into manufacturing. A massive wave of foreign investment occurred, and the Peruvian bourgeoisie quickly developed satellite firms around subsidiaries of North American firms. Foreign investment in manufacturing trebled between 1960 and 1966.[19] Industry grew at a rate of 9 per cent a year in 1960–5, so that the share of industry in GNP rose from 17 per cent in 1960 to 20 per cent in 1968.

Industrialisation came late to Peru, however, and produced both distortions in the economy and increased technological dependence. The industrialisation process was neither integrated nor self-sustaining, for the import content was high and increasing, and the sector became more vulnerable to foreign exchange constraints. Industrialisation relied heavily on artificial props to its profitability; it was not carefully planned and it quickly ran into problems of scale. Neither did it create a new class of dynamic industrial capitalists. As on numerous earlier occasions, the elite Peruvian capitalists took advantage of market opportunities and occasionally manipulated policy to their own advantage, but in welcoming overseas capital they showed no signs of playing a role as a national bourgeoisie determined to defend Peru's national interest.

Meanwhile the dramatic reallocation in investment meant that the classic agricultural exports of cotton and sugar declined, and some of the irrigated coastal land was planted with food crops to meet the demands of the burgeoning cities. With less than 3 per cent of the budget invested in agriculture, both agricultural and foodcrop output per capitum fell in the 1960s.[20]

As the crisis in the economic structure began to become evident, a growing consensus developed that tended to place the blame for the situation on two powerful groups. Foreign firms, it was alleged, had steadily displaced Peruvian businessmen and drained resources out of the country. Second, the top group of the elite (described as the 'oligarchy') acted, it was believed, to block reform in the country's social structure, preventing a more egalitarian society from emerging. In the rural sector, the great Sierra *gamonales* (landlords) were seen as an archaic, reactionary group that stood in the way of land reform which would not only free the repressed rural classes but would also open the way to modernisation and economic progress. On the coast and in the cities the upper classes, backed by powerful foreign allies, were seen as promoting only their own narrow self-interest and obstructing the initiatives of the new middle groups and upwardly mobile working classes.

SOCIAL AND POLITICAL ISSUES OF THE 1960s

The failure of Prado's government to deal with pressing social problems ensured that it was the last government dominated by the oligarchy. The 1962 elections, which appeared to be the closest in history, gave a victory to Haya (backed by Prado) by less than 1 per cent over Belaúnde, with Odría running a close third. The armed forces, however, declared voting frauds had occurred and took over the government for a year. Only lack of cohesion among the armed forces prevented a longer period of military rule and in the 1963 election Belaúnde, favoured by the armed forces, was the victor, although APRA and Odría forces controlled both houses of congress between them.

The Belaúnde government (1963–8) represented the last, pre-Revolutionary attempt by a populist, reformist administration which, in principle (though much less in practice), appeared to accept a mixed economy model. Belaúnde (an 'architect of hope') surrounded himself with a dynamic group of young technocrats and ministers, and in his first two years of office managed to have more than 500 reform bills passed by Congress.

Most impressive of all was his social programme, including education, housing and health, the Cooperación Popular projects of self-help community development and the new developmentalist role established for the armed forces in which they built many new public works and even adopted a kind of Peace Corps role (working, for example, in squatter settlements).

Unfortunately, however, Belaúndism was always much stronger on style than on substance. His government was finally undone by a serious constitutional flaw which had also hamstrung other reformist governments. The residual forces of populism and conservatism represented by the coalition between APRA and the Odría party had a clear majority, and when they determined to abandon the role of a constructive opposition and resort to mischievous obstructionism it was very difficult for Belaúnde's government to make any headway.

The fate of Belaúnde's agrarian reform policy represented both the inadequacy of his approach and the obstructionism of the APRA–Odría opposition. At best Belaúnde's agrarian reform would have benefited only one-tenth of the country's land-poor peasants, and he had decided that the reform should apply mainly to the troubled Sierra and not extend to the efficient large plantations on the coast. The military government of 1962–3 had calmed the situation in the countryside by granting agrarian reform for the La Convención and Lares Valleys, where a serious peasant movement had developed under the leadership of the Trotskyite Hugo Blanco. When Belaúnde's Minister of Agriculture introduced a far-reaching agrarian reform within a month of the government taking office, other parties unveiled rival agrarian reform bills and it seemed unlikely that the President's plan would emerge from the legislative labyrinth. Belaúnde received tacit support from the peasantry and their syndicate leaders, and land invasions intensified in 1963, with an estimated 300 000 people participating in seizures.

The APRA–Odría opposition demanded that law and order be enforced. Belaúnde hoped to avoid bloodshed, counting on the peasant mobilisation to give him political leverage over his rivals, but when in January 1964 the first major invasion took place on the coast, involving the occupation of about 30 000 acres in Puira by 10 000 people, Belaúnde sent in the heavily armed civil guard to evict them.[21] In the next week, 17 squatters were killed by police in Cuzco and 200 peasant leaders arrested. The final agrarian reform law, which was eventually passed in May 1964, was a vaguely worded administrative nightmare which provided numerous opportunities for administrative sabotage. Only 3 per cent of national revenues were allocated to finance the agrarian reform, and although its limited effects were not apparent in 1965, only 607 000ha and 20 000 farmers were to benefit under it by mid-1968.

After a study of strikes, land invasions and the proliferation of revolutionary parties, the General Staff School concluded in 1964 that Peru was 'in the stage of revolutionary war'.[22]

After 1965, the momentum of Belaúnde's reformist programmes began to falter. Unrest began to mount over the economy, and a decline occurred in investment. The conservative stance of APRA and its negativism led some of its remaining radicals to desert the party; for the first time it lost its hegemony in the universities to the emerging revolutionary left. Meanwhile the armed forces had gained in confidence, and easily eliminated three bands of rural guerrillas in the Central Sierra in 1965. Within another year or two, the army had reached the position of ceasing to believe that change could be achieved democratically.

Graft, declines in aid,[23] the slow-down in the rate of growth of exports, the deteriorating balance of trade, the fall in overseas investment and massive growth in the government's deficit[24] seriously weakened Belaúnde's government. A mismanaged devaluation in 1967 split the Acción Popular leadership, and a crisis over a long-standing dispute with the International Petroleum Company led inevitably to the October 1968 military coup.

MODERN DEVELOPMENT AND THE INDIAN PEASANT

What effect have these various policies in modern Peru had on the Indian peasant? They are still isolated economically, socially and politically from the mainstream of Peruvian society.

At the beginning of the modern period, probably the most outstanding analyses of the Indian problem were contributed by Gonzalez Prada and José Carlos Mariátegui. In his most famous essay, '*Nuestros Indios*' ('Our Indians'), Gonzalez Prada developed his theme of exploitation, showing how one or two thousand whites and *mestizos* had succeeded in subjugating 3 million Indians by means of an alliance between politicians and the wealthy of the coast and Sierra regions.[25] He pointed out, correctly, that this power structure denied Indians education because it viewed them as animals; moreover, education might undermine the systematic oppression perpetrated upon them. Mariátegui, on the other hand, rejected the idea that Peru suffered from a 'racial' problem and hence that Indian needs could be met by education. Instead, the Indian question was essentially one of economy and class, having its roots in the land tenure system. Whereas Prada focused on the rampant injustices of the system, Mariátegui saw communism as the solution, and formulated an indigenous brand of it based on the ancient Inca *ayllu*. The ideas of Neopositivists, such as Gonzalez Prada, had little (if any) effect on the Indians themselves, but did promote a new brand of *indigenismo* which influenced several generations of Peruvian intellectuals. In fact, Mariátegui's writings foreshadowed the Peruvian Revolution in that he believed that only by destroying the *hacienda* system could the shackles of feudalism be broken, enabling the Indian to progress.

Leguía's inauguration in 1919 and the Constitution of 1920 ushered in a new era in Indian legislation. Though Leguía is often portrayed as a great *indigenista* president who initiated humane, benign policies, he made little more than empty gestures. When circumstances became pressing, he showed that his basic support was for *hacendado* interests and compulsory conscription for road construction.

In spite of his great popularity with Indians, Sánchez Cerro did not achieve one piece of Indian legislation. His successor in the 1930s, Oscar Benavides, boasted that his road programme would be of 'incalculable benefit to the nation'. While it undoubtedly increased opportunities for peasants to market their goods, it proved to be a two-edged sword. As had happened under Leguía, road construction led to forced labour, and men between the age of 16 and 60 were forced to work in rotations of 15 days with one month off at a daily wage of one *sol*.[26]

The Constitution of 1933 was the only example in the decade to continue the 1920 concept that the state had a duty to protect the Indians and to provide for their welfare. Undoubtedly the most important event of the 1930s was the emergence of APRA as a major political force and Haya de le Torre as a very significant, and potentially revolutionary, leader. During his years of exile abroad Haya developed the ideology of his revolutionary movement which included an *indigenista* campaign. However, APRA never developed programmes of reform for the Indians that were operational or likely to be effective.

More to the point, they never gained the opportunity to try to do so. The alliance between the elite and military outlawed APRA, exiling, gaoling or killing its leaders. During the years 1945–8, when Bustamente legalised APRA, it was forced to choose between its middle-class supporters and its *indigenista* policies. When it chose the former and opposed both agrarian and Indian reform, it seriously damaged its reputation as an *indigenista* party. Furthermore, in its increasing desperation to gain power, APRA made compromises with Prado in 1956 and after 1962 with Haya's hated enemy, Odría, thus in effect turning APRA into a conservative party which seriously eroded its support from the masses and intellectuals.

Belaúnde's government was undoubtedly the most truly populist administration for many years. Belaúnde's appeal for Peruvians to embark on their own conquest of Peru, and the need for Indian integration, attracted large voting support in the Sierra in 1963 (including 64 per cent of the vote in Cuzco and 74 per cent in Puno).[27] His programme of Cooperación Popular was to be one of the means by which the Indians were to be brought into the mainstream of Peruvian life. He argued that modern Peru should emulate the cohesion, organisation and discipline of the old Peru in the era of Inca greatness. He wanted to encourage self-help, with support from the central government, and undoubtedly this achieved considerable success in villages. More roads, more teachers and more land for peasants were undoubtedly good policies, and the primacy given to interests of the Sierra was certainly new and refreshing even if the nature of the political economy made this unattainable.

Yet Belaúndism after 1965 began to fail, primarily because the massive increases in government spending were not accompanied by a commensurate increase in government revenue. Private investment began to decline substantially as export growth for the first time began to encounter serious physical or structural bottlenecks.

State paternalism among the poor had begun with Odría's populist policies in the squatter settlements, and these were extended and elaborated in the 1960s and 1970s. But state action to benefit the rural poor, which began with Cooperación Popular, ran into the problems of bureaucratic paternalism. Graft, inefficiency and stifling red tape did much to discourage Indian interest and support, as did a continuation of these practices (but on a much larger scale) under the agrarian reform in the 1970s. Although hundreds of projects were begun, only a small percentage appear to have been completed because of these problems and because of Congressional opposition, which cut off funds for the programme in 1968. By the time Belaúnde was deposed by the military coup of 1968, it was clear that most of his Indian programmes had largely failed.

Accompanying and often underpinning Cooperación Popular was the Alliance for Progress, the largest overseas aid scheme to the developing countries of the world to date. Yet, in spite of the massive infusions of aid funds, the whole programme seems to have been seriously flawed in its approach. Based on principles of Western liberalism, it provided transfers of technology on the assumption that the classes most in need would respond just as quickly, if not more quickly, than the *cholo* and *mestizo* rural classes who were more literate, better educated and more aware than the masses of rural Indian poor. However, very little of this aid reached those who needed it most: as much as $21.8 million of the loans went largely to hire American contractors to build jungle highways, $30.6 million for projects that reinforced the predominance of Lima, and $31.1 million on various agricultural projects (mostly coastal irrigation works).[28]

In the last resort, all modern development efforts have failed because they have not involved Indians centrally in the development process. While this would be difficult to manage, as village society is racked with much of the divisiveness that characterises Peruvian society as a whole, it is absolutely essential that Indian attitudes and perspectives be the foundation of development efforts. At frequent intervals the white and *mestizo* fear of bloody Indian revolts has been used as a scaremongering tactic, either to induce the government to institute reforms or to strengthen the forces of law and order in the Sierra. Throughout the 1950s and 1960s Peru seemed to be moving closer to general social revolution. Failure to achieve widespread social reform and integration of the Indians into the nation made that prospect an inevitability.

Part II
Village Community

6 Chilca in 1964

Chilca lies in the Pampa de Anta at an altitude of about 3200m, 32km north-west of the district capital of Cuzco. Chilca is fortunate to be located on the Pan American highway which links it to Cuzco and which winds on through the Central Andes to reach Lima some 650km away. The Pampa is also crossed by a highway that links Cuzco with the Urubamba and Convención Valley in the hot wet tropics to the east, and the Cuzco–Quillabamba railway crosses the Pampa with a stop at Izcuchaca, a thriving market and trucking centre (see Figure 3.5). The district, Anta, had a total population, at the 1961 census, of about 26 000, and comprised a number of small hamlets (*aldeas*), three townships, several *haciendas* and numerous communities.

Chilca thus has good access to markets and favourable prospects for receiving outside help: in short, while it is typical of many Quechua communities, it also enjoys better prospects for development.

In 1964, the community consisted predominantly of Quechua Indians who together comprised an *ayllu*, modified, reworked and probably consolidated by the other institutions of the colonial period. Surrounding and confining the community were the great *haciendas*: Hacienda Sullupujio to the west and north, and Hacienda Condebamba (both owned by the brothers E. Luna) to the east. Much of the life and work of the community and its fortunes over the years were deeply affected by these *haciendas* and the power wielded by their owners.

Chilca in 1964 was characterised by clustered *adobe* houses of mostly one or two rooms with dirt floors, and walled compounds (see Plate 5) interspersed with a few larger two storey houses belonging to the richer (*vecino*) families. A small plaza (see Plate 6) with a modest whitewashed church and two or three small stores formed the centre of the community.

POPULATION

In 1964 the population of 1100 people comprised 180 households. While almost all people apart from the school teachers were *comuneros* who identified with the community and hence were generally classed as Indian, Hispanic influences were more marked with some, and most of the small number of *vecinos* were bi-lingual.

While well over 90 per cent of the people saw themselves as *campesinos*, a few of the larger landholders saw themselves as *agricultores* (farmers), denoting a rather superior position. Above this, however, the people were conscious of their nationality and were proud to call themselves Peruanos (Peruvian citizens).

The considerable socio-economic differences which existed made it appropriate to distinguish three groups: the rich, middle and poor peasants.

LITERACY AND EDUCATION

About 30 per cent of the population of Chilca understood and spoke a moderate amount of Spanish, although only about 10 per cent were fluent in the language. The head teacher estimated that about 65 per cent of the population were illiterate; few of the 35 per cent who could read and write could do so well. Only about 15 men, and no women, had had more than five years at school.

Most people in the community recognised the value of education, at least in instrumental terms, but on the other hand there was a vast cultural gulf between the school, a national institution purveying the values of the dominant *mestizo* culture, and the Indian *comuneros*. This class and ethnic difference was reflected in the suspicion, at times even hostility, with which villagers viewed some of the teachers. Some teachers cultivated an air of superiority, or even showed contempt for the ignorance and superstitions of the villagers. At best, teachers remained strangers who could never be members of the community. For these reasons, school attendance was poor and erratic; often only 50 per cent of a class was present. Moreover, in an open field agricultural system and in a peasant economy, children did not enjoy childhood in the Western sense. Many children were regularly required to guard the few household sheep or cattle (see Plate 7); if these livestock wandered on to *hacienda* land they could be impounded, and payment of a fine would be required to recover them.

PEASANT ORGANISATION: THE HOUSEHOLD

Peasant organisation is rooted in the household which is the essential consumption unit, and the sustenance and survival of all members is the ultimate objective underlying peasant economic strategy. The people who share the same 'hearth' or 'eat from the same cooking pot' are the people who comprise the peasant household, and in the Cuzco area this is usually identical with the nuclear family (plus, occasionally, one or two relatives) or, in some cases, the extended family.

The household is also the main production unit, exploiting the 'family farm' (though the small *chacras* or plots of fragmented land, worked primarily for subsistence, cannot properly be termed 'farms') for sustenance and occasionally for the sale of surplus produce. Just as land plots are pooled to meet the needs of the household enterprise, so is the income gained by family members who undertake non-agricultural activities, whether earned within the household through crafts, or outside by working on *haciendas* or in mines or market towns or cities (see Plate 8). In general the family members, working individually or collectively, provide the labour force necessary to sustain and reproduce the household; where necessary non-wage traditional forms of reciprocity (*ayni* and *minka*) are utilised for major tasks (such as irrigation works, or harvest).

It is only in recent decades that capitalistic forces within the village community have become sufficiently strong to compete with or challenge this non-capitalist system of production.

LAND CLASSES

The people of Chilca recognise four distinct land classes, each corresponding to distinct types of terrain, land use and tenancy: *maizal*, *temporal*, *puna* and *pampa*.

Maizal land is irrigated maize land on the edge of a plain adjacent to the houses (see Plate 9). This gently sloping land consists of predominantly alluvial soils crossed by a number of small streams which are tapped inefficiently for irrigation. Occasionally, *mawai* or early potatoes destined for sale are planted but this land is usually sown in maize. The land, split into small *parcelas*, is worked intensively. Almost all of it is privately owned.

The *temporal* land is where limestone hills rise sharply from the *maizal* land and on these poor eroded slopes, at about 3300–3400m elevation, the peasants have small *chacras* in which barley and wheat are usually sown. This unirrigated or *temporal* land is usually unfertilised, and in 1964 one year of cropping was followed by only one year of fallow. Most is owned privately.

The *puna* or high land lies above the *temporal*, where an undulating plateau can be found at about 3550–3650m. In this poor, colder zone there is a considerable variation in soil type depending on drainage, or sunny or shady aspect, but *ichu*, sedges and inferior grasses are dominant. This land is communally owned and households are allotted *parcelas* by the *personero* (someone holding a position in community government) in which to plant crops; families with little land or many mouths to feed are granted more. The land is used mainly for potato growing, with three or four years of fallow following one or two years of cropping. The ancient grains *quinoa* or *cañihua*, or more commonly the traditional tubers *oca* and *olluco*, are occasionally planted. Many of the *chacras* in this zone can be reached easily, being about 40–50 minutes' walking time from the village some 400m below.

Pampa land is the poorly drained flatlands adjoining the *maizal* area, which consists of humic clays or peat soils, and this area – deprived of valuable topsoil by centuries of *adobe* making – provides natural grazing land. This is communal land, regained by the community in 1961 from neighbouring *hacendados* who had occupied it illegally for decades.

The tenancy system also includes rented land, and 15 men in 1963 were *arrendatarios* (lessees) of *hacienda* land nearby. They each held 1 *topo* of land in return for which they had to work on the *hacienda* for one day a week, receiving the nominal salary of 2.5 *soles* per day. (If a man held 2 *topos* on the *hacienda*, two days' work on the *hacienda* would be required each week.) Sharecropping was also practised (to work *en compañia*) when one man with land was joined by another who provided the seed and usually the labour, the crop being halved. This form of tenancy was helpful for the landless or land-poor families, as well as those with sufficient land but a shortage of labour. Finally, there was a category of church land worked by communally organised groups or *faenas*.

The lands used by 50 households are indicated in Table 6.1.[1]

Table 6.1 Land use in Chilca, 1964
(Mean of 50 households, in *topos**)

	Irrigated cropland Maizal	Mawai	*Unirrigated* temporal *lands*	Puna *common lands*	*Other community*	Hacienda†	En compañia	*Other*‡	*Total*
Total	37.13	4	38.75	38.73	13.1	8.7	14.8	1.3	156.51
Mean per household	0.82		0.77	0.77	0.26	0.17	0.29	0.03	3.1

*A *topo* in the Cuzco region is 1000 sq. m., about one-third of a hectare.
†Applies to men who receive some *hacienda* land to use in exchange for work on *hacienda*.
‡Includes rent of land.

It can be seen that a mean of about 0.8 *topos* of *maizal* land, slightly less *temporal* land and about the same area of *puna* were held per household. In total, households averaged 3.1 *topos* of land (or just over 1ha) each. The table includes land held in another community; often a spouse from another community owned land, which the household could work if it were nearby. The range in lands between households in the sample varied markedly, however. While many used 2–3 or 3–4 *topos*, three households had over 6, five had under 1 *topo* and one had none.

MINIFUNDISM

Minifundism is a system of agriculture that depends on a number of tiny, fragmented pieces of land that are worked primarily for subsistence. As it exists in Chilca, it is primarily a consequence of land hunger, which in turn is a result of the extensive ancient exploitation of land by surrounding *hacendados* and the rapid rate of population increase. In addition, the system of land inheritance divides privately owned land among sons, which results in smaller and smaller plots measured by the number of furrows. The fact that land is normally owned in two locations (*maizal* and *temporal*) also leads naturally to land fragmentation.

Each household, with its allotted *puna* land as well, usually has a total of only three or four *chacras*. In general, a man's status will be greater if he possesses a relatively large number of *chacras*. Clearly, on this basis of fragmented plots separated in different locations, it is extremely difficult (if not impossible) to modernise agriculture, yet there is sufficient uniformity of physical conditions within each land class to apply some common modern agricultural techniques (for example, tractor cultivation or improved irrigation of the *maizal*) which, by considerably increasing output, might induce a change in tenure and other archaic institutional rigidities.

THE CROPPING CYCLE

The two main staples of Chilca were corn and potatoes, although milk products were almost as important. Throughout Latin America, corn has high status as a food and accompanies most meals, and it is the crop to which the best land is given. Yellow, white and red varieties are cultivated, with the first (*maiz amarillo*) preferred.

The gentle slopes of *maizal* land are carefully prepared for planting. Two ploughings are carried out with a man working with a plough team (*yunta*) of two oxen pulling the ancient 'Egyptian' plough. Sowing takes place straight after the second ploughing in September, at the start of the wet season. Four to five men work on each *chacra*: one man with the *yunta*, a second man sowing, a third man with another *yunta* covering up the furrows, a fourth distributing cow manure and a fifth helping, including bringing food and *chicha* to the workers. Eight days later the *rastrojo* (harrowing) is carried out by two men. In November the first *lampa*, or tilling, occurs. About four or five men work with *lampas* (hoes) to weed the *chacra*, form furrows and build up the rows. Two months later a second *lampa* occurs, heaping up the earth around the growing stalks. At the beginning of March *yauchiy* (weeding with a sickle) is carried out by four or five men. *Cosecha*, or harvest, occurs in April or May when about eight men use sickles to cut the cobs from the plants, collect them in piles and each carry about 15 *cargas* (loads) of the cobs back to the house to be stored.

While maize is the favourite food (the food of the gods), the most important staple and the crop which grows best at this altitude is the potato. By far the most common and highly favoured for its flavour is the traditional *ccompis*. A more modern variety suitable for marketing because of its greater response to fertiliser is *mantaro*. An even better price can be gained for *mawai*, early potatoes grown on the *maizal* especially for cash sale. Preparation of the land (*barbecho*) follows a similar cycle to that for maize, with groups of men working together throughout the growth cycle.

The tasks associated with barley and wheat are also similar. These crops are much more marginal in Chilca, for flooding or drought often destroy much of a crop and the poor eroded *temporal* plots produce only niggardly harvests.

TECHNOLOGY AND CROPPING TECHNIQUES

The technology used reflects traditional modes of exploiting *chacras*, in this case through ecological zones which can be

Table 6.2 Livestock, Chilca
(data from 50 households)

	1964 Total	*Losses, foot-and-mouth disease 1963*	*Mean per household*		*1979 Total*	*Mean per household*
Cows	104	100	2.1			
Bulls	18	19	0.4	2.7	393	7.6
Calves	8	23	0.2			
Guinea pigs	312		6.2		413	7.9
Sheep	121	98	2.4		53	1.0
Pigs	57	46	1.1		108	2.1
Horses	45	7	0.9		85	1.6
Donkeys	13		0.3		14	0.3
Roosters	29		0.6			
Hens	130		2.6	4.0	228	4.4
Chickens	41		0.8			
Ducks	12		0.2		26	0.5
Goats	1		0			

reached easily from the village. Each household attempts to control lands in the three zones, to diversify their production, maximise their success with varied crops and diminish the environmental problems of any one zone.

Livestock are also kept (see Table 6.2), predominantly on the *pampa* while feed lasts in the wet season and later in the *puna* during the dry season. Cows, sheep or horses and sometimes oxen are also grazed on the *maizal* plots after the harvest. Unlike many Andean communities, Chilca does not specialise in raising *llamas* or *alpacas*. Guinea pigs as feast food are kept inside the houses, while pigs and poultry forage in the house compounds.

The agricultural cycle is determined by the two seasons. The rainy season begins in September; general cloudiness and maximum precipitation extend from December to March. High pressure conditions then prevail from May to August; this is the cold dry season characterised by clear sunny days, cold nights and early morning frosts. The mean annual temperature is about 11.8°C, varying from a mean of about 8.8°C in the coldest month of July to 12.9°C in the warmest month of November.[2] Diurnal variations are very great at this altitude and may differ by 20°C between the warmest and coldest hours. The zone is rather dry,

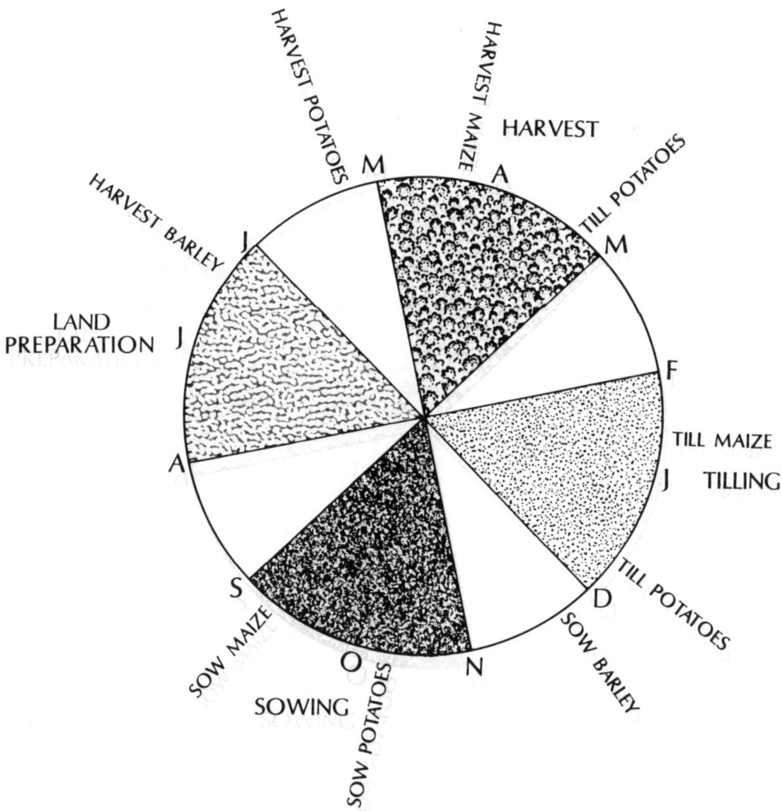

Figure 6.1 THE AGRICULTURAL CALENDAR, SHOWING SEASONAL WORK

with precipitation averaging between about 720 and 840mm. Variability is, however, a major characteristic of this climate, for pronounced droughts occur occasionally and severe frosts, floods and hailstone storms are quite frequent, adding to the hazards of cropping.

The peasants recognise four main cycles throughout the agricultural year: *roturado* (ploughing and tilling the soil) in the dry season from June to August, *siembre* (sowing) from September to November as the rains become more frequent, *aporqué* (hilling up the earth around the stems of the growing plants) from December to February and *cosecha* in the dry season from March to May (see Figure 6.1).

Traditionally the ground was broken after a period of fallow by using the *chaquitaclla*. A long-handled, spade-like tool, it has had an iron point added to it since the Conquest; above that there is a foot rest. Land worked with the foot plough creates a double layer of topsoil with grass and organic material concentrated at roughly half the depth of the raised row, a level suitable for tubers. As Freeman[3] has noted, however, a field prepared in this way is actually only half ploughed, consisting of built-up rows of sod about 45cm wide separated by furrows about 30cm wide and 30cm deep. On sloping land the furrows usually run downhill.

By 1964, however, the *chaquitaclla* was less commonly used in Chilca, except on the *puna*. By far the most important implement for working the *maizal* was the Egyptian plough. This tool is virtually unchanged from the light sixteenth-century Spanish plough which was evolved for Mediterranean soils, not the heavier loams and clays of the Andes in which deeper penetration is needed. It turns the soil over to a depth of only about 23cm, which is adequate on the lighter soils, but the heavier, dark brown, silty clay loams of the *maizal* would benefit from deeper ploughing; in 1964, only one man (a rich peasant) used a tractor and discs, hiring them from a nearby *hacienda*.

The other main limitation on adequate ploughing is the availability of plough teams. In 1964, the number of oxen and bullocks in the village was greatly reduced, for in the previous year a catastrophic outbreak of foot-and-mouth disease had wiped out about 80 per cent of the livestock population, including working animals. Even in normal times, plough teams were rarely owned by poor peasants; they had to hire them or, more likely, ask to borrow them from a *hacienda*. Delays were frequent and the season was sometimes well advanced by the time the land was ploughed and ready for sowing. This meant that climatic hazards were more likely and poor harvests might result. This situation illustrates the inter-relatedness of practices in Andean communities: common grazing on the open *pampa* greatly increases the danger of serious stock losses owing to disease, which in turn affects the preparation of land and leads to later poor harvests (see Plate 10). Enclosure would not only reduce the danger of heavy losses through disease and so assist cropping, but would also pave the way for other agricultural improvements and a crop rotation system.

The *lampa* (*corana*) is perhaps the only tool to have a pre-

European origin: it is a broad-bladed hoe with the blade set at an angle of 45° to the short haft. The *lanzon* or *allachu* is a narrow-bladed hoe. The sickle (*ujana*), a wooden mallet (*icosuna*) used for breaking sods, the spade and the machete virtually complete the inventory of agricultural tools.

Fallowing was a key feature of land use. Although the *maizal* plots could be worked permanently with irrigation apart from four or five months' fallow each year, I was told that the *temporal* lands 'would not produce' without fallowing. One year of rest was needed after each year of cropping wheat or barley. A few fortunate people owned 3–5 *parcelas* of *temporal* land, working one each year.

In the *puna* a collective *laymi* system was practised on the communal land. The *puna* was divided into named sectors and every year a new sector was selected. A rest of seven years was regarded as necessary after a year of cropping, but the average period of fallow was only three or four years. Formerly more peasants cropped unused *hacienda* land, but quarrels in recent years between the community and the *haciendas* had confined villagers to their own lands and population growth had led to shorter rotations. The good price for barley offered by the Cuzco beer company was the main reason for overcropping of steep *temporal* land in recent years. It was clear in 1964 that this period of fallowing was insufficient for an adequate build-up of organic matter in the soil before the land was cropped again.

YIELDS

In the great majority of *chacras* yields were low, occasionally disastrously so. Discussion with 52 households revealed the precariousness of the livelihood of many. Clearly, it was necessary to seek access to additional land on the *haciendas*, supplementing income by casual work in the nearby towns or resorting to migration on the part of some family members.

It must be emphasised that harvest data is only approximate, based on memory of the number of *cargas* gathered at the previous harvest, but the high degree of concordance of yields from similar land gives confidence in the results. Moreover, mean yields are difficult to estimate since harvests vary considerably in response to the wide range of climatic conditions experienced from year to year. Corn harvests on *maizal* land in 1963 varied mostly between 200 and 300kg per *topo* (600 and 900 per hectare), with the mean of 78 plots being only 266kg. *Mawai* grown for sale on the same land averaged about 747kg. By far the most satisfactory and dependable harvests were gained from potatoes grown in the *puna*: the mean of 53 *chacras* was 1090kg. The extreme marginality of the poor *temporal* land was revealed in the excessively low harvests for barley (mean of 86kg per *topo* on nine plots) and wheat (82kg on nine plots). A small number of *campesinos* grew *habas* (broad beans) in 1963, averaging only about 93kg per *topo*, and *olluco* in the *puna* (270kg).

The most convincing evidence of the inadequacy of yields is provided by the planting/harvest ratio. All *campesinos* are only too aware of the proportion of the stored harvest that has to be retained rather than consumed in order to plant the new season's crop. In 1964, the planting to harvest ratio reached its lowest in the poorest land of the *puna*, where the ratio varied from 1:3 to 1:8. Planting to harvesting ratios that were nearly as low applied to some of the *temporal* plots of barley and wheat.

CAUSES OF POOR HARVESTS

Several factors contribute to low harvests. Highly variable weather conditions and natural hazards loom large, while soil limitations,[4] inadequate water supply for irrigated lands, a high incidence of insect pests, fungus and other crop diseases, shortened fallow systems and overcropping, and the abandonment of some traditional rotational patterns all play a major role. Inadequate application of animal manures has been common, while artificial fertilisers, insecticides and fungicides are largely not used. The growing incidence of sheet erosion and gullying testifies to a man–land relationship that is no longer in balance.

The large-scale *Plan Regional del Sur* of the 1950s estimated that the Southern Sierra suffered crop failure owing to hail, frost and drought that amounted to the loss of one complete crop every seven years for the area as a whole. Ninety per cent of the informants at Chilca had in 1963 lost more than 25 per cent of the normal harvest through these hazards. On 16 out of 78 *chacras* of corn, for example, the crop was totally wiped out either by flooding or heavy frosts, or a combination of the two. Several plots of *temporal* crops were also destroyed. Climatic hazards were much less dangerous in the *puna* where the potato, *oca* and *olluca* are traditionally adapted to this climatic zone.

Lack of water[5] is almost as serious as lack of land to many *comuneros*. Production on the small *maizal chacras* is quite intensive, but inadequate water distribution from the small streams that descend from the *puna*, and intense competition between households for the desperately needed water, cause chronic problems. *Campesinos* who have plots near a stream source at the base of the hills are specially favoured, compared with those further off who must wait until the scarce water has passed across the plots of several others. Cleaning and maintaining the irrigation (*riego*) ditches is one of the more important *faenas* for which labour from all households is regularly mobilised. Better levelling or grading of slopes and ditches would achieve a much more efficient distribution of irrigation water; this was an innovation that some Andean communities welcomed in the 1970s.

After weather hazards, *campesinos* identified a considerable number of plant pests, insects, worms (*gusanos*) and fungus diseases which ravaged their crops. A list of the pests reported at Chilca is shown in Table 6.3.

Although standard insecticides or fungicides would have controlled these pests economically, no one in the community had ever used sprays and only a few had ever heard of their existence. Some men used ash made from cow manure as a traditional technique of combating plagues that infested maize. On low-lying land, waterlogging caused problems in the rainy season and here standing water can accumulate in the *pampa* fields, stagnate and cause root rot and disease. Maize is more resistant to these conditions than potato. A considerable problem occurs, too, because of the high ground water level; the parasitic snail *callotacca* thrives in these conditions and attacks growing plants. Clearly major drainage of the Pampa de Anta would not only allow more land to be used for cropping, but would also lessen the depredations of a number of crop pests.

Many *campesinos* asserted that harvests were lower than in previous years, and the principal reason was said to be the shortened fallow period on the various classes of land.

On the *maizal* and *temporal chacras*, low yields indicated low chemical fertility. On the former colluvial land fallowing is not necessary, given intensive tillage and the use of adequate animal

Table 6.3 Biological pests affecting agriculture at Chilca

Common name	*Quechua name*	*Scientific name*
MAIZE		
rancha	*illa*	*Acordulecera* sp.
otoscuro	*gorgojo*	*Heliothis* sp.
gusano negro	*socra*	*Pococera* sp.
	qoto	
	sillhui kuru	*Laphygma frugiperda*
		Feltia experta
		Copitarsia turbata
loro	*raca*	*Diabiotica decolor*
rata rata		*Racumin* sp.
paku		
	q'oto	*Diplodia zea*
		Ustilago maydis
POTATOES		
pequena mosca	*callotacca*	*Perfecthion metasystox*
		Liviomyza sp.
	carhua	*Epicanta willex*
illa kuro	*huaylu*	*Gnorimosche* sp.
taladro		*Terastia meticulosalia*
la rancha (leaf)	*seca seca corcho*	*Phytophthora infestans*
tapura		*Polyrania combi*
	sillhui	*Laphygma frugiperda*
		Xylomiges evidania
	papa piqui	*Epitrix* sp.
	yurac kuro	*Bothynus maimon*
	loro loro	*Diobiotica decolor*
	raka kuro	*Perfecthion metasystox*
	koya	*Puccinia* sp.
putrefaction	*ichu kuro*	*Pseudomonas* sp.
		Podrialumbre parda
	q'oto	
	ccarhua	
WHEAT		
roya		*Puccinia graministratia* (tallo)
LUPIN (TARWI)		
gusano		*Azodmia* sp.
BARLEY		
rancha		*Puccinia graministratia* (tallo)
roya		

Table 6.3 continued

Common name	*Quechua name*	*Scientific name*
PIGS		
		Trequina sp.
pig fever	*callotacca*	*Fasiola hepatica*

Source: Fieldwork. Scientific names were identified at the Servicio de Investigación y Promoción de Agricultura, Cuzco, in October 1964.

manure as fertiliser. Yet these *maizal chacras* received on average only about 250kg of animal manure per year per *topo* together with some household ash. Although the value of fertilisers was recognised, the supply of animal manure was inadequate and the use of manure for fuel (because of the great shortage of firewood) made inroads on the supply. Cultivators complained that the ears of maize were smaller than formerly, and the tiny cobs certainly displayed evidence of nutrient deficiency. Apart from one corral on the *puna*, Chilca did not use corrals to herd animals at night and so did not practise the moving of corrals each year to optimise soil fertility, as is common in many high altitude communities. Only two or three men with horses used the *puna* corral for collecting manure, applying it only to *maizal* plots, not to land in the *temporal* or *puna*. People did, however, recognise the advantages of relieving themselves in the fields next to their homes to improve soil fertility. Not much use was made of intercropping, and neither were legumes grown (*tarwi* was a major crop for many villages on poor land at high elevations).

A year earlier a new fertiliser factory had been built nearby at Cachimayo, a project funded by West German aid, but in 1963–4 no *comuneros* of Chilca had purchased any of the new phosphate fertilisers. One man nearby had bought some that a middleman had acquired from the factory, but as the fertiliser had been diluted with talcum powder the *campesino* got no result on his plots. A local *hacendado* occasionally bought *guano*, acquired from the coast through a Cuzco merchant and resold at a profit to *campesinos*. Only about three men from Chilca had bought and used *guano* on their land, but they were well aware of its value.

The *Plan Regional del Sur* estimated that 47 per cent of the cultivated area of the Southern Sierra suffers substantial handicaps to crop production, and the Food and Agriculture Organisation and the International Bank for Reconstruction and Development (IBRD) found that depleted soil fertility and erosion were among the most significant problems of the Sierra.

THE GOALS OF PRODUCTION

Overwhelmingly, the heads of households saw their main task as subsisting and providing a livelihood for their families. Life is often seen as a constant struggle against nature, and against other people.

Only three households out of 52 in the sample produced a sufficient surplus of crops to indulge in cash sales or conversion of corn into *chicha* for sale. Since most households possessed or had access to only one or two small plots of land, the battle to survive dominated their lives. When, as in many cases, the area of land available was inadequate to feed the household, supplementary measures were necessary: the *campesino* might choose to gain the use of a *topo* or two of *hacienda* land; or he might engage in casual *jornal* in Izcuchaca or Cuzco; or resort to pendular or circular, semi-permanent or permanent migration by one or two family members to obtain income externally.

Thus although Chilca, like other communities, was proud of being 'free' and 'independent' (no *comuneros* conceded the validity of the *hacendados*' claims to own a portion of the *pampa* and of the *puna*), the economic strategies followed by the peasantry revealed the hollowness of their claim. Their poverty and the ever present processes of pauperisation (whether caused by natural hazards, crop or animal disease, population growth, the aggrandisement of the *hacendados*, ill health or misfortune) either forced dependence, through a relationship of servitude to more powerful local property holders, or meant seeking opportunities in the modern capitalistic world through the labour market. The apparently self-contained, isolated character of the closed corporate community is thus partly illusory, for it is closely and deeply involved with the outside world.

The degree of importance in gaining money incomes in Chilca is indicated in Table 6.4. Although *campesinos* largely saw their lives as tilling their *chacras* and gaining a living from the earth, the most common source of income in 1964 was working on the

Table 6.4 Sources of monetary income, 1963 and 1978
(Number of households)

	1963	*1978*
Daily labouring		
Labour on nearby *hacienda*	19	
Other *haciendas*	1	
Woodcutting, or work in *hacienda* plantation	17	2
Planting trees, Forest Service	10	
Construction work, Izcuchaka	8	13
Construction work, Cuzco	6	4
Porter, Cuzco	1	
Harvesting and seasonal labour, Urubamba Valley	5	6
Road work	2	
Household sales		
Cheeses	12	17
Milk	2	27
Cows	6	13
Bulls	4	5
Sheep	2	1
Pigs	3	
Poultry	1	
Skins	1	
Eggs	4	
Maize	1	5
Habas		2
Potatoes	1	6
Chicha	5	
Wheat		1
Village store	4	2
Crafts		
Tailor	3	
Weaving	2	
Pottery	–	1
Making *adobes*	2	1
Knitting ponchos	–	1
Making tiles in nearby village	1	
Carpentry	1	2
Sewing	–	1
Buying and selling livestock	2	
Repairing huts	1	
Stonemason	1	
Blacksmith	1	
Butcher	1	
Remittances		
From 2 relatives	6	1.6
From 1 relative	5	

continued on p. 100

Table 6.4 continued

	1963	*1978*
Wages		
Salary, administrator of *hacienda*	1	
Wage, fertiliser factory hand	1	
Rent		
Team of bullocks	2	6
Land	1	1
Total of individual items of income	146	

local *haciendas*, either as general agricultural or plantation labourers, or as woodcutters. An important new source of income also appeared: planting trees in local communities in an afforestation programme run by the National Forest Service on Alliance for Progress aid funds. Table 6.4 lists all other sources of income.

INCOME LEVELS

The method of calculating incomes is rather suspect, involving recall of periods of day labouring in the previous year, and the sale of stock or other items. It may be that the figures presented underestimate real incomes to a degree. The mean income of 47 households is 1547 *soles* (US$62) with a range from 240 to 5240 *soles*: at an average size of 5.8 people per household, at 25 *soles* per US$ in 1964, this gives a mean per capitum income of 268 *soles* ($10.7). Households can be placed in a relative category of 'rich', 'middle', or 'poor' peasants. On this basis, nine households in the sample are categorised as 'rich' (above 2500 *soles*), seven as 'middle' (1000–2500 *soles*), and the remainder, 31 (below 1000 *soles*), as 'poor' peasants.

In terms of the *campesinos*' own self-view, however, wealth and poverty are perceived primarily in terms of land. Moreover, land *owned* is of much greater security and status than land used. Only four households in the sample of 52 can be said to be rich in land according to local perceptions, holding 5 *topos* or more (2ha).

What relationship, if any, is there between richness or poverty in land held and monetary incomes? A word of caution is necessary in interpreting income data. Income is best looked at alongside household composition and age structure and the various social, economic and ceremonial needs that each household faces in a year. Much income earned (or gifts requested from wage-earning relatives) is for specific 'target income' ends. Such targets may not be repeated for some considerable time so that a household that has a relatively high money income (and expenditure) in one year may earn and spend no more than the rest in the succeeding year. The transient nature of the 'rich' category of some households therefore becomes clear.

Consideration of the details of household budgets supports this view. Four out of the nine so-called 'rich' households in money income in 1963 achieved a good part of their earnings by the sale of a cow or bulk capital stock. One man was fortunate to possess one of the few salaried positions in the neighbourhood, earning 4800 *soles* as administrator of a nearby *hacienda*. Two men possessed special skills upon which they could capitalise: one was a good house builder and the other was a tailor. Three men showed greater commitment than usual to labouring jobs, one making tiles in a nearby village and two labouring on a *hacienda*. Indeed, a considerable proletarian aspect to peoples' lives is indicated in the fact that 40 per cent of households indulged in wage or salary work and in total this contributed about 26 per cent of monetary income. One household benefited marginally from a tiny village store, which appeared to make a profit of only about 20 *soles* per week. Two households benefited substantially from remittances: in one case two daughters in Lima sent a total of 300 *soles* three or four times during the year, and in another case a son employed in a business firm in Lima sent 100 to 150 *soles* to his parents every two or three months.

There is, therefore, little relationship between high money incomes and the possession of a relatively large area of land: only two households out of 44 were rich in both. The possession of a special skill, more assiduous work in paid employment, the sale of livestock or being the recipient of remittances were the key factors. There did, however, seem to be some inverse relationship between having access to a relatively large area of land (over 4 *topos*) and low or medium income; 15 households were in this category. It appears that when sufficient land is available to ensure a reasonable subsistence livelihood in normal years, the need for money income is accordingly slight. This group would appear to represent the 'core' peasantry of the closed corporate community model, maintaining a relatively self-contained existence. Sixteen households were poor in both land and money incomes.

The people themselves recognised a number of social differences within the community. Those who could read and write were considered to be superior to those who could not. A group of about 10 men (the *vecinos*) were considered to be 'rich' since they possessed more than 4 or 5 *topos* of land. This same group of people was expected to organise and sponsor the *fiestas* celebrated in Chilca. As the outlay on the food, *chicha* and other expenses was considerable, only people of substantial means were able to serve as sponsors. A group of poor people was also vaguely distinguished from the mass of *comuneros* because they had less than 1 *topo* of land and they found it difficult to maintain their status.

LABOUR AND RECIPROCITY

Reciprocity in the community is an historical expression of a social relationship which links persons as individuals, households or groups with others, and links groups and communities with each other.

Labour exchange is common in Andean communities, but it occurs only when the resources of family labour are inadequate for the task required. Commitment of family members to household labour is total and unquestioned and the household head will exploit this labour pool to the limit during busy times of the year, such as planting and harvest. If more labour is needed, the household head will probably approach other households, choosing siblings, relatives or friends first, and request help through *ayni*. Help requested in this way is difficult to refuse and once given must later be repaid. Workers assisting a *comunero* under *ayni* will be provided with a free meal, *chicha* and sometimes a *picante* (chilli flavouring).

Ayni is a highly calculated system of reciprocal obligations; the number of days' work given will later be repaid to the same extent. It is the main institution for mobilising labour within the loosely reciprocal pattern of broad *ayuda*, or seeking aid from fellow kinsmen.

In 1963, 44 households out of 50 in the sample used *ayni*, with brothers, brothers-in-law, fathers, sons, nephews and other relatives called on more often than non-relatives to supplement household labour.

Reciprocity was much weaker as a principle for gaining access to scarce capital equipment, such as a *yunta* of two oxen. Of the 42 households that lacked a *yunta*, only six acquired the use of one to plough their plots by *ayni* (later repaying the loan by work). Four received the use of a *yunta* from close relatives, no repayment being required. Thirteen hired a team for 10 *soles* a day (the price usually required from an owner in another community) while 11 hired for 5 *soles* a day. In two cases, a peasant paid 5 *soles* and also contributed a day's labour to ensure that he got the team when he wanted it. For use of this important capital equipment, capitalist relations seemed to be becoming common in the community.

MOBILISING LABOUR

A second type of work engagement or labour mobilisation is that of *jornales*. In this case, the *peones* receive a wage and employment is on a daily basis. It is essentially a *mestizo* and monetarist approach and therefore, in contrast to *ayni*, does not involve social obligations.

It is often assumed that the persistence of 'pre-capitalist' labour relations results from the low degree of integration of the peasant with the capitalist system. In reality the situation is more complex. *Ayni* persists even when peasants have sufficient income to employ *peones* by *jornal*; the key factors are trust between partners in labour exchange, reflecting close kinship or neighbourhood ties, and rough equality in income and status. Where there are pronounced income differences between households, *ayni* is likely to become less common; richer households tend more regularly to utilise *jornal*.

Larger mobilisations of labour, involving up to 15 to 20 people, is achieved by *minka*, which requires a lot of food and drink. *Minka* might be used to build a new house. *Faenas* are much more common for community purposes, such as public works. The officers of the Junta Directiva (Board of Directors) take the lead in organising *faenas* about once a month or more, frequently to clean out irrigation ditches, mend roads and repair the church. Females prepare food and make *chicha* for the *faena*. Often *traga* (Sp. *aguadiente*, or sugar cane alcohol) is supplied too, in liberal quantities, so that as the day advances very little work is done as people become too drunk to stand.

LABOUR INPUTS

Labour inputs per hectare are high, reflecting intensive work directed at individual plants. Especially with maize and potatoes, care is taken in seeding and mounding each plant twice in the growing season. This does not, however, apply to barley, which is sown broadcast on steep land and not weeded. Where land is prepared by foot plough rather than by *yunta*, several additional days are needed. Labour inputs per *topo* are shown in Table 6.5. As few *campesinos* planted wheat, figures are not given, but the labour input would be very similar to that for barley.

If the mean figures for labour input for each crop are multiplied with the mean area planted in each crop by each household, it can be seen that about 117 man-days on average are expended by the average peasant, who crops a mean area of 3.1 *topos* of land (1.02ha: see also Figure 6.2).

These figures, which are probably on the generous side, give an indication of the time needed to gain a livelihood in Chilca. Time spent tending animals (often carried out by young children) must of course be added, but it is clear that, in spite of the intensity of production, the average household that comprises just over two adults (or rather more in worker equivalents) has much more labour available than the tiny land area requires. Labour surplus or labour shortage are concepts that can be tested only by considering the agricultural cycle month by month with the varying seasonal requirements.

DEPENDENCE ON EXTERNAL RESOURCES: THE *HACIENDAS*

Classically the peasantry and the *hacienda* existed in a symbiotic relationship, expanding or contracting in relation to each other,

Table 6.5 Labour inputs in man-days (per *topo* and per crop)

A. *Labour inputs per* topo *in man-days*

	Ploughing or foot ploughing	*Sowing*	*Harrowing*	*First tilling*	*Second tilling*	*Weeding*	*Harvest*	*Total*
Potatoes	6–8 or 12*	4		7–8	7–8		5–6	29–38
Maize	2	5	1	5	5	4	4–7	26–29
Barley	12	8–10					8–10	28–32

B. *Labour inputs per crop in man-days per* topo

	Labour input	*Mean area of land*	*Total*
Potatoes	32	1.145	36.64
Maize	29	1.965	56.98
Barley	31	0.77	23.87
Total	92	3.88	117.5

*Foot ploughing.

Source: Fieldwork.

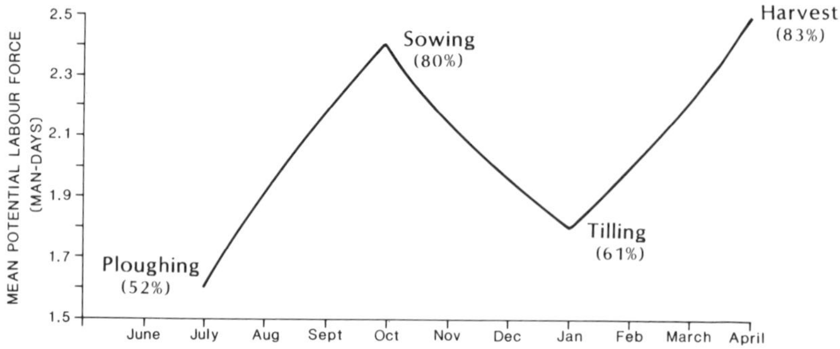

Source: PROYECTO HOLLANDAIS (1978): 162-63: FIELDWORK

Figure 6.2 POTENTIAL LABOUR FORCE AND HOUSEHOLD LABOUR FORCE UTILISED IN AGRICULTURAL AND LIVESTOCK ACTIVITIES, PAMPA DE ANTA (Standardised Man-Days, Mean of 10 Communities)

representing archaic, quasi-feudal institutions nourished by an ecotype unredeemed by the opportunities of a modernising capitalism. But by 1964 the ecotype was changing because of improved infrastructure, the spread of education and new ideas, and the opening-up of new market opportunities. In Chilca, at least, some of the richer *campesinos* were aware of the opportunities in the outside world and were becoming 'proto-*cholos*' about to break out from the confines of peasantry. And at the same time, the *hacendados* had been keen for some time to make their properties more commercial, more modern and more efficient.

In discussing life at Chilca with members of households and in listening to the debates at the weekly village assembly attended by household heads, it was abundantly clear that the role of the *haciendas* and their absentee owners governed many aspects of life. Their power was expressed in at least five ways. First, the *haciendas* had dominated the community in times past by using various sanctions or even brute force; second, they possessed the key resource, land, which the *campesinos* needed above all else; third, they provided opportunities for employment; fourth, the *patrones* frequently used their greater knowledge of the law and their acquaintance with influential judges or lawyers to expand their *haciendas*, laying claim to communal lands possessed by people whom they regarded as ignorant and servile; and finally, the *gamonales* were ever ready to espouse the fashionable philosophy or dogma of the day, appearing as wholly rational men urging the acceptance of positivistic beliefs or posing as harbingers of a new dynamic capitalism needed to sweep away the useless, traditional detritus of the past. Shortly after I arrived in Chilca I met the *mayordomo* of one of the Luna brothers riding along the road. After enquiring about the purpose of my study, he asserted that it was not in the interests of Peru for land to be left in the hands of idle, ignorant Indians.

The power of the *hacienda* system reached a peak towards the end of the nineteenth century and was revived during the 1930s. Ezequil Luna, the most prominent landowner in the Pampa de Anta, was elected a senator during President Leguía's regime. Luna used his administrators to enlarge his landholdings by seizing the land of adjoining peasant communities.[6] In this way, most of the *pampa* at Chilca and a sector of its *puna* land was forcibly occupied in spite of the strong protests of the community. In fact, the *personero* and *presidente* (head of community government) of Chilca fought with the elected officers of the other communities against Luna's representatives who were sent to quiet them, and the *personero*, after being imprisoned several times in Cuzco, persisted in his campaign and eventually petitioned the President for help. A decree from the President guaranteeing the inalienability of the communal lands was finally won in 1961, terminating the long struggle with the Luna brothers.

When I arrived in Chilca in 1964, *comuneros* told me of their long and bitter struggle against the *patrones* to recover their land. But although the intense importance of land was obvious, the *comuneros* were hesitant to talk about their relations with the *haciendas* and their attitudes to them. This reluctance was scarcely surprising since I was a strange *gringo* (foreigner) who had only recently arrived in their community. I had read in *Time* magazine, while flying to Peru, of the large number of land invasions (allegedly carried out by communist-influenced peasants) that had occurred in the Cuzco Department from September 1963.[7] The police had been used to evict large numbers of illegal *ocupantes* (squatters) who had seized *hacienda* land. This was part of an important chain of events stretching from the struggle in the La Convención Valley between *colonos* (resident or tenant farmers) and coffee *hacendados*, to the Junin land invasions in the Central Sierra, the influence of radical leaders like Hugo Blanco, and the more general social mobilisation of the peasantry in the 1960s that was to pave the way for the Peruvian Revolution of October 1968 and the later agrarian reform. In retrospect, the *comuneros*' taciturn stance on the *haciendas* appears to reflect the sullen view of a temporarily repressed, but by no means cowed, peasantry.

Of the five ways in which the power of the *haciendas* was expressed, we have already illustrated the first, fourth and fifth. By far the most important in 1964, however, were the second and third (those involving land and employment).

It is only in recent decades that *campesinos* have finally begun to realise that their labour resources, needed by the *gamonales* to work *hacienda* lands where mechanisation is impracticable, are a source of power. Moreover, more and more *ocupantes* who illegally occupy or graze *hacienda* land have come to see there is strength in numbers, especially if their actions are backed by a growing awareness of their situation and a growing sense of class solidarity.

Only in the very long term can one view modernisation in the Andes as involving the transition from a 'feudal' to a capitalist mode of production or, at the same time, as involving at the local level a transition in labour relations from 'pre-capitalist' or traditional forms of reciprocity to capitalist relations. Martinez-Alier (1974) and Bertram (1974) have emphasised that the choice of one or the other system (wage-labour or labour-service tenure) rests upon the landowner's calculation of efficiency and profitability in producing for external markets, and on the *colono's* comparison between the cash wage and the value of the usufruct access to land. To this I would add the element of security: it is probably less usual for a man to be evicted from his plot used under labour-service tenure than to lose wage employment.

Underpinning this rationale is the nature of the peasant enterprise, in comparison with the wage labourer and his family. The peasant household is a unified entity in which the labour and output of all members are pooled. Moreover, labour will be used even when its marginal product is substantially lower than the prevailing wage rate in the wider economy, unless the shortage of labour is so great as to guarantee any member of the peasant family employment at the prevailing wage rate if he or she leaves the household enterprise.

Of course, the labour-service system is likely to survive only as long as the usufruct access to land remains of equal value to the hiring of free labour at the prevailing wage rate. In other words, if land use could become more profitable by increased value of cash crops, or any technological innovation, the landowner may be induced to abolish, wholly or partly, the labour-service system.

In 1963–4 such conditions were beginning to occur in the Cuzco area. Although the labour-service system was still largely intact, a good number of peasants were seeking external wage employment by circular migration or migration for seasonal employment. Nearly half of those surveyed (23) preferred to use *en compañia* production to increase their *access* to land, planting the land of a fellow *comunero* who had adequate resources in return for sharing half the crop, rather than to take up usufruct rights on *hacienda* land. Such attitudes of stubborn independence, of pride in being a free *comunero* bound to no *patrón*, seemed to be a common characteristic.

Thus some men with only 3½ *topos* asserted they had enough land. There were others, however, who seemed willing to accept the role of *peón*, of being a *colono* on *hacienda* land. Such men voluntarily accepted the inferior status and traditional role and duties of a *peón* in return for perceived advantages and the security that the whole patronage structure afforded.

A minimum wage law existed in 1964 and had been generally observed for a year or two, yet there was wide variation in labour-service tenure conditions. One man who particularly valued the independence of the community complained that only five years earlier, people who wanted grazing rights had been forced to provide five days' labour for only 2½ *soles*. If the worker did not turn up, a *hacienda* employee would come to look for him with his whip. I was unable to check the accuracy of the allegation. Variations also existed in the number of days' labour required in return for the use of 1 *topo*.

It is interesting to note the circumstances of Lucio Huaman's[8] household; the attitudes and values seem to reflect not only the ideology of the little community, but also the context of the peasant household economy in which decisions are made. This household of seven members had access to only 1½ *topos* of its own land and the maize crop had failed entirely. Lucio worked for 3–4 days of the week on the *hacienda* all year for 2 *soles* per day, the use of 1 *topo* and grazing rights. The latter enabled him to pasture as many as five cows and five sheep, and his income of 1100 *soles* was about average. He pointed out that Chilca 'did not belong to any *hacienda*' and the people were 'tranquil'. In discussing future prospects he rejected the migration option; he said he had enough security with his house, his employment and grazing rights on the *hacienda*.

INNOVATION, TRADITION AND CHANGE

To the outsider in 1964, little change appeared to have occurred at Chilca for many years. In the few small stores, Coca Cola could be purchased, but almost the only other recent innovation appeared to be the compulsory adoption of a new variety of barley about five years earlier, a change required by the beer company in Cuzco. One man, who was a part-time tailor, had received the gift of a new sewing machine from his sister-in-law employed in Lima. In one household, the family had a primus stove which made food preparation much easier than cooking on an open fire.

Of course, changes had come over the years but they had been imposed by powerful outside authorities and were often accepted unwillingly. Andean culture has survived and remained durable partly because of the relative weakness of modern capitalist forces in the Sierra until the last five decades or so, and partly because of the effective closed corporate community structure that the peasant *comunidades* crafted for themselves as a major instrument of defence. Both Wolf's (1955 and 1957) concept of this closed corporate community, and the argument of Martinez-Alier and Gow[9] that Andean culture has been used as an instrument of defence in the class struggle, are convincing. Moreover, the peasant is not averse to subtly manipulating the *mestizo* stereotype of the peasant as ignorant, slow-witted and dishonest, if this image will serve to protect his interests.

When I began my fieldwork it quickly became obvious that questions posed about innovations or the voluntary acceptance of change from the outside were quite meaningless to a majority of peasant households. Crops had been cultivated and livestock grazed according to time-hallowed methods and procedures. The idea of supplying inputs to the land was not foreign, however, in the sense that people recognised the value of using animal manure as fertiliser. From this, the introduction of artificial fertiliser would appear a logical progression, but '*No soy acustumbrado a usar fertilizante*' ('I am not accustomed to use fertiliser') was a common response. In this sense we can say that a considerable number of the peasants of Chilca were 'traditional' peasants, defining 'tradition' in Horton's sense of 'the attitude which sees what is handed down to the current generation as an immutable, timeless heritage'.[10]

One young man who had already assisted the Forest Service in organising the tree planting campaign in Chilca was persuaded by the Ministry of Agriculture and especially by an American Peace Corps Volunteer to try a mixture of NPK (nitrogen phosphate potash) artificial fertilisers on a small plot of *maizal* land. Fortunately, the experiment succeeded and natural hazards did not take their customary toll; at harvest time in 1964 the innovator, Justo Quispe, was rewarded by an unusually tall, healthy stand of maize that all could see. As Justo was an enterprising young man well regarded in Chilca, the experiment was influential, and within a few years a growing number of peasants began to follow his example. Although the other results were less spectacular, they were not ineffective; another man who received credit to purchase fertiliser gained a harvest of 20 *cargas* of potatoes per *topo* instead of the usual nine or 10. Two others declared they were interested in fertilisers but did not use them because of the cost. The potential for social change in Chilca suddenly appeared exciting in August 1964, for Justo was now eager to follow up his initial success in innovation by trying insecticides, fungicides, improved seeds and other modern scientific methods in a snowballing process of modernisation, and it appeared that he could be utilised by the Ministry of Agriculture extension service as a 'leader farmer', whose example other villagers might follow.

Unfortunately, however, Justo soon perceived that whatever he might gain from adopting agricultural innovations in Chilca (his family possessed only 1½ *topos* of land) was small compared to gains to be won in the exciting *mestizo* world outside. He left the community to live the life of a *cholo*, engaging in a small trucking business. After a few years he obtained a job in the

Ministry of Agriculture in Lima, where he enjoyed a living standard and status vastly superior to that of the richest man in Chilca. With his departure the rate of innovation slowed and the scope for modernising many areas of life diminished greatly.

The use of supervised credit by development agencies is one of the most widespread strategies for encouraging innovation and the use of modern techniques. The notions of credit and usury are widely known and families occasionally borrow, although at high rates of interest, from rich people when faced with a large household expense.

At Chilca only four households out of 52 had received any agricultural credit in 1964. In one case the Ministry of Agriculture had provided improved potato seed but the harvest was still low and the peasant was left to pay back the loan plus an additional 60 *soles* of interest. Another man had been provided with a loan of 750 *soles* with 7 per cent interest from the bank to buy potato seed, but since he purchased the traditional *ccompis* variety rather than one of the newer, more high yielding varieties, he obtained no benefit. A third recipient also received a loan of 750 *soles* with 35 *soles* interest but had a total loss of his harvest owing to natural hazards. Only one man out of the four appeared to benefit.

In none of the cases in which credit was given was any supervision or technical advice provided; without this the value of the credit is dubious. People who had received credit found the burden of paying back the loan and interest to be a major problem. As many recipients in the Anta area had defaulted from paying back the loans, no more credit was being extended by the Ministry of Agriculture late in 1964.

Probably the most important innovation in Chilca in 1964 was the eucalyptus afforestation campaign carried out by the Forest Service on US Alliance for Progress aid funds. This project, one of a series throughout the Sierra, aimed at planting steep, eroded land with eucalyptus trees to replace the natural vegetation which had almost everywhere been removed long ago in the search for pit props for the mines. The lack of timber in the bare, treeless Sierra had long been a problem; it had to be imported into the region at considerable cost. Not only would a plantation provide useful timber for house building, furniture and other needs and income, but it would also provide fuel and so free up supplies of manure to be used on the fields.

The eucalyptus afforestation programme was successful in many areas because it met a genuine need, and it also offered the prospect of resources for the future. The programme was successful, too, because it was well organised and made an effort to involve the villagers and acquaint them with its goals. It also employed 40 men in tree planting under the supervision of Forest Service staff. Households in Chilca rotated in supplying labour for the tree planting and were paid partly in cash and partly in nutritious foods. Most villagers were aware that after 20 years the eucalyptus trees would be big enough to harvest; at that point 70 per cent of the proceeds of the cut timber would go to the community and 30 per cent to the Forest Service to repay their costs. Moreover, some saw that the project would provide opportunities to diversify occupations and achieve added value in Chilca: sawyers, carpenters and others would be encouraged and more wealth would be earned in the community. All households welcomed the innovation and some gave credit for it to the Acción Popular government of Belaúnde. As one peasant said: 'At least this government has tried to give something to poor people – other governments haven't. It will be something for my sons.'

PROBLEMS AND SOLUTIONS

Discussions with household heads revealed that people were very much aware of their poverty, the problems of gaining a livelihood and some of the factors that impoverished them. In an attempt to identify the major problems and possible solutions, household heads were asked in an open-ended way what they saw as the problems or difficulties in Chilca. A very diverse range of topics was identified.

The forced repression of the peasantry in the Anta area has undoubtedly had a marked effect on attitudes in Chilca, and it is likely that this led many people to feel reluctant to identify land as a major issue (only six out of 66 responses), to point to the *gamonales* as a group or class who oppressed them, or to speak of the class war that had, in effect, recently broken out against the *hacendados*. For example, in the answers to this question, the problem of grazing rights on the *haciendas* was not even mentioned. About 23 per cent identified agricultural difficulties of one sort or another (for example, lack of seed, irrigation and water, a shortage of ox teams needed for ploughing and the like); and clearly, there was recognition that yields had declined over the years. But to voice the true grievances to an outsider would be to make overt, in political terms, what was largely latent. Eighteen responses identified improved community facilities as needed.

The most significant facts arising from this survey are both the striking omissions and the large number of responses which claimed that 'there were no problems' in Chilca (23 out of 66). Although most households depended on muddy spring water for drinking, nobody raised the issue of *agua potable* (drinkable water), or instituting a system of hygienic piped water. (Later, when the issue was raised as a possible project, only a few households appeared to be genuinely interested.) The danger of rabies was not mentioned, although about 10 dogs died of the disease each year. Even the dreaded foot-and-mouth disease was not mentioned as a 'problem', and neither were the killing frosts, hailstones or savage droughts that wreaked havoc on the crops. The high infant mortality in the community caused mainly by bronchial pneumonia was not referred to. The reason, of course, is that because these occurrences were seen as part of nature, as 'given' and unalterable, they were unquestionably accepted. The same was true of the peasants' attitude to their social position in relation to land use and the *haciendas*.

As Evans-Pritchard (1973) reminds us, it requires a great mental change to begin to reason outside the scope of the local belief system and its idiom of thought, for up until recently Indian peasants at Chilca had no other idiom in which to express their thoughts. The few people who did not understand the point of the question or even the word *problema* in Quechua (four out of 66) reinforced the acceptance of the round of life with all its vagaries. Some of the responses may also reflect the tenacious defence of the closed corporate group, or their choice not to seek a livelihood in the outside world.

Identifying and confronting problems, making decisions about them and attempting to find solutions raises the issue of leadership. In coping with their present situation and dealing with the future, who would the *comuneros* look to for leadership? An attempt was made to gauge whether people distinguished between institutionalised leadership roles and the personalities of particular people who showed leadership qualities or commanded authority. Who wielded the greatest authority in the community? At another time questions were posed to establish who was most active in trying to solve problems in the community. What had they done for the community? Responses revealed that the man who wielded the greatest authority in Chilca was the *personero* (44 responses), the trustee or legal representative of the village in all land disputes. He was assisted by the Junta Directiva, elected, like him, for a four-year term. The paramount importance of land in the community and of defending communal land against the claims of encroaching *hacendados* was indicated in the time and energy that was devoted to defending local interests in this area. About half the number of responses were accorded to the authority of the *presidente* and *teniente-gobernador* (lieutenant governor), followed by the vice-president.

Almost uniformly these officers were imbued with authority and status because 'they were named by the people'. Clearly officers attempted in the main to carry out the roles expected of them, such as defending the rights of the community, consulting with lawyers to this end, visiting engineers in Cuzco about local public works, dispensing justice, distributing communal land to all households in a manner that was compassionate yet deemed to be fair, and so on.

In essence three broad solutions could be suggested for the problems of the community: (1) the initiation of a genuine, integral[11] agrarian reform that would not only provide more land for the peasantry and drastically alter the social structure of the country, but which would also provide capital and training in modern agriculture so that the peasantry could utilise the land productively in the national interest; (2) the achievement of a sufficient rate of economic growth to pay for the massive investments required under (1), as well as to meet the needs of the nation as a whole; and (3) out-migration.

The first solution would require, in effect, a national revolution as well as a radical agrarian reform (see Chapter 10) if any chance of success were to be achieved, and would also depend in the long term on success in (2). Solutions (1) and (2) clearly lay at the national level, although (1) might be partly stimulated by a massive peasant social mobilisation (see Chapter 15). The only solution that lay in the hands of the peasants themselves was (3): out-migration. This is usually a conscious choice not taken until people are ready (and possess the skills) to attempt social mobilisation from the largely Indian or *comunero* peasant status of the village to the *cholo* status of the non-Indian wage worker of the town or city.

OUT-MIGRATION

The majority of household heads expressed a clear preference for living in Chilca, although many occasionally left for three months' temporary work. Seven heads of households said they had never considered leaving; for them, at least, migration was not an option. These households represent a large group of peasants who appeared to be the most traditional and most Indian people in the community. They were also among the poorest in monetary terms, spoke only Quechua and in almost all cases were illiterate. They appeared to be strongly committed to life in Chilca and did not evince that quality of 'psychic mobility' or empathy which Lerner (1958) has argued is essential to imagining life and work in a quite different environment.

The real options for migration were (1) to work in the nearby market town of Izcuchaka; or, more likely, (2) in Cuzco only 32km away, (3) to migrate for a few months to work at harvest time in the Urubamba Valley, or on a coffee *finca* (farm) in the *selva*; (4) to migrate to the large plantations of the coast; or to move to the coastal cities of (5) Arequipa or (6) Lima. These six options embrace short-, medium- and long-distance step and stage migration,[12] and pendular (or circular) migration of three or four months, and semi-permanent and permanent migration, including urbanisation.

In Table 6.6 the responses to out-migration are categorised; however, some people expressed several reasons for their reactions and such responses are thus difficult to classify. However, attitudes overwhelmingly indicated a strong preference for life at Chilca; while pendular or circular migration was quite common, it merely represented a short-term excursion to seek out some cash income to supplement the subsistence-based production of the household in the village. It did not, in itself, indicate any weakening of commitment to living in the village or to a rural, peasant livelihood. The paramount factors were the possession of land and of a house in the community, together with crops and

Table 6.6 Attitudes to out-migration

Characteristic attitudes	*Number*
Born in Chilca	4
'This is my *pueblo* and the land of my birth.'	
'We have been here since the time of my great-grandfather.'	
'My wife was born here.'	
Land and house	8
'Content with my plot and house.'	
'My house and land are here – if I didn't have lands here would go elsewhere.'	
'Here have own house, land and food. Would be difficult living in Cuzco – would have to buy all food.'	
'This is wife's land – but doesn't know how much her father will inherit.'	
'Can't leave my house and land to anyone.'	
'Plenty of lands for crops and pasture.'	
'There is a lot of land on which animals can graze.'	
'I have land, plenty of water, wheat, barley and maize, therefore don't want to leave.'	
'My lands are here.'	
Capital equipment	1
'I have a *junta* and animals here.'	
Kinship and demographic	7
'Because my sons are here I could not leave.'	
'My wife and children are here.'	
'We have a lot of children, so don't want to leave.'	
'No – my husband is old.'	
Accustomed to Chilca	3
'Spent my childhood in Chilca – now we are accustomed to it.'	
'I am accustomed to living in Chilca – wouldn't feel right living in other places.'	

continued on p. 118

Table 6.6 continued

Characteristic attitudes	*Number*
Employment	3
'Employed on *hacienda* – have house and grazing rights here.'	
'Difficult to get work in the city.'	
Independence of community	5
'Community doesn't belong to anyone.'	
'Content here – when I want to work I can, when I don't want to I needn't – in city I would have to work all time.'	
'I am a free man in Chilca – don't have any desire to leave.'	
'Like it better now than before, when *hacienda* controlled more land – not obliged to work for *hacienda* now – feel free and therefore content now.'	
Ideology	6
'Good people here – because everybody helps one another.'	
'Because I am joyful living in the fields.'	
'I didn't feel right in other places. This is my land.'	
Other	
'Location is good – transport available to Cuzco when we want it.'	
Rejection of migration option or possible destinations	8
'I'm afraid my son would fall sick in the city and be unable to work.'	
'My husband doesn't like the hot valley.'	
'He is afraid of dying if he went.'	
'Because there are many diseases in the *selva*.'	
'I didn't like the *selva* – many flies and hot.'	
'He wouldn't feel at home there.'	
In favour of migration; not content with Chilca	2

animals. Ownership of a plough team or other capital equipment was also relevant. Finally, the basic sense of belonging that makes people regard a place as home was significant.

At the same time an investigation was undertaken into the actual number of people who had left the community in recent years, and a very different picture emerged. Over the previous five years about 80 people had migrated from Chilca, leaving on a semi-permanent or permanent basis, although about half had owned land in the community. Usually they rented their lands to relatives, at 1000 *soles* for 1 *topo* over a period of two to three years. A few allowed relatives to use land without charge. Most men who left took their families with them, or sent for them after obtaining employment; a few who left their families in the village were away for lengthy periods. Returned migrants were usually people who possessed land, or hoped to inherit land in the community. Some migrants were minors who had gone to Lima to stay with relatives while furthering their education.

The main destination of migrants from Chilca was Lima where a group of ex-*comuneros* now resided, either permanently or semi-permanently. Next in importance as destinations were Cuzco, followed by Arequipa. Five or six people had gone to live permanently in the La Convención valley in the *tierra caliente* (tropical lands), and one or two to Quincemil, also in the subtropics. A few of these migrants returned occasionally to Chilca to visit relatives, spreading news of their new lifestyles.

Another (probably smaller) group of migrants was composed of the very poor and destitute. If an entire crop failed unexpectedly and the family had no other options and could expect little help from others (that is, were poor in kinship as well as in resources), the man might leave to seek work elsewhere.

Although people expressed a largely positive view of living in Chilca, it is important to distinguish these attitudes about *where* they lived from the way they viewed their livelihood. If the former approaches 'the good life', the latter involved, in no uncertain terms, a recognition that peasantry goes hand-in-hand with poverty and deprivation; while these were scarcely new conditions, there was a feeling that they should no longer be tolerated. It may well be that Redfield himself slightly confused the two issues. Attitudes involve values and aspirations which, as Firth (1959) has noted, comprise a different level from expectations as to what will happen, and expectations themselves may be rather different from the actual happenings. Hence, in a community which is not entirely static and in which change is beginning, the structure of aspirations will differ from the structure of expectations and also from the structure of action. Although the image was one of unchanging stability and peace, Chilca was beginning to change, and migration as an indicator of change was already becoming significant. While the surface appearance was of the *passive* peasant, awareness of the peasantry in 1964 as a temporarily repressed rural class prepared the way for recognising the peasant as an *active* participant.

In a structural sense, the rise in out-migration from Chilca also probably reflects the inability of the land use system to cope with growing population pressure and the insidious ramifications of land ownership and commercialisation arising from the impact of capitalism. Past communal production practices, such as the *laymi* collective rotation system, no longer survive, and several modern practices have had a detrimental effect on land use. The effect of this set of factors was that Chilca in 1964 was ripe both to accept technological change to lift productivity (and enhance incomes) and to respond to the growing pressures by increased out-migration. 'Push' factors, in short, may have been combining with 'pull' factors associated with the allure of external sources of employment.

The decision to migrate on what might turn out to be a semi-permanent or permanent basis involves far more than a physical shift of location; it is an important cultural process and one affecting socio-economic or *class* position. Since the world outside Chilca is a non-Indian world dominated by *mestizos* who possess or control most resources and employment, who occupy positions of power and status and, most importantly, who define the rules of the game, Indians who hope to make their way in this world must divest themselves of their 'Indian-ness' and attempt a process of movement to '*mestizo*-ness'. While they are in this long drawn-out process they may be termed *cholos*. Once they leave the community and begin the process of change they can take certain actions that openly declare their intentions and their *cholo* status: they can speak Spanish rather than Quechua, they can cease wearing the community's distinctive 'Indian' dress and adopt the more nondescript 'poor white' clothing, stop chewing *coca* and so on and generally try to behave in a more '*mestizo*' manner.

In these various ways the *cholo* pattern indicates a *cultural* change, but it also denotes a *class* change insofar as attempts to achieve upward social mobility, to attain more wealth, power or status are *perceived* to have involved movement from the Indian level to some position a little 'higher' on the social hierarchy. *Cholo* status is determined, at least partly, in a subjective way, referring in a derogatory sense to someone whose position is inferior, and emphasising the social distance between this person and the one who does the name-calling. But although society is strongly hierarchical and class differences are great, cultural barriers are few once someone has decided to leave their Indian culture behind, become a *cholo* and commit him- or herself in the long run to *arribismo* (the desire to get to, and be on the top) by a process of 'cholofication', in an attempt ultimately to become a *mestizo*.

Most people probably do not aspire so highly, seeking perhaps merely the relative advantages of *cholo* status and regular paid employment. Culturally the situation is fluid, although the class barriers are difficult to surmount; the transition from Indian to *mestizo*, when it does occur, usually takes two or three generations. While many who leave the Sierra to move to Lima or Arequipa may remain for a long period relatively unchanged 'urban peasants', as Lewis (1952) has suggested, others, whether acting consciously or unconsciously, will be leaving both their peasant and Indian lifestyle for ever. As will be argued below, migration to the cities and cholofication are the fundamental processes that are slowly destroying the peasantry and creating a new society.

CONCLUSION

The findings of the 1964 household survey are that the peasants of Chilca were not a homogeneous society, for there were substantial inequalities in land, capital resources and money incomes. The degree of 'Indian-ness' also differed: a group of the most traditional peasants, who were illiterate and spoke only Quechua, earned, on the whole, the lowest money incomes. Apart from one or two *vecinos* who were regarded almost as non-peasants because of their higher incomes and status, the rest of the community comprised middle or rich peasant groups (although the distinction between the two groups is rather blurred in the community). Some members of these two groups were, in effect, proto-*cholos* who were evaluating life with other alternatives in the world outside.

As Gonzalez de Olarte has explained, peasant families are the minimal mercantile units which have the objective of reproducing themselves on the basis of limited resources and under a conjunction of restrictions: of property, ecology, markets and cultural and ethnic conditions. Since their subordination to these factors is so complex, to reproduce themselves as families they must base their economic and social behaviour on the combination, which is often very changeable, of a heterogeneous conjunction of variables: climate, soils, water, prices, salaries, crops, technologies. Family efficiency in the use of their resources constitutes the basis of their survival and reproduction. Peasants seek a monetary income proportional to their production and consumption costs, preferring usually a low but secure average income to a high but insecure marginal income.[13]

Traditional practices adapted to the local ecology had stood the test of time, but the impact of capitalism was causing repercussions throughout the whole system. The trend to private land ownership and a tendency, for example, to consolidate separate land *parcelas* struck at the heart of a rigid (though effective) communal land use system which did not tolerate individual non-conformity. Complementarity and specialisation of different ecological niches is an approach diametrically opposed to the consolidation, uniformity and scale economies promoted by modern commercial agriculture.

In the last resort, the peasants were grindingly poor because of a lack of *entitlement* to land, capital resources, employment, modern technology and knowledge, and to education and the means of either transforming their situation by mobilising as a class to promote peasant interests, or of escaping by out-migration.

7 Chilca, 1964–76

It is difficult to establish the nature of changes and the exact pattern of events in Chilca in the later 1960s and in the 1970s. My data are crude and fragmentary, or depend on the memories of informants looking back over these years. I returned to the village for one-day visits in mid-1966, 1974 and 1976, these occasions providing only tantalising glimpses of the community in those years. Meanwhile, however, great changes were occurring in Peru, and from 1968 to about 1975 the Peruvian Revolution and its associated agrarian reform deeply affected the country, although not always in positive ways (see Chapters 10 and 13). At the same time, other forces had been unleashed that greatly affected the situation of the peasantry and its relationship to the modern world (see Chapter 9).

CHILCA IN 1966

After I left Chilca in 1964, I wrote a short report on the community which was used by the Peace Corps. In the climate of the times when 'New Frontiers' ideology was rampant and the Peace Corps was vigorously attempting to post volunteers into many areas within Latin America, Chilca appealed to the regional Peace Corps agency as a village which might well have considerable potential for community development. They were perhaps conscious of its favourable situation near Cuzco, it showed some signs of willingness to modernise and my report provided some background data. Moreover, the community had responded most positively to the Forest Service's tree planting campaign of the previous year, a project to which a Peace Corps volunteer had been attached. Accordingly, two volunteers (both women) were posted to live and work in Chilca for two years.

On my visit to Chilca in 1966, about one year after the Peace Corps volunteers had begun work there, a number of innovations were immediately obvious. Most significantly, the volunteers had rallied the community in a campaign to build a new school with government money. Considerable enthusiasm was generated and households appeared to have willingly contributed labour to the communal *faenas* needed to build the large, partially two-storey building. The upper storey contained a library. A kindergarten was also started and a school garden was instituted to encourage new crop varieties. A significant innovation was a water pump which drew up ground water and enabled some pipes to be installed so that clean water could be obtained from two or three taps at different locations within the village.

Clearly, the Peace Corps women hoped that this would not only improve health, through making clean water available (instead of households using often polluted water from small rivulets and irrigation channels), but also improve hygiene. A few showers were installed. A number of minor innovations were attempted in agriculture, such as importing superior poultry stock. In order to discourage people from defecating in the fields, two or three pit latrines were dug. Books were obtained so that the library could become operational.

When Peace Corps activity was at its highest level, an event occurred that was to give Chilca considerable fame throughout this region of the Andes. When Robert Kennedy came to Peru, Chilca was chosen as one of the two or three villages that he would visit. On the memorable day, Kennedy walked through the village, talked to some of the leaders through an interpreter, inspected the school and other innovations, and gave a speech to the assembled villagers on the *pampa*. He urged villagers to increase their efforts to initiate self-help development. A highlight of the day was the scattering of many American one dollar notes in the air, like confetti, for the villagers to pick up.

At the time of my visit, the community was still glowing with pride over the new school. It was not only much bigger and better equipped, but it now had nine teachers to deal with a greatly expanded roll of pupils. The volunteers encouraged improved nutrition, urging peasants to consume more milk, butter and cheese. Villagers were pleased, too, at the limited piped water system that the installation of the pump had made possible, but it was already obvious that the showers and latrines were unused and were turning out to be meaningless irrelevancies. A few villagers who had become the beneficiaries of the introduced poultry valued the birds. One man, however, was at a loss to know how to keep them inside the new wire netting fence of his compound. I was able to show him how to clip one wing of each of the birds to prevent them from flying over the fence.

The villagers in general treated the volunteers with courteous respect. They regarded the Americans as well-meaning people who were sincere in their efforts to assist Chilca's community development. As we will see in Chapter 12, many villagers remained amiably cynical about the value of many of the attempted innovations, but they appreciated the good intentions, efforts and friendship displayed and acknowledged the real improvements made with the school.

I did, however, find some disillusionment in the volunteers. While still determined to work hard in the community, they had been frustrated by the lack of unity and by the attitudes of a number whose self-interest and lack of concern for communal well-being caused considerable handicaps to the various projects or led to less than whole-hearted participation in voluntary work parties. One or two were believed to be more concerned with cultivating their ties with *hacendados*, and at times of peasant mobilisation and land disputes with the *hacendados* were believed to act as informers, or to come close to betraying the cause of the community. The volunteers had come to realise fully how daunting and difficult it was to bring worthwhile innovations into an Andean community and to gain their acceptance.

CHILCA IN 1974

By 1974, the agrarian reform was still in its earlier stages and the community had been one of the first in the Pampa to respond to the opportunities of joining the new co-operative. In the last years of the 1960s, the Luna brothers had not acted like harsh masters. Villagers would pay only a few *soles* for the right to graze each sheep on the *hacienda* and some now regarded them as 'kind masters'. While some villagers declared it was too early to say if the agrarian reform was good or bad, there was considerable enthusiasm for it. When the *haciendas* were expropriated and the Co-operative set up, some men felt safer now that the old *hacienda* system no longer existed. However, since men from many households were frequently seeking work on the Co-operative there had been a serious clash with community projects, as people now had less time to work on improvements for the village.

By this date the substantial achievement of the Peace Corps volunteers in education was apparent. Now only about 40 per cent of the population of Chilca was illiterate compared with 65 per cent in 1964, and about 80 per cent of the population now spoke a little Spanish (compared with about 30 per cent in 1964). The school was considered to function well and the people's enthusiasm for education was apparent. Many children had passed through the school and had gone on to upper primary or secondary schools in Izcuchaka or Cuzco. Some had even become teachers themselves or had obtained skilled or semi-skilled jobs, ceasing to be peasants.

Apart from the great impact on education, the other innovations were now barely apparent. The pump had long since broken down and was now rusty. Since clean drinking water was no longer available, the teachers who had resided in the village since 1967 now lived in Izcuchaka. No sign could be found of the other innovations. The school garden no longer functioned. The library still existed but appeared to be unused. Although a new building had been completed, the kindergarten had lapsed. What people wanted most of all was a medical post, placing a permanent nurse in the community. *Faenas* were being held regularly to build the clinic and the sum of 100 *soles* was to be levied from each household to assist with the cost. It was believed that when the building was finished the government would provide the nurse and pay her salary. (Although the building was completed, this did not happen.)

Thus change and ferment were still in the air as a result of the Peruvian Revolution, and peasants had been dislodged from their perennial slumber. But many of the gains resulting from the Revolution or from agrarian reform were insubstantial or had not been consolidated. Little rural investment occurred other than that initiated by government agencies, and current data suggested that agricultural output was not improving.[1]

CHILCA IN 1976

The visit in 1976 came well after the end of Velasco's reform initiative period (1969–73), and by then there were even more visible signs of the agrarian reform and Revolution. A large barn had been built on what Chilca regarded as communal land but which was now part of the Co-operative. Various other buildings, warehouses and silos had been constructed on the *pampa*; *tecnicos* (technicians) drove their shiny new trucks to visit the communities; and numerous colourful posters exhorted the peasants to achieve new development goals. But the frenetic activity seemed to be confined to the plethora of bureaucrats and administrators and the smothering output of official paperwork and red tape.

By now the Revolution had moved into its attempted consolidation phase (1973–6) but, according to many criteria, it might already be declared dead. Velasco, whom many peasants believed to be sincere and genuine in his ideals, had died a year earlier and the Revolution was now moving towards the right. The failures were becoming more obvious and, while some ex-villagers had returned to Chilca in the hope of capitalising on the opportunities offered by the agrarian reform, it was patently obvious that agricultural output on the *pampa* had fallen dramatically. A good deal of the earlier euphoria had dissipated and the huge Social Interest Agricultural Societies (SAIS) and Agrarian Production Cooperatives (CAPs: formed often from 5–15 former *haciendas*) appeared to be grossly large and inappropriately cumbersome.

Although the 1976 visit was again fleeting, the mood of a number of villagers was somewhat disquieting. New hopes, aroused by revolution and reform, had largely been dashed and the village appeared to be more unsettled than before. Villagers bemoaned the decline in unity. Representatives from various political parties occasionally visited the village, raising contentious issues and increasing the tendency towards factionalism. Harsh economic pressures were becoming insistent, affecting the price of agricultural inputs, for the International Monetary Fund (IMF) was beginning to exert pressure on the government to lower or remove subsidies. For more and more villagers, the best prospect for escaping from grinding poverty appeared to be migration to the *barriadas* of Lima or Arequipa.

These trends will be considered in more depth in Chapters 8, 9, 10 and 12.

8 Chilca in 1979

By 1979 the community had changed considerably. The years since 1964 had involved not only widespread peasant mobilisation, but also the initiation of the Peruvian Revolution of 1969–75. A major goal of this revolution was agrarian reform, which aimed not only at liberating the peasant from exploitation but also at laying the basis for a more modern, productive commercial agriculture, and at speeding national economic growth. Equally significant, however, were the universal forces of change: the steady expansion of capitalism, the extension of roading, communications, electrification and other changes of infrastructure, improvements in schooling, the growth of literacy and the spread of Hispanic culture in its Peruvian national form, the erosion of vestiges of the archaic 'feudal' structures and further 'destructuration' of traditional Quechua culture.

Two other forces in particular were of great importance in the 1960s and 1970s. The first was the replacement of the old patrons by new patrons, a class of 'modernising' doctrinaire bureaucrats who succeeded in burying the old order without putting a new structure in the social vacuum created. They extended the dominance of the state, with all its associated bureaucratic confusion and red tape, without building new functional relationships that would enable healthy economic and social growth: 'development from below'. And second, population movement and urbanisation, which represented the impact of many of the new dislocating changes, grew to a new, significant level.

POPULATION

A Dutch development project estimated the population of Chilca in 1978 to total 1699, an increase of about 54 per cent over 1964. This rapid increase represents an average annual growth of nearly 3.9 per cent, which is great when compared to the growth rate of the province of Anta in the period 1961–72 of 0.2 per cent, or 1.5 per cent for the department of Cuzco as a whole. The number of households had increased even more, to 293, with the mean number of members per household declining slightly from 5.11 in 1964 to 5.08 in 1978.

AGRICULTURE

The total area of cropped land in 1979 was 224.5 *topos*, or a mean of 4.3 *topos* (1.3ha) per household.[1] This comprised 3.1 *topos* of owned land together with 1.2 *topos* of *en compañia* land. This mean area was made up of the following lands in the three ecological zones:

Maizal	1.7 *topos*
Temporal	1.3 *topos*
Puna	1.2 *topos*

The increase from 3.1 *topos* in 1964 to 4.3 *topos* in 1979 probably reflects the eviction of the *hacienda*. The sample was perhaps a little skewed towards the larger and richer landowners: although the largest class of people is represented by peasants using 3–3.9 *topos* (27 per cent), 19 per cent held over 6 *topos* and another 19 per cent from 5–5.9 *topos*. In all, 48 per cent of the sample used over 4 *topos* and 25 per cent less than 3 *topos*.

Yields of households are shown in Table 8.1.[2] As in 1964, an enormous range of harvests was gathered in 1978, with the main crops being corn, potatoes, wheat, barley and broad beans. A small number of households planted *olluco*, *oca*, *arveja* (green peas), cabbage or *quinoa*.

COMPARISON WITH 1964

A good deal of caution is needed in comparing 1978 yields with those of 1964. While it was originally intended to return wherever possible to the same households used in the 1964 sample, this was achieved in only some cases. Several of the household heads and other family members had died, a considerable number of families had broken up largely because of out-migration, or on the days of fieldwork the household head could not be located. Demographic change and other circumstances had also altered the labour force/consumer balance greatly in many cases. Socio-

Table 8.1 Crop production, 1963–4 and 1978

Crop	*Land class*	*Year/Number of plots*	*Yield per* topo *(kg)* *1963*	*1978*	*Yield per hectare* *1963*	*1978*	*Dutch project data (1977) (kg per hectare)*	*Yepez de la Ross data* (kg per hectare)*
Corn	Irrigated	1964/78						
	maizal	1978/62	266	366	798	1098	376	
Mawai		1963/6						
Mawai		1978/11	747	771	2241	2313	1175	
Potatoes	*Puna*	1963/53						
	(unirrigated)	1978/48	1090	702	3270	2106	2030	4000–5000
Olluca			270		810			6000
Wheat	*Temporal*	1963/9						
		1978/33	82	336	246	1008	193	
Barley		1963/9						
		1978/9	86	439	258	1317	201	800
Broad beans		1964/3						
		1978/24	93	486	279	1458	1779	

*Taken from Freeman (1963): 59.

Sources: Fieldwork; Dutch Project, Tables 21 and 22 (the Dutch study was based on a sample of 30 households); Freeman (1963): 59.

economic differences had become marked between the ageing parents who were usually illiterate and monolingual and the comparatively well-educated children, some of whom had travelled out of Chilca for work or education, who had mostly become Spanish-speaking *cholos*.

The increase in mean corn yields from 266 (1963) to 366kg (1978) per *topo* (798 to 1098kg/ha) probably reflects the undoubted technological progress achieved by some *campesinos* over the 15 years, especially their use of chemical fertilisers and weedkillers. An increase in the number of plots planted in *mawai* can perhaps be attributed to growing commercialisation.

Little significance should be attributed to the apparently substantial increase in yields of wheat and barley over the period as the sample included only a relatively small number of plots. In part these higher yields might represent an effective response to the use of fertiliser and weedkiller on *temporal* land, and in part they represent an abandonment of the steeper land that was being affected by accelerated erosion in 1964 (some of this land was planted in the afforestation project) and the use of less eroded plots. The yield data of the Dutch project for 1977 are much closer to the figures of 1963. In 1978, far more plots were planted with wheat compared with barley, reversing the 1963 situation. This would appear to be a response to the better market price for wheat and the glut in the barley market with the beer factory in Cuzco being oversupplied. Broad beans were planted on more plots than in 1964.

The yield figures for potatoes are lower in 1978 than in 1963, falling from 1090 to 702kg per *topo* (3270 to 2106kg/ha). However, it should be appreciated that the soil types vary considerably in the *puna* according to the sectors (*tiray*); under the *laymi* system of land rotation and fallowing the community shifts each year. The sector used in the *puna* for planting potatoes and other tubers in 1978 was different from that used in 1963; it appeared to be an area of lower soil fertility and to suffer somewhat from drainage problems.

In assessing the yields of Chilca, both the severity of crop and livestock disease and weather hazards are relevant (see Figure 8.1). As expected, the biological pests are the same in most cases as those reported in 1964 (Table 6.3). The data are a reminder of the continual danger of pauperisation to which even richer peasants may be subjected if catastrophic weather or very severe

CLIMATIC

Frosts	Heavy rain	Flood	Hail	Drought
22	21	2	14	9

MAIZE

Rancha	*Raca*	*Sillhui*	'Maize worms'	'Putrification'	*Q'oto*	*Paku*	*Choclo*	*Rata*	'Fungus'	*Otoscuro*	*Gorgoju*
5	5	3	3	5	1	1	1	1	2	16	1

POTATOES

Taladro	*Illa kuro*	*Sillhui kura*	*Rancha*	*Royo*	*Tapura*	*Carhua*	*Loro loro*	*Piqe piqe*	*Yurac kuro*
14	14	5	23	3	4	11	3	2	1

WHEAT

Roya	*Q'oto*
2	1

BROAD BEANS

Rancha	*Roya*	'Insects'	*Piqe piqe*
10	2	7	1

LIVESTOCK

Cows and Calves (*Callotacca* and Carbuncles)	Sheep	Guinea Pigs	Chickens	*'Porcina'*	Pigs Cholera	*Trecina*	Horses *Suflla*	Unknown Fevers
29	7	29	24	19	1	1	1	3

Note: For scientific names, see Table 6.3.

Figure 8.1 BIOLOGICAL PESTS AND CLIMATIC HAZARDS AFFECTING CROPS AND LIVESTOCK AT CHILCA, 1978
(REPORTED DAMAGE IN NUMBER OF HOUSEHOLDS)

pest problems destroy a large portion of their crops or decimate their small herds of livestock. To counter this danger, ever present in this palaeotechnic ecotype, modernising peasants seek to modify the ecotype by spraying with the appropriate insecticide or fungicide. One important criterion of technological progress is the use of such techniques to counter such problems.

LIVESTOCK

By far the most significant feature of agriculture at Chilca in 1979 was the raising of cattle for dairying. The mean number of cattle per household was 7.6, having nearly tripled in the course of 15 years. The figures for other livestock were about the same as in 1964. Guinea pigs, at about eight per average household, continued to be a source of feast food, being raised on household scraps.

As noted in Chapter 6, population pressure and an acute shortage of land, especially in the *pampa* and *temporal* zones, would seem to be a constraint on the increase in the numbers of cattle. However, in the intervening years, peasant mobilisation and invasion of *hacienda* and co-operative lands had provided access, albeit illegally, to the necessary pasturage. As we shall see, much of the meaning of the agrarian reform and the relationship of the community to the new co-operative was determined (as it had been in the past to the *haciendas*) by the issue of grazing rights.

On the damp *pampa* land, where the water table lies only 2–4m below the surface, dairy farming is ecologically appropriate. Since the 1960s there has been a steady demand for dairy products, and Chilca's location near Cuzco and other towns has made the Pampa de Anta an important area of specialisation in dairying. Furthermore, as poor rural folk the world over have realised, the breeding of cattle provides one of the surest means of raising capital (of amassing wealth 'on the hoof', as it were). Cattle raising, and especially of relatively highly valued dairy cattle, provides the mechanism for capital accumulation, and at the same time facilitates 'depeasantisation' (the escape from the constraints of a meagre peasant existence).

In 1978, three households possessed over 20 head of cattle and another 13 owned between 10 and 19 cattle. On the other hand many poor, traditional peasant households had only two or three cows. We examine below the relationship between the number of dairy cattle owned and income, and the trend towards dairying as a form of specialisation.

INCOME AND INTERNAL DIFFERENTIATION OF THE PEASANTRY

In the household interviews, an attempt was made to assess the approximate total monetary income for 1978, following the same approach as 1964. Since the method was crude, depending on informants' memory, and yields could not be weighed, the money incomes calculated can only be approximate. Subsistence income was at least as important as monetary income for many households. For the middle peasant group it is estimated that at least half of their total production comprised subsistence income (calculated at current market value), while for the poor and very poor peasant groups subsistence production was probably two-thirds or more of their total production.

The sources of money income in 1978 differ in a number of respects from the same data for 1964 (see Table 6.4). The most significant change is the greater specialisation in dairy products in 1978–9, with much more income (and a far higher proportion) coming from the sale of milk and cheese. The sale of cows is also much more important.

Remittances and gifts were rather more significant, and some families had three or four sons or daughters (rather than one or two) sending money in return for *encomiendas* (gifts) of food. About 27 per cent of households benefited; remittances comprised between 5 and 6 per cent of total income. Moreover, sources of money earning were rather less diverse in 1978 compared with 1963 since day labouring, which involved a smaller range of jobs and contributed a smaller proportion of money income, was important only to the middle and poor peasant groups. Again the range of crafts had narrowed, with only five households (compared with 15 in 1963) receiving income from this source. In sum, the table shows the growth of quasi-capitalism within the community – for, in contrast to 1964, there were now genuine marketable surpluses with the expansion of dairy production – and the community's closer involvement with external markets.

The sample of 52 households gives a total estimated monetary income of 2 688 300 *soles* for the 1978 year, or a mean of 51 698 *soles* or US$243 per household. Mean figures are not very useful, however, because of the pronounced socio-economic differences within the community. The effects of class formation will become apparent from the data presented below.

The 1964 survey indicated three distinct socio-economic groups within the community – rich, middle and poor peasants – and the distinction between these groups was clearly recognised. In 1979, these distinctions were even more pronounced and the gaps between groups wider. Five 'groups' were distinguished for 1978–9.[3]

The main data on the economic status of peasant households in 1978 are summarised in Table 8.2. The table includes land area and number of cattle owned, since these are obviously linked to wealth or income, and three indicators of innovation or modernisation (use of artificial fertiliser, insecticide and receipt of agricultural credit) as well as criteria of capitalist production relations (columns 7 and 9).

RICH GROUP

As the table indicates, seven households had a mean income of 196 000 *soles* (or US$903) which is nearly four times greater than that of the 'moderately rich' category (51 000 *soles*).

They enjoyed a more comfortable lifestyle and were in almost all cases accorded higher status in the village. Indeed, of the seven, only four (households 24, 34, 4 and 49) should, in effect, still be classed as 'peasant' in terms of style of life, culture, occupation and values. The group includes the most powerful and highly respected man in Chilca: Honorato Charves, Justice of the Peace, who had been a former senior employee of a *hacendado*. In 1978, he had an estimated income of 204 700 *soles*. Honorato, classed as a *vecino*, enjoyed a status slightly superior to that of a peasant and played a role in which he was well versed in exploiting the local peasants.[4] Moreover, the heads of households 1 and 52 are classed as *cholos*, fairly close to *mestizo* status.

The former was an absentee landowner employed in Cuzco as a chauffeur for the Ministry of Education. He was an urban sophisticate in his second year of university studies, and his

Table 8.2 Economic status of peasant household types, Chilca 1978
(Percentage of households in each class)

	1 *Income*	2 *Land area* (topos)	3 *Cattle*	4 *Use artificial fertilizer* (*per cent*)	5 *Use insecticide* (*per cent*)	6 *Received agricultural credit* (*per cent*)	7 *Use of wage labour* (*per cent*)	8 *Selling/buying hire of plough* (*per cent*)	9 *Rent plough* (*per cent*)
Rich Group (over 80 000 soles) *(7 households, or 14 per cent)*									
Range	83 260–468 500	4.5–9	5–20	86	57	0	28	28	14
Mean (in *soles*)	195 946	6.6	13						
Mean per capitum	33 784								
(in US$)	156								
Moderately Rich (50 000–79 900 soles) *(10 households, or 20 per cent)*									
Range	50 000–62 080	2.6–16.5							
Mean (in *soles*)	51 013								
Mean (in US$)	235	6.6	10.9	80	60	50	40	20	10
Mean per capitum	8 795								
(in US$)	40								
Middle (30 000–49 900 soles) *(10 households, or 20 per cent)*									
Range	30 200–47 920	2.3–5.75	2–14						
Mean (in *soles*)	38 354	4.3	7.2	50	60	10	0	50	10
Mean (in US$)	177								
Mean per capitum	6 613								
(in US$)	30								
Poor (10 000–29 900 soles) *(13 households, or 25 per cent)*									
Range	15 700–29 250	1–7	1–10						
Mean (in *soles*)	23 677	3.5	5	31	38	23	0	69	0
Mean (in US$)	109								
Mean per capitum	4 082								
(in US$)	19								
Very Poor (under 10 000 soles) *(11 households, or 21 per cent)*									
Range	0–8 400	0.5–4	0–6	27	27	18	0	27	0
Mean (in *soles*)	4 890	2.5	3.2						
Mean (in US$)	22								
Mean per capitum	843								
(in US$)	4								

dependable salary contributed over 200 000 *soles* of an income of 254 000 *soles*. Ricardo Ravelo of household 52 was also an urbanite and entrepreneur, who perceived the genuine opportunities for expanding dairy production and was keenly interested in the possibility of restarting a marketing co-operative. His experience, motivation and respected status made him the main economic leader in the community, for as a *limaco* (a person who had returned after living for several years in Lima) he was an intermediary between the village and society, a cultural broker adept at dealing with the dominant *mestizo* culture.[5] Equally he possessed the skills for exploiting the peasantry and for evolving a new *campesino* 'bossism' (*caciquismo*) like Honorato and *vecinos* generally, although his capacity for genuine leadership limited this tendency because of his respect for local people and his desire to identify with the community and work for its betterment (see Chapter 12).

As Table 8.2 shows, the rich group held an average of 6.6 *topos* of land and grazed about 13 cattle. Their superior wealth or income and rather high level of literacy and education were no doubt relevant factors in a high proportion (86 per cent on average) of their households using chemical fertilisers. Over half (57 per cent) used insecticides or fungicides on their crops. Some growth of capitalist relations is suggested in their use of wage labour (28 per cent on average) instead of *ayni*, and 14 per cent hired out their plough teams. However, the fact that these figures are still low shows the persistence of customary forms of reciprocity within the village where face-to-face relationships predominate.

MODERATELY RICH PEASANTS

Some of the data in Table 8.2 appear to suggest that these households are similar to those of the 'rich' group: on average they hold 6.6 *topos* of land and about as many (80 per cent and 60 per cent) use chemical fertilisers and insecticides. It must be stressed, however, that there is a substantial difference in the mean income of this group compared with that of the rich group. The main difference is the absence of non-peasant *vecinos*, or *cholo* members who were *limacos* or urban sophisticates. If land were the sole criterion for obtaining a higher income, this group would be as comfortably off as the rich group; one member, Santiago Puma, held 16.25 *topos* of land and had been a popular and determined *personero* in the community in the 1950s and 1960s; he even went to prison in his battle to recover the village *pampa* expropriated by the *hacendado*.

Although Santiago was regarded as a good and selfless leader, dedicated to the community's interest, he had in fact taken it upon himself to allocate 5 *topos* of communal land in the *puna* to his own household. The holding of extra land in the *puna* was usually limited to those households which were especially impoverished (for example, a widow's household), yet Santiago's family enjoyed an income of 54 500 *soles*, above the average for Chilca as a whole. While the holding of some additional communal land was considered legitimate (a perk of holding the office of *personero*), 5 *topos* is excessive. Clearly Santiago had profited from his position of power and higher status. However, his relatively poor level of literacy and education and lack of business acumen meant that he was incomparably poorer in money income. He had not 'planted' family members in permanent jobs in the co-operative, his 16.25 *topos* of land was underused, and because he had only three cows he received little return from dairying.

The moderately rich group possessed significantly fewer cattle per household (10.9 compared to 13), although 40 per cent hired wage labour rather than using *ayni* and 50 per cent had received agricultural credit from the Banco Agricola at some time. Capitalist relations of production, though not highly diversified, were more pronounced than in the poorer socio-economic groups.

MIDDLE PEASANTS

The middle peasants had an income on average about two-thirds that of the 'moderately rich' group: a figure of about 38 000 *soles* or US$127 (about $30 per capitum). The mean land area held was 4.3 *topos* and about seven cattle were raised per household. Half the households used artificial fertiliser and about 60 per cent insecticide, and clearly the lower income of this group was the main constraint on advancement, rather than lack of knowledge or awareness of the desirable innovation. These peasants were far too poor to be able to hire wage labour, being totally dependent on *ayni* for large labour tasks.

The main characteristic of the middle peasantry (and even more of the poor peasantry) was their dependency. Since they were so poor they inevitably sought access to resources elsewhere: by working *en compañia* on the lands of richer peasants and, until the land reform, by seeking employment or pasturage rights in a client status to a *patrón* on one of the nearby *haciendas*. To illustrate their condition and economic strategy, two case studies will be presented.

Jenaro, a Progressive Peasant with Adequate Land and Labour

Jenaro, a man of 46, had four children (including two dependants). He was better educated than most of the middle peasants, for he had completed primary school and spoke a little Spanish. His wife, Maria, was illiterate and had not gone to school. Like most villagers, Jenaro valued education, seeing it as a key to obtaining paid employment. Two adult daughters had completed primary schooling but had not obtained jobs, and a son of 17 was halfway through secondary school. They possessed a radio. The family was fortunate in having a relatively large area of land – 5½ *topos* including 3½ *topos* of prized *maizal* land – and the large household was needed to work these lands although there was only one son of working age. Jenaro had capitalised on his land area by raising 10 cows and four calves, as well as three horses (of little economic use) and one pig, and he had allowed a poor *comunero* to use one of his plots *en compañia* to plant wheat. He complained of the lack of water for irrigating his *maizal* land; much of the water was used by peasants whose land abutted the hill slopes where the streams were tapped.

Although frost, hail and drought had not been especially severe he had got only 10 sacks (400kg) per *topo* from his *maizal chacras* in 1979 and eight sacks (320kg) in 1978, a planting/harvest rate of about 1:14. Much of the blame for the poor harvest he attributed to *gusanos*. In the *puna* he had fared a little better, obtaining 20 sacks of potatoes (about 1000kg per *topo*), albeit at a planting/harvest ratio of 1:7. Potatoes and broad beans had suffered badly from *la rancha*. The wheat crop had been almost a total failure, producing only 1½ sacks.

Jenaro was a relatively progressive cultivator, however, and he had applied a sack of nitrate of ammonia to half a *topo* of *mawai* before the insect pest ravaged the crop. He attempted to combat pests by using 15kg of the insecticide, aldrin, at a cost of 180 *soles*/kg. The costs of production worried him, and he had calculated that *guano* from the islands off the Peruvian coast (at 950 *soles* for 60kg) was cheaper than nitrate of ammonia purchased at the nearby fertiliser factory. He could not afford to buy chemical fertilisers for his maize crop, so used only manure from the corral. Four years earlier he had received agricultural credit from the Banco Agricola, and the loan of 3500 *soles* at 6 per cent interest was used to purchase superior seed and fertiliser. Since the credit was not supervised by extension officers, however, no benefit was received; now he no longer considered taking credit as the interest rate had risen to 15 per cent.

Normally Jenaro's main source of income was the sale of cheese, earning 4000–5000 *soles* annually, but as he wished to replace the old thatch roof of his house with a tiled roof, he had sold two cows for 30 000 *soles* to enable him to buy the tiles. He sold some surplus potatoes for 1125 *soles* and had undertaken day labouring in Izcuchaka for 4–5 days at a time on three occasions during the year for a wage of 75 *soles* a day plus food and fare. He had also earned a little money through hiring out the use of his *yunta*.

Jenaro had worked for 30 years on the *haciendas* and regarded the *hacienda* system theoretically as good, with mutual benefit to the *patrón* and client; when the *peón* worked well the *patrón* might give him food and meat, although when he was idle he could be punished. However, in his experience, punishment loomed larger than benefits received. His view of the agrarian reform centred on the dispute between Chilca and the co-operative over access to grazing. He saw the agrarian reform as favouring the new co-operative rather than the peasants, who should be the rightful beneficiaries.

Jenaro, a reasonably progressive peasant, was content on the whole with life in Chilca. Although he wished to visit Lima at some time, he did not contemplate migration as an option unless some of his children obtained paid employment there. He saw the main problems of the community, apart from the dispute with the co-operative, as being the need for *agua potable*, and a college for school children to continue education after the primary level.

Matias, an Ageing Householder with Inadequate Labour

Matias, a middle peasant of 59, had been interviewed in 1964. Neither he nor his wife Rosa had received any schooling. They were illiterate and could not speak Spanish. Again, however, they appreciated the instrumental value of education: their oldest son, 30, had gone to college and in 1979 was employed as a tailor in Arequipa; another son, 25, had finished *media* (middle) school and was employed as a clerk in the Ministry of Fisheries in Cuzco. Only one son, who had also finished *media*, was at home in the village, so that although the household possessed 4 *topos* of land the two ageing parents lacked labour resources within the household.

Livestock raised in 1964 can be compared with the numbers in 1978 (see Table 8.3). There was a logical, though modest, increase in the number of cattle and pigs (which required little labour input), but sheep had been discontinued as the *pampa* was poorly drained.

Table 8.3 Matias's livestock, 1964 and 1978

Animals	*1964*	*1978*
Cows	2	4
Calves	–	2
Sheep	2	–
Pigs	–	2
Horses	2	1
Guinea pigs	6	–
Chickens	3	–

Again, the sources of income in 1978 compared with 15 years earlier are instructive (see Table 8.4). Dairy products comprised about a third of the household income in 1963–4; in 1978 they amounted to 89 per cent. Total income had almost quadrupled (from US$40 to $158) but in real terms had probably increased only moderately. In crop yields, Matias had had an even more disastrous season than Jenaro; heavy rain had destroyed a fifth of his maize crop and he had harvested only about 100kg. *Otoscuro* had infested the maize and *rancha* and *illa kuro* had plagued the potatoes which yielded only 650kg/*topo* at a planting/harvest ratio of 1:6.

Table 8.4 Sources of income, 1964 and 1978

1964	soles	*1978*	soles
Sale of cheese	300	Sale of milk	27 900
Making *adobes* on *haciendas*	350	Sale of cheese	2 700
Jornal in Izcuchaka	288	Remittances	500
		Jornal, neighbouring communities	3 200
Total	938		34 300

In spite of his illiteracy, Matias believed in the value of artificial fertilisers and insecticides. He had used two sacks of nitrate of ammonia (at 1200 *soles* each) and two sacks of superphosphate to supplement the use of ash and cow manure, and also applied 10kg of aldrin. Like other middle peasants, Matias could not afford to hire wage labour and used *ayni* to mobilise five to 10 workers when the household labour resources would not suffice.

Matias and his wife declared they were happy in Chilca and would never leave. The two absent sons provided a link with the outside world (the household did not possess a radio), writing about five letters a year, sending 100 *soles* per letter and sometimes sending *encomiendas* of clothes, rice and sugar. Although Matias believed the size of harvests was rather lower than in earlier years, the cost of living was too high to contemplate living elsewhere. He believed Chilca was the most fortunate community in the Pampa de Anta. Because of his reliability he had been entrusted with the responsibility for a small government agro-veterinary shop in Chilca, and he gave out forms to peasants who wished to apply for inoculation of their cattle. Matias declared that the agrarian reform had had 'good ideas' but had not fully carried out its intentions.

In contrast to his father, who did not recognise problems in Chilca, Matias's 22-year old son complained of the dispute over grazing rights with the co-operative, dirty drinking water, and the deterioration in the school and the standard of teaching since the days of the Peace Corps. The *mestizo* teachers seemed to despise the *campesinos*; they often failed to turn up at school and took little interest in educating the pupils.

POOR PEASANTS

Poor peasants averaged a money income (23 677 *soles*) less than half that of households in the moderately rich group, or about two-thirds that of middle peasants. Their land resources were very meagre – only about 3.5 *topos* – and on average they possessed only five head of cattle. Again, the indices of innovation are generally lower: 31 per cent of the sample used chemical fertilisers, 38 per cent used insecticides and 23 per cent had received agricultural credit. The fact that they lacked capital resources and could not acquire them through customary reciprocity is revealed in the fact that 69 per cent were forced to hire plough teams.

Eusabio: Dependence on Remittances

A typical poor peasant household is that of Eusabio, also interviewed in 1964. At that time, as an illiterate, monolingual man of 41 with a household of 10 and only 3¼ *topos* of land, he had had abundant labour but inadequate land. He had supplemented his low income (which appeared to have totalled about 500 *soles*), gained through occasional *jornal* labouring on the *haciendas*, by acting as a sheep buyer and butcher. He bought animals in neighbouring communities at 5 *soles* per pound and sold at 10 *soles* or often for 5 *soles* for the meat but retaining the hide, head and entrails for his profit. He also occasionally received small gifts of 10–20 *soles* from his wife's brother. An attempt in 1962 to maximise the value of his small land area by gaining agricultural credit had not been successful. He had hoped to purchase superior potato seed and also sheep for his butchery business, but when the harvest failed totally he was unable to pay back the loan of 750 *soles* plus 35 *soles* interest. His father helped by lending him half of a *topo* which he had to pass to a richer peasant for one year in exchange for 750 *soles* cash in order to repay the loan. The loan had been totally unsupervised by the bank and Eusabio vowed never to seek any further agricultural credit.

By 1978, Eusabio was 56 and had a family of 14 children, nine of whom were living in Lima and one in the Urubamba Valley. All of the *limaco* children could speak Spanish and four were literate. Although this was a relatively traditional family, they possessed a functioning radio and each child wrote every two or three months and took time on the occasion of a parent's birthday or Christmas to return to Chilca for a visit. Since Eusabio's 3¼ *topos* did not produce very large harvests, and he had in 1978 only three cows and one pig, it was as well, now that he and his wife were becoming old, that they had these external contacts. Five calves, 10 guinea pigs and 20 chickens had recently died of *callotacca*. Frost had affected the maize crop planted in his 1½ *topos* of *maizal* land, and he had garnered a harvest of only about 214kg/*topo*. *Illa kuro* had been bad and the black worm *taladro* had plagued his potatoes, which yielded only about 300kg/*topo*. Eusabio could only fertilise his land with ash from the hearth; artificial fertilisers and insecticides were now too expensive to purchase.

Being poor, the household depended entirely on *ayni* for the two to five additional people needed during the busy times. With respect to earning money income, Eusabio declared that there was little *jornal* labouring available in the surrounding area for a man of 56. The loss of the five calves had been a severe blow to his main local source of income, while his low harvests provided barely enough food for existence. In 1978 the household cash income was comprised entirely of remittances. Each of the 10 children sent money, varying from 300 to 1000 *soles* per letter, and clothes and other gifts were also occasionally sent. Such a total dependence on his family members for income through remittances was unusual but not rare: it was a logical economic strategy for ageing parents, who lacked adequate land or labour resources. At the same time the external assistance represented 'investments', in the broadest sense of external kin refortifying family ties and strengthening their village interests which could be affected by inheritance. With so many children, Eusabio was clearly worried over the inheritance problem when he was gone: 'On death land is divided into equal parts. Many plots are so small you measure it by the number of furrows.'

Eusabio had never personally worked on the *haciendas*. He viewed the system as an exchange relationship and valued the *personalismo* (personal qualities of leadership) of good *patrones*: 'The times of the *haciendas* were very good, because if one lacked money or animals or food, the *patrón* would give it to them, and when a person died, many goods were given to the family.' He deplored the fact that, with the agrarian reform, the human touch no longer existed but only capitalist relations: 'The co-operative only gives us work.'

VERY POOR PEASANTS

These *campesinos* experienced chronic poverty and insecurity; at times the condition of some households became desperate. As Table 8.2 shows, the mean money income of this group was almost nil: only 4890 *soles* (US$22 or about $4 per head). They had access to an average of 2.5 *topos* of land (owning much less); eight households out of 11 had only 3 *topos* or less. Each household possessed about three cattle. Only about a quarter used any artificial fertiliser or insecticide, and in most cases only very tiny amounts. Most households lacked a radio. In addition to the lack of land as the basic source of security, cultural and educational factors loomed large among the very poor peasants. Five of the households were headed by illiterate parents who spoke only Quechua, and the close correspondence of *Indio campesino* status in the poor and very poor groups with illiterate, monolingual people is striking compared with the greater prevalence of proto-*cholo* status associated with bi-lingualism, literacy and some years of schooling in the relatively richer grades of peasantry.

There are, of course, many causes of poverty. One of the most basic, and one that induces much anguish, is the poverty experienced by people who are poor in kinship. Widows who do not have husbands to earn the livelihood for the family may experience hardship if other family members or *compadres* (friends) ignore their plight. Marta was such a case.

Marta: The Poverty of Kinship

An illiterate of 60 years in 1979, Marta had been widowed twice. I had met her and her first husband in 1964. At that time they possessed one cow, two calves and a bull, but they had access to only 3 *topos* of land. Marta owned 1 *topo* in another *ayllu*; her son-in-law had cropped it and given her 60 *soles* in return. At that time the household income was about average for a poor to middle peasant family: about 1000 *soles*, of which the sale of cheese and eggs comprised half, and the balance came from *jornal* labouring on the *hacienda*, stonemasonry and working on the forest project. Marta had commented that they were content with life in Chilca in 1964, but after the loss of two husbands her standard of living had deteriorated markedly. The *maizal* land her family had used in 1964 had belonged to the first husband, and this land was inherited by the sons of his first marriage. In 1978 she had no *maizal* land; her total resource was only half a *topo* of *temporal* land that was cropped in potatoes and *habas*. The yield had been only about 250kg of *habas* (a stray pig had eaten much of the crop) and 290kg of potatoes. *La rancha* and 'putrification' were said to have wrought much destruction. Two cows were lost from *callotacca* and one was killed to eat; her remaining livestock was only two cows, two hens and two guinea pigs. Her total income in 1978 was about 7000 *soles*, earned from the sale of a bull calf. Marta's son was earning a little money by illegally felling some of the eucalyptus trees of the afforestation project to sell for timber.

Marta had three sons, two of whom were employed in Lima. This situation, considered an asset in most families, was of no assistance to this household for they did not send any remittances. Although she sent gifts of maize, meat, wheat and potatoes to them when small surpluses existed, they sent no money or goods in return, as they had many children of their own. Marta visited her *limaco* sons each year, but they never visited or wrote to her.

Marta's views on the *hacienda* system and agrarian reform reflected her lonely status and lifelong dependence on patronage. She had formerly worked on the *hacienda* as a dairy maid for 1.20 *soles* per week. She declared it was a good system as there had been plenty of meat to eat. The time of the older Señor Luna (the 1930s) had been the best, although he punished people severely, sometimes whipping them.

Martín: A Landless Household

Another household, that of Martín's, was very poor because they had no land at all in the village. He had worked before as a small trader, selling clothes in the Cuzco market, but as his wife Maria came from Chilca they had returned to the village. So far Maria's father had not allocated them any land. Although they could both read and write (he had reached the third year of primary school and Maria the fifth), they had little income. They could graze only two cows (one on loan from Maria's father), two pigs and two piglets, one horse and three chickens on the communal *pampa* or in the house compound. They had eked out their food resources by working *en compañia* on the land of a richer peasant, but their share of the harvest was only four sacks of maize. Martín could afford to buy only 1kg of insecticide (190 *soles*) to protect the crop.

In 1978 their income was only about 4800 *soles*, earned by Maria sewing garments which she sold (about 10 each month for 40 *soles* each) in the Cuzco market. However, if some land were left to them, or Martín could find more *jornal* employment, their position would become somewhat more secure.

* * *

Thus family is differentiated from family by the wide variation in resources available, by the conjunction of production and commercial activities and the role of potential workers and their capacities to generate monetary as well as subsistence income. The various sources of income and relations of production established by each family define the character of the transition in which it is involved.

As Gonzalez de Olarte (1984) has explained, the *comunero* family economy is a complex one in which various social rationalities are mixed with different economic calculations. It is comprehensible only when viewed in its totality and in its functioning over time.

EXPLOITATION WITHIN THE COMMUNITY

Although the grossest exploitation of the poor no doubt occurred outside the community – where the Quechua *campesino* was often treated by the 'decent people' (*gente decente*) not only as *Indio* but as an inferior, even sub-human creature – exploitation also occurred within the community, reflecting and legitimising class formation.

In this process the use of pejorative terms, the lack of respect and the perpetuation of forms of behaviour continually reinforced the inequality or the inferiority of the poor and the *Indio*. Such attitudes are every bit as important as any so-called 'hard' or 'objective' data on pauperisation and poverty. Socialisation and enculturation lead to a low self-image among many poor Quechua peasants and to apathy, resignation and acceptance of their lowly, abject status. Village assembly meetings are vivid illustrations of their powerlessness, hopelessness and even their irrelevance (except as free labour on village *faenas*), and the callous disregard in which many *campesinos* from the richer, more articulate, more powerful groups hold them.

Fortunately the presence of the partly-educated Martín in the very poor group acts as a reminder that not all *campesinos* are conditioned passively to accept their status, grinding poverty and gross inferiority. However, if Martín or others like him succeed in engineering an escape from the trap of poverty, it is likely to be through purely individual efforts – in a semi-capitalist way and through cholofication (like that of Justo in 1964: see Chapter 6) – that will do nothing to redeem the living conditions of other members of his class. Such an escape might, however, serve to remind other *campesinos* of the harsh reality and cruel choice that confronts them: without basic resources, economic betterment and a degree of liberation can be achieved only by rejecting their traditional culture and peasant lifestyle.

9 The Unequal Exchange Model of Peasantry

Historically, peasants have been beholden to powerful outsiders and outside forces. As long as they were not politicised or socially mobilised they remained economically fragmented, operating as atomistic independent producers who were largely at the mercy of external appropriators or market trends.

The common view among non-peasants in Peru is that peasants are slow to appreciate either that there is a shortage of some product for which there is a clear market demand and tardy in demanding a higher price or, alternatively, that there is a glut from overproduction. For example, a *vecino* in Quoquepata gave me this assessment of peasant economic calculations:

> The *campesinos* are like animals with four hooves. They don't think of anything, are blind men who are not aware of what happens. They don't take account of the cost of living to protect themselves. They sell their products at the same price as before whereas now the costs are much higher.

In the short term, peasants may not be very quick to adjust to price changes, and the inflexibilities built into the household labour force and the narrow range of choice imposed by their meagre resources do not permit rapid or drastic changes in strategy. However, over the medium term, macro-economic data suggest that considerable change does occur in the peasant economy. The Peruvian peasant who appears immobile, as rooted to the ancient earth as the few gnarled trees that still grow in the Andes, does in fact move readily to other locations in search of employment. Second, there appear to be periods in which a 'proletarianisation' trend is dominant, with peasants moving to take up unskilled wage employment, followed by times when 'peasantisation' again occurs.

In this chapter we will investigate the hypothesis that, over the two to three decades before 1979, external forces outside the peasant community tended to constrain any economic growth which may have been possible in peasant areas of the Southern

Sierra. The evidence to be examined is the evolution of average prices received for peasant crops sold at the market, the growth in *jornal* rates, and the ratio between the two (prices for peasant produce expressed in numbers of man-days of labour). The rate of increase in the cost of key inputs such as artificial fertilisers, insecticides and fungicides needed for commercial production will be examined in relation to returns from peasant harvests. The changes in peasant crops in the Southern Sierra compared with other regions of Peru will also be presented, and the growth and change in the pattern of agricultural credit extended to peasants and other rural producers in the 1960s and 1970s will be examined. Finally, a comment will be made on the provision of agricultural extension or advisory services.

CROP PRICES AND *JORNAL* RATES

What was the trend in average prices received by the peasant producer for his crops over the period 1942–76?[1] The data are presented in Table 9.1. Wheat increased in price by 3500 per cent, or 509 per cent for the period since 1964. The increase for barley was 4498 per cent from 1942 to 1976 or 395 per cent from 1964 to 1976. The rise for the two major crops of maize and potatoes, and for broad beans, was less, however: maize increased by 3965 per cent from 1942 to 1976 or 390 per cent from 1964, and potatoes by 3482 per cent or 319 per cent since 1964. Broad beans increased by 71 per cent from 1953 to 1976 or only 13 per cent from 1964 to 1976.

The daily wage rate for agricultural labouring in the years following 1940 (and especially in the 1970s) grew rather rapidly. Furthermore, while the national wage level grew by a factor of 108 from 1940 to 1977, and the Sierra wage level even more, by 143 times, the cost of living increased in this period by a factor of 64, implying an increase in real wages of 27 per cent for the nation as a whole, or 48 per cent in the Sierra.[2]

When the evolution over time of mean prices for each peasant product is related to the changing mean rate of *jornal* labour, the altered basis of the peasant economy becomes clearer (see Table 9.2). Maletta has suggested that the price of wheat, for example, when calculated in the value of man-days of labour (*jornales*), did not vary much from the level of about 250–260 *jornales* per metric

Table 9.1 Prices to the producer of 'peasant' crops, 1952–76
(*soles* per tonne)

Year	*Potatoes*	*Wheat*	Quinoa	*Barley*	*Dry beans*	Oca	Mashua	Olluco	*Maize*
1942	179	300	882	171	–	–	–	–	210
1943	273	334	980	200	–	–	–	–	236
1944	299	400	1 090	262	–	–	–	–	287
1945	305	440	1 210	270	–	–	–	–	334
1946	274	440	1 350	400	–	–	–	–	402
1947	456	565	1 500	500	–	–	–	–	534
1948	730	790	1 520	810	–	–	–	–	650
1949	700	800	1 200	650	–	–	–	–	900
1950	751	1 260	1 196	750	–	–	–	–	881
1951	850	1 300	925	870	–	–	–	–	920
1952	800	1 100	1 720	700	–	600	–	–	900
1953	900	1 100	1 500	719	800	620	–	–	900
1954	870	1 150	1 550	730	900	650	–	–	979
1955	1 001	1 300	1 667	1 026	2 000	700	–	–	1 049
1956	1 000	1 300	1 798	1 040	2 000	750	–	–	1 060
1957	1 020	1 300	2 200	1 100	2 000	780	–	–	1 078
1958	1 100	1 320	1 300	1 100	–	790	–	–	1 100
1959	1 050	1 350	2 350	1 120	–	800	–	–	1 150
1960	1 340	1 700	2 400	1 360	1 670	786	–	–	1 300
1961	1 340	1 640	3 190	1 250	1 670	750	820	850	1 660
1962	1 402	1 700	3 277	1 250	1 780	940	1 040	1 070	2 432

continued on p. 152

Table 9.1 continued

Year	*Potatoes*	*Wheat*	Quinoa	*Barley*	*Dry beans*	Oca	Mashua	Olluco	*Maize*
1963	1 530	1 750	2 860	1 500	1 980	990	1 090	1 120	1 950
1964	1 531	1 772	2 862	1 587	1 875	988	1 092	1 122	1 741
1965	1 645	2 049	3 043	1 689	3 025	1 026	1 047	1 417	2 105
1966	2 057	2 843	2 363	1 855	2 971	1 500	1 201	1 798	2 353
1967	2 011	2 903	2 453	1 876	3 087	1 594	1 553	1 934	2 520
1968	2 474	3 909	4 338	1 743	4 233	1 854	1 767	2 287	3 366
1969	2 405	4 414	4 149	2 570	4 835	1 666	1 632	2 346	3 390
1970	2 254	4 090	3 850	2 462	4 682	1 644	1 509	2 290	3 730
1971	2 160	4 270	4 048	2 609	4 898	1 562	1 536	2 303	3 516
1972	2 815	4 944	4 054	3 119	3 556	1 943	1 792	2 558	3 923
1973	3 422	5 655	4 824	3 591	5 834	2 392	2 052	2 867	5 052
1974	4 546	6 619	6 231	3 923	6 981	2 940	2 516	3 550	6 168
1975	5 645	10 482	13 803	7 576	12 141	3 937	3 580	4 540	8 177
1976	6 411	10 800	15 233	7 863	12 577	4 735	3 928	4 854	8 537
Increase 1964–76	319 per cent								390 per cent

Source: Maletta (1979).

ton in 1882 until the 1940s, when a ton of wheat was equivalent to 308 *jornales* (the average of 1942–4 in Table 9.2). It is interesting to note that after 1942 this trend was reversed: by the mid-1970s a ton of wheat had fallen[3] in equivalence to only 149 *jornales* (average of 1974–6). When we compare data for 1976 with 1964, we can see that the same general trend occurs for all crops except broad beans and for wheat (which was static from 1964 to 1976). Thus, the price of potatoes fell from 116 *jornales* in 1964 to only 82 in 1976, maize from 131 *jornales* to 109 and barley from 120 to 101. The fact that dried broad beans were the exception to this trend, rising from 142 to 161, is probably because they had become a crop of minor importance in Chilca in 1979 whereas I did not see the crop growing at all in 1964.

The great difference in the escalation in daily wage rates, and the only slight increase over the 34-year period in current prices received by peasants for their crops (an increase that was in fact a substantial fall in real value), indicates the reason for the popularity of *jornal* work. Indeed, when coupled with the growth of population in the Sierra and the increased pressure placed on the tiny plots of the *minifundio* system, the increasing tendency to favour daily wage labour and also to participate more fully in circular, semi-permanent and permanent migration to city employment seems thoroughly rational. The very considerable demand apparent in the peasant communities of the Pampa de Anta for *jornal* labour during the agrarian reform period of the 1970s (see Chapter 11) illustrates this preference.

The one exception to this trend – albeit an important one – is the favourable demand for dairy products during the 1960s and 1970s. The official statistics on livestock products are, unfortunately, confused and unclear so it is difficult to estimate average prices to the producer. Rearing livestock is one of the most basic and dynamic processes in the peasant economy, since livestock (and especially cattle) provide the most valuable form of capital. In difficult times, when a rural economy based primarily on cropping for subsistence and some cash sales shows signs of increasing pauperisation, the consequent trend towards proletarianisation might be delayed by decapitalising the peasant household's herd of cattle. In 1978, as many as 18 households (35 per cent of the sample) in Chilca had exploited their fund of capital 'on the hoof' by selling one or more cows, bulls or sheep to raise cash, and in most cases this was the main source of income

Table 9.2 Equivalence in daily wage rates of prices to the producer of peasant crops, 1942–76
(*Jornales* of the Sierra per metric ton)

Year	*Potatoes*	*Wheat*	Quinoa	*Barley*	*Dry beans*	Oca	Mashua	Olluco	*Maize*
1942	201	337	991	192	–	–	–	–	235
1943	235	288	845	172	–	–	–	–	203
1944	225	300	819	197	–	–	–	–	216
1945	188	272	747	167	–	–	–	–	206
1946	141	227	696	206	–	–	–	–	207
1947	194	240	638	213	–	–	–	–	227
1948	238	258	497	265	–	–	–	–	212
1949	191	218	327	177	–	–	–	–	245
1950	171	286	272	170	–	–	–	–	200
1951	155	236	168	158	–	–	–	–	167
1952	116	160	250	102	–	87	–	–	131
1953	106	129	176	85	94	73	–	–	106
1954	98	129	174	82	101	73	–	–	110
1955	108	140	180	111	216	76	–	–	113
1956	105	136	188	109	210	79	–	–	111
1957	102	130	220	110	200	78	–	–	108
1958	108	129	225	108	–	77	–	–	108
1959	98	126	219	105	–	75	–	–	107
1960	112	142	200	113	139	65	–	–	108

1961	107	131	255	100	134	60	66	68	133
1962	111	135	260	99	141	75	83	85	193
1963	119	136	222	116	153	84	84	77	151
1964	116	134	216	120	142	75	82	85	131
1965	122	152	225	125	224	76	78	105	156
1966	132	182	151	119	190	96	77	115	151
1967	106	153	129	99	162	84	82	102	133
1968	115	182	202	81	197	86	82	106	157
1969	90	165	155	96	181	62	61	88	127
1970	78	141	133	85	161	57	52	79	129
1971	70	138	131	84	158	50	50	74	113
1972	83	145	119	91	104	57	53	75	115
1973	92	153	130	97	158	65	55	77	136
1974	101	147	138	87	155	65	56	79	137
1975	88	163	216	113	190	61	56	71	127
1976	82	138	195	101	161	61	50	62	109

Source: Table 9.1 and Maletta (1979).

Figure 9.1 PEASANT TERMS OF TRADE, CUZCO

gained during that year. Later, if the price of some peasant crops were to improve substantially, if more *jornal* labour became available, or if remittances or other forms of income came readily to hand, the peasant household could be expected to replenish its herd.

It is interesting to note that the recent study on Cuzco agriculture carried out by Guillén (1983) confirms the deterioration in peasant terms of trade identified by Maletta (see Figure 9.1).

INFLATION AND THE RISING COST OF INPUTS

In the latter years of the 1970s the annual inflation rate was often around 60 per cent. As non-wage workers, peasants could not benefit from the frequent devaluations of the currency and wage rises which enabled most workers in the economy to catch up on their standard of living. Table 9.3 indicates the rapidity with which prices rose for four basic foods in a period of less than four years. The average rate of increase was 568 per cent, or far greater than the rise in value of peasant crops over a much longer period. Few peasants, of course, could afford to buy store goods.

The fall in real terms of the prices received for eight out of nine

Table 9.3 Evolution of prices for products in greatest demand in rural areas, July 1975 to March 1979 (*soles* and *centavos*)

	July 1975	*May 1978*	*March 1979*	*Increase (per cent) July 1975–March 1979*
Bread (loaf)	0.65	2.20	2.50	385
Sugar (kg)	5.65	29.50	50.00	885
Rice (kg)	13.30	35.00	59.00	444
Vermicelli and spaghetti (kg)	17.90	69.00	100.00	559

Source: Alvarez (1984).

crops produced by peasants in the Sierra for cash sale, as well as the major crops sold from Chilca over the period of 1964–76, was even harder to bear when prices of artificial fertilisers, herbicides, insecticides and fungicides were increasing over these years.

By the late 1950s there had been enough field trials of crop response to artificial fertiliser on some of the major soil types in the Cuzco area for agronomists confidently to predict that average yields of major crops on arable land could be increased, with appropriate fertilisation, by up to 10 times for potatoes, 5 times for maize and 3½ for cereals.[4] Widespread realisation of the advantages to be gained from agricultural modernisation through investment in fertilisers and other innovations came through a diverse range of development efforts in the 1950s and early 1960s – including the American Alliance for Progress, the activities of many international development agencies and not least by the Peruvian Government's own efforts through its Ministry of Agriculture, Bank of Agricultural Credit and other regional institutions – to implement the findings of the *Plan del Sur* and many local regional surveys. As a result, the consumption of artificial fertilisers increased steadily throughout the 1960s, and it seems clear that by the late 1960s or early 1970s many peasants in favoured locations began to purchase at least small quantities for the first time. By 1975, the use of artificial fertilisers per hectare in Peru was a little above the average for the Andean group of countries.[5]

After 1972, however, the consumption of fertilisers became

somewhat erratic. The first reason for this was a supply and demand problem. The Cachimayo fertiliser factory near Cuzco began functioning properly in 1965. Before that, there were only two small fertiliser factories. Although Cachimayo had a capacity of 12 000 tonnes, it was something of a 'white elephant' at first and did not operate to its full capacity until 1971, owing to high costs of production and lack of demand for its product. In addition, costs and supply were controlled by the fact that, until 1971, 60 per cent of nitrogenous fertilisers and all phosphatic and potassium fertilisers were imported into Peru.

Fertilisers increased in price in 1974 and 1975, which had serious repercussions for agricultural production.[6] In August 1975, a subsidy was announced which reduced the cost of fertiliser by approximately 40 per cent, and in April 1976 a single price was created for all fertilisers at national level. The Empresa Nacional de Comercialización de Insumos (ENCI) provided a state distribution system which also subsidised freight. However, by 1978 transport costs had risen so much that there were further sharp increases in fertiliser cost, so that they represented about 20–31 per cent of the costs of production of most crops.

As Peru's economic situation and balance of payments worsened during the late 1970s, there was increasing pressure from the IMF and other international banks for the government to cut spending and adopt 'more market'-oriented policies. *Sur* suggested that a subsidy of 40 per cent of the normal price of fertilisers was essential to maintain usage so that agricultural output would continue to increase. However, the government, faced with huge transportation costs, decided to remove its subsidies progressively from 1978 and completely by 1980.[7]

From December 1976 to December 1978, the price of four major artificial fertilisers increased by an average of 212 per cent, while potatoes increased in price by only 81 per cent. Over the longer period of July 1975 to July 1979, five fertilisers increased in price by an average of over 600 per cent. Early in 1978, 10kg of nitrate of ammonia (the most commonly used fertiliser) from Cachimayo could be bought by 4.6kg of potatoes. By November 1978, the purchase of the same amount required 9.3kg of potatoes, and by August 1979 as much as 22.4kg of potatoes were needed.

In the Cuzco zone artificial fertilisers were used mainly for the cultivation of potatoes, maize, coffee and wheat. However, in view of this price trend, it is not surprising that as many as 25 out of 52 peasants in the sample (all the poor and very poor peasants in Chilca) gave up using artificial fertiliser by 1979. The impact of the government's pricing policies was not detrimental to all rural producers, though; in contrast to the mass of peasants, *agricultores* who grew crops for export were favoured. Producers of white maize could purchase 10kg of nitrate of ammonia with 1.88kg of their crop in 1976; two years later only 1.45kg of white maize were needed. Overwhelmingly, the main users of fertilisers were the CAPs and SAIS and medium-sized farmers.

AGRICULTURAL CREDIT

It is interesting to note the changing pattern of agricultural loans in the Cuzco Department over the 20 years from 1957 to 1978.[8] In 1957, during the oligarchical government of Prado, small *agricultores* comprised 92 per cent of all beneficiaries who received loans from the government Banco de Fomento Agropecuario (BFA). They received only 22 per cent of the total loans, however, with the balance going to large producers or *haciendas*. Five years later, though, when Belaúnde's Acción Popular government came to power, the small *agricultores* were 98 per cent of the beneficiaries and received 81 per cent of all agricultural credit. Over the period 1962–8 (which was marked by peasant mobilisation, the land invasions of 1963, repression and instability) the number of loans fell from over 7000 in 1962 to less than 1300 in 1965, with the total value dropping from 68 million *soles* to under 22 million. The value of loans from private commercial banks grew over the same period, from 125 to 184 million *soles*. The number of properties with access to bank credit dropped in these years by 70 per cent, and the value lent by 52 per cent on average. In 1968, the BFA provided 67 per cent of all bank loans to the agricultural sector.

The period 1968–76, coinciding with the Peruvian Revolution and with agrarian reform, has been termed the 'Great Leap' in agricultural credit. There was a rapid expansion in the services of the BFA. In less than three years from 1968 the value of loans grew by 300 per cent, increasing by 24 times by 1976, an unprecedented growth (see Table 9.4).

Although private banks gave out loans of 191 million *soles* in

Table 9.4 Agricultural credit in south-east region

Year	*Number of loans*	*Total Value of BFA (000s)* soles *and* centavos		*Total*	*Total value of loans from commercial banks*
		Large agricultural producers	*Small agricultural producers*		
1968	2 174	13 606	19 259	32 865	184 152
1970	2 062	302 098	28 606	330 704	191 763
1974	8 010	396 780	65 138	461 918	608 059
1976	7 751	626 425	90 104	716 529	883 249

Source: *Sur*, 1, 3 (June 1978): 6–8, 28.

1970, the loans of the BFA almost doubled this. However, private sector loans more than quadrupled from 1970 to 1976, and outstripped the loans of BFA after 1974. From 1968 to 1976 the preference shown to small farmers over large producers in 1961 and 1968 was reversed, with large properties receiving from 86 to 91 per cent of total bank credit. This tendency that began with the agrarian reform was consolidated by channelling the major part of resources into the new huge CAPs and SAIS enterprises. It is interesting to note that peasant producers formed only a part of the 'small producers' who received only 9–14 per cent of agricultural credit in this period: a good portion of these producers were *pequeñas propiedades* (small farmers) or *vecinos* who owned larger holdings and were more commercialised than the mass of peasants.

An attempt in late 1979 to inspect records of government rural credit policies in Cuzco Department proved largely abortive. Officers who were personally embarrassed at the new policies declared that the records were not available, but it was clear that the great majority of loans that were not going to the large enterprises went to assist medium or small export producers, such as coffee holdings in the sub-tropics.

AGRICULTURAL EXTENSION

What assistance was provided by agricultural advisory services to enable peasants to increase production? In Chapter 12 we will discuss innovation. In general, agricultural extension officers visited Chilca infrequently; when they did so, they usually contented themselves with talking to a group of peasants, exhorting them to use artificial fertiliser or insecticide or to adopt improved crop varieties. It was rare for *tecnicos* to visit the *chacras*, to take off their kid gloves and demonstrate how to apply fertiliser correctly without burning the stalks of the plants. (Some peasants doubted the *tecnicos*' competence in practical farming techniques.) Up to the 1970s, the most valuable service provided by the Ministry of Agriculture was undoubtedly the vaccination of cattle against foot-and-mouth and other diseases. This innovation resulted from the lobbying of an association of cattle producers that included the peasants, although led by a number of *hacendados*.

With the initiation of the agrarian reform, enthusiasm for innovation increased as several villagers became representatives on the committees of the new co-operatives or undertook training in regional seminars designed to teach modern agriculture. Throughout the 1970s, many more *tecnicos* visited the villages, haranguing the peasants to produce greater outcomes. For all this eloquence, the villagers remained largely cynical and unmoved. These new *mistis* of the agrarian reform were no different from the middle-class *tecnicos* of the Ministry of Agriculture before the Revolution; indeed, they were now even more theoretical, suffering often from urban bias and lacking the political experience and local knowledge of the *mistis* employed by the former *haciendas* (see Chapter 13).

The commitment of the government to assist only commercial agriculture or export cropping was expressed at Qolquepata in the policy that prevented the extension officer from visiting individually the peasants who owned less than 3ha of land, even though some progressive peasants were desperate to receive advice. Basically he was limited to working with the official units of the agrarian reform: the local co-operative societies, the 'nuclear community' of Qolquepata and about 552 *agricultores* who held over 3ha.

Apart from the success of the eucalyptus planting campaign of the Forest Service, development extension did not make a great impact. Although the national policy should have been uniform throughout Peru, the individual efforts, skill and degree of rapport achieved with the peasants varied greatly among extension officers of the Ministry of Agriculture, and this affected the success of their involvement.

CONCLUSION

The evidence clearly suggests that there is much in contemporary practice to confirm the peasant view of the outside world as hostile, unfriendly or exploitative. The terms of trade have usually moved strongly to the disadvantage of the peasant. The prices of the eight major peasant crops in the Cuzco Department fell substantially in real terms over a 34-year period. One of the few favourable trends was the considerable rise in real terms of daily labouring wage rates, but this was countered by the fact that the economies of scale achieved by the agrarian reform meant a marked contraction in the demand for *jornal* labour during the 1970s (see Chapter 13).

Although, with improved organisation, the power of peasant syndicates became greater through the 1970s, the peasant still remained defenceless in the face of rapid inflation. Apart from resorting to complete withdrawal from the market, the peasant possessed little leverage in the national economy. Although there was a substantial rise in the volume of agricultural credit from 1968 to 1976, it was invariably unsupervised; the great bulk of the loans went to the large enterprises. Rural credit increasingly favoured producers of export crops, such as coffee growers. Agricultural extension activity in peasant areas was either non-existent or infrequent. Where it did operate, it was confined to the new agrarian reform units, or to *pequeñas propiedades*. As the economic conditions worsened in the late 1970s and the utopian visions of the Revolution evaporated, renewed pressures by international bankers brought a new era of relative austerity; what little help had been made available to the peasants in the early 1970s was transferred to the producers of export crops.

Part III
Peasant Solutions?

10 The Peruvian Revolution and its Aftermath

To what extent, it must be asked, could the endemic problems of Peru – its chronic poverty, backwardness and underdevelopment, its gross social inequality and exploitation, its dependence on foreign capital – be solved by a far-reaching national revolution? And since these conditions both characterise and underpin the situation of the peasantry, would their amelioration assist the peasants to escape from the poverty trap and evolve to a status approaching that of small farmers, who might expect to enjoy a lifestyle of simple but modest decency and self-respect?

Nearly every revolution relies on a rhetoric of freedom and strives to bring about change; revolutions are also vitally concerned with the problem of new beginnings, and of remaking or transforming society. They often aspire to bring back a golden age and, as Octavio Paz (1961) has reminded us, the 'eternal return' is one of the implicit assumptions of almost every revolutionary theory. Certainly the Peruvian Revolution was imbued with attempts to reclaim the Incan past and thus to legitimise the nation. In terms of *intentions*, there is no doubt that thoroughgoing revolution in Peru was attempted by the military government. In terms of *implementation*, some structural changes and drastic alterations of policies achieved considerable, perhaps substantial, success.

It is beyond the scope of this book to review the full significance and achievements of the Peruvian Revolution.[1] However, apart from the agrarian reform, two important features warrant special attention: first, the attempt by the military government to build a new model of accumulation, which is possibly coherent enough to be termed a 'state capitalist' model of development;[2] and second, the evolution of the ideology of an 'organic corporate state'.[3]

First, we shall consider the agrarian reform, the most significant aspect of the Peruvian Revolution to affect the peasantry.

THE AGRARIAN REFORM

Above all else, the agrarian reform of 1969,[4] its implementation and ultimate fate must be viewed in the context of the crumbling economy, the growing loss of direction and conviction of government policy, and the government's mounting confusion in the face of increasing social divisiveness as class struggles in the countryside were unleashed.

In the words of the military government, the agrarian reform was to be 'radical, massive and rapid'. For it to succeed, the gross inequalities in Peruvian society, and especially the servitude and poverty sustained by feudalism and the *latifundia*, had to be overturned:

> Today, the Day of the Indian, the Revolutionary Government presents the peasant with the best of tributes, . . . a law that will end for all time an unjust social order that has maintained in poverty and iniquity those who have always had to till someone else's land, a social order that has always denied this land to millions of *campesinos* . . . To these men of the land we can now say in the immortal and libertarian words of Tupac Amaru: '*Campesino*, the master will no longer feed on your poverty'.[5]

Not surprisingly, President Velasco's speech on nationwide radio and television on 24 June 1969 greatly aroused peasant expectations, adding to the momentum of the Revolution. Whether this momentum could be contained and channelled constructively was, however, an entirely different matter.

Although *equity* appeared to be the dominant theme of the agrarian reform, the government was primarily committed to an anti-oligarchical ideology and to an economic plan in which agriculture would finance industrial growth. Pre-capitalist forms of exploitation had to be eliminated; the coastal oligarchy had to be broken since they monopolised the country's wealth and were the accomplices of powerful foreign interests; and 'feudal' obstacles to capitalist development had to be removed by land reform. It was thought that a wide-ranging modernisation process could then develop, and that a reduction in the concentration of landownership would lead to a redistribution of income which would expand the internal market, encourage industrialisation and reduce social tensions. Although the regime was at pains to point out that the revolution was 'neither capitalist nor communist' but Peruvian (emphasising its authentic and nationalistic character), it was clearly primarily capitalist in design.

The revolutionary potential of the working class and rural violence perpetuated by the peasants were seen to be internal threats which could best be allayed by social and economic development initiated by agrarian reform. The agrarian reform would incorporate the peasantry into the national economy, thus expanding the internal market, and co-opt them politically, thus building support for the revolutionary process.

The Revolution was flawed by a basic contradiction: the average rural income was very low and, to rectify this, incomes and/or investments would have to increase. On the other hand, one of the underlying ideas of the agrarian reform was that agriculture should finance industrial growth. The government never made it clear how it would reconcile these two contradictory objectives.[6]

Other conflicting elements in the reform became more obvious over time. Towards 1973 it became clear that equity was less important as an objective and expropriations were reduced. The reform became more conservative in its aims, and issues of consolidation or stability became more prominent.

The wide scope of the process can be seen by classifying the agrarian reform into seven objectives, as outlined below.[7]

(1) *The exclusion of both the Sierra landowners and agrarian bourgeoisie from the production and appropriation of surplus in agriculture*

The maximum area that landlords were allowed to keep following expropriation was fixed at 150ha of irrigated arable land in the Coast, and between 15 and 55ha (irrigated) or their equivalent in the Sierra and *selva*.

(2) *The promotion of owner-operation and the removal of land from the market*

The law aimed to eliminate absentee landlordism and various forms of renting and servile relationships. Also, direct producers were not to be placed in a position where, in cases of indebtedness, market forces could strip them of their land. The state was made legally responsible for all transactions in land.

(3) *Co-operative collectivisation was preferred to the distribution of land to families*
There was a clear intention to establish, as far as possible, large production units with centralised management. These would facilitate the achievement of scale economies and mechanisation. Especially from 1972, new 'associative enterprises' were seen to be the principal agents of agricultural development under the reform.

Two main forms of associative enterprise were created: CAPs and SAIS. There were four different categories of CAPs: the agro-industrial sugar CAPs of the north coast, coastal CAPs producing mainly for the internal market, Sierra CAPs including both subsistence and cash crops, and high *selva* CAPs producing for the local market and the international coffee market. The SAIS were intended to combine one or more ex-*haciendas* with neighbouring indigenous communities. They were predominantly concerned with grazing livestock and, as with the CAPs, the beneficiaries were expected to make annual agrarian debt payments to the state.

On most Sierra *haciendas*, the 1969 law gave priority to the claims of *cólonos* and small tenants to the plots they worked. There was also the expectation that it would prove possible to strengthen the centralised part of the *hacienda* and extend the centralised management of resources to include and proletarianise the peasant members.[8]

(4) *The allocation of expropriated land in such a way as to incorporate neighbouring peasant communities and lessen differences in income and access to resources among peasants*
It was intended that a greater number of people would be included in the newly created associative units than had been involved in the expropriated estates. This policy was put into effect, with mixed but usually very limited success, in the creation of the CAPs and SAIS. It was also one of the aims of the establishment, from 1972, of Integral Rural Development Plans (PIARs). The PIARs, incorporating several associative enterprises (usually villages) within a given region, were designed to promote regional economic integration and planning by centralising marketing, processing, use of machinery and service provision for a group of enterprises.

(5) *Administrative and economic incorporation of indigenous communities*
The communities, to be called Campesiñas Comunidades (Peasant Communities), were to be encouraged to transform their traditional forms of economic organisation and internal government into entrepreneurial or co-operative forms, which could assist their economic and political integration into the nation.

(6) *Participation by land reform beneficiaries in the production decisions of the new enterprises*
As we shall see, such 'participation' in terms of the corporate state ideology had clear limits. It was intended that production and technocratic considerations would be uppermost in the minds of the co-opted members.

(7) *State intervention and control*
A high degree of state intervention was written into the 1969 law and subsequent legislation. Economically, the state was given control over land use, wages, marketing and investments in the associative enterprises. The participation of the beneficiaries was greatly limited. Politically, the state attempted at first to limit union organisation; later it tried to channel mass mobilisation into government-approved structures under the umbrella of SINAMOS (Sistema Nacional de Apoya a la Movilización Social).

How did the plans of the agrarian reform work out in practice? The government's greatest weapon for reform was expropriation of land, and at the end of 1978 practically all the big farms in Peru had been expropriated and almost 50 per cent of the agricultural land had been involved in the enormous transfer (see Table 10.1). Unfortunately the military leaders were largely in ignorance of the complexity of peasant farming organisation and ecology, and they believed that expropriation and redistribution would cure all ills. Although a minimal 'family agricultural unit' was allowed, the rest of the land was meant to be worked communally. The government believed it was applying traditional, communal socio-economic principles congruent with their overall organic statist philosophy.[9] In fact, however, individual ownership or tenancy had long superseded communal

Table 10.1 Land redistribution under agrarian reform, 1969–75

	Area allocated		*Value of land allocated*		*Beneficiary families*		*Average land value per family (thousands of soles)*
	Hectares	*Per cent*	Soles	*Per cent*	*Number*	*Per cent*	
SAIS	2 494 427	43	1 388 727	14	59 210	25	23
CAPs							
Agro-industrial	126 474	2	3 713 285	38	27 497	12	135
Other coastal	577 028	10	3 545 594	37	40 153	17	88
Sierra	1 100 587	19	484 130	5	26 602	11	18
High jungle	128 948	2	95 867	1	3 829	1	33
All CAPs	1 933 037	33	7 838 876	81	98 081	41	80
Peasant groups	919 210	16	349 996	4	26 405	11	13
Communities	420 373	7	99 428	1	46 025	19	2
Individuals	71 712	1	–	–	10 721	4	7
Total	5 838 759	100	9 677 027	100	240 442	100	40

Source: Héctor Martínez, *La Reforma Agraría Peruana: las Empresas Asociativas Andinas* (Lima: Ministerío de Agricultura y Alimentación, 1978); p. 21, cited by Havens, Lastarria-Cornhiel and Otero (1983): 33.

ownership as the dominant form, and while the government believed that the redistribution of land would stimulate the economy in general and reduce the land hunger of the rural masses, there was not enough land available to achieve this: 'A redistribution of all or part of the land farmed by large farmers (*latifundios*) could add on the average no more than one-fifth of a hectare to each small holding if the land was distributed evenly.'[10] Unfortunately the arithmetic of land tenure did not permit a solution, and in fact minifundism was even more pronounced in 1972 as the agrarian reform was being carried out.

Almost 400 000 out of a total of 1.4 million rural families benefited from the reform. In terms of sheer numbers this was impressive: perhaps about 2 million people were involved. But it can be argued that most of the families benefiting from the reform already belonged to the richer strata in Peru. While poor *colonos* became co-operative members of Sierra CAPs and SAIS, in the large agro-industrial CAPs of the coast most of the beneficiaries were unionised workers who were already relatively well paid. The poor majority of Peruvian peasants received very little land, credit and technical assistance.

Available information suggests that income distribution worsened in Peru during the period 1961–75,[11] in contrast with the goals announced by the Revolutionary Government. The internal market for agricultural and livestock production grew between 1970 and 1976 by only 0.9 per cent, and redistribution seems to have been quite limited, most of it occurring among the most favoured quartile of the population.[12]

While agriculture received higher inputs from the national budget in the first years of the agrarian reform, these inputs fell from 1977[13] and continued the historical trend towards neglect of the agricultural sector. In addition, surplus from agriculture continued to be extracted to finance industrial-urban growth. Private investment also remained insignificant.

The agrarian reform did not significantly raise the level of employment. Though accurate information is not available, the number of jobs that existed by 1976 was completely out of proportion to the target set. Ministry of Labour estimates gave an economically active population in agriculture in 1976 of 2 150 700 workers, or 43.3 per cent of the country's total economically active population. Of that number, only 815 000 workers (37.9 per cent) had adequate jobs, while 6500 workers

(0.3 per cent) were unemployed and 1 329 200 (61.8 per cent) were underemployed.[14] These results were so serious that the government decided to implement a special project in 1976 to create jobs in rural areas. It was, of course, well known that the Sierra was an area of acute land shortage and excess labour. It is paradoxical, therefore, that the chief thrust of the reform was to establish giant new production enterprises which were to be highly mechanised, providing relatively few jobs. The sad results of this policy will be described in Chapter 13.

Institutionally, too, the agrarian reform has not been successful. Although a minority of the SAIS and CAPs is operating as intended, as efficient agro-business enterprises, the great majority is far too large and cumbersome. Before 1969, large areas of the *haciendas* (often one-third or one-half of the total land) were effectively controlled by the *colonos*, who used this land in exchange for work for the *patrón*. The SAIS and CAPs have tried to deny peasants use of this land. Ironically, although it was intended to destroy the *latifundio* class, the reform has accentuated the concentration of territorial property by combining perhaps 5–15 former *haciendas* in great new collective enterprises (mainly at the expense of the useful intermediate-sized properties of 5–500ha). Many of these are far too large to be managed efficiently and it is significant that in the late 1970s there appeared to be some decentralisation down to sectors (former *haciendas*).

What are the effects of these various unfavourable factors? After the agrarian reform, producers were not inclined to invest in their properties or become more sensitive to market stimuli. Lazy farmers did not respond to the supposed new opportunities. Massive migration to the urban centres continued, despite a short phase of return migration in some areas at the time of land redistribution. And probably only a small percentage (under 25 per cent) of the SAIS and CAPs in the Puno zone were sound and progressive in 1979, agronomically speaking.[15]

While there was an attempt to ensure that the reform was not simply *agrarian* (redistribution of land) but also integral and *agronomic*[16] (ensuring the input of fertilisers, insecticides, new seeds, credit, technical advice and so on), too much faith was placed on the management of the new giant enterprises and no real support was given to the peasants. The failure of peasant training and the lack of their full (rather than formal) participation in the running of the enterprises is reflected in their continued poverty and the surviving class structure.

The Peruvian agrarian reform was pushed to the left in its programme of land expropriations by pressures from rural groups excluded from it. The aroused expectations of different rural sectors were not satisfied and conflicts were created between the rhetoric of self-management and the reality of central control.[17] At the same time, the 'right', composed of medium-sized commercial farms, proved to be unexpectedly strong and determined. In view of these trends, government planners became more convinced of the advantages of a centrally planned and controlled agricultural economy with all directives, inputs, credits and so on emanating from central authorities to regional offices.

At one level, official attempts to contain and direct the struggles in the countryside implied an extension of the state capitalist role in rural areas to all aspects of rural social and economic organisation. At another level, the idea of the organic corporate state emerged in the promotion by the government of the National Agrarian Confederation (CNA). The intention of the CNA was to join together all people who worked in the agricultural sector, both to communicate their interests to government and to co-ordinate regional and national agricultural policies. It soon became clear, however, that the CNA was 'basically a mechanism to enhance the labors [*sic*] of the government' since peasant interests were to be defended by the CNA only to the extent that they were 'compatible with the national interest as determined by the Military Government'.[18] Genuine participation of local peasant groups would not be permitted. Even in the name of the Peruvian Revolution, the dominance of coastal *mestizos* would be perpetuated over Indian peasants of the Sierra.

THE STATE CAPITALIST MODEL OF DEVELOPMENT

Economically, the situation in Peru in 1968 pointed unequivocally to the state needing to adopt a new role. Since the industrial bourgeoisie was weak and dependent, the state itself had to emerge as the centre of a state capitalist model of accumulation, burdened though it was with all the demanding tasks of economic and political organisation.[19] The required change was immense, involving historically the transformation of an export-led economy based on natural resources to one based on industry serving domestic markets. This necessitated extensive restructuring of capital, including changes in the pattern of production, in the ownership of assets and also in the relationship between capital and labour.

The first task was to destroy the export oligarchy which had been closely associated with foreign economic interests. The day after the agrarian reform law was passed in June 1969, eight huge enterprises controlling approximately 90 per cent of sugar production were taken over by the government.[20] The regime not only destroyed the power of the oligarchy, but also hoped to discredit the Aprista trade union leaders whose main strength was also in this north coast area. Next the state replaced private ownership with public ownership in key branches of the export sector, in heavy industry, in banking, and in transport networks and their infrastructure, co-ordinated through a national planning system.

In the cities, new 'social property' firms were established in the light manufacturing and service sectors. Co-ordination was to be provided by central state-controlled boards which supplied finance and marketing arrangements. The industrialisation drive was to be spearheaded by the manufacturing sector, but private Peruvian industrialists were to take the lead, supported by guaranteed markets, import protection, subsidised inputs, cheap credit and fiscal incentives, although subjected to worker participation in management and profits. In its social aspects the state was to institute a new and more subtle system of class domination, based on carefully manipulated mobilisation. The model emerged gradually over the 1969–75 period, but the main outlines were apparent as early as 1970.[21]

The very considerable changes in the economy between 1968 and 1975 and the trends which led to the call to restrict and reverse foreign penetration and control over the economy are broadly indicated in Table 10.2. While the military rulers were sincere in their intentions to alter and develop the country radically, the changes they made did not fundamentally alter Peru's economic structures. The emphasis on redistribution of property did not change the economy's essential rules of behaviour, which sustained inequality and maintained a wide gap between wealth and poverty. Thus, although the redistribution

1. Inca terraces at Chinchero.

2. Historically the expanding *haciendas* monopolised most good land, including often valley floors, pushing land-hungry *minifundistas* up on to the steep valley sides. Urubamba Valley, near Urcos.

3. A priest and his flock. Note the *varayoc* with his staff of office on the right. Near Pisac.

4. The heavy cost of the ceremonial fund. A peasant returns home with an elaborate coffin (costing as much as his annual monetary income) for his wife's funeral. Near Izcuchaca.

5. A peasant *adobe* house and courtyard. Maize cobs are drying on the roof of a store house on the right. Near Maras.

6. The plaza of a peasant community. Chinchero.

7. A peasant girl guarding the family livestock. Urubamba Valley.

8. A peasant market, including fruit and vegetables from tropical as well as temperate altitudes. *Cholo* men can be seen left and centre foreground. Chinchero.

9. Irrigated *maizal* land with terraces in the background. Urubamba Valley.

10. Peasant shepherds guarding their sheep. Open field grazing near Ayaviri.

11. A family of Chilca. The old head of the household and his wife, both illiterate, had spent their lives on the *hacienda*. Their *comunero* son, second from right, was also illiterate. There is a marked contrast, however, between his two sons: the younger one on the left is illiterate, but the one on the right is a literate, bi-lingual secondary school student.

12. Rapid, uncontrolled urbanisation. A *barriada* of Lima with older dwellings and pig sty in the foreground. In the background some houses have a second storey and some have been upgraded.

Table 10.2 Changes in the structure of ownership and control of the Peruvian economy indicated by corporate sector (per cent of GDP)

Date	*Domestic private business*	*Foreign enterprise*	*Public sector*	*New co-operative*
1950	72	17	11	
1968	51	33	16	
1975	40	17	31	12

Source: Fitzgerald (1983): 70, based on Appendix in Fitzgerald (1976) and Fitzgerald (1979): Chapter 4.

instituted by the Revolution may have shifted around some of the inequality, it nevertheless left the poorest 60 per cent of the population empty-handed. A change in property ownership did not automatically change the distribution of income, since income was based primarily on the efficiency with which resources were used. For any real change to occur, it was essential that investment be resuscitated and capital shifted towards industry.

However, the Peruvian private sector was badly shaken by the nationalisation and increased government interventionism; as a result private investment grew only slowly.[22] In addition, the government assumed that nationalisation of profitable foreign firms would give it access to the surplus. However, many enterprises before nationalisation had been run down, and dividend distribution and capital flight had increased so that the government received very little.[23] It was believed that foreign investment could continue on new terms compatible with the government's policies. In practice, however, it proved very difficult to persuade foreign companies to invest on the scale required in view of the nationalisation and new regulations on worker participation and the transfer of technology. Finally, it was believed that the reforms would, in total, rapidly rectify various disequilibria within the economy, but nationalisation did not, for example, do much to improve the balance of payments. Some profit outflow might have slowed but, since no serious attempts were made to reduce dependence on foreign firms or technology, the balance of payments worsened; the external public debt deteriorated to \$3 billion (3 thousand million) in 1975 and \$4.2 billion in 1977.[24]

There were real difficulties in the Peruvian economy. Long-run structural problems were becoming serious: the gradual exhaustion of natural resource projects, the crisis in fishing, the long lead time needed to establish new mineral projects before they became export earners, and the transference of more coastal land from export crops to domestic food production.[25] By 1976, real demand in the economy had grown by about 60 per cent above the 1966 level, yet the purchasing power of exports was almost the same as in 1966. Price rises in Peruvian imports seemed to be excessive, increasing by 98 per cent between 1973 and 1976, and the terms of trade generally became more unfavourable. A combination of internal factors and more unfavourable external factors meant that only very limited achievements were gained in pursuing the economic goals. As a result of over-optimistic planning and misallocations in investment, export returns in 1977 fell well below the government's projections.[26]

Since there was no basis for a full transition to socialism in a late developing country such as Peru, the 'middle road' of state capitalism provided the only alternative to further penetration by multinational corporations. In view of the weakness of local private enterprise, its failure to respond to the new opportunities and the restrictions placed on foreign capital, the public sector was forced to grow far beyond original government intentions. In an attempt to prevent Peru lapsing back into the old pattern of dependence, an overlarge state bureaucracy, rather Eastern European in type, emerged to play the role of economic entrepreneur. Sadly, as Eric Hobsbawm has remarked, without an effective national bourgeoisie, 'military decisions are unlikely to create what several centuries of history have denied the country'.[27]

AN ORGANIC, CORPORATE STATE?

The regime's largest and most interesting effort which illustrates the inclusionary policies of a would-be organic corporate state concerned the urban poor and the squatter problem.[28] From 1956 to 1970, the squatter population of Lima had grown by an estimated 600 per cent, to reach 760 000 or 26 per cent of the population. There had been much debate as to whether the massive waves of urban migrants who came to live in the shanty towns represented a radical force. While academics were later to conclude that the first generation of migrants, for a host of reasons, were more concerned with instrumental goals (gaining employment, secure title, cheap housing materials, transport, education, clean water and so on) rather than radical political action,[29] the military officers showed a considerable concern with the potential threat of urban violence that might originate in the rapidly spreading *barriadas*.[30]

During the First Phase of the Revolution there was a definite attempt to give functional groups an economic base. The state established a new co-operative sector which, together with the state sector (which included much of the mining, telecommunications and new metallurgy industries) and the private sector, provided the 'economic pluralism' that would preclude domination either by the state or by capitalism according to the regime's official doctrine.

In theoretical terms, this organic corporate state model of government differs from the command-socialist model in offering greater political pluralism and greater decentralised self-management within the 'organic' structures. The real predicament of such systems, however, becomes one of how to reconcile government control inherent in the model with the high degree of participation in the new structures. The stormy disputes of different interest groups on many CAPs illustrate the problem of reconciling both class differences and centralist versus local interests. Regimes with an avowed ideology of organic statism or inclusionary corporatism may be able to manage a degree of limited pluralism, but in the last resort the authoritarian political structure is likely to assert itself to achieve 'reconciliations', eliminating significant participation by functional groups. Velasco's affirmation that only a 'minimum' of government 'intermediaries' would be required to manage the new enterprises was belied by the excessive growth of government bureaucracy.[31]

THE FAILURE OF THE REVOLUTION

The Peruvian 'experiment', as it has aptly been termed by Lowenthal (1975), was a complex, wide-ranging process, fraught with contradictions and difficulties.

If the First Phase of the Revolution (1968–75) is to be judged on the Junta's objectives of (1) increasing the rate of economic growth and (2) improving the distribution of income, it must to a large extent be considered a failure. Although it included some good planning, its general vagueness and the priority of political expediency over economic considerations meant that the revolution became neither a popular democratic capitalist revolution nor a move towards socialism. In 1973 the number of strikes escalated to 788, double the number in 1970. The armed forces' implacable enemy, APRA, who were never subdued, re-emerged in the union movement. Velasco's ailing health was matched by the serious deterioration in the economy. A growing crisis in the import-substituting industrialisation strategy developed, and by 1975 foreign lenders were becoming insistent that debts be paid off.

Velasco was overthrown in 1975 by a coup of more right-wing officers, led by General Francisco Morales Bermudez, who were committed to more conservative fiscal policies designed to improve the country's national accounts. This period is often called the Second Phase (1976–80), and it is characterised by the force of economic necessity and retrenchment under the influence of the IMF and international bankers, the developing character of the right-wing military government, concerted population pressure and renewed peasant mobilisation. The government stressed that the coup merely changed the personnel and did not signal a rejection of the Revolution or of its goals.

It seems likely, however, that historians might well conclude that the Revolution ended in 1975 rather than in 1980 when the military officers finally handed over to a civilian government. The so-called Second Phase reordered government priorities, reduced the influence of reformist officers and began to emphasise the themes of national sacrifice and labour discipline. A draconian austerity package announced in June 1976 set the tone for much of the Morales Bermudez administration. A devaluation of 44.4 per cent, a steep increase in consumer prices, a 12.4 per cent cut in government investment in state enterprises, a 12.8 per cent reduction in the national budget and a wage increase of only 10–14 per cent led to a violent popular reaction. The attempts by the Second Phase government to rationalise First Phase programmes usually entailed increasing the profitability of public enterprises and adopting wage or employment policies injurious to the working class.

How then, on balance, are we to assess the Peruvian Revolution? The regime's claim that it would accelerate Peru's economic growth clearly failed. Peru's external debt climbed to unprecedented levels. In spite of much rhetoric of redistribution, of social justice and of carrying out fundamental structural reforms, the income of the lower half of the national population was virtually unaffected by measures taken, while the lowest quarter were worse off by the late 1970s compared with their situation in 1968. The government did not even overhaul the regressive tax system, which became more regressive. Per capitum calorie consumption of low and middle income families declined in this period, and the incidence of typhoid, malaria, dysentery and other diseases associated with poverty increased.[32]

Apart from the agrarian reform and a few gains that were made in education, very few of the innovative social, cultural and economic experiments survived into the 1980s. Government recognition of Quechua as a national language in the 1970s seemed to herald a new era of greater respect and lessening inequality for the Indian peasant, but this, sadly, was undone at the end of the decade when this recognition was withdrawn, marking the renewed political, legal and official dominance of Spanish, the language of the *mestizo* masters.[33] The regime's claims of changing national values and creating a 'new Peruvian man' led to a good deal of heady excitement and euphoria, but little substantial change appears to have been achieved. The social property sector which was once expected to become the predominant part of the economy gradually lapsed, and was replaced bit by bit late in the 1970s. And while the government's industrial development policy was intended to expand production, improve equity and police undesirable actions by entrepreneurs, it led mainly to capital flight, unenthusiastic 'co-operation' mainly aimed at getting round the system, the consolidation of an aristocracy of workers and the blocking of new job creation.[34]

At the moment of triumph, at the height of the revolution, revolutionary leaders dreamed dreams and believed that almost anything was possible. The sober reality, however, was that the social transformation of Peru had to deal with a country largely composed of mountains, remote jungle and coastal desert, and with social groups differing vastly in respect to class, ethnicity, education and values. Planning was not likely to be sound unless the intractable geographic and cultural conditions were taken fully into account and the country's political economy fully appreciated. Because these considerations were often ignored, some plans and programmes were too doctrinaire, if not downright fatuous.

Many of the limitations of the agrarian reform arose from failure to deal with the dual nature of the economy, and of agriculture in particular. Traditional sectors of agriculture which were rooted largely in the conditions of the closed corporate community could not be expected to respond to new initiatives in the same way as modern coastal agriculture. Disarticulation of the two segments, and the yawning gulf between the domestic household economy largely concerned with subsistence and export agriculture relying on massive capital inputs, required a mix of appropriate, precise policies. Unbalanced economic growth occurring over centuries could hardly be overcome in a few short years, and the interests and understanding of illiterate *colonos* and sophisticated urban *tecnicos* could not be harmonised without a great deal of community education simply by lumping them together in the new enterprises.

We must conclude, therefore, that the Revolution was not enough. Poverty, inequality, deprivation and the many distinctive household, community and cultural characteristics which are typical of and which underpin peasant economy and society are not so easily eliminated.

BELAÚNDE'S RESTORATION, 1980–5

Belaúnde's second administration was elected to power in 1980 on a wave of anti-militarist feeling, and its declared intent was to reverse the reformist legislation of the Velasco years. Belaúnde's government, however, achieved little, for the 'architect of hope' seemed now to be lacking much of his former zeal and energy. His government adopted a pragmatic approach and tried to avoid conflict with the trade unions, the industrialists, the bankers and the farmers. It was plagued by various immediate problems: a very severe economic crisis in 1983, and the Sendero guerrilla threat, whose existence it refused to recognise for some time.

Peru suffered the worst slump for 50 years in 1983. Real gross domestic product (GDP) fell by 10.7 per cent after growing at the average rate of 1.5 per cent in 1976–82. In a country in which less than half the national workforce of 6 million people was fully employed, 900 000 jobs were lost, although 150 000 new jobs were needed each year to keep pace with population growth. Inflation doubled to 130 per cent while real wages fell to only three-fifths of the 1973 levels.[35] Soup kitchens became essential for the survival of some people in the shanty towns.

The immediate causes of the crisis were the deteriorating prices for Peru's exports in 1982 and the cut of tariffs in 1980 which led imports to escalate to $335 million a month in early 1982, well ahead of exports at $260 million. At the same time Belaúnde had launched a populist but excessively expensive public works programme, and had committed one-quarter of all government spending to the military (which was demanding an additional $4 billion). With the military waiting in the wings and the Sendero Luminoso guerrilla threat mounting, Belaúnde was not able to reduce this expenditure. The reappearance of the warm current El Niño at Christmas 1982 signalled the disappearance of the cold Humboldt current on the Peruvian coast; the anchovy catch declined by two-thirds and floods in the north of the country and the worst drought in the south for decades left 2 million people hungry.[36] About 70 per cent of all crops in Peru were lost, at a value of about US$152 million.

By the end of his administration, Belaúnde had completely lost the confidence of the electorate, his government was in disarray and, after the draconian IMF-led austerity drive of 1983, the mood of the country was bitter and resentful.

ALAN GARCÍA: ANTI-IMPERIALISM AND ECONOMIC HETERODOXY

The dynamic, youthful Alan García became president in 1985, calling, like Belaúnde in 1956, for national renovation, sacrifice and effort.[37] Proclaiming himself a revolutionary and a socialist, García led an APRA party that had finally achieved power after moving to a slightly left of centre position (and discrediting itself in the eyes of many of its original followers). However, in spite of a considerable resemblance to earlier populist leaders, García proved to be made of sterner stuff. Despite his flamboyant style and a considerable discrepancy between his avowed policies and their implementation, García committed the government to meeting the people's basic needs and seemed sincere in his claim to be a democrat. The role the state would play in planning a reorientation of the productive base was reasserted. Large public works projects were cut and new priority was given to agriculture and light engineering industries. Soon after his inauguration he took on the military, castigated the bureaucracy for its waste and inefficiency, fired corrupt police officers and initiated raids against narcotics traffickers. He set up a peace commission and offered to negotiate with Sendero Luminoso.

In his dramatic speech at the United Nations in 1985, which rekindled the nation's sense of pride, García adopted a foreign policy stance based on three principles: anti-imperialism, non-alignment and support for Latin America unity. In contrast to Castro's emphasis on East–West conflict, García focused on north–south inequality. He noted in his speech that the richest industrial countries and the poorest, undernourished countries share a single unjust economic order. The external debt has been one of 'the blatant means of extracting and transferring resources' from the Third World to rich industrial countries, and he noted that in 1984 many countries devoted over half of their export revenues to servicing it. The object of his ire was the IMF.

García's most famous and apparently radical action was to limit Peru's debt payments to 10 per cent of its export earnings (a payment ceiling on the $14 billion foreign debt which was not, in fact, enforced, for some observers claim it was 20–30 per cent or more of exports).

García attempted to formulate a new economic model which would try to end the repeated cycle of export-led boom, overspending and runaway inflation, followed by financial crisis and collapse. His programme reflected the more progressive populist and anti-imperialist principles on which Haya de la Torre founded APRA in 1924. He was also trying to revive the nationalist and reformist themes of Velasco's revolutionary government in the early 1970s, based on a finer and unorthodox tuning of the state capitalist model. With the hardening of international market prices in 1986, the opportunity increased for Peru at last to break out of the dependent export-led model.

What success did García's heterodox economic programme

achieve? Orthodox economists believed the policies were not only heretical but suicidal. Initially they achieved spectacular results through reactivating the economy, including a mass employment programme in the shanty towns and 30 billion *soles*' assistance to communities in the poorest parts of the Andes.[38] The GDP grew from 1.5 per cent in 1985 to 8.5 per cent in 1986 – the fastest in Latin America – while inflation dropped from 158 per cent to 68 per cent. Since much of the growth was consumption fuelled, and particularly by consumers in the lower socio-economic classes, their additional spending encouraged food production. Fears that the economy could not continue to grow and inflation remain tolerable, proved, however, to be correct. Inflation reached about 110 per cent in 1987 and galloped away in 1988. While economic growth was still impressive in 1987 at 7 per cent, recession returned; in 1988 the economic growth rate was near zero.[39]

After two years of proffering carrots to the private sector to expand investment, García showed he was prepared to use the stick in 1987 by suddenly nationalising private banks, finance corporations and insurance companies. This provoked intense opposition from the business community, much of García's own APRA party and allegations from a new right-wing political front led by the famous novelist Mario Vargas Llosa of dictatorial, unconstitutional actions. Although many of García's actions suggested that he was not essentially left-wing but very pragmatic and flexible, the nationalisation irredeemably alienated the business sector as the military government had done in the early 1970s. In 1988 little new investment occurred, reserves fell rapidly and public sector enterprises deteriorated in their performance. By this late stage of his presidency, García was dependent on the response of the top 500 companies, and one conservative critic gloomily predicted that by 1990 15 powerful industrial groups would again own large sectors of the economy, 'like the old oligarchy'.[40]

Socially and politically García faced much greater problems. The gaol massacre of rioting Sendero prisoners in June 1986 which involved torture, summary executions and at least 250 deaths, provoked international outrage at the President's apparent approval of quick action to crush the revolt. Fears grew of military influence over his government. Although his human rights record was much better than the previous government's, the growing militarisation of the war zones led to various atrocities which were hushed up.

Massive labour unrest increased as austerity policies began to bite. Real wages were eroded by about 15 per cent in 1987, and about one million workers went on strike. After 18 months of the government's domestic economic programme, 65 per cent of the labour force got only US$40 per month in wages. Although García was adroit in settling some strikes quickly, his quest for solutions looked likely to fail, and the use of short-term policies to try to obtain medium-term results in the long run proved counterproductive.

THE END OF GARCÍA'S PRESIDENCY: FINANCIAL CRISES AND THE POLITICAL ECONOMY

García found it increasingly difficult to placate the more militant right-wing and left-wing parties. In addition, he had the world economy to contend with and the demands of the IMF. It has been persuasively argued by Scheetz (1983) that the recurring financial crises of 1948, 1958, 1968 and 1978 have parallel causes, that the IMF played a major role in those of 1958, 1968 and 1978 (and, I would add, in 1983), that its stabilisation role followed a predictable monetarist approach to the balance of payments crisis and that the social and political effects were also parallel and predictable.[41]

Basically it can be argued that in an export-led dual economy such as Peru's, the conjunction of interests between foreign economic forces, the IMF[42] and the Peruvian oligarchy backed by the armed forces often prevails over the rising force of allied working-class, middle-class and peasant interests, although the whole system shows frequent economic and political volatility. There is a deep, unrelenting social and political struggle between the mobilised working classes and the demands of the exporting oligarchy, and since no wide-ranging social accord is ever agreed to, the problem is merely patched over, and inevitably re-emerges a few years later. The classic nature of the dual economy expresses itself in the country's political economy, and recurring financial crises which create political volatility and topple governments merely reflect the failure to bridge the great chasm that divides Peru's social classes.

Clearly Alan García did more to assist the peasantry than many other modern governments, but the fate of his longer-term economic programmes was doomed. Meanwhile the civil war, now thirteen years old, is as serious as ever. Furthermore, the slide of Peru into a vast black economy of drug trafficking has enmeshed the country in international crime networks, earning the enmity of European and American governments. And for all his courage, enthusiasm and ingenuity, García's approach was essentially personalistic, in the long tradition of Latin American *caudillos*, rather than institutional.

11 Agriculture, Government Policies and Food Import Dependency

The legacy of 100 years of dependent dualistic development is nowhere more evident than in the dualistic character of the Peruvian food system which is made up of (1) an agro-industrial sub-system, and (2) an agro-food sub-system. The first centres on a core of no more than two dozen processing firms supplied by inputs imported by the state as well as the inputs of tens of thousands of Peruvian farmers. Most of the marketing is also highly concentrated, and many of the prices of inputs and products are still set by the state. The second centres on over a million farmers and peasants who supply the agro-food sub-system through many wholesale and retail marketing channels. The majority of prices are determined by the free play of market forces.

It seems paradoxical that in such a large, apparently underpopulated country as Peru, food imports have long been important. Yet, as we noticed in Chapter 3, environmental factors cause an excessive scarcity of land, and the indigenous agricultural system has been predominantly subsistence. At the same time, in the face of massive urbanisation, the steady rise in urban demand for food could only be met by increased imports.

LAND TENURE, PRODUCTION AND THE PRODUCERS[1]

By the early 1970s, agrarian reform had been largely implemented in Peru in an attempt to remedy the unequal distribution of land. Table 11.1, which covers the period of the Revolution, presents a summary of the distribution of agricultural property in Peru in 1961 and 1972 among different kinds of producers. It shows that the agrarian reform did not have a great effect on the area of total lands in the reform sector (*haciendas* and so on), and that the *arable* area owned dropped substantially:

Table 11.1 Distribution of land and livestock in Peru, 1961 and 1972

A. *Land*	*Farms (1)*				*No. of plots per unit (2)*		*Average ha per plot (3)*‡		*All types of lands per cent (4)*		*Agricultural land including natural pastures, per cent (5)*		*Arable land excluding pastures, per cent (6)*	
			per cent											
	1961	*1972*	*1961*	*1972*	*1961*	*1972*	*1961*	*1972*	*1961*	*1972*	*1961*	*1972*	*1961*	*1972*
Minifundio (less than 5 ha)	699 427	1 083 775†	82.9	78.0	3.3	4.6	0.4	5.8	6.6	7.9	7.9	7.0	30.9	36.0
Medium-sized properties (MSP) (5 to less than 100 ha)	132 491	291 432	15.8	20.9	3.7	3.9	3.7	3.7	10.4	18.0	10.8	15.2	29.4	47.0
Reform sector* or former large *haciendas* till 1969 (100 ha and over)	1 132	15 081	1.3	1.1	2.4	2.5	552.9	475.3	83.8	75.4	81.3	77.8	39.7	17.0
TOTAL	833 050	1 390 288	100.0	100.0	3.5	4.4	5.9	4.9	100.0	100.0	100.0	100.0	100.0	100.0

continued on p. 188

Table 11.1 continued

B. Livestock	*Livestock (7)*		*Beef cattle (8)*		*Sheep (9)*		*Horses (10)*		*Auchenedas*[§] *(11)*		*Pigs (12)*		*Goats (13)*		*Donkeys (14)*	
	1961	*1972*	*1961*	*1972*	*1961*	*1972*	*1961*	*1972*	*1961*	*1972*	*1961*	*1972*	*1961*	*1972*	*1961*	*1972*
Minifundistas	62.5	55.8	60.2	52.2	56.3	52.8	70.7	60.6	57.8	53.1	79.2	64.8	66.1	73.7	77.3	69.6
MSP group	24.3	30.3	25.7	34.2	27.3	24.3	21.4	33.3	21.3	20.9	17.9	32.6	28.8	24.0	19.6	28.3
Reform sector (former large *haciendas*)	13.2	13.9	14.1	12.6	16.3	22.6	7.9	6.1	20.9	26.0	2.9	2.6	5.1	2.3	3.1	2.1
TOTAL	100.0	100.0	100.0	100.0	100.0	100.0	100.0	100.0	100.0	100.0	100.0	100.0	100.0	100.0	100.0	100.0

* The actual number of reform enterprises does not coincide with the number of units compiled in the 1972 Agriculture Census data. This is the case because co-operative units were created by either joining together former independent farm units or partitioning farm units.

† For the computation of the number of plots per unit in 1972, 307 649 farm units, in the less than 0.5 ha category, were excluded, making the total number of *minifundistas* 776 126 units. This was done because according to the 1972 Agricultural Census, these units were not asked about the number of plots or had actually no agricultural lands (National Bureau of Statistics (ONEC), (1975); p. xv). An agricultural unit may have several plots. In 1962, for instance, *minifundistas* had an average of 3.3 plots. The total number of plots in 1961 was 2 959 946 and 4 741 207 in 1972.

‡ This is the average size of the different plots comprising an agricultural unit, and should not be confused with the average size per unit. This last indicator comprises the overall size of an agricultural unit, regardless of the partitioning of the farm unit in different plots.

§ *Llamas*, *alpacas* and *vicuña*.

Sources: Alvarez (1984): Table 2.1, citing National Planning Institute (INP) (1965), tables 2, 4, 8 and 9 for 1961; and National Bureau of Statistics (ONEC) (1975), tables 1, 2, 11 and 12 of Part A for 1972. The livestock data come from Hopkins (1981), pp. 100–1, Tables 18 and 19.

from 39.7 per cent in 1961 to 17 per cent in 1972, a difference of 23 per cent.

The medium-sized producers (MSPs) increased from around 16 per cent to 21 per cent of producers between 1961 and 1972. Their access to all types of lands rose and their gain in arable lands (column 6) was very marked, rising from 29 to 47 per cent. By the early 1970s the MSP group, not the *haciendas*, had acquired the largest share of arable land as well as a significant proportion of the livestock.

The *minifundistas* (peasants), who comprised the great bulk of Peru's farm units in both 1961 and 1972, increased their access to all types of lands by only about 1 per cent, owning only about 8 per cent of all types of lands (column 4).[2] While the table shows 1 083 775 units in 1972, it should be noted that a further 307 649 units recorded in the census have been excluded as they were less than 0.5ha (1 acre). Although such extremely small units do not qualify as 'farm units', they are highly relevant to our overall concern with peasantry since they are important for the subsistence (and indeed survival) of the very poor peasants, most of whom could not live without some wage labour.[3]

Table 11.1 also indicates that an important feature of Peruvian agriculture, and especially of *minifundio* agriculture, is its highly fragmented character. The average number of plots per farm unit increased from 3.5 in 1961 to 4.4 in 1972 (column 2) and for the *minifundio* category fragmentation occurred to an even greater degree, rising from 3.3 to 4.6. This would seem to suggest increased population pressure in peasant areas, in the absence of change in the system of inheritance.

In considering agricultural production in Peru, it is important to bear in mind the regional distributions between the coast, the Sierra and *selva*. In two of the three regions the *minifundio* is by far the most numerous agricultural unit, comprising over 70 per cent of all units on the coast and in the Sierra. MSPs are the most important unit in the *selva* (55 per cent). Large enterprises or reform sectors comprise only 1–2 per cent of all units in all three regions but make up 62 and 45 per cent of the agricultural area in the coast and Sierra respectively.

There were considerable changes in the distribution of land and livestock between 1961 and 1972, whether or not lands were standardised. There was a decline in proprietorship of large *haciendas* or plantations and the corresponding improvement of smaller groups, and especially of MSPs.

CHANGES IN AGRICULTURAL PRODUCTION AND PRODUCTIVITY

The Peruvian agrarian structure changed markedly over the period 1950–79. The great growth of the internal market, accompanied by a huge urbanisation process, fluctuations in the terms of trade and government policies, altered the allocation of resources in agriculture and the pattern of agricultural production. The strong predominance of restricted markets (mainly peasant) and export crops in the early 1950s gave way to the rapid expansion of producers concerned with direct urban consumption and led to agro-industrial production. More and more coastal land was switched from planting export crops to urban-consumed items and the *selva* agricultural frontier expanded by producing for the same market (for example, rice), while peasants and small townsfolk increasingly began to acquire more 'urban' consumer tastes.

During the early 1950s, over 70 per cent of agricultural production was distributed equally between restricted market production and export crops. This changed dramatically, however, when the military government came to power: direct urban consumption and agro-industrial imports doubled and there was a substantial decline of both restricted markets and exports. By 1976, after a period of intense urbanisation, urban consumption products made up as much as 65.1 per cent of all agricultural production. By this date a large portion of former export products (for example, sugar cane and cotton) were being consumed in the domestic market. Government policies (as we saw in Chapter 5) and the substitution of food crops for export crops were the main reasons for the decline in export production. Exports had dwindled to only 7.9 per cent.

The most striking fact about agricultural productivity[4] is the major difference between regions. In 1961 Diebold made a rough estimate of productivity, comparing the coast with the Sierra. He gave a gross return of US$470 per man per hectare for Ica on the coast, compared with only US$90 at Ayacucho in the Sierra. Per head of population, the ratio was even worse: $186 in Ica and only $21 in Ayacucho, or nearly nine times greater in the former.[5] A comparison made by Golte (1980) of 1000 working days applied to the production of coastal potatoes showed an average 7.4 times greater yield on the coast compared with the western highlands of the Andes, or an average 9.5 times greater than in the eastern highlands.[6]

These figures would seem to confirm the widespread view of the inferiority of the traditional Andean production system. While this may be partly true, it is considerably modified by more careful comparison of average yields, and especially of net margins, for the production costs of the Andean peasant are much lower than those of the coastal producer.

Comparisons between *selva* and Sierra are often rather facile, because different crop varieties appropriate to each ecological zone are planted. With present technology, modern varieties have a considerable yield advantage over native varieties on the coast, but this is not always the case in the Sierra, where traditional varieties are more highly resistant to frost and hail and often produce reasonably well with low applications of chemical fertiliser and pesticides (Brush, Carney and Huaman, 1981). Their use allows farmers to minimise losses in an environment characterised by frequent crop failure. Moreover, in recent years it appears that native varieties are considered a luxury item in urban areas, fetching a higher market price than modern varieties.[7] In the Sierra, where native varieties yield almost as much as modern varieties, some producers are now deriving a substantial income from marketing native potatoes.

Other factors are relevant for the persistence of native varieties in the Sierra even when modern varieties produce substantially higher yields. In sparsely populated areas where retail outlets are few and little money is spent on food, the superior storing quality of traditional native varieties is a significant factor. Moreover *chuño*, the dehydrated product of frost-thaw in Sierra regions which experience night frost and sunny days, is an excellent food product made from inedible bitter, small potatoes. Light in weight, *chuño* can be easily carried by herders during seasonal migration to high altitude pasture lands and, as it can be stored for years, it provides them with a degree of food security in this uncertain environment.

A traditional low-input system can offer producers economic advantages over a modern higher input system. D. E. Horton (1984) compared, in the intermediate and high altitude zones, the *ticpa* system, which employs native varieties, no tillage before planting, hand power (using the *chaquitaclla*) for all cultivation and harvest operations, and very little chemical fertiliser and

Table 11.2 Yields, costs and returns in two potato-production systems in the intermediate and high zones

	Barbecho *system** (*N* = *8*)	Ticpa *system*† (*N* = *9*)
Yield (t/ha)	9.4	7.3
Total returns (US$/ha)	1 102	1 030
Direct input costs (US$/ha)		
Seed	278	235
Labour	186	218
Pesticides	67	14
Tractor/oxen	64	0
Chemical fertiliser	62	18
Manure	15	59
Total	672	544
(Purchased)	316	114
Gross margin (US$/ha)		
Total return (direct input costs)	430	486
Total return (purchased inputs)	786	916

* Modern varieties grown; tractor used for ploughing.
† Native varieties grown with no tillage before planting; all cultivation done by hand.

Source: D. E. Horton (1984): 42.

pesticides, with the *barbecho* system, which employs modern varieties, tractor power and high levels of chemical fertiliser and pesticides. In these zones the *ticpa* system produced higher net returns than the *barbecho* system. The net return over direct input costs was higher in the *ticpa* system because higher valued native varieties were produced. At least of equal importance, bearing in mind the predominantly subsistence character of many peasants, is the fact that the *ticpa* system employs only about one-third of the value of purchased inputs compared with those used in the *barbecho* system. The traditional system exposes producers to a much lower level of financial risk (see Table 11.2).

Although there are problems with the data base, it appears that changes in productivity have not been significant over the 1960s and 1970s. Peasant crops such as wheat, barley and potatoes decreased in yields in the 1960s, but slightly increased, for wheat and potatoes, in the 1970s, the period of agrarian reform (see Table 11.3). The reasons for this are unknown, but govern-

Table 11.3 Index of yields for some Peruvian crops, 1960–80 (Index (1960–4) = 100)

	Peasant crops			*Urban direct consumption*	*Agro-industrial and export crops*		
	Wheat	*Barley*	*Potatoes**	*Rice (rough)*	*Coffee*	*Sugar*	*Cotton*[†]
1960	96.9	94.3	94.8	99.7	94.0	103.9	97.4
1961	102.0	105.2	100.0	98.8	100.2	103.3	97.6
1962	101.0	100.5	96.6	108.8	101.1	99.9	100.2
1963	101.0	98.8	100.9	89.5	101.7	98.2	104.6
1964	98.0	99.7	107.7	103.2	103.0	94.5	100.6
1965	98.0	99.2	101.5	93.6	108.2	100.0	106.5
1966	94.5	84.5	108.6	94.2	105.0	106.5	110.2
1967	100.0	91.1	109.9	104.4	108.4	102.9	91.1
1968	84.7	82.1	101.4	90.9	116.5	85.6	112.2
1969	88.8	87.9	105.5	97.7	119.6	83.2	97.4
1970	93.9	88.9	106.0	100.9	119.6	95.4	117.8
1971	89.8	85.0	109.0	96.8	119.6	110.4	110.9
1972	90.8	126.4	110.4	98.6	114.4	110.1	109.8
1973	91.8	88.0	110.9	99.1	115.0	105.4	112.2
1974	93.9	87.1	112.8	103.0	114.8	109.1	112.4
1975	96.9	89.2	113.7	105.8	112.7	104.4	100.4
1976	96.9	89.9	112.9	103.4	112.7	101.3	106.3
1977	102.0	84.1	118.2	106.7	124.4	97.0	97.2
1978	102.0	83.6	120.8	98.8	129.0	95.4	122.0
1979	108.2	84.1	122.5	102.9	141.8	77.3	127.6
1980	114.3	na	na	105.8	138.7	65.6	121.7

Annual average growth rate of yields (1960–4 = 100)

Periods	*1960–70*	*1970–80*	*1960–80*
Wheat	–0.12	2.0	0.9
Barley	–0.3	0.9[‡]	0.4[§]
Potatoes	–0.8	2.0[‡]	1.6[§]
Rice	0.7	0.5	0.6
Coffee	2.5	1.6	2.1
Sugar	–0.5	–3.1	–1.8
Cotton	2.7	1.9	2.3

* Includes both highland and coastal potatoes.
[†] Cotton fibre.
[‡] 1970–9.
[§] 1960–79.
na = not available

Source: Alvarez (1984): Table A.1, based on information from Hopkins (1981: 44) and official data from the Ministry of Agriculture.

ment provision of price incentives and fertiliser transport subsidies until the late 1970s may have had an effect. The yields of urban consumption items, such as rice, barely increased in the period 1960–80. The yields of export crops and agro-industrial inputs such as coffee and cotton increased throughout the two decades. The exception was sugar, which suffered from a variety of government interventions; yields decreased steadily throughout 1960–80.

THE PRODUCERS

It is clear that substantial class restructuring occurred in the Peruvian countryside between 1950 and 1980 as urbanisation and land reform made their effects felt. There was a great and growing market for urban consumer foods and for crops required by the transnational food industry. Many producers, especially on the coast, in the Central Sierra and in the most accessible parts of the *ceja de la montaña* as well as *selva baja* (low forest), succeeded in adapting to the new urban demands (for example, for rice and bananas). But many producers, and especially the mass of the Sierra peasantry, failed to adapt both because of the nature of peasantry and because of the difficult ecological conditions of the Andes. Of those who failed to adapt, some joined the rural exodus to the cities, while others persisted as peasants, involved in subsistence or restricted market production.

By far the most important agricultural group of producers by the late 1970s were the MSPs, a disparate and heterogeneous mix of former large *hacendados*, landowners, colonists of the *ceja de la montaña*, and richer peasants (Alvarez, 1984). Geographically located in areas which made profitable agrarian accumulation possible, by 1976 they produced about 50 per cent of the gross value of Peruvian agricultural production.

The traditional *minifundista* was, in 1976, still by far the most numerous agricultural group, comprising over 1 million units. The peasants did, however, divide their time among a variety of activities: local wage labour, marketing and transportation, and seasonal or circular migration. They provided in total a rather small share of the total Peruvian agricultural output (28 per cent).[8]

The reform sector – the former *haciendas* or large coastal plantations expropriated by the agrarian reform – produced the smallest share of the total agricultural output (about 22 per cent), revealing the economic failure of the agrarian reform. They provided half the agricultural exports and agro-industrial crops, almost all the sugar cane, over two-thirds of the cotton, over four-fifths of the soyabean and over two-thirds of the grapes grown in the country.[9]

CHANGES IN FOOD CONSUMPTION

Consideration of food consumption raises the issues of the importance of food imports, the growth of processed food items from the agro-industrial sector and the significance of peasant production, especially in the rural diet.

Major differences exist within domestic patterns of food consumption, ranging between the extreme poles of the self-subsistence or on-farm consumption of the Andean peasant through to the almost entirely store-bought sophisticated modern diet of Lima. Over the last 25 years the diffusion of urban tastes in food consumption has tended to spread, while the rural pattern is showing a tendency to disappear. In the long run, the trend appears to be for land use to switch, where ecological conditions permit, more to urban-consumed products or items in demand for the agro-industrial sector. The expansion of the urban diet is limited, however, by the availability of foreign exchange, by government policies on subsidies and by the availability of discretionary income in rural areas.

It has been estimated that every Peruvian family consumes a daily average of 6.4kg of food. Up to 278 food products are in demand in towns and cities in the coast, but only 142 in rural areas or towns in the Sierra. Ten products account for 50 per cent of total food consumption by Peruvian families, the most important being potatoes, rice, milk, sugar and noodles. The urban diet is composed predominantly of processed foods which derive from the agro-industrial sector and from imported foods. Only one of the major food products (potatoes) is produced by both restricted market and medium-sized producers. Even sugar, one of Peru's most famous exports, had to be imported in

1981; and there is a very pronounced and increasing dependence on imported wheat, although wheat has been grown in Peru for centuries.

There is a definite change in consumption patterns in the countryside. Higher prestige is associated with urban and Western cultural influences, while the class discrimination against Indians, peasants and the Sierra extends also to their food patterns. Moreover, although the urban diet is generally more expensive than the characteristic rural diet, some of its components are relatively cheap. The unit price of calories and proteins supplied by rice and imported wheat, for example, is lower than those of traditional Andean staples. The urban diet is superior in terms of convenience (for example, the ease of preparation of noodles or the smooth *mantaro* potatoes compared with the small knobbly *ccompis* potato of the Anta area). The rural diet is much more limited than the urban diet and is totally dominated by the white potato; only very small volumes of meat or fish are consumed, while purchased rice, brown sugar, noodles and bread are growing in importance.

FOOD SUBSIDIES

Although various subsidies were granted over the period 1950–80, most were allocated at the consumer rather than at the producer level.

It is clear that governments since the 1960s were becoming increasingly worried about the food supply and cost of living of the growing urban masses. The Ministry of Food was created at the beginning of the 1970s to control inflation in food prices, to attempt to programme the most important crops and to maintain an adequate supply of staple foods for the population, especially the urban population. The process of importing many foods was nationalised and state participation in the domestic marketing of some staple foods increased. EPSA (regulating certain agricultural inputs and products to ensure availability and price stability in urban areas) and several other state marketing institutions were created. The government thus set up a state monopoly in imports of wheat, milk, maize, oilseeds, rice and fertilisers, and in domestic marketing of rice and yellow maize from the *selva*, and state participation in exports of coffee, sugar and fish products. Also tried by the government were price controls, prohibition of farm storage, and control of inter-regional movements of agricultural products, in an attempt to achieve the goal of reasonable prices for both producers and consumers.[10]

A government study in 1975 showed that 56 per cent of subsidies were concentrated in metropolitan Lima where they benefited 20 per cent of the country's population. The medium and upper income brackets appropriated 40 per cent of the funds: only 10 per cent of the country's total population benefited.[11]

Since stress, antagonism towards the military government and growing immiseration of the working classes in the large cities were pronounced in the 1970s when Peru experienced what has been termed its 'deepest and most persistent crisis of this century',[12] any relief was welcomed. It has been estimated that, in the absence of food subsidies, the price of cereals in 1980 would have been between 13 and 18 per cent higher.[13] But subsidies were clearly detrimental to internal producers, acting as a kind of negative tariff imposed on the peasants of the Sierra and on the medium and large coastal livestock producers.

Along with the other Andean countries of Bolivia, Colombia and Ecuador, Peru began to import increasing quantities of wheat in the mid-1950s, commonly under special arrangements to alleviate food price increases generated by demand–pull inflation and to reduce the need to divert scarce foreign exchange resources from importing capital goods. Government importing agencies could generate a profit from such agreements since domestic prices were set well above import costs, and the consumer was still left better off.

After nearly 20 years of externally subsidised wheat prices, it is scarcely surprising that wheat became a basic food, with levels of consumption per person more than double those of Ecuador or Columbia. In 1975, Peru spent US$5 million per month on subsidising wheat imports, which represented 40 per cent of the final price to consumers.[14] Under these circumstances, imports have come to account for nearly 90 per cent of total wheat consumption. The remainder has been supplied by a steadily decreasing domestic production.

It is particularly unfortunate that, while wheat could be grown easily in appropriate zones of the Andes, the national variety was not the one utilised by the food industry. Moreover, the domestic price of wheat was higher than the imported one. Although there was no need to subsidise imported wheat as foreign producers already had sufficient incentive to sell in Peru, a subsidy was granted. Peruvian wheat producers were therefore displaced from the urban markets.

Beef was imported at an undervalued foreign exchange rate for a few years in the 1960s while the domestic beef price was controlled. The subsidy worked out at varying rates of 1.6–5.6 *soles*/kg.[15] The culmination of the negative impact on domestic beef occurred in the 1970s when beef was banned from the market for two weeks each month, giving an opportunity for other animal proteins, such as poultry, to replace it. During the period 1975–8 the state paid, on average, 36.5 per cent of the final price of fertiliser,[16] before it could no longer afford to.

Dairy products provide an interesting illustration of government subsidy policy. Moreover, this commodity is highly relevant to our topic since 62 per cent of national dairy production is located in Southern Peru, 75 per cent is produced by peasants or smallholders and, as we have seen, dairy products have provided the main source of cash earning in the village of Chilca. Subsidies have been given mainly to evaporated milk producers. Since 1976 the subsidised dairy inputs (powdered milk and milk fat) were imported by the public enterprise in charge of marketing and sold to the agro-industry at prices lower than those formerly paid by the public agency. Milk for urban consumption was produced largely by the food industry and strongly controlled by branches of two powerful transnational corporations, Perulac SA (Nestle, Switzerland) and Leche Gloria (Carnation, USA). Foreign capital concentration was 90 and 48 per cent respectively in 1973. In the period 1972–4 both firms produced approximately 60 per cent of the dairy industry's gross value of production.

In the milk producing districts monopoly is a fact of life, owing to the great distance from the urban markets where milk is sold direct to the consumer, the excessive fragmentation and wide dispersal of many small producers, the existence of extremely competitive cheese and butter markets (open to low-priced imports), the highly perishable nature of the product, and the fact that milk production has become the main (or at times the only) source of regular monetary income for many peasant producers.

All this lessens the primary producers' market power to the extent that, in all plants, the weighing and analysis of fat and acid content of the milk is carried out without the participation of the producers or of their representatives.

In recent years strenuous efforts have been made by bodies similar to service co-operatives and led by intermediate producers (although also representing small producers) in bargaining to obtain state subsidies or better prices. However, milk producers generally are not vertically integrated into the processing industry, so the two giants can still dominate.

Many small producers are specialising more fully in milk production. While, as peasants, their whole livelihood does not depend on dairying, the increasing specialisation leads, as at Chilca, to increasing dependence on the external firms buying and processing their product. Since processing plants usually pay producers for two-week periods, two weeks after collecting the milk daily from the producers, the primary producers are in effect providing credit to the industry. Given the volume of average two-week collections, its cost and the interest rate prevailing (51 per cent in 1981), the amount of this credit is substantial.[17]

The industry as a whole and its processing is highly concentrated. During the 1970s the processing companies were assigned imported milk supplies in proportion to their share in the domestic market. Since imported milk was cheaper than local milk, these quotas were keenly sought, and in periods when imported milk was sold at less than the international price, enterprises have attempted to replace domestic inputs by imported ones. During the 1960s the average ratio of imported inputs to total dairy inputs for evaporated milk plants was 41 per cent; during the 1970s the figure rose to 58 per cent. Only since 1980 have imports of whole milk powder for direct consumption become important. In general, canned evaporated milk predominates over all other dairy products (58 per cent of total consumption).

One theory on the milk industry is that there is collusion between the two giant companies since the two arrived in the country at the same time (at the beginning of the 1960s) and there has been no price war for more than four decades. Despite the fact that the income of Gloria depends exclusively on evaporated milk sales, the company has not had to spend money on advertising for many years; import prohibition or high tariffs on imports of whole milk powder and other processed milks kept its market ensured. This was strengthened by the subsidy policy which reduced the relative price of evaporated milk.[18]

In general the effect of these policies was to stifle milk production in Peru. During the period 1964–9, milk production was growing at the impressive rate of 8.9 per cent annually, but in the period of 1969–76 the rate fell to only 1.1 per cent. The stagnation of milk production showed up regionally in the important producing areas of Southern Peru, including the Sierra and Cajamarca, contributing to slow regional growth rates. This situation seems to have been caused mainly by the large increase in subsidies for imported dairy inputs. In the late 1970s this situation led to a strong campaign by dairy livestock breeders to win government support for the national dairy producers.

Subsidies as a whole therefore acted largely as a negative tariff on producers. Those who benefited were primarily the urban consumers, especially those in the medium and upper income levels, the food industry and the transnationals to which the firms were closely linked, as well as the more competitive foreign farmers whose access to the Peruvian market was enlarged by government subsidies.

CONCLUSION

It is clear that the government's macro policies have, on the whole, worsened rather than ameliorated the plight of the peasantry, and especially those peasants with sufficient resources to produce for the local market. In recent years the importance of staple food imports, of state enterprise in food imports and of state monopoly of some products has become characteristic. The agro-food industry is a major component of the industrial sector, and prepared food processing has become highly concentrated. While the extremely low amount of arable land per capitum and the wide class differences in Peru have led to food importing being important, at least since the beginning of the century, massive urbanisation in the last three decades has accelerated the trend. Today, there is considerable food dependence on essential imports.

In general food subsidies have acted as a substantial barrier to Peruvian producers. While the government assisted the urban population through its food policies, blunting the full bite of poverty and malnutrition, the policies were far from successful. This judgement does not criticise government intervention as such, but rather the manner of the intervention, which imposed negative tariffs and disincentives through inadequate and unfair prices on rural producers, many of whom struggled on in conditions of acute poverty. Many distortions were created in the economy, and virtually nothing was done to make marketing through private channels more efficient and less costly.

There was recognition of the policies' failure before the military government handed over to Belaúnde's administration in 1980. However, in the face of increasing urban poverty, by 1985 the World Bank was recommending nutritional interventions and the provision of low-cost meals by popular canteens targeted specifically at the extremely poor.

12 Innovation and Leadership

The peasantry endures, the peasants survive. This capacity to survive has coloured the specific traditional culture embodied in each small rural community. The *comunidad* had been crafted as an instrument of defence. The environment, within this self-contained 'moral community',[1] was on the whole certainly not conducive to innovation. Tradition appeared to reign supreme and innovations that threatened well-accepted values and norms could arouse envy and invoke brutal, summary 'justice'.[2]

If innovation is to offer scope for modernisation, we must consider the context in which innovators have to operate and the local principles which they cannot violate if they are to have any hope of success.

THE CASE OF THE HUNGRY CALVES

A classic and instructive case study of attempted innovation in a Peruvian peasant community has been provided by W. Stein (1956). While staying in the community of Hualcán, Stein noticed that two recently born calves were not very strong. Although cattle diseases, parasites and poor fodder were probably the main reasons for this, it seemed to Stein that the calves might become stronger if they were allowed to suckle from their mothers for longer. He offered to purchase the cows' milk production that would be lost to the household for six weeks and, with the agreement of Miguel, the head of the house, the experiment began.

Stein noted that Hualcainos' knowledge of animal husbandry was not 'scientific' but traditional. Folk remedies, charms, divination and prayers to the saints were part of the herding complex. The idea of human control did not apply; often the peasants would watch their animals die, feeling impotent to save them and commenting philosophically that at least they would have some fresh meat. In such a situation an experiment that might improve calf rearing and place it on a more rational basis appeared to be worthwhile.

In the event, the 'experiment' failed after a week when morning milkings were renewed. As his knowledge of local culture grew, Stein was able to discern a number of faults or deficiencies in the experiment that played a part in its failure. First, he had not paid for the milk in advance. Second, he had not made any compact with the owner. In all interpersonal relations, the 'principle of compactual responsibility' appeared to be important and a situationally-structuring gift, the *derechun*, would have been appropriate. If the subject wished to avoid responsibility he had but to refuse the gift. Stein had not made a *derechun* to the household head, which, if accepted, would have required him to accept responsibility for supervising the experiment.

Moreover, the question of the 'ownership' of the milk was a fraught one. In the peasant household economy all resources and income are pooled, so that in practice the milk of the cows was 'owned' by the whole household. Instead of allowing the calves to suckle for a longer period, the women of the household gave away a good portion of the milk as part of a traditional custom of gift giving. In addition, people who looked after the cows, even if they were not the owners, were entitled to keep some milk for themselves (for example, children guarding cows while they grazed on the hillsides). In no sense could the cows' milk be said to 'belong' to the calves; rather, by applying the principle which induces people to share with those who 'count', the cows were obligated to their human herders, who protected them, nursed them when sick and fed them. If the milk was 'due' to anyone, it was to the people who took care of the cows.

Stein also identified supernatural factors that were relevant to animal husbandry. God was conceived as the supreme power who arranged the world for His own reasons, placing good and evil forces in the world in a kind of balance. While the Hualcaino might intercede with God through the saints as mediators, or Santa Ursula, the patroness of Hualcán, the household economy depended upon destiny, which was equated with God's will. Bad luck in agriculture was a sign that something was lacking in one's obligations so that one had become contaminated with evil power. Therefore, if one's animals were in a poor condition, the matter was between oneself and God, to be mediated by God's representatives, the priests, or Santa Ursula. In a religious sense, the avenue to controlling the condition of the livestock was defined as supernatural: 'God, not more milk, is the deciding factor in the maturation of calves.'

In terms of Western logic, it might seem that a number of basic principles on which Hualcaino behaviour was based were mutually inconsistent or incompatible. However, they all reflected the status quo of self-sufficiency, sharing and compactual responsibility within a context of peasant survival, peasant belief systems and the 'moral community'. For innovation to work and to become practice, it is necessary for it to adapt to or reflect local conditions and to make only reasonable demands on the peasants. If it fails, it is because it is not compatible with the local traditions and population, it demands too much of them, or it denies their belief system.[3]

Although Hualcán's lessons are relevant to Chilca, Chilca in 1964 was less traditional and more open to change than Hualcan in the early 1950s. Provided innovations could be seen to enhance the well-being of the community or the household economy and did not challenge established values, they could be accepted. The eucalyptus afforestation scheme was a great success in Chilca, for example. It was a massive, well-organised aid programme that offered employment during the planting phase. Moreover it was unusual in that the peasants had been consulted and involved throughout. Although initially set up under the American Alliance for Progress, the fact that the project was carried out by the Peruvian Forest Service meant that the peasants became involved in a constructive way with one of their own government departments, and were influenced by efficient, well-motivated technicians.

There is no doubt that in agriculture, tradition minimised innovation, yet even here we have noted that acute population pressure and perhaps exposure to outside influences had made Chilca ripe for change by 1964. The example of Justo showed the community that some progress could be achieved through their own efforts by adopting some modern techniques.

Justo's superior tall maize crop with its fine large cobs provided the objective evidence that Stein specified. Clearly villagers could now see that greater control over the production of crops was possible rather than relying on supernatural beliefs. The fact that Justo was well regarded and had worked selflessly to assist the community in the afforestation scheme meant that the demonstration effect of his new innovations was considerable. Working indirectly through Justo and one or two others like him, the Ministry of Agriculture seemed well set to start a chain reaction process of innovation and agricultural modernisation. Unfortunately, when Justo decided to leave the village, the modernising upsurge that he had initiated was nipped in the bud.

The routine avenues of agricultural progress offered little. In the years following 1964 and the largely ineffectual innovations attempted by the Peace Corps volunteers, a few changes occurred. The incremental nature of the change process, especially after 1971, boosted by the euphoria for modernisation and agrarian reform which were promoted by the Revolution, brought new elements into the community. Although the attempts to improve the school, establish a school library, introduce improved poultry breeds, build showers and even to introduce clean piped water all failed at that stage, it may be that some positive legacy ensued or arose, phoenix-like, from the ashes of failure.

There was proof by 1979 that the benefits of improved technology were generally accepted by many households: by this date 26 households out of 52 in the sample used artificial fertiliser, 25 used insecticides, and a few paid for vaccinations to protect livestock from disease. And although the rich and middle peasant groups adopted these modern innovations to a greater extent than the poor and very poor peasants (see Table 8.3), the fact that reasonable numbers of the latter two groups used fertilisers and/or insecticides shows that they were *aware* of the value of the innovations. The reason why more poor peasants did not use them (or use them in greater volume or frequency) was their high cost.

LEADERSHIP

It became clear that the quality of leadership would be significant in influencing the acceptance of worthwhile innovations, the welcoming of constructive external initiatives and in encouraging people to work hard to achieve community goals. Attendance at meetings of the village assembly indicated not only what issues were held to be important by village households, but also provided evidence of the ideas and goals espoused by several leaders or would-be leaders and the tactics they seemed to be employing to win supporters.

At all assemblies attended it was noticeable that villagers divided themselves into three distinct groups: the rich, middle and poor peasants. This underlined the three-tiered nature of society. At meetings the rich peasants generally dominated, although middle peasants also contributed to speech-making. The third group of poor peasants, and also all women present, formed a largely passive and silent group. On the rare occasions on which a member of this group might try to speak, he was often rudely interrupted or talked over by the more articulate and more confident villagers of higher status.

The household survey showed that some half a dozen men of the rich peasant or upper middle group were identified as the main leaders of this community. These were the people who regularly rotated in the elected roles of *presidente*, *personero*, vice-president, *teniente-gobernador* and as members of the Junta Directiva. They were mostly men in their 40s or 50s who had had some experience in dealing with agents from the outside and who had acquired their position of leadership by supporting community goals, accepting sponsorship of *cargos* for *fiestas* on Saints' Days and appointment to the civil–religious hierarchy. Although they were not above benefiting themselves or relatives while filling office, they knew the limits of acceptable behaviour.

In the survey, household heads were asked to identify the person or persons who had the most authority in the community. Why? Was he also the most active person in wielding his authority?

By far the greatest number of votes were accorded to the Justice of the Peace and the president, to the roles themselves rather than to the individuals who held them. Generally there was recognition that the nominal power reflected actual power, but there was also some recognition of authority based on class, and on 'achievement leadership' (that is, the ability to solve problems). Three people, however, said that nobody had authority, and some expressed the view that office-holders did not really take the lead. Two of the undoubted leaders of the community pointed out that the official regulations for governing communities were at fault since office-holders were elected for a term of only one year. Even if successive office-holders were to pursue the same policy, achieving continuity would be difficult.

Householders were also asked to identify the person who was most interested in helping people resolve the problems of the community. What had they done for the community?

Again there were some stock answers: the president was named (seven times), and also the 'directors', *personero* or *teniente-gobernador*. However, villagers repeatedly asserted that the leaders were not interested in the welfare of the community, but only concerned with their families' personal concerns: 'No one here is good as a leader'; 'All work only for their own family'; 'There is not much unity in the community.' Several villagers, while identifying certain leaders, cynically remarked that they 'had not rendered account' to the community, a task that leaders were expected to perform when finishing their period of office. While the idea of accountability of leaders to the community as a whole was not widely mentioned, it did greatly concern some people.

There were a number of villagers who clearly felt a deep sense of rejection or alienation and who did not identify anyone as having an interest in helping the community. These respondents were lowly Indians whose answer represented their class and ethnic condition; the lowest rung of village society did not identify with the interests of the more enterprising, upwardly mobile, more *cholo*, richer peasants. The greatest number of people, however, genuinely expressed a sense of sadness and frustration at the decline of community; leaders seemed to be unable to counteract this dangerous trend.

While there was little perception of 'achievement leaders' or of leadership linked to the requirements of modernisation or innovation, there was a sense that leaders should defend the interests of the community from outside enemies (who are often linked to the forces of modernisation). There were in Chilca a few relatively articulate, ambitious men who sought to become leaders for their own reasons of enrichment or aggrandisement, or political entrepreneurship. Most of these people, who were invariably *cholo*, would make themselves useful through serving as cultural brokers to help the community confront and deal with a new event or complex proposal (see Chapter 13). But generally they had little lasting influence, for villagers invariably saw through their false claims.

In Chilca there were three leaders of considerable stature and ability, whose altruism and concern for community interests were usually unquestioned. They possessed far greater potential influence than the normal village office-holders referred to above. We shall call them Honorato, Ricardo and Victor. Although all three actually lived in Chilca, they represent major types of leaders who exist in villages of the Sierra, and who need to exist if social harmony, constructive local development, effective organisation and purposeful political action are to occur in the future. Their various and competing leadership roles need to be seen in the context of village life and the changing external scene.

Honorato: The Importance of Order

Undoubtedly the most powerful and respected leader in Chilca was the Justice of the Peace. Honorato was the biggest landowner in Chilca, holding 8 *topos*, and was one of the richest men. With 18 cows, he had one of the largest herds of cattle and, until 100 of his sheep died a year earlier of *callotacca*, he had grazed the largest flock.

As a successful and literate person he was proud that his children were doing well in the world: three were attending university, two were teachers, another was a merchant, and another was a police investigator on the Ecuador border. As Justice of the Peace Honorato was concerned with the maintenance of peace and order in the community and was held in some fear and trepidation by many *comuneros*. While basically conservative in outlook, Honorato had shown himself to be pragmatic in the face of changing circumstances.

For 48 years Honorato had worked on one of the largest *haciendas* in the area, ending as an administrator. While he supported the *hacienda* as a system of production, noting its higher productivity in comparison with the waste and inefficiency of the new co-operative under the agrarian reform, he had been flexible when the Revolution brought new opportunities. He accepted the highly paid position of administrator of the co-operative for two years, a post that was an acknowledgement of his skills, experience and prestige compared with other leaders in the Anta zone. However, growing resentment by members at lack of progress under the co-operative and with his high salary led to his dismissal.

Honorato considered Chilca to be a relatively peaceful village but he was concerned about the incidence of crime. The main problem was drunkenness, which frequently caused fights; a drunk man had recently murdered his grandson. With the greater availability of insecticide, there had been more than one suicide. Robberies also occurred and Honorato believed that lack of employment led to stealing.

He basically supported the older patrimonial system which had allowed the village access to pastures on the *hacienda*. He was, like many other villagers, disenchanted with and cynical of the co-operative; in spite of the fact that his had been the first village to join, he considered the community had received little benefit: 'The co-operative does not permit day labouring – it impedes it.'

In discussing goals that Chilca should attempt to achieve in future years, Honorato thought piped drinking water to be of high priority. The community should also seek to obtain an electric lighting system like the *pueblo* of Anta a few years earlier. There was also a great need for an agronomist possessing veterinary skills to be stationed in the locality. The problem that worried him most, however, was the declining unity and growing dissent within the community. The problem, which was one of factionalism, could be attributed, he claimed, to the activities of the young leader Victor, who had come back to Chilca two years earlier. He regarded Victor as a political extremist and regretted that so many young people followed his lead.

While Honorato's authority was largely unquestioned and he was widely believed to be a 'good man', some villagers regarded him as too conservative and thought that he had acquired his enviable status mainly by theft and deceit. I was told that rather than being employed as 'administrator' on the *hacienda*, he had in fact occupied the lowly position of 'killer of flies' in the dining room of the *patrón*. And one villager gained some malicious pleasure from recounting a story widely believed by many members of the community. According to the story Honorato once stole an ancient golden statue (Inca or pre-Inca) from the house of the *patrón*. Many people believed that the statue drank human blood and one person claimed to have seen it covered with blood. A well-educated young woman declared she had seen the statue walking one day outside Honorato's house. It was believed that Honorato achieved promotion from his formerly lowly job on the *hacienda* partly by raising loans on the security of the golden statue. He gradually became rich and used the loans to buy land to attain a position of considerable prestige and authority. There was a note of ambiguity both in his personality and in the furnishings of the room in which we conversed: on the wall was a large golden crucifix, symbol of the ecclesiastical system that legitimated much of the older order. On another wall was a large inflammatory poster of Che Guevara uttering a call to revolution.

Ricardo: An Indispensable Outsider

Ricardo, an astute and enterprising *cholo*, worked on *haciendas* for 15 years and later in Cuzco in a variety of jobs for two years. He then moved to Lima where he drove buses, and eventually acquired a pickup truck of his own. His private trucking business flourished and he expanded to operate three trucks, using relatives as drivers. Then he moved into operating micro buses for commuters. His wife owned land in Chilca and he had lived in the community for short periods since 1950. In 1977, he left Lima as a return migrant, coming back to Chilca in the hope of capitalising on some of the new opportunities arising from the agrarian reform. He hoped to operate micro buses in the Pampa de Anta area, but had not been able to obtain a licence to operate.

Ricardo was a successful entrepreneur who brought many skills and some accumulated savings back to the village. With these he had been able to buy some plots of land in the community so that by 1979 he and his wife owned 7½ *topos*. He grazed 15 cows, one of the largest herds. He had become a *comunero* through marriage, and through many instances of working for the interests of the community he had become a leader of a constructive, moderate kind. In business skill and experience he was unrivalled in the community, but because he had not recently lived in Chilca for long, and because of the great social distance between his urban sophistication and the older villagers, he had not as yet achieved widespread recognition as a leader, or much popularity. In 1979 he received an allocation of half a *topo* of communal land in the *puna* for the first time, recognition of his status as a *comunero*.

Ricardo's agricultural techniques were the most efficient and innovative in the village. He had introduced superior potato seed from a neighbouring community, and in the 1962 outbreak of foot-and-mouth disease, he treated his five cows with a mixture of carrot juice, grated squash and boiled linseed; none died. Although he appreciated that onions were the most lucrative cash crop in the Cuzco region, he saw that there was inadequate irrigation water in Chilca to grow them successfully, and that dairying was the most rational land use. Through selective breeding he believed one could amass wealth so long as there was access to grazing land. Ricardo identified the most critical problem facing Chilca as access to pasture land, and he provided a detailed account of the long dispute between the community and the *haciendas* and then with the co-operative over this issue. He also saw the real need to establish a milk marketing co-operative to centralise the operation, and to obtain economies of scale that would regularise transport and enable a higher price to be paid to the producer.

Ricardo declared that the other main needs of the community in 1979 were a system of piped *agua potable*, provision of electric light and improved layout of the village with construction of streets, allocation of recreation areas and designation of other uses. When villagers asked me to assist them in gaining a government loan to install *agua potable*, Ricardo came forward as a willing and logical leader to press for the 4 million *soles* loan to purchase the materials and then to supervise the work of installation. He also identified one of the greatest needs to be the appointment of an administrator who could supervise the distribution of scarce irrigation water. This would minimise the continual friction and improve the distribution of water. And he acted as a sensible moderating influence during a land boundary dispute with a neighbouring community in 1979, helping to avert possible bloodshed.

Ricardo believed Chilca to have no great potential for achieving progress in the future, although it was fortunate in its location. He believed the community to be 'disorganised' and some people, he declared, 'never changed': they were exactly the same as they had been 15 years ago before peasant mobilisation. He was not greatly impressed by other leaders in the community, although he respected Honorato as a man of experience. He expressed distaste, and perhaps some envy, for Victor, whom he declared did not have enough experience to be president.

Ricardo alleged that Victor had retained 2 *soles* per litre in the milk marketing co-operative, ostensibly to build up a community fund. At the end of the project, however, no trace of the fund could be found and 70 000 *soles* were missing. He warned darkly of the danger of Victor and his colleagues of the left if they became influential. He believed they would resort to violence, if necessary, to gain their ends.

Victor: Moderniser and Political Activist

As soon as I returned to Chilca in 1979 I was told about the activities and influence of Victor, a young man of about 25. It immediately became apparent that Victor was a controversial figure in the community. Some greatly admired him for his bravery, ability and his personal analysis of the whole situation of the peasantry in the Cuzco region, while others who believed in more cautious political strategies regarded him as a dangerous and disruptive figure. The significance of Victor's role as a peasant leader and his apparent influence even outside Chilca was underlined by the fear expressed by his mother and sister that they daily expected visits by the police to arrest him. Police had already visited Chilca, saying they 'wished to speak to him'. It was obvious whenever I spoke to him that he and his relatives were constantly keeping an eye on the road to Cuzco. During daylight at least, any approaching vehicle caused a cloud of dust to arise and Victor was always eager to learn who the approaching visitor might prove to be. From his house some 150m from the road he was ready to retreat rapidly to the plantation behind the village where he could escape to the rugged hill country, but he was fearful that the police might visit at night.

Victor was well educated, having studied at university and worked in Lima. His sophisticated, cosmopolitan ways were unmatched even by Ricardo, the main entrepreneurial leader. He brought many outside ideas to Chilca and had been particularly active in local development projects in the community as well as being concerned with wider social mobilisation and political action. In 1978 Victor had organised a milk co-operative in Chilca, and with two other members had formed a small committee to run the project. Before the scheme, villagers had received only 26 *soles* per litre for their milk; but Victor planned that with better organisation and transport he would be able to pay 32 *soles* per litre. For a while the scheme operated successfully but then the community insisted that it be run by the Junta Directiva.

Victor commented that if people did not accept the idea of centralised control for marketing they would lose out. After the Junta Directiva began to run the project, prices began to fluctuate and then fall, and transport became a problem, with the truck no longer being contracted for each day of the week.

Victor shared the same concerns about Chilca's needs as Honorato and Ricardo, and also believed that Chilca's population of over 1000 people warranted the services of a full-time nurse.

He had been elected to the six-member committee in the village, a body that was required to work with the officers of the Junta Directiva on community affairs. Although he was glad to serve on this body, he remarked that the *comuneros* 'maintained many customs' and 'were not progressive'. He lamented that the Junta Directiva undertook no preparation before meetings, even though the issues to be considered might be important and complex.

The strength of Victor's leadership was his sincerity and integrity, and his obvious sophistication and relative competence in organising and managing the dairy co-operative and other similar projects. Villagers recognised his skills as a *limaco* and as an educated and cultured man, though some may have suspected his knowledge was based on book learning rather than tried and true practical experience. Although fully accepted as a villager, a member of the moral community, his education and cosmopolitan ways had made him very much a non-peasant; the social distance between him and fellow-villagers was very great. His analysis of and solutions to local problems were very different from those of most villagers, and many were not yet willing to accept the risks involved in committing themselves to his ideas and proposed course of action. It was not that Chilca could not commit itself to radical action, for the village had been both the first community to join the new co-operative and then in 1977 one of the first to invade co-operative lands; rather they were beguiled by other pressing short-term goals, such as the question of purchasing the stable from the co-operative, or of milling a portion of the eucalyptus plantation, instead of pursuing consistently larger longer-term goals.

There were, however, more basic objections to Victor's leadership. Hitherto most peasant leaders had been characteristically concerned with classic peasant goals: either those of development within the little community (such as whitewashing the church or enlarging the plaza), or of occupying *hacienda* land to which they claimed the title, fighting the *haciendas* over land titles to their *pampa* or joining other peasant communities in the invasion of co-operative land. Such latter actions were part of the on-going class war of Indian peasants versus *mestizo* middle- and upper-class people, of trusted insiders of the moral community against untrustworthy or exploitative outsiders. But now Victor and visiting *politicos* (political activists) had introduced a new dimension into peasant politics.

Victor and the *politicos* had been toughened in the fires of revolution. They were second-generation revolutionaries, for they had read about or witnessed the ideas and strategies of Che Guevara, Regis Debray and their local hero, Hugo Blanco, in the La Convención campaign, as well as studying the earlier ideas of José Carlos Mariátegui and Haya de la Torre. Now Maoist ideas were in the ascendancy as ideologues sought a strategy that would at once increase the awareness of the peasants of their objective conditions, provide 'conscientisation' of the masses and rally them behind a new Marxist–Maoist programme. Clearly these strategies were complex and difficult, embracing major philosophies and depending essentially on middle-class leadership and specialised political education and indoctrination.

The new goals were too ambitious for most peasants, given the low level of literacy and education. The ideas were not contiguous with peasant traditions, ideologies, belief systems or customs. Instead, they were products of the world 'outside', outside the moral community, even as it struggled to grasp any advantages directed by the Revolution towards it. Some in the community felt they were stretched to the utmost to accommodate Victor's revolutionary ideas, even though he was a member of the moral community; other visiting *politicos*, allied to Victor, were too much to stomach. Moreover the community was all too aware of the costs of political revolution that might spill over into bloody conflict; the Pampa de Anta had often been the scene of ruthless repression by the authorities, of imprisonment, confiscation of property, even death. It is interesting to note that the Sendero Luminoso movement which led the civil war in the

1980s began in 1980 in the mountain fastnesses of Ayacucho, Apurimac and Huancavelica Departments; in contrast the Pampa de Anta is much less remote and could easily be reached from Cuzco city if a recalcitrant peasantry needed to be punished and repressed. Villagers were aware of this.

The most basic objection to Victor, however, was a feeling of deep resentment for the new level of divisiveness that had been brought into the community. Chilca was still fighting its most basic battle of accepting valuable innovations that came from the outside; as in most traditional communities there was no compelling need to search for a rational scientific explanation of why an innovation (such as the milk marketing project) had failed. Failure was confirmation of traditional perceptions that external things are evil or dangerous. Victor had not really won his most basic battle as moderniser, although success was perhaps close at hand through the widespread recognition of his skills in business practice and management. Success as a *political* leader, however, was much harder to achieve, given the complexity and the middle-class links required, at a time when his leadership in modernisation had not been fully established. If he had restricted his leadership role to achieving success in innovation and modernisation, he would have established a solid platform from which to launch political activities. In the political ferment of 1979 Victor's enemies were ready to use him as a scapegoat and to blame him for the declining unity of the village.

By this time he showed increasing signs of impatience with the conservatism of the villagers and their commitment to unsound short-term goals. Although he still retained strong support among the young and better educated people, Victor's long-term success as an important political leader or as a moderniser became increasingly a matter of doubt.

NEW ROLES AND MODERNISATION

The roles played by the three leaders, Honorato, Ricardo and Victor, and the degree of influence each wielded provide an interesting commentary on the process of modernisation in Chilca. The distinction between a traditional and a modern society is determined largely by the extent to which people can accept the need for single-interest relationships and specialised roles (as, for example, in economic management of the dairy marketing co-operative, entrepreneurial business leadership, or political leadership) rather than persisting with multiplex relationships. The rejection of Victor's business-like management of the dairy co-operative as well as his political leadership, and the non-acceptance of Ricardo's entrepreneurial leadership, indicate that Chilca remained, on the whole, a relatively 'traditional' community, since they were both men who possessed considerable skills as well as being reasonably altruistic. Both, however, had been back in the community for only two years, compared with the longer residence of the more popular Honorato.

Always in the past, proposals or commands to adopt new political or economic roles, or to adopt some new innovation, had come from the outside; hence it was only natural for the community automatically to categorise the actions of outsiders as dangerous or sinful. While friends and relatives were proud that Victor had acquired status, education and sophistication during his years in the outside world, it was important that when he returned to Chilca he ceased to behave like an outsider, so that he could retain his place in the moral community of peasants.

The conclusion is thus sad and pessimistic: Victor could act neither as a mediator between the two worlds nor as an effective modernising agent among his own people; he could, in fact, only retain the tie with his own people as long as he acted in accordance with their values. The true innovator is often seen both by himself and by others as a deviant, or perhaps as a 'role-hybrid', who straddles the two groups, being both inside and outside the recipient or acceptor sphere,[4] but the actions of a deviant have to be accepted if an innovation is to occur.

The long saga of attempting to install a piped water system testifies to the difficulties of innovation within the closed peasant world. Eventually it was achieved, but only after 25 years' agitation. Having innovative leaders in the community was not sufficient to achieve more rapid success. The role of cultural broker, such as Ricardo tried to fill, may not necessarily serve as a conduit for modernisation of the community; it is a device which enables the peasants and the *mestizo* officials of the outside world to avoid a meeting of minds, a convenience that enables the peasant leaders to avoid dealing with outsiders whom they fear and who often dupe them. Certainly ability to act as a cultural broker does not automatically promote a person to a position of leadership.

In contrast to Victor and Ricardo, Honorato was not really a moderniser, although he professed to seek a number of goals for the community. In part, support for him reflected agreement with his conservative viewpoint, but in part it derived from his role as Justice of the Peace. In this role he was placed in a position that was accepted as being largely *above* the values and conditions (such as nepotism and corruption) characteristic of the community at large. As the legal guardian of peace and order he was regarded as usually working for the harmony and well-being of the community. Once he gave up this role, however, Honorato lost a great deal of his authority as a leader.

As the 'Case of the Hungry Cows' reminds us, belief in supernatural forces is a strong factor that often acts as a levelling mechanism. However, to a much greater extent than in modern society, peasants blame failure upon the malevolence of human agents. This is significant for innovation and modernisation, for while it is acceptable for a *mestizo* to adopt new ways and become rich, if a peasant does so he is said to have cheated, or to have exploited his fellows. To that extent he should be punished or put outside the moral community. The accusation that Honorato had stolen the golden statue which he could then use as security to raise loans to buy land, asserted that his wealth and status were based originally on theft. And the charge that Victor had embezzled part of the funds of the milk co-operative indicates the strength of envy and malevolence that exists between competing leaders and which is directed at modernisers whose innovations threaten the stability of the status quo.

Yet this sombre, bleak picture of Chilca's stance towards modernisation and innovation, while largely true of the early 1960s, is not adequate for the 1980s and 1990s. By 1979, social differentiation had proceeded a good way, the community was very diverse and it was becoming more difficult to generalise about people's attitudes and values. Many peasants had learnt new techniques of crop and animal husbandry, and they knew that if they were to escape the fearful ravages of the elements or plant or animal disease, they might now produce much larger harvests. Justo's tall crop of golden corn had taught peasants a fundamental, new lesson that many had now absorbed. The successful afforestation project provided another lesson in rural development, showing villagers that an arm of government could be beneficial rather than oppressive. And Chilca also includes Julio, the storekeeper, whose son is a university student, and Ciprian, the proud father of a professor of Quechua. The change in values and education between generations is great and sometimes dramatic, even within one family (see Plate 11).

The difficulties and pain experienced in attempting to accommodate, let alone resolve, the clash between the values of the educated, *cholo* and young, compared with the traditional, Indian and old are great, and it is scarcely surprising that there is an unfortunate mismatch between the needs of the community and the ability to organise, plan and accept certain kinds of leader in order to achieve these goals. Choice of unsound goals might lead to a serious setback and disunity but, in numerous insignificant but incremental ways, change is slowly seeping into Chilca through many cracks in the old edifice. Indeed a new structure, grafted uneasily on to the old, has in fact emerged in the village, with new people – non-peasants born to peasants in the community – now living there, and new roles being played in local life.

13 Agrarian Reform in the Pampa

BACKGROUND TO THE REFORM

The Pampa de Anta was in the national spotlight as one of the first Sierra regions to experience the effects of the sweeping new agrarian reform. This area of a dangerously volatile peasantry became something of a showcase. Even in the 1960s part of the infrastructure for agrarian reform had been laid in the Pampa: an aerial photo and a cadastral survey had been completed and a socio-economic survey carried out. In August 1968, two months before the military junta headed by General Velasco swept Belaúnde from power and initiated the Peruvian Revolution, a group of engineers and topographers from Lima travelled to the Pampa de Anta.

The agrarian reform[1] had two phases, *afectación* (legal expropriation of the land) and *adjudicación* (distribution of the land to beneficiaries), carried out by the agrarian reform section of the Ministry of Agriculture. The first wave of expropriations – of 53 *haciendas* – was completed by December 1969, and the second wave involved nine. An *ad hoc* commission was appointed to study the region and carry out a census to determine who the beneficiaries would be. The 1970 report of this commission (COMARCA) specified two particular goals for agrarian reform in the region:

(a) to integrate the diverse peasant groups in the Pampa into a unit to enable them to participate in discussions concerning their well-being; and
(b) to stimulate economic growth to enable a rise in the per capitum income of peasant beneficiaries and also an increase in the output of the ex-*hacienda* sector of the regional economy.

At first it appeared that the expropriated *haciendas* might be dismembered and fractionated among the peasant population, which led to much early peasant enthusiasm for the idea of agrarian reform. However, in view of the first goal identified above, COMARCA specified that a co-operative would be the mode of exploiting the redistributed lands. All expropriated resources – land, cattle, installations, crops and equipment – were to be owned and exploited by members recruited from among the beneficiaries. Members were to provide labour and monetary contributions for the operating capital of the co-operative, and a loan of 7 million *soles* was provided by the BFA.

ORGANISATION OF THE CO-OPERATIVE

Formally, the co-operative was headed by a general assembly of 120 elected delegates representing all the different geographical units. It met twice a year to decide major issues, set policy, determine priorities and formulate an annual work plan. Wherever a nucleus of co-operative members was to be found (as in the ex-*hacienda* population or in *comunidades* like Chilca), a local assembly of members existed to elect their delegate to the general assembly and to discuss co-operative policy. Execution of policy set by the general assembly was the responsibility of the administrative council, a group of 11 elected members who met monthly. It hired temporary and permanent workers, let contracts and constructed an operating budget. The administrator (*gerente*) covered all technical operations of the co-operative. He had the final decision concerning a specific crop-planting programme, selection of seed potatoes or field procedure, insect control or stock purchases. He had considerable power, therefore, and more than anyone else was responsible for the success or failure of the annual work plan.

CAP Tupac Amaru II was established in June 1971. In six successive adjudications from June 1971 to 1975, a total of 38 437ha were assigned to the new co-operative, an area that represented over 63 per cent of the Districts of Anta, Zurite and Huarocondo. Before the agrarian reform the lands belonged to 63 *haciendas*, 23 Campesiñas Comunidades and 170 *pequeñas propiedades*. It is important to note that not *all* of this land represented expropriated *hacienda* land: Campesiñas Comunidades were persuaded to enter communal lands from each village, so that the *comunidades* thus ceased to be formal entities in the CAP Tupac

Amaru II and some of their population could opt to become members of the co-operative (*socios*).

Indeed, it is a moot point whether 'persuade' is an adequate description of the process by which *comunidad* lands were included in the huge new co-operative: Lovón Zavala stated that the bureaucrats in effect 'demanded' that they cede their lands to the co-operative and that the process was one of 'usurping' their lands. Certainly the age-old adherence of the peasants to their land and the enormous social change required for them to accept fully and adapt to modern capitalistic principles lay at the heart of the growing difficulties experienced by the new co-operative.

COMMUNICATION IN THE REFORM PROCESS

Any hope of success of the agrarian reform depended not only on the soundness of the planning and the appropriateness of the goals set, but also on the new revolutionary elite carrying the people with it. Rapid social change required a massive re-education campaign. As with revolutions everywhere, utopian ideas flourished; in the heady excitement of the time it was believed that a new rural society would arise from the ashes of the old order. It was the challenging task of the new bureaucrats – who quickly became the new *patrones* – rapidly to diffuse information about the radical new agrarian reform, the maze of new laws and regulations and to re-educate all peasant, *cholo* and *mestizo* classes in how the new co-operative should function. This re-education process led to the most visible aspects of the agrarian reform process. There was a substantial expansion in the bureaucracy and most aspects of the reform were heavily 'bureaucratised': ONRA (Oficina Nacional de Reforma Agraria) became the main national agency for the agrarian reform.

In June 1971 the umbrella organisation SINAMOS was created, ostensibly to implement the reform more effectively, to hold in rein a potentially incompetent and expanding bureaucracy, and especially to enable the popular classes to satisfy their needs by achieving power to make decisions affecting their lives. In practice most observers attribute a much less philanthropic role to SINAMOS; it appears to have been designed to hold in check the new revolutionary forces let loose in the countryside and to guide them in directions desired by the national government.

A media programme was carried out in newspapers and by the Ministry of Agriculture, which also broadcast a radio programme twice a week in Quechua during the dinner hour. The theme of each programme was chosen to stimulate discussion among the assembled peasants. A van equipped with a public address system criss-crossed the Pampa, broadcasting news about the co-operative. Many striking posters displaying slogans of the agrarian reform and quotations from President Velasco soon appeared, adorning the walls of stores or peasant houses.

The most basic approach in the re-education programme was the *concientización* campaign (consciousness raising) carried out in communities by representatives of the Ministry of Agriculture. They stayed in each community in turn, explaining the goals of the agrarian reform, the structure of the co-operative and encouraging the beneficiaries to join. Peasants were asked to send representatives to local or regional seminars where the workings of co-operatives were explained in detail. They were then expected to return to their villages to share their knowledge. After 1970, a series of more specialised seminars for co-operative administrators was organised by the new national training and research unit of the agrarian reform, CENCIRA.

In the early years, interest in agrarian reform remained high and generally positive. The peasants of the Pampa appreciated that a real revolution had occurred. Many were impressed by the genuine sincerity of Velasco and his determination to bring social justice to the Indians. A number of new institutions appeared to bear out this promise: for example, the creation of a new independent judiciary to consider almost any type of peasant land complaint and the exoneration of peasant litigants from paying any legal costs. For the first time a land judge and tribunal could objectively rule on land matters, in contrast to the former system dominated by the *mestizo* class and served by the notorious *tinterillos*, who made a living by forging or falsifying land titles and documents used to exploit peasants. Many peasant representatives eagerly attended seminars and courses on the working of the co-operative, keen to learn the new skills.

By the early 1970s, however, rumours abounded as to the real nature of the agrarian reform. Guillet[2] reports a conversation in which one peasant asserted that the government was aiming at a Cuban type of socialist model in which private property was abolished and all property evenly distributed. Another version held that the government would become the 'new Inca', acting as governor and patron of all. Most peasants, however, did not know whether the agrarian reform would turn out to be good or bad; in the meantime they waited with considerable anxiety.

In fact, the substance of the change was much less impressive than all the showy surface activity. The large numbers of bureaucrats on the Pampa, the coastal *mestizos* posted to Cuzco, the many shiny new pickup trucks, the euphoric verbiage in the newspapers, the great output of stamped paper and profusion of red tape indicated much public spending but had little to do with achieving increased agricultural output. When I returned briefly to Chilca in 1974, I found the peasants surprised and confused at the complexity and overmanning of the co-operative bureaucracy, with its accounting division, general services division, cattle operations, agricultural operations and others.

The problem of communication in implementing the agrarian reform was indeed formidable. As the 1970 Peasant Communities Census showed, about 46 per cent of the adult population of the Pampa had no schooling whatsoever and 34 per cent of the remainder had not completed *primaría*, the lowest grade of schooling. The lengthy, complex legal documents and legislation on the co-operative and how it functioned required a level of education far higher than that of most peasant speakers of Spanish. Moreover, direct translation of the new law into Quechua would have achieved little, as Quechua is an unwritten language and correct interpretation of law based on Spanish concepts and legal thinking would have been very difficult. The vast quantity of rules and regulations made it almost impossible for the interested peasant to understand and digest them; even the labour legislation passed by the general assembly of the co-operative contained over 309 separate provisions on the obligations and responsibilities of co-operative members.[3]

As time passed, it became increasingly obvious that real power had passed to the new bureaucrats and that a centralisation process had occurred. Technicians and advisers were responsible to bodies at the national level and there was a lack of feedback to the local people. Members felt they could not make their voices heard through their delegates on the general assembly.

Friction was, of course, to be expected.[4] Technicians feared that peasant control of the co-operative would see it converted to purely local, short-term ends. On the other hand, peasants suspected that the technicians were ideologues, perhaps well meaning but nevertheless suffering from urban bias, and bent on promulgating untested theoretical ideas. The division was again one of class as well as ethnicity, with a new breed of *mestizo* technicians replacing the earlier *mestizo* oligarchy.

ECONOMIC PERFORMANCE OF THE CO-OPERATIVE

Even before CAP Tupac Amaru II was functioning, it became apparent that the technical decisions of the Provisional Administrative Commission (PAC) were being made by *tecnicos*, rather than by trusted peasant members. Furthermore, although these outside advisers were meant to be agricultural experts, they demonstrated their incompetence on a number of occasions. A *tecnico* ordered ploughing to begin as the last date for planting would soon arrive, against the advice of the assembled peasants. They knew that the soil was already soaked and with tractor cultivation it turned into a gluey mass that baked hard as the sun rose. On another ex-*hacienda*, a good harvest was obtained when, under the new PAC reform authority, the land was first seeded in potatoes. However the *papa blanca* (white) potatoes were piled up without being graded according to size. As the peasants knew, no buyer would bid for them in this form, and before they could be graded the potatoes rotted. Consequently a large part of the harvest had to be fed to pigs.

The peasants were wrong and the *tecnicos* right when it came to the choice of potatoes for new sowings. Although the peasants preferred the superior flavour of the *ccompis* potato, there was greater demand in urban areas for *papa blanca*, which also gave a greater yield with the use of artificial fertilisers. However, a serious error occurred when the *tecnicos* set a price of 4.5 *soles* per pound, which was a price much higher than buyers were prepared to pay. This crop went largely unsold as well and eventually had to be dumped.

In the first season after expropriations, it was quite rational to plant many of the ex-*hacienda* lands in potatoes rather than to retain them as pastures, but no arrangements were made for the *yerbajeros* (graziers) who had used the land. Several members petitioned the co-operative on this matter, but months of bureaucratic delays ensued. The dry season arrived and some peasants were forced to take their animals to the *puna* to find pasturage. A number effectively gave up their membership of the co-operative from this point.

Later the co-operative recognised the problem and allocated pasturage, but members found to their dismay that the land was also to be used by members of several other communities. There were allegations that the theft of cattle was now much more common and the request to build a hut so that the stock could be guarded had to wait for several weeks till the next general assembly meeting. When a guard was finally appointed, he turned out to be a member of another community: a person who might avert his eyes from cattle thieves so long as the stock of his own community were safe.

In general, the often promising possibilities for wage labour seldom materialised; work was sporadic, or obtainable only in distant locations, and there continued to be a lack of cultivated land anyway. Of course, as a form of agro-industry the co-operative aimed in the long term to reduce its dependence on local labour, relying on mechanisation and labour-saving technology (by 1976 it had 14 tractors and several other machines and threshers). In the short and even medium term, such a policy was not likely to win the support of the peasantry.

Peasants complained that the co-operative brought new differences between *comuneros* and *socios* that had not existed to the same degree with *colonos*. Fixed labour costs increased from 645 000 *soles* in 1971 to 3 580 000 *soles* in 1974, and wage differentials between co-operative members and non-members (already high at 2:1 in 1971/72) widened to 12:1 in 1977.[5] It would have been much more realistic to design appropriate small-scale technological solutions to increasing productivity and to use current *jornal* rates for hiring labour.

In comparison with some other agrarian reform enterprises, it has been asserted that CAP Tupac Amaru II was not particularly inefficient. Certainly massive government investment led to some valuable new innovations: co-operative store houses, a large cattle complex, a new dairy herd of 150 cows, a set of silos and a great extension of eucalyptus planting on the surrounding hill country. But the major shift in land use from the pre-reform pattern, when dairy farming was dominant, to arable farming –

first, mainly for potatoes, and then, when the price of grain rose, to grain cultivation (enabling the application of mechanisation and scale economies) – was not successful. The changes in land use were dictated by economic considerations and took little account of ecological factors. Only after several years of poor harvests did a trend emerge after 1976 back to greater reliance on dairying.

The precarious financial management of the co-operative was becoming more obvious from 1976. Although the volume of sales was said to have grown from 2 million *soles* in 1971 to 17.5 million *soles* in 1979, the co-operative still used the same exploitative marketing channels of *comerciantes* (merchants) as had operated in the days of the *haciendas*. Indeed, with the investments of the agrarian reform, the economic position of the middlemen in the regional social structure strengthened. A growing debt crisis seemed to be drawing near as the first instalments on reducing the principal were due in 1977. Better financial management was desperately needed, and belt-tightening appeared likely. While wage reduction was logical, this would probably be rejected by co-operative members.

In 1979, it seemed it might be too late to save the co-operative. It had reached an almost impossible situation; as with many other CAPs and SAIS throughout Peru, it appeared that massive debt write-offs and drastic changes might be necessary if it was to continue. This, however, would not be a solution, but imply even more centralisation and an autocratic form of development from above. From 1979 to 1986, the government had in fact no policy at all on the co-operatives and SAIS; they clearly did not know what to do, but did not want to liquidate the co-operatives as it would be a confession that the agrarian reform had failed.

SOCIAL AND POLITICAL FACTORS

Poor communication and tension between growing centralised control and the demand for more democratic, local autonomy led to increasing disunity in the co-operative and ultimately to an unleashing of class conflict. Even in the first year of land redistribution, the *comunidades* showed their discontent by joining FUCA (Frente Unico de Campesinos de Anta) to press their case on the reform authorities. Some compromise was achieved by bringing back a few of the more experienced ex-*hacienda* staff. The other approach was to establish links with the peasantry through individuals who were perceived to be leaders. Such men seemed much more appropriate as intermediaries with the peasantry than the former *mestizos* or *cholos*; they seemed to be genuine peasants, ideologically opposed to the old *hacendados* and able to articulate the interests of peasants.

In the fluid social situation of the early 1970s, however, many would-be 'peasant leaders' appeared to be in a kind of 'political cholofication' process, aiming to reap the rewards available in a time of unrivalled government investment in the region and seizing opportunities to enhance their status and power.

At least some cases occurred in the Pampa area of the successful transferral of the co-operative organisation into the socio-economic structure of a small *hacienda* community. In this case the ex-*colonos* or *feudatarios* (labour-service tenants on *haciendas*) perceived their best interests to be served if the co-operative continued to provide the benefits they had gained in the past from the *haciendas*: the provision of a plot of land, access to pasture for grazing and opportunity to work on co-operative lands for a *jornal* wage (much higher with the co-operative). Their security was thus largely assured and risks minimised by accepting the co-operative and becoming *socios*.

The socio-economic structure of the community was an important determinant. For the richer, more independent communities there were few compelling reasons why *comuneros* should join the co-operative. Furthermore, from 1970 onwards new trends in the class pattern on the Pampa complicated the situation, making it more difficult for communities to respond constructively and uniformly to the agrarian reform.

One important element was provided by the *pequeñas propiedades*. The reform eliminated the power base of *mestizo* landowners. Although in most cases the *mestizo pequeñas propiedades* did not own enough land to be expropriated, they feared expropriation under articles of the Agrarian Reform Law, especially when neighbouring peasant communities lacked sufficient land to cover their needs. Accordingly, many *pequeñas propiedades* shifted their residence into peasant communities, began to participate in community affairs and successfully sought admission to *comunero* status. Their *mestizo*, bi-lingual and superior educational status made them an important new component in the population of some of the communities. Some of their members became notable new *misti* leaders.

In addition, with the initiation of the agrarian reform, migrants who had entered sharecropping arrangements or other forms of indirect tenure with fellow villagers began to fear that their lands in the village might be expropriated under certain clauses of the Agrarian Reform Law. In an attempt to protect their lands (some of which had not been used but lain fallow) and perhaps capitalise on other agrarian reform opportunities, many migrants returned to their home communities in the Sierra. Return migration was an important characteristic after 1969, and an estimate of three communities suggests that 14 per cent of the population in 1971 was comprised of return migrants.[6] Since the return to the village from Lima or some other city implied downward social mobility, the decision was not undertaken lightly. Nevertheless these return migrants who resumed cultivation of their *chacras* and sought legitimacy by participating in community affairs became another important element in local society. Not all should be assumed to have resumed peasant status; the more literate, bi-lingual, sophisticated members, like Ricardo, were *cholos* who at times reached new *misti* status.

Some communities that absorbed several *pequeñas propiedades* as well as various return migrants became socially more diverse and less unified. The traditional mechanisms – envy, rumour and gossip and threats of witchcraft – became less adequate to contain the centrifugal, disequilibrating forces. In their decision to re-establish themselves in their communities, and perhaps motivated by altruism and a desire for power, some return migrants sought office in political organisations. Again, when the agrarian reform bureaucrats sought a link to explain the co-operatives to the community, they found some of these new *mistis* to be propitious cultural brokers; as literate bi-linguals with some urban experience, they were better fitted to explain the workings of the co-operative than some of the older, traditional leaders. Some of the new *mistis* accepted this additional role of serving as a link with the co-operative as well as continuing with traditional office-holding roles, although at times the two roles might be quite different and conflicting.

There was competition for the new positions of responsibility, and *comuneros* perceived that cultural brokers were in reality more concerned with their own personal enhancement than the community's real interests. In such a situation (which in fact occurred at Chilca in the case of Honorato) factions emerged, and it became increasingly difficult for the community to act together. Moreover, where the threatened *pequeñas propiedades* spread rumours that the agrarian reform was designed to exploit peasants and most of the new co-operative members in the community were the richer peasants, it is scarcely surprising that the poorer *runa* peasants who had not joined remained sceptical.

THE DEMISE OF THE CO-OPERATIVE

When the co-operative was formed and people in the surrounding communities were invited to join, Chilca was the first to step forward, with about 80 members. However, disillusion soon set in for the various reasons described above. The co-operative became more and more concerned at the chronic illegal grazing by *comuneros* from Chilca and other communities, and eventually the Director of Agriculture announced in a ministerial edict that they would have to take all their animals off the co-operative land if they wished to continue as *socios*. The people of Chilca rebelled, stating that the co-operative had lured them with benefits (a hospital, new school and clinic had been built for the zone), while their cattle had been occasionally injured while grazing on the co-operative *pampa*. For their part, they did not at that stage believe they had 'invaded' the co-operative lands as they had been granted access to enter these lands under the *hacienda*. The co-operative paid only 8 *soles* per litre for milk and payment was often very late (up to two months), so Chilca withdrew their milk supplies to obtain a higher price elsewhere. They received no division of the profits from the co-operative in spite of paying the high membership fee of 550 *soles*, and began to resent the compulsory unpaid monthly *faenas* by which the co-operative mobilised labour.

As time passed the failure to reconcile divergent class interests and to meet the genuine interests of the peasantry became serious. The vast size and strange incongruous structure of the co-operative seemed to be very inappropriate. The concentration of lands by the huge new enterprises was seen to be incompatible with, and antagonistic to, land-hungry communities. In December 1976 and throughout 1977 a series of land invasions occurred.

Chilca, together with six other communities of the District of Anta, occupied over 4255ha.[7] The strength of these invasions lay in the social mobilisation of the peasantry who consolidated themselves through the close alliance of various peasant syndicates. Police and soldiers were sent from Cuzco and people were killed in the fighting.

In March 1978, a commission met with all the communities to adjudicate the disputes with the co-operative. In the face of peasant refusal to give up the lands that they believed they occupied legally (if *socios*) or illegally, it was decided in April 1978 to introduce a programme of redivision by which the size of the co-operative was reduced by over 7000ha. Chilca sought access to two blocks of land of 700 and 300ha, which would represent less than 2ha per family. After protracted negotiation, the co-operative retained about 240ha of these blocks, with about 700ha of pasture land being passed to Chilca. However, peasants from Chilca felt they had won no great victory, for some other communities had gained much more land per family (up to 7–8ha).

In view of its low production, costly bureaucracy and the huge loans that would ultimately have to be repaid (if not written off by the government), the co-operative tried to realise some of its assets. Land occupations continued, however, after the disputes of 1976–77, and in 1978 a further massive dismemberment occurred, leaving the CAP with only 7540ha (or 20 per cent of its original size). All the *socios* of Chilca had been expelled as members so nobody considered themselves as belonging to the co-operative.

In September 1979, co-operative members aided by a battalion of Guardia Civil reoccupied the *fundo* (rural property) Ancachuro on the *pampa* which had been invaded a fortnight earlier by *comuneros* of Zurite. The *fundo* had the most important cattle installations of the co-operative. The reoccupation was violent and bloody with 20 people being wounded.[8]

PERCEPTIONS OF THE AGRARIAN REFORM: CHILCA IN 1979

In 1979, when the agrarian reform was widely perceived to have failed and a greatly reduced co-operative, having been largely dismembered, barely survived, I discussed with each household how they viewed the reform and how they compared conditions under the co-operative with the former *hacienda* system. To some extent perceptions of the co-operative depended on whether peasants had had fortunate experiences of their own in dealing with the co-operative (such as obtaining paid employment), just as their view of the *hacienda* system was coloured by the terms of labour service that they experienced or their position in the status hierarchy. Apart from three informants, all who had worked on *haciendas* had occupied lowly positions.

Eighteen peasants considered the agrarian reform in general to have been a failure. Although most peasants had a poor perception of the co-operative and believed it had provided them with few benefits, nine thought that the agrarian reform was preferable to the older *hacienda* system that preceded it, while five stated that the *hacienda* system was better than the co-operative. While most peasants had a mixed view of the *hacienda* system, a majority of answers (11) considered it on the whole a 'bad system'. Most commonly the *hacienda* system was criticised for being tyrannical: 'on the *hacienda* there was no liberty'. Several peasants referred to the intolerance of the old *patrones* who preferred to keep the peasants ignorant by refusing permission to have a school on the *hacienda*. Others remembered that they had to work very hard on the *hacienda* (from 6 am to 4 pm for five days each week) with only two days on which to work their own *chacras*. If they did not work well in the old days, or complete a task, they might be whipped.

However, a number of peasants praised the *hacienda* system and most conceded that it had advantages. Above all it gave them a measure of security. In comparison with today, when Chilca is more fully involved in the market system, the autonomy of the near-subsistence system of the *hacienda* protected them against massive price increases. Invariably, when aspects of the *hacienda* system were commented upon favourably, it was seen as an exchange system, providing the peasants with land, employment and even help or food when in need; these benefits in their eyes mitigated much of the harshness of the system. Moreover, aspects that were praised involved humane treatment, whereas the co-operative and modern capitalistic trends were seen to be coldly impersonal, operating in ways oblivious to individual human needs.

Many peasants recognised that in the first year or two the reform was 'good', promising some genuine new opportunities. The Revolution led to an attack on illiteracy and the opening of more schools. A number of peasants believed that President Velasco was genuine in his determination to free the *campesino* from his bondage, but were cynical about the middle and later stages of the revolution (after 1972). Many were bitter at the broken promises. The co-operative had offered them a lot – a division of profits to the members, jobs, use of equipment, better agricultural returns, security, health benefits and so forth – but they believed it had deceived them, for it had 'provided none of these things'.

In showing their hostility to the co-operative, the peasants were expressing not only their resentment as a class of Indian *campesinos* to the new *patrones* of *mestizo tecnicos*, but also their view that the new agro-industrial enterprise was quite inappropriate for the situation. Many of their individual allegations were probably true or partially true. Members of the co-operative were deemed to be 'robbers', guilty of defalcations or of enriching themselves at the expense of the peasants who were meant to be the true beneficiaries. The heavy fines (100 to 500 *soles*) levied on stray cattle wandering on to co-operative cropland were particularly resented, as was the high membership entry fee. The peasants were not slow to criticise the shortcomings of the unwieldy co-operative bureaucracy, or the incompetence of some of the staff.

Almost all peasants were aware that harvest yields and total output from the former *hacienda* lands were now much lower than under the *hacienda* system. One of the *haciendas* on the Pampa de Anta had been one of the best in the south of Peru: in the 1930s it supported about 7000 cattle. However, by 1979, under the co-operative, its livestock totalled a mere 400, supplemented by about 1000 head owned by peasant *yerbajeros*. Competition among the various peasant groups had increased throughout the 1970s, reflecting growing socio-economic differentiation, and this caused friction and exacerbated a feeling of inequality and unfair treatment.

Overall, four issues dominated the thinking of Chilca people. To be viable, the co-operative had to serve as an exchange system, providing land, wages or security in exchange for work or other inputs. The instability of the co-operative in the social fluidity created by the Revolution meant that it never achieved any real credibility; the *hacienda* system, on the other hand, for all its injustices had at least functioned in ways that were well understood. Complaints over *jornal* labour were equally important: the scarcity and unreliability of work was accompanied by the failure of the co-operative to pay for labour for three or four months. The people objected to working unpaid on co-operative *faenas*, for in no sense were they working for their community. Finally, Chilca's concern with access to pasturage coloured views on the agrarian reform as a whole. Disputes with the co-operative over pasturage rights dragged on for years, and if the co-operative could not solve this problem it would not achieve any acceptance by Chilca. As one of the most respected traditional leaders stated: 'The agrarian reform hasn't aided us with our land. There are many problems with the co-operative. Now times are worse – no respect is shown and there are many robbers.' And among those who saw the main goal of the Peruvian Revolution as the elimination of servitude, the agrarian reform was seen to be abortive: 'The co-operative is the new *gamonal*'.

Clearly the agrarian reform in the Pampa de Anta had failed: its goals were inappropriate, its planning was not sound, and the revolutionary elite failed to carry the peasantry with it.

14 Migration, Empathy and Schooling

SOCIAL CHANGE AND URBANISATION

The process of social change *within* the village parallels, and is often closely linked to, the processes of change *outside* the village. Rural–urban migration is occurring on a massive scale in Peru, as in many other Third World countries that are also experiencing rapid social, economic and political change. An important study by Skeldon (1977) on nine micro regions of Cuzco showed that the changing nature of the link between urban and rural areas causes and is caused by transformation in the social structure of the areas of origin and areas of destination. In my household survey, it became quite clear that there were important feedback influences from the city to those Chilca households which had sons or daughters employed in Lima, Cuzco or Arequipa. Not only did the link often affect the household's income, but it also meant migrants relayed perceptions and news of the socio-economic life of the city, and fragments of their evolving view of urban culture.

It became clear during fieldwork in 1964 that decision-making on migration was not purely an individual matter, since it did not occur in a social vacuum but as a result of interaction with others, including relatives who had earlier moved to live and work in the city. This social network[1] provides the link that bridges the gulf[2] between the village and the city, for the networks encourage, regulate or otherwise influence the migration process (see Figure 14.1).

Dependent capitalist development is highly uneven in Peru; its main benefits are concentrated in the larger urban areas, and principally in Lima. The main 'pull' factor appears to be awareness of the advantages of modern development and the expectation that urban wages will be greater than rural earnings, the central idea of the Todaro model of migration.[3] Diffusion of the migration transition occurs down through the urban hierarchy. Generally, areas close to cities on the whole supply the majority of the migrants to those cities. Chilca, for example, has been

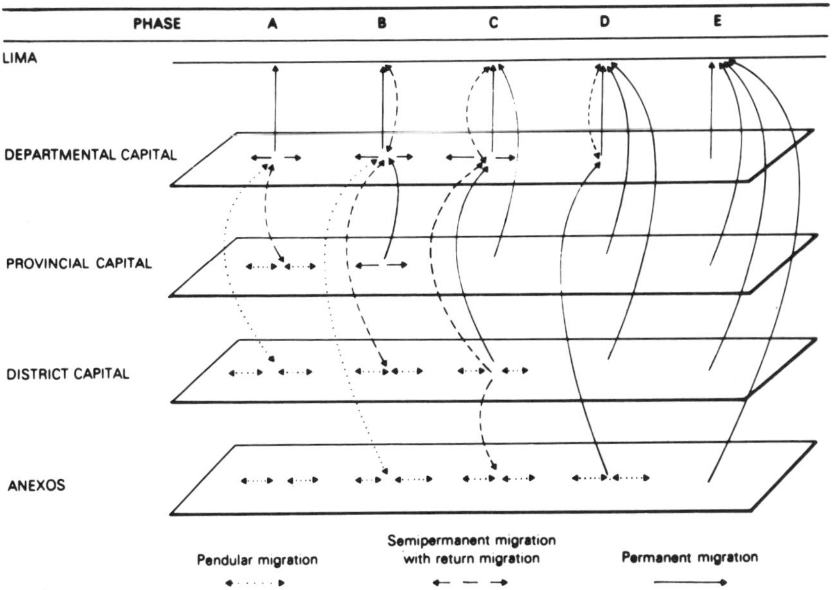

Source: Skeldon (1977).

Figure 14.1 A MIGRATION SCHEMA

urbanised by Cuzco and supplies it with many migrants. Some villages close to cities may, however, be at a low stage in the migration transition and this has to be explained.

There are also 'push' factors which cause out-migration: for example, the man–land ratio (or population pressure), differences in livestock resources, and the effects of natural hazards or irrigation. Skeldon found that the migration transition was more advanced in the better endowed villages. Residents of such communities were generally aware of a shortage of land (and of the advantages of urban living), whereas residents of some more traditional communities were not. Where *Indios* outnumbered *mestizos* by a large ratio (for example, nine to one) migration began much later.

What is the relationship of migration patterns from Chilca to this migration model? In 1964, Chilca seems to have been in a transition between phases B and C in Figure 14.1. 'Seasonal' pendular migration to the Urubamba Valley and *tierra caliente* still occurred, although semi-permanent local migration was common and a few long-distance, semi-permanent or permanent

Table 14.1 Chilca 1979: migration network

Households with no relatives residing elsewhere	18
Households with at least one relative residing elsewhere	34
Total	52

	Destination of Migrant					
	Lima	*Cuzco*	*Arequipa*	*Tropical valleys**	*Elsewhere*	*Total*
Number of households	24	12	4	2	2	44
Number of people	72	18	4	2	4	100

* Both in Quillabamba.

migrants moved to Lima. By 1979, however, it was close to phase D, with many long-distance, permanent migrants to Lima (see Table 14.1).

Travel over considerable distances has long been commonplace in Cuzco Department: trade in *chuño*, potatoes and beans to the sub-tropical valleys to obtain the narcotic *coca* in return dates from the 1920s, and in some villages dates back to the nineteenth century. In the 1920s and 1930s, seasonal movements and circular migration of up to three months involved trade and often a few days' labouring in Cuzco on the way, or on construction of the railway line to Cuzco. Movement to Lima was under way from some communities by the 1940s.[4] In general, in 1964 people left the village to seek cash income to supplement the subsistence production of the household; a commitment to a Redfieldian rural, peasant lifestyle was still dominant, although signs of urbanisation influence were becoming strong. By 1979, Chilca had moved a good way from the situation in 1964, when 48 out of 50 heads of households had stated that the village was a good place in which to live. By this time, the group of traditional peasants for whom migration was not a realistic, conscious option had shrunk greatly; only 35 per cent of the sample had no family member residing outside Chilca. As Lerner (1958) points out, the traditional peasant accepts, he does not have an opinion. The remainder, however, seemed to be at a stage of making carefully calculated decisions about whether to migrate or to remain in the village.

Part of the 'secularisation' process that affects traditional societies undergoing change is the dissociation of economic from social and political aspects of life. Such a dissociation is an intrinsic part of the process by which people not only acquire greater awareness of and familiarity with the outside world, but also experience a change in cognition. It also appears to accompany greater 'psychic mobility', or an increase in empathy.[5]

By 1979, Chilca was enmeshed even further in the wider economy and the life of the nation. As Table 14.1 shows, 65 per cent of the households in the sample had at least one family member living elsewhere; many had several migrants. Moreover, more than half of the families who had no migrants had only young children (who were being educated at the village school) or no children at all. As many as 100 people, or 38 per cent, were living outside Chilca permanently or semi-permanently, out of a total population of 266 in the 52 households. Furthermore, the movement of people was overwhelmingly part of the process of urbanisation, for 95 per cent of the migrants had moved to cities. And the pull of the largest urban 'pole' had dominated, for 72 per cent had moved to Lima, 18 per cent to Cuzco and 4 per cent to Arequipa.

While the role of migrants and their significance to the household economy varied considerably, remittances were received by 14 families and were an important component in total household income for seven households. Even where migrants sent no remittances, peasants from Chilca might visit them in their city home, and migrants' trips back to the village and letter writing maintained an important and continuing kinship link. Reciprocity was characteristic: in return for the receipt of a few hundred *soles* with each letter three or four times a year, villagers despatched *encomiendas* of potatoes, maize or other produce.

Economically, the migrants fill an important niche in the modern capitalist economy, enabling resources to be funnelled back to the village to supplement meagre local resources. Culturally they provide a direct channel for the dissemination of new ideas, values and tastes back to the peasant village. From the migrants' viewpoint, the continuing link with relatives in Chilca represents an investment in a broader sense, maintaining a place to which they can return.

Skeldon shows the intimate link between education and migration, in that schooling creates new aspirations. It often leads to income expectations that can be fulfilled only outside the village and primarily in cities, and schools disseminate information about job opportunities in towns and the urban way of life in general. But migration and education (in its broader sense) are mutually reinforcing processes, for migration aids the spread and acceptance of education.

Thus, Indian peasants in the community who have a largely self-contained household economy and share a relatively traditional culture have the lowest levels of literacy, schooling, empathy and awareness of the wider world. People higher up the social ladder, at the middle or rich peasant rungs, are more oriented towards *cholo* and ultimately *mestizo* values and less towards traditional Indian culture; they are also more literate, more likely to speak Spanish, more likely to possess a radio and are more aware of cities, of job opportunities outside the village and of the wider world. They appear to possess more empathy, which is both a cause and consequence of these mutually reinforcing factors.

The correlation between the traditional, relatively closed social system, and poverty, illiteracy and monolingualism is shown in Table 14.2. On the other hand, the rich peasant groups and middle peasants have a higher percentage of literacy. Their exposure to media and to the outside world is greater than the traditional, poor peasantry, and accordingly their empathy and awareness of employment opportunities are likely to be greater.

Skeldon's work is an important explanation of the spatial and temporal movements of people in a modernising peasant society. It is a step towards (but stops well short of) being a theory of social change. He does not explicitly recognise the cultural dimension differentiating stages in the migration transition, and fails to relate spatial mobility to upward social mobility – the cholofication process – with which it is usually associated.

In the light of Skeldon's model, it is interesting to compare the five socio-economic 'groups' of peasants in Chilca with respect to their propensity to migrate. In Table 14.3 the average number of migrants per household is given for each of the five groups. In line with Skeldon's model, the two rather richer (and more literate and aware) groups have more migrants per family than the middle peasants, and a relatively low percentage of households with no migrants. On the other hand, the very poor households have a lower number of migrants in comparison with

Table 14.2 Class level, literacy, education and out-migration (Percentage of households or persons in each socio-economic class, or mean figures, Chilca, 1979)

Literacy (per cent)		*Some years of schooling (per cent)*		*Speak Spanish (per cent)*		*Per cent functioning ratio*	*Mean income of households* (soles)	*Mean number of migrants per household*
Head of Household	*Wife*	*Head*	*Wife*	*Head*	*Wife*			
RICH PEASANTS								
71	16	71	16	83	16	71	195 942	1.7
MODERATELY RICH PEASANTS								
90	10	90	10	90	20	80	51 013	1.4
MIDDLE PEASANTS								
60	10	60	20	50	10	60	38 354	1.2
POOR PEASANTS								
36	16	36	25	36	16	69	23 677	3.1
VERY POOR PEASANTS								
40	18	40	18	40	18	36	4 890	1.5

Table 14.3 Number of migrants and socio-economic class

Socio-economic group	*Number of migrants, mean per household*	*Percentage of households in group with no migrants*
Rich group	1.9	12.5
Moderately rich	1.6	33
Middle peasant	1.2	45
Poor	3.1	31
Very poor	1.5	45

the rich group. However, there appears to be an anomaly in the high rate of migration (at 3.1, the highest of all groups) from the poor peasant group. It would seem that 'push' factors might be relevant for these people who experience a chronic shortage of resources.

'Push' factors prompting people to leave an overstretched *minifundio* system might be expected to relieve population pressure somewhat, but it is interesting to note that of the approximately 80 people who left Chilca between 1959 and 1964, about half were landowners and many of these had sufficient resources to ensure sustenance for their families (that is, the same characteristics as most 1979 migrants). It seems likely, therefore, that 'pull' factors combined with 'push' factors were, in most cases, probably more decisive in explaining the motivation to migrate. In the late 1960s and 1970s, however, as people from Chilca began to occupy *hacienda* and co-operative land and avoid eviction, the pressure of 'push' factors seems to have diminished.

What is the effect of out-migration from Chilca on social mobility? Since to be an Indian peasant is to be on the lowest rung in society, migration in search of any occupation virtually implies some ascent on the social scale and an attempt to improve living standards. The most frequent jobs gained by out-migrants in the city were domestic servants or labourers, but the range of jobs was considerable, including a number of semi-skilled and skilled occupations. Some girls left Chilca at marriage and accompanied their husbands to the city. Up to 1979 at least, these attempts usually met with some success as the life of peasantry was left behind.

The largest group of migrants became students, which had the potential of giving them the best means of acquiring employment. Although many observers have seen the link between schooling and rising expectations, the connection needs to be examined in depth as Hazen (1974) has done in the *altiplano*. Although Skeldon recognised the importance of awareness for migrants, he did not see that awareness is closely linked to empathy – 'the lubricant which facilitates the modernisation process' – in which literacy, mass media exposure and other variables alter a person's traditional lifestyle. Empathy can prise loose mentalities from the closed world of the subsistence household economy and traditional culture. The polar types are represented in the withdrawn, shy, subservient *encogido* and the thrusting, confident and enterprising *entrón*. The more advanced the secularisation process, the more conscious the choice which will guide the peasants' decision-making and the closer the individual comes to the point at which he or she will opt to become a *cholo*.

We have already referred briefly to some of these qualities in describing some types of peasant, but since we argue that the modernisation process creates appropriate personality types which represent important niches in the transition from traditional Indian peasantry to modern capitalistic roles, the characteristics need to be clearly set out. Case studies of actual individuals suggest the elements of ideal types that serve as poles in the social change process.

ENCOGIDO AND *ENTRÓN* PERSONALITIES

In the course of fieldwork, we can see how culture and personality are inter-related in real life situations. *Encogido* types avoid persons of higher status, except for social brokers who provide patronage, and they invariably adhere to customs which stereotype them, maintaining a lowly self-image which is adapted to their social position. These qualities have, however, usually been described in cross-cultural situations involving *mestizos* or powerful outsiders, or in market, urban-industrial situations. The probability remains that in a purely Quechua, traditional situation where the peasant feels completely at home, different and more out-going qualities might be evident. Nevertheless, most situations involving development or urbanisation are characterised by market opportunities, commercial situations, the possibility of change and the introduction of various Western criteria. In remote, small villages where the palaeotechnic ecotype reigns supreme, many *encogido* peasants can be observed.

Clearly *encogidos* accept their situation. They do not compare life as a peasant with a possible alternative life in the town or city. As they are not literate and probably speak very little Spanish, their awareness of the outside world is very limited. The process of secularisation has not yet proceeded very far for such individuals: a livelihood of subsistence agriculture, supplemented perhaps by craft making and unskilled wage labouring and the nurturing culture of the little community have provided enough security, a life sufficiently satisfying and meaningful. The old peasant order has changed little, the older order of priorities is unaltered, the possibility of hunger still exists and peasant values dominate.

The *entrón* is the polar opposite of the *encogido* personality (Hagen, 1964). We have described an upward thrusting, socially mobile individual in the person of Justo Quispe. The *entrón* is often a leader, keen to try innovations, to experiment with new seeds, new crops and new techniques. He or she is enterprising and outward-looking and, while still retaining a sense of the value of communal unity and solidarity, is also keen for the community to progress. Laziness and drunkenness are despised; hard work and enterprise are admired.

An *encogido–entrón* dichotomy has been criticised as an ethnocentric, Western-biased conceptualisation. There can be little doubt, however, that the two types represent polar opposites on a continuum, and empirical examples are readily identifiable. Traditional peasants in remote areas of the contemporary Sierra approximate the *encogido* syndrome, and while only a small number are fully *entrón*, most are placed somewhere between the two, usually lying closer to one or other pole.[6] To some extent personality types reflect the cultural situation which surrounds the peasantry, and as social change proceeds they will alter accordingly.

Indeed, one is reminded of Oscar Lewis's (1964 and 1967) classic account of the peasant Pedro Martinez, whose life was stirred by the great events of the Mexican Revolution. The story of Felipe, the son of Pedro Martinez, is centred on the conflict between old and new ways. Influenced by ideas unleashed by the

Revolution and modernisation, he adopted a new religion and acquired education, humble though it may have been. However, the old peasant lifestyle in which his father, as head of the household, was boss, dominated: he seemed destined for a future toiling in the fields. The result was a decision to abandon the fields for urban life, a move that was followed by the other children in the family. In the life of Felipe, urbanisation can be seen as an interplay between Revolutionary ideology, personality type and peasant culture, leading to abandonment of peasant life and migration to the city. The situation in the Peruvian Andes is broadly similar.

15 Mobilisation of the Peasantry

PEASANT MOVEMENTS[1]

Power has always included the components of violence and consent. While the violence imposed by rulers has, at times, been so overwhelming that it has annihilated civilisations, the consent of the ruled to their domination is sometimes an even stronger element in the nature of power.[2] The numerous variations of patron–client relationship in Peru probably express not only regional and historical differences in the relative force of the various institutions of the Conquest, but also the varied ways in which Indian communities evolved their own sub-cultures of repression.

Since the Conquest, three other tactics have been followed by Indian peasants in their struggle with domination and alienation: flight to inhospitable areas, ambivalent behaviour, and revolt. This chapter considers peasant revolt, involving social mobilisation, unionisation, protest and growing class solidarity.

Since the Peruvian Revolution of 1968–75, burgeoning interest in peasant mobilisation has led to the discovery that many apparently quiescent populations had revolted in the past, and studies have revived knowledge of nearly forgotten events.[3]

Many historians have explained these revolts, and the more famous ones led by Tupac Amaru in the late eighteenth century and by Juan Bustamente in the 1860s, almost solely in terms of the objective conditions of exploitation and cruel oppression which the Indians suffered. But, as several scholars have shown, a messianic or millenarian aspect was closely associated with the violent response of peasants to injustice and exploitation.[4] The strength of this interpretation is reinforced by the particular measures adopted by the Spaniards to stamp out revolts. These involved a policy of ethnocide against Andean culture and Inca practices.

In the 1970s the revolutionary government used Tupac Amaru II's name, portrait and pronouncements to give credibility to its stand on the peasantry and land reform. Throughout the Andes, many colourful posters displayed Tupac's stern face and carried the message: '*Campesino, el patron no comera mas de su probreza*' ('Peasant, the landlord will no longer live off your poverty').

Recent peasant social mobilisation has been admirably documented by Handelman (1975). The growing instability and fluidity in the countryside reached a stage that he described as 'social effervescence'. The widespread nature and range of peasant movements in Cuzco and the neighbouring department of Apurimac since 1945 are shown in Table 15.1, which is a chronology of organisation and action by peasant groups involving 40 events between 1945 and 1978. The leading role of the Anta region in peasant mobilisation in the two departments, and indeed in the nation as a whole, is evident in the fact that 35 of the events occurred in Cuzco Department and 10 of these in Anta. While the table mainly marks the steps in founding various *campesino* syndicates or constituting new groups and federations of syndicates, it also documents the struggle to recover legally the ownership of lands lost to expanding *haciendas*, the authorisation in La Convención of the eight-hour working day, strikes in 1960 against gratuitous work for *hacendados*, strikes for the liquidation of archaic feudal services and numerous incidents of reoccupation of lands. The table also notes several events between 1962 and 1964 in which a total of 86 peasants were killed in the course of the struggle.

The peasant movements of the early 1960s depended on the enfeeblement of the *patrón* and the spread of modern capitalism and liberalism on the one hand,[5] and on the condition of the peasantry and their perception of their status on the other. Clearly, there must be a certain social milieu to allow the rise of such movements: when the local landed elite begins to lose its grip, usually because of larger economic or political circumstances, peasant activism often springs up rather quickly.

At this time peasant unions were formed throughout the Southern Highlands, and especially in Cuzco, in both *hacienda* communities and in free *comunidades*. The *colonos* demanded better working conditions and their principal tactic was strike action, while the *comuneros* sought the return of communal lands usurped by expanding *haciendas* and their weapon was land invasion. It has been estimated that over 300 000 peasants were involved and at least 114 *haciendas* were invaded; it was certainly the largest peasant mobilisation in recent Latin American history.[6]

Table 15.1 Chronology of the organisation and mobilisation of the peasantry in Cuzco and Apurimac (1945–78)

Date	*Place*	*Province*	*Department*	*Organisation*	*Mobilisation*	*Others*
1945	Lauramarca	Quispicanchis	Cuzco		Recovery of lands	
1948	H. Honorura	La Convención	"		Authorisation of 8-hour working day	
1948	Maranura	"	"	First Syndicate of Peasants		
1948	H. Churo	Paucartambo	"	" " " "		First Sat. Huillca
1949	Manahuañunca	Cuzco	"	" " " "		
1949	San Jerónimo	"	"	" " " "		
1949	Lauramarca	Quispicanchis	"		Recovery of lands	
1951	Maranura	La Convención	"		1st meeting of peasants	
1958	Quillabamba	"	"	Foundation of Federation of Syndicates of Peasants of La Convención and Lares		
1958	Lauramarca	Quispicanchis	"	Constitution of Peasant Syndicates		First Miguel Turpo
1958	Cuzco	Cuzco	"		Meeting with peasant party	Death R. Huaman
1960	Pachac Grande	La Convención	"		Strike against gratuitous work	
1960	Chancamayo	"	"		" "	
1960	Chaupimayo	"	"		" "	
1961	Cuzco	Cuzco	"	Foundation of Cuzco Peasant Federation	First regional peasant convention	First Sumira
1961		La Convención	"	Cuzco Peasant Federation and Lares	General strike	
1962	Echarate	"	"		Strike for liquidation of archaic feudal	

					commitments	
1962	Pujyura	〃	〃		(as above)	
1962	H. Sullucuyoc	〃	〃		〃 〃	
1962	H. Chaullay	〃	〃		〃 〃	43 peasant deaths
1963	Ccapacmarca	Quispicanchis	〃		Recovery of lands	3 peasant deaths
1963	Ongoy	Andahuaylas	Apurimac		〃 〃	15 peasant deaths
1963	H. Minabamba	Quispicanchis	Cuzco		〃 〃	7 peasant deaths
1963	Cuzco	Cuzco	〃		General strike	
1964	Huarocondo	Anta	〃		Recovery of lands	1 peasant death
1964	Sicuani	Canchis	〃		〃 〃	17 peasant deaths
1973	Andahuaylas	Andahuaylas	Apurimac	Foundation of regional peasant syndicate	Recovery of lands	1st Nauto
1974	Cocharcas	〃	〃		〃 〃 〃	Occupation 13 h.
1974	Andarapa, Pacucha	〃	〃		〃 〃 〃	〃 7 〃
1974	Chincheros	〃	〃		〃 〃 〃	〃 11 〃
1976	Equeco Chacán	Anta	Cuzco		〃 〃 〃	Occupation Tupac Amaru II
1977	Equico Chacán	〃	〃	Constitute regional peasant syndicate		
1977	Huayllacocha	〃	〃		Recovery of lands	Recovery 700 hectares
1977	Chaquilcasa	〃	〃		〃 〃 〃	〃 120 〃
1977	Quewar	〃	〃		〃 〃 〃	〃 350 〃
1977	Pinacay	〃	〃		〃 〃 〃	〃 300 〃
1977	Conchacalla	〃	〃		〃 〃 〃	〃 2198 〃
1977	Tambo Real	〃	〃		〃 〃 〃	〃 180 〃
1977	Anta	〃	〃		〃 〃 〃	〃 2000 〃
1978	Cuzco	Cuzco	〃	III Congress Cuzco Peasant Federation		

Notes: H. = Hacienda

Source: *Sur*, Año 1, No. 5 (August 1978).

CHILCA AND PEASANT MOBILISATION

My main findings were that the peasantry was *not* an undifferentiated mass. Furthermore my findings completely support Alavi's view[7] that the real question is not whether or not the peasants are revolutionary, but under what circumstances they become revolutionary and what roles different sections of the peasantry play in revolutionary situations.

Before my arrival in Chilca in 1964, the middle peasants had clearly been 'active' peasants and indeed revolutionary since they were involved in the land invasion of nearby *haciendas* in 1962. In 1964, however, following severe repression, they presented many of the attributes of a classic passive peasantry (Chapter 6), and only a few pieces of evidence suggested that this was not the whole truth. Later in the 1970s, they again became revolutionary and highly 'active'. In short, the issue of whether they were basically active or passive must be viewed in terms of the changing relationship between the community and the wielders of power in the local region. It is a matter of situation-analysis, including the changing power relationship between an emboldened peasantry at the time of a weakening elite, alternating with a repressed peasantry when renewed power is asserted by the local or national authorities.

Of critical importance as well is whether or not the national government chooses to support the local elite in the face of the challenge by a strong solidarity movement of peasants. While later the entire Peruvian Army was at times deployed to snuff out some local uprisings, Presidents Odría and Belaúnde were sometimes intent on gaining political capital or international support, and so denied guns to the local *hacendados*. The point is that such small-scale movements did more good for Peru's international standing than they did harm to the actual balance of power.[8]

We have seen, however, that the ability of the middle peasantry in Chilca (the only potential revolutionary group) was severely circumscribed in 1979. Although the village would and did take part in land invasions, the village had not yet reached the stage of accepting specialised roles (see Chapter 12). Multiplex roles dominated, and although Victor, as part of the moral community, possessed some influence both as a would-be revolutionary and as a moderniser, the social distance between him

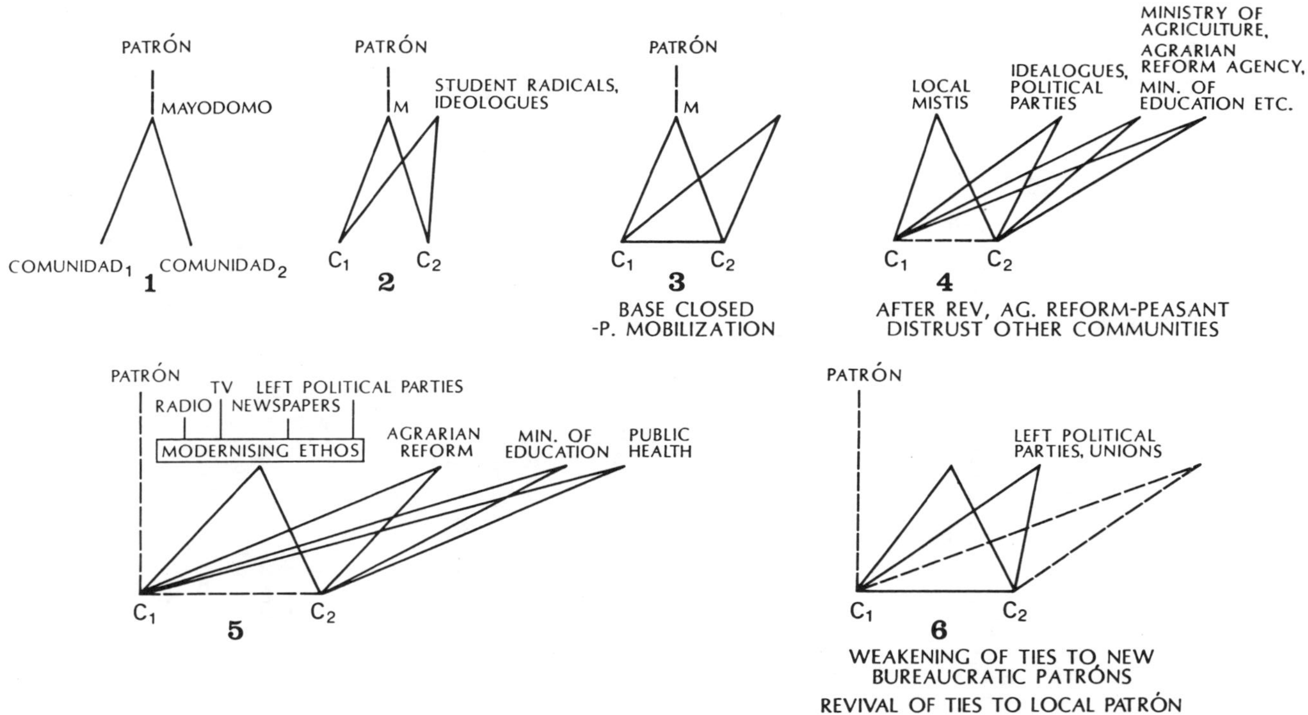

Figure 15.1 SEQUENCE OF PATTERNS OF PEASANT MOBILISATION

and other villagers was great and prevented him from achieving social mobilisation.

The sequence of patterns of peasant mobilisation is shown in Figure 15.1 through a series of diagrams of triangles without bases. The discovery of new apexes to the triangle in the form of new, external *patrones*, enables communities to lessen their ties to the traditional *patrón*, weakening his position. 'Closing the base of the triangle' (stage 3) signifies peasant mobilisation and a feeling of class solidarity. Peru in 1990 can be exemplified by stages 4–6, with often a revival of distrust for other communities, and disillusion with bureaucratic *patrones*.

AUTOBIOGRAPHY OF A GUERRILLA LEADER[9]

> I was born in 1935 . . . the son of a bourgeois father who owned *haciendas*. He abandoned my [peasant] mother.
>
> [At that time] the famous executioner Perdiz Nuñez del Prado and [his brother] Benjamin Nuñez del Prado were in charge of the first settlement of the *selva* at Cosñipata. [They] were in charge of finding husbands and wives for the settlement and [recruiting] people from different provinces. Seventy per cent of migrants didn't return. If they didn't die of diseases, they died of the [arduous nature] of the work or were shot or abused. The brothers Nuñez del Prado brought people, especially from Paucartambo Province. People who didn't pay debts are sent to the Valle[10] and people didn't return. In that time people were brought, including my mother and people who weren't 16 years old [legal age for accepting work]. [My] mother escaped by [following] a muleteers' trail to Paucartambo.
>
> Hacienda Ccachipita was despoiled by [its] owner Jose Fernandez – while I was a boy it was invaded by *colonos*. [My] mother became a *politico* – there was tension between my parents, [and] my father took me away from my mother several times. [My] mother had suffered from abuses at Cosñipata that had killed many of her comrades.
>
> At school, the teacher had his favourites; the children of *hacendados* [sat] in one row, the rest, including myself [sat] behind and were despised.

At that stage my struggle began, but I didn't have the comfort of syndicalism or freedom of Marxism to comfort myself. I was punished a lot. At that time Apristas walked around at night[11] and I talked about the canings [I suffered]. When I was 14 or 15, about 1949–50, one man in particular influenced me; he [took] charge of a group of people supporting Haya de la Torre. I left school in the second grade of primary school.

I continued working for my father in the country and came to know Communist groups in Paucartambo [about 1952] headed by Cesar Vilchez. A lot of people joined secretly, including an uncle of mine. I accompanied him to meetings and listened to what they said about the Russian Revolution. They spoke of Lenin, Marx and Stalin. Then I started to study all the books – especially books on Russia.

I left my father's [*hacienda*] and rented 20 hectares of land on a property in Pucara. At this time, 1959–60, a rumour began that I had formed a syndicate to struggle against the *hacendados* and I listened to a lot of stories about abuses and the people wanted me to see all the abuses (I had seen them already in my father) committed by this *gamonal* Oscar Fernandez, which my mother had talked about and suffered. In my mind I saw everything in a mirror and I thought of doing something for my *campesino* brothers in their lifetimes.

In Pucara I lived almost beside the [peasants] but I had no one to leave my house and income to. I was a bachelor. Then I decided to get a wife to love. Later in 1960 I travelled to Cuzco and searched for [two of the first syndicate organisers] to ask for help [to form syndicates]. Many years earlier they had gone out to form syndicates in Paucartambo [they had only established them in Lauramarca]. [A few organisers] in Paucartambo were in a state of litigation with the Haciendas Sispascancha, Alta and Baja. Peasants asked that the [place] be recognised *not* as a *hacienda* but as a *comunidad* and that the same situation [also should apply] to Hacienda Churo.

The communities of the Districts of Qolquepata and Cuycuy were converted into *haciendas* by the brothers Nuñez del Prado because they had 'carte blanche' with the Government and had orders to send the people of the communities to the *Valle*. The majority never returned. Through fear, the people of *comunidades* became *colonos* on *haciendas* so they would have a *patrón* to save them from being sent to the *Valle* and this [surplus value from the additional labour] helped many *gamonales* to buy their land, at the same time converting *comuneros* into *colonos*. This applied to Churo, Sullapata, Videochoni, Kica, Ccototoclla and Miramarca and many others. [We] began to demand that these *haciendas* be declared new communities as this would be less inflammatory. Each year more and more communities reclaimed their rights as their own *comunidades* and some continued as *haciendas*.

In the year 1960 when I intervened I met in litigation of this type Saturnino Huillca, initiator and director of the community in Haciendas Sispascancha, Alta and Baja, which was leaning [for support] on the Federación Departmental de Trabajadores. In this situation the Federación Departmental de Campesinos de Cuzco [FDCC] was formed in 1961, with Eduardo Sumire Huillca as General Secretary. Then the initiation [of syndicate organisation] was established for the peasantry and in an assembly I was named as the delegate of the Province of Paucartambo to the FDCC, [charged] with promoting the organisation of syndicates in Paucartambo, dealing rapidly with reproofs, accusations such as detentions [of peasants], denunciations of agitators, sometimes sending [messages] from Paucartambo to the Prefecture of Cuzco, sometimes to the Police, and at other times to the 5th Region [Headquarters] of Police.

[This gave me breathing space] and liberty for intervals at times of two days, eight days or sometimes a month before more repression was suffered. Repression [led us to] organise syndicates, for then our work was to demand and denounce against the patrons to the Judge – [for example] for work for which the *hacendado* had promised to pay 1 *sol* 50 *centavos* but then didn't comply. At this time [1964], the Ley de Reforma Agraria [Belaúnde's law] was authorised [enabling] an infinity of memoranda denouncing all the abuses of the *gamonales*, and so I succeeded in organising a Provincial Assembly of [syndicate organisers]. [A list of twelve syndicates and names of their directors follows.]

These syndicates [were] the first organised in Paucartambo. The rest lacked organisation. The 14 directors constituted a Federación Provincial de Campesinos de Paucartambo [which had the objective] of dealing with repression and abuses in the

Province. They called for a meeting of *campesinos* of the Province on 22 December 1962. But it had to be co-ordinated with the directors of the different federations such as the President of the University of Cuzco, and comrades of the Federación de Trabajadores . . . and others of the Federación de Campesinos de Quillabamba . . . and many others of the FDCC.

They gave an invitation to different *campesino* sectors to attend the meeting and to assist obligatorily all those *campesinos* of Paucartambo who had not yet organised [to attend] [for whatever reason] . . . some for reasons of fear of the *patrón*. But the announcement of the great *campesino* meeting 'spread an electric current' which each one commented on in his own way, and some said this day would be a day of deaths and assaults and that it was the end of the *gamonales*. The drunks in some stores said that if we were to become like white dogs and have to kill, this would contribute even more to the protest of the peasantry. Meanwhile I personally worked with different co-ordinators in the countryside and in the city of Cuzco.

On their part the *gamonales* headed by . . . the Sub-Prefect of the Province did what was possible to cause our great meeting to fail. They made an infinity of scurrilous accusations to incite all the population of the town not to allow our meeting to take place, because they said that on that day the Indians were going to assault [property] and pilfer everything in the shops.

Then in the town a meeting was held by the Sub-Prefect who denounced me and said everything was my responsibility and then sent a memorandum to the Prefect in Cuzco with two signatures requesting that the meeting be banned. A complaint was made by an official of the Frente Liberación Nacional [FLN] which was a political party which comprised lawyers of the Federación [presumably FDCC] and others. I had to live in secrecy because of the many accusations [made about me] and [my concern] about the FLN [which was] headed by Dr Jacinto Caceres [right wing] in Paucartambo, and Dr Ferdinand Cuadros.

[They were to carry out an investigation] by 10 December revoking an assembly of the FLN party and they invited me and Eduardo Sumire. Since we knew the problem and the wishes of these señors, we went and assisted. The leaders of the debate asked for a report to be commissioned. J. Caceres was from Paucartambo and in his report which was supported by the people of Paucartambo and the Society of Artisans of Paucartambo, [they declared they] didn't want such a [peasant] meeting. They accused me of being a delinquent because of the activity then [occurring] in Paucartambo – not even in dreams did they know of [the scale or nature] of the protest meeting which was to be held for the first time in the history of Paucartambo. Caceres' report accused me and [tried] to frustrate the announced meeting. In this case I did not want to participate if the FLN [as a whole] did not participate.

Then I protested and immediately talked with Eduardo Sumire, leaving the assembly when we did not wish to be bound [by its conclusions]. But we left because the next day, 21st, we had to be in the Prefecture [in Cuzco] for discussions on permission for the meeting. Even more I was worried [about] the amount of work on my *chacra* which had been abandoned and the poultry left to the [attention] of my wife [who suffered] delicate health. On 16 November 1962 my son was born in solitude since we were not married, with another woman delivering the baby [and complications occurred]. We had a lot of problems and at the same time did not have enough money. Next day I went to get a person to look after my wife and then was struggling to save the meeting and the constitution of the Federation.

At the meeting at the Prefecture, the Prefect showed me the memorial presented by the Sub-Prefect and the *pueblo* stating that the meeting should not be held, for whatever reason. All this time [we] raised many points over two hours to convince them about the meeting in order to gain authorisation. In the end we got permission under the following conditions:

1. That I promised to accept responsibility for whatever happened during the meeting.
2. The Prefect guaranteed that the armed police would stay away during the meeting to prevent any reaction of the *campesinos* who thought of them as enemies – if they thought they were being watched.

Afterwards the Prefect telegraphed the Sub-Prefect telling him the meeting was authorised. This fell like a disaster on the

Sub-Prefect as he had been assured that he had achieved success and that there wasn't going to be a meeting. [Indeed they] had recently notified the people that. At the same time they did not delay in assuring all the shopowners about the mobs around the town, that they should take care over their things, they should hide their eggs and some maybe their money, believing that [during] this meeting even assaults, etc. [might occur]. From the day of the meeting, some [storekeepers] stayed locked in their shops with shotguns.

When we gained authorisation all the directors from the different Federations travelled to Paucartambo in a truck. [We] took an express truck at 3 p.m. but were kept at the Guardia Civil control post at San Jerónimo and on seeing this we called by phone to Dr Ferdinand Cuadros who sent us the written order of the Prefect and [presented us] with three bottles of rum, cakes and sweets, inviting us to proceed by road to Paucartambo. [We did so], singing some Cuban protest songs and joking a little on the [circumstances of the permit], and at about 10 p.m. arrived at Paucartambo and then slept in the truck since we did not have any houses in the town where we could sleep.

On the following day, 22 December, we began walking in groups like visitors going through the town for the first time, wanting to look and walk. Naturally the streets were silent, the shops closed and people walking (non-Indian) were quite nervous.

At this time, around 9 a.m., it was full of groups of *campesinos* who came from high altitudes playing cornets and drums of pig skins. [Peasants had come] from the southwest, others from the north, also the high lands of Tahuanpata, and also from the east, the *campesinos* of Llaycho. It looked like an army of *campesinos* arriving, commanded by Melquiades Huaman, director of the FDCC and a native of Urubamba. Women carried stones and the men slings. Approximately 2000 *campesinos* [arrived]. [They] went into the building of the Society of Artisans for a list of the syndicates assisting and other communities and *haciendas* participating. A rumour [spread] that those who didn't participate would be declared 'yellow' [traitors] – enemies of the *campesino* – and their animals would be confiscated. The list showed 110 *comunidades* participated and later at 12 o'clock everyone assembled in the Plaza de

> Armas and each group expressed their protests using papers, and small Peruvian flags and posters were brought with the signs '*Tierra o Muerta – Mueran los gamonales*' ('Land or Death – Death to the landlords'). At the head of the demonstration was the Syndicate of Carpapampa including women and children and I was directing. They filled the Plaza and put a wool bale on a pile of stones and *adobe* bricks that they had made in a corner of the Plaza near a shop doorway. From here each orator denounced the infinity of abuses and injustices and we installed a microphone [so we could] sing national songs.

While the above extracts from Domingo Cruz's autobiography are not always coherent, they are interesting in that they express the views of an important peasant leader and organiser. There is a self-conscious quality about the material and a feeling that the author is taking part – and a leading part at that – in a very significant social movement. There is little doubt that the 1960–2 peasant movements in Cuzco Department and in Paucartambo Province are of historic importance in the struggle for peasant and Indian rights, and it is thoroughly understandable that the climax at the peasant assembly was seen as a great triumph and symbol of the peasant awakening, a striking illustration of what might be gained by peasant solidarity.

While the influence of communist 'Russia' and Cuba appear to have played some part in the evolution of this would-be revolutionary, the overwhelmingly important factors were experiences affecting his family, class and region. The account is strongly charged with a sense of outrage at the cruel exploitation of his mother and other peasants who had to submit to harsh, inhuman treatment and oppression in undertaking forced labour in the *tierra caliente*, under conditions that most often led to death. Although he does not specifically say so, it seems clear he understood that the underlying forces motivating this callous treatment sprang from the expansion in the 1930s of an inhuman, rapacious capitalism that was determined to establish (at low economic cost) cashcropping in the virgin areas of this region. The tension between his parents and his treatment as an inferior at school added to his bitterness and his growing feelings of deprivation. Increasingly, he saw his father as heartless. Although he remained on his father's *hacienda* for some years after committing himself to left-wing solutions, it is clear that he rejected his father both on personal grounds (for the treatment of his mother, and perhaps of himself) and on class grounds (as a bourgeois, whom he saw abusing or exploiting the peasants).

What is significant in the account is the strong class-based nature of the analysis. Although Cruz would be categorised as a 'rich peasant', he aligned himself with his mother and saw himself as a peasant. He shows an awareness based on class that the inhuman brutality of the behaviour, whether instigated by labour recruiters and directors (who in some cases were notorious figures in their own right) or by *hacendados*, was motivated by changes occurring in Paucartambo Province and in the neighbouring tropical lowlands. Paucartambo served as a convenient labour reservoir that made possible the opening up of new virgin lands. Whatever the cost might be in terms of human suffering,[12] the economic cost was very low, given the great power of the local elite (and the disinterest of a distant government) to enforce their wishes, whether by direct force, threats and punishment or through guile by techniques such as *enganche*. Yet such a process of capitalist expansion not only led to colonisation and agricultural expansion in the *selva*, but also reworked and fundamentally altered the nature of master–servant relationships in Paucartambo. To escape the fate of being sent to work in the *selva*, peasants increasingly sought to become *colonos* on *haciendas*, subordinating themselves in new relationships in exchange for patronage and protection from labour recruitment. The above account is valuable in describing this changing relationship between *comunidades* and *colonos*, and the changing nature of *haciendas* in the 1930s and 1940s.

The autobiography makes it clear that great stress was placed on organisation as the key to growing class consciousness and solidarity. Although the great mass of peasants involved were illiterate, the organisers regarded as very important the forming of unions or syndicates with lists of members and proper constitutions. While part of the importance of constitutions to the Indian peasants might have been symbolic, cementing solidarity, the organisers placed considerable faith in the national system of law and of legislation, as tools in the struggle to obtain justice.

The whole struggle is depicted in class terms against the abuses and repression of the *gamonales*. (It is interesting that this word is used more often in the account than the word *patrón*.

Gamonal implies in its Peruvian sense, as we have noted above, an accumulator of land.[13]) The account details the growing alliance of individual syndicates with others in Paucartambo Province and the careful and successful attempts to secure lateral support and alliances not only with peasant syndicates at the department level (FDCC), but also with urban workers and university students at Cuzco. As the struggle moves towards its climax, there is a growing polarisation between the peasantry, seeking their 22 December assembly, and the increasingly nervous and frightened townspeople of Paucartambo, comprising mainly petit bourgeois *cholos*, and some lower middle-class *mestizos*. However, it is interesting to note that at the climax in the town plaza, when the possibility of confrontation and bloodshed was perhaps still imminent, the Indians asserted their nationalism, that they were Peruanos (an implicit appeal for recognition and redress of their differences).[14] And again there was the classic peasant cry: 'Land or Death'.

Finally, it is interesting to see that the Prefect in Cuzco and some of the authorities and lawyers who appear to have been involved in the dispute adopted responsible and reasonably impartial roles. By 1962, it is clear that the provincial authorities could no longer be accused of being the stooges of a powerful, self-interested elite.

It is important, however, to view the peasant triumph of 22 December 1962 in perspective. Although nearly 20 years later *haciendas* no longer existed and the abuses of the *gamonales* had passed, peasantry as a social type persisted with few signs of impending dissolution. Today poverty and social humiliation continue. Moreover, in spite of his victory in 1962, in 1979 Domingo Cruz felt like a hunted man, living a precarious existence in daily fear of arrest by the authorities. This situation continued in spite of the evident goodwill or even magnanimity that large numbers of middle-class people felt towards peasants by this time. (Most urban middle-class people were probably largely indifferent to the fate of the peasantry.) Although serious discrimination and exploitation continued, especially through the paternalism of the new bureaucrats and the petty malevolence of *vecinos* and other lower-class rural people, in the isolated fastnesses of the Andes where the palaeotechnic ecotype was little disturbed, the defence mechanisms of the traditional communities and the ongoing strength of peasant culture enabled peasantry to persist.

SENDERO LUMINOSO AND THE PEASANTRY

The outbreak of guerrilla warfare in Ayacucho in 1980 which escalated into a civil war by 1982 demonstrates the most extreme form of peasant mobilisation and the major threat that a deprived peasantry can pose when organised by committed intellectual leaders who employ excellent hit-and-run guerrilla tactics.

Not a great deal is known about the philosophy, goals and origin of Sendero Luminoso[15] because of the secrecy of the organisation, the isolation of the peasant communities, and the militarisation of the affected zones. It is argued by Degregori (1988 and 1989) that Sendero Luminoso has arisen in a region where traditional power was based not only on a monopoly of the means of production but also on a monopoly of knowledge and manipulation in the domination of an ignorant, illiterate Indian peasantry. The ideology arose from interaction between an intellectual *mestizo* provincial elite and *mestizo* Andean university youth. The latter are described as young people 'who meet in a land of nothing between two worlds': the traditional Andean world of their parents whose myths, rites and customs they no longer share, and the urban–*criollo* world which rejects them as provincials, *mestizos* and Quechua speakers.

In the 1960s, when the traditional power basis was crumbling and the old monopoly on knowledge was undermined, education acquired an explosive character. It became not only a search for truth but also a very pragmatic instrument in what students conceived to be a democratic struggle against the *mistis* and local power holders. There was a large expansion of Marxist thought in the universities and a diffusion of anti-capitalist ideology among fringe juveniles. Lacking a sense of identity of their own, students at the University of Huamanga in Ayacucho adopted a simplified version of Marxism–Leninism–Maoism, defined it as the only scientific truth and legitimated it by reference to the Marxist classics.

The Sendero Luminoso movement has three main ideological bases: José Carlos Mariátegui, Mao Tse-Tung, and *indigenismo*.

The guiding spirit was probably Abimael Guzmán (*nom de guerre* Camarado Gonzalo), a philosophy professor at Huamanga University. An important role was also played by Diaz Martinez, who was one of the first to see that a small group of rich peasants was sabotaging the Peruvian Revolution by taking advantage of non-commercial opportunities at the expense of others. In 1969 he advocated the total transformation of Peru's semi-colonial and semi-feudal structures. After a visit to China to study Mao's revolution, he returned to Peru to write a book which may have provided some of the ideology and language for Sendero Luminoso to use in their escalation of a peasant war designed to liberate 'the semi-feudal, semi-colonial masses' of Peru from bureaucratic capitalism.[16]

The original nucleus was drawn from the Ayacucho regional committee of the Communist Party, which later inherited the influence in the region of Bandera Roja (Red Banner), Peru's first Maoist party. Sendero believed that Mariátegui's 1920s analysis in *Seven Interpretative Essays on Peruvian Reality* still applied to Peru in the 1970s. Lima-based left-wing parties, trade unions and peasant federations were all dismissed, for their policies were contaminated by 'parliamentary cretinism' and 'revisionism'.[17] The guiding thought of Camarado Gonzalo was seen as 'the Fourth Sword of World Revolution', his predecessors being Marx and Engels, Lenin and Mao, and both the debt to Mariátegui and the name of the movement are revealed in its full title: 'Peruvian Communist Party – for the Shining Path of José Carlos Mariátegui'.[18]

Sendero thinking appears to have been strongly influenced by leaders of peasant risings in Ayacucho who believed that external leaders were required to give them orientation and guidance. Such ideas were developed into a new hierarchical order, in place of the old hierarchy, of teacher(urban–*mestizo*)–pupil. As Sendero ideology developed, including the sacralisation of 'Gonzalo thought', the role of the *caudillo*–teacher came to be fundamental in education, since he was the guide, truth and virtue incarnate. For Sendero, 'proletarian ideology' came to acquire almost divine attributes, so society was now confronted with a new diversity capable of defeating the old Viracocha gods which had dominated them for centuries (Degregori, 1989). The guerrillas saw themselves as new evangelists who would not only guide and teach, but also rid the peasants of ignorance and vices, such as drinking, *coca* and smoking.

Guzmán has been described as a discreet and respected professor. He gradually consolidated Sendero's political control over the university and especially over the teacher-training department, so that Quechua-speaking sons and daughters of richer peasants and traders could return to the countryside to work for the party. Sendero's primary statement, a 32-page pamphlet distributed in 1982, characterised Peru as a semi-feudal society in which the peasantry, and especially its poorest sector, must form the principal motive force of revolutionary change within a worker–peasant alliance, with the petit bourgeoisie being attracted as a minor partner. The Velasco and Morales Bermudez governments were termed 'fascist' and said to be engaged in constructing a corporate state and 'bureaucratic capitalism'. Belaúnde's government was seen as the 'continuation of fascism' behind a 'masquerade of apparent democracy', serving the 'deepening development of bureaucratic capitalism'. The capitalisation of the 'great landlords, the great bankers and the magnates of the *comprador* [buyer] bourgeoisie' were seen to be oppressing and wounding the people.

In 1977, Sendero declared that its reconstruction of the Peruvian Communist Party was complete. It had lost control of the university in 1974, but in 1977 its cadres went underground. In 1980, it began armed action in isolation from the rest of the left in the belief that the conditions for revolution existed and that a prolonged popular war would build a road to communism in Peru. An assault on the Chuschi polling station during elections was followed by various dynamite attacks. In accordance with its Maoist philosophy, Sendero attempted to foster a revolutionary situation, opposing reform and promoting extreme action. It has destroyed rural co-operatives, prevented peasants selling their produce on the market, mutilated and murdered informers and rich peasants, and slaughtered prize cattle in a university research facility.

At first, President Belaúnde minimised the threat posed by the guerrillas, dismissing them as a handful of delinquents who could safely be dealt with by the police. Sendero Luminoso, however, quickly showed that such optimism was completely misplaced, for the guerrillas soon demonstrated that they were a tightly organised and disciplined movement, virtually impenetrable by the intelligence services. Moreover, their superior knowledge of the local terrain, the rapid mobility and surprise achieved by their small strike forces and their close links with the peasantry proved to be invaluable advantages as the war escalated.

It is abundantly clear that, despite aspects of truth in its analysis, Sendero's characterisation of Peru is distorted, its goal to return peasants to a non-monetary primitive communism utopian, and its plan to cut off the food supplies to cities quite unrealistic. Nevertheless, the movement has been remarkably successful. Although overwhelming military force has been mobilised against it, and in spite of defeats or military occupation of zones formerly held by the guerrillas, they continue to bounce back, more audacious than ever. As we argue below, much of the success of Sendero can be attributed to a widespread sympathy for the movement held by sections of the peasantry for the first few years, as well as a profound unease about, distaste for and often hatred of the government, police and armed forces. A consequence of the deployment of large numbers of military personnel has been the brutalisation of the civilian population in the emergency zones. While the guerrillas have committed many terrible acts, it is widely argued that the paramilitary forces have surpassed the guerrillas in their violence against civilians. In a particularly dirty war, there have been documentations of 'disappearances', hidden mass graves and systematic torture of political prisoners. The effect has probably been to turn the peasants more against the military than against Sendero. By the end of 1982, a substantial portion of rural Ayacucho was effectively controlled by Sendero and seven provinces were put under martial law. By mid-1985, the guerrillas were attacking targets in virtually all parts of the country, and the Emergency Zone had expanded to 24 provinces. In February 1986, after a series of bombings, Lima itself was put under a state of emergency.

By the end of 1985, a leaked government intelligence report contradicted official propaganda that the war was waning. By then, 8256 deaths had occurred and 3524 subversives had been captured; by late-1990, the deaths had reached 26 000. These figures made Sendero Luminoso one of the largest and most persistent guerrilla forces in Latin America. Moreover, the number of 'subversive acts' rose from an average of about 2500 per year in 1983 and 1984 to 3079 in 1985, although the overall death rate fell. The strength of the organisation was indicated by its representation at a Paris press conference, successful recruitment of illiterate peasants to replace university-trained militants being moved out of Ayacucho, prison training schools, penetration of shanty towns, and the procuring of food by levies on street vendors, extortion and assaults.

Any explanation of Sendero must emphasise the characteristics of the peasantry in its original core area of Ayacucho. The role of the university in the movement was crucial, just as the University of Cuzco, either directly or indirectly, had influenced various peasant movements in the Cuzco region in the 1960s. But this isolated provincial university was able to radicalise students from peasant backgrounds only because of the chronic poverty, economic stagnation and relative deprivation of the region (McClintock, 1984). In most assessments of regional economic growth in Peru, based on socio-economic indicators of consumption levels, Ayacucho, Apurimac and Huancavelica are ranked, along with Puno, as the poorest, most deprived departments in the country, coming lower even than Cuzco.[19] Annual income per head in the region in the 1970s was scarcely more than US$200, with an average life expectancy at birth of only 45 years, while state investment per head was the lowest in the country.[20] McClintock argues that there was a subsistence crisis, marking a decline in standards of living in the region.

The province of Andahuaylas lagged behind the rest of the country in the process of agrarian reform, and when the *haciendas* were finally expropriated they had been seriously decapitalised. The peasantry, embittered by this situation, hoped for a radical grass-roots reform in which they could participate widely, but this was blocked by the formation of co-operatives. The co-operatives displayed the same characteristics of poor administration, waste of funds or embezzlement and apathetic, poorly organised workers that were described in Chapter 13, and they began to take on some of the role that the *haciendas* had adopted towards the communities. With the boom in investment, some enterprising return migrants and some rich peasants began to prosper as local entrepreneurs. The peasants' resentment grew as these entrepreneurs became affluent, acted in capitalistic ways showing insensitivity to local norms, allegedly 'stole' land in some cases or were guilty of profiteering; they were seen to lack generosity in cultural terms or defy customs of reciprocity.[21]

When the guerrillas became active in Andahuaylas, their first major action was to destroy the machinery of a co-operative; later the transport was destroyed and the produce distributed among nearby peasants. Several public figures were assassinated and death threats made to various local merchants and entrepreneurs. Other state agencies were attacked and infrastructure such as electric power, telephone and telegraph stations and airports dynamited.

Although the hard-core Sendero forces have not numbered more than 5000–7000, they have frequently out-maneouvred the police and army, using steep trails on the edge of the jungle or a line of march inaccessible to wheeled vehicles. They have also been successful in setting one village against another, utilising ancient local grievances, boundary disputes or disputes with the agrarian reform authorities to their advantage, and have recruited masked villagers to attack their traditional enemies. Clearly the movement of guerrillas has been facilitated by a network of safe houses, sleeping spots and sources of supply, while peasants not sympathetic to Sendero may have been neutralised by the practice of shooting informers.

How did the peasants view Sendero Luminoso? Berg (1986–87) argues convincingly that there was a good deal of passive support for the guerrillas when political assassinations or public whippings began. Invariably the victims were seen to have 'deserved it' because they were cattle thieves from enemy villages, or were rich and corrupt officials who had taken advantage of their political power and had accumulated wealth without remaining involved in relations of reciprocity. Some were described as egoists who only looked after themselves, acting like *mistis*, refusing to speak Quechua and adopting the culture of the towns. They were, in effect, no longer *campesinos* and so were outside the boundary of the moral community. It was rare for people to discuss Sendero's communist principles; when they did, they generally disapproved of redistribution and collectivisation. Generally their attitudes seem to have been a reaction to the particular attacks. Since the co-operatives and leaders were seen to have been exploitative, peasants welcomed the bombings. But peasant support was not always forthcoming: 'I have nothing against their killing the rich, but I don't like it when they kill peasants.'[22] Indeed, it is significant that when people debated the morality of killing a person, the discussion centred on whether or not he or she was a *campesino/a*.

The strong class dimension that influenced peasants' perceptions emerged clearly when the South-Central Andes became heavily militarised. While many peasants recoiled at some violence perpetrated by the guerrillas, their reaction against the cruel and arbitrary behaviour of the police and army was a good deal stronger. Beatings, electric shock treatment, near-drownings in the muddy river, execution of villagers suspected (often on the flimsiest evidence) of being guerrillas and many disappearances became common. The group which particularly bore the brunt of paramilitary repression were the young adults, especially returned migrants who had spent time in Lima or in educational institutions, as they were suspected of harbouring left-wing ideals. The growing sympathy for the guerrillas was shown by the changing terminology used by peasants to describe Sendero Luminoso. In 1982, they were known as 'terrorists', or sometimes sarcastically as *los universitarios*, but by 1985 they were often called 'comrades' (*compañeros*).[23]

However, Sendero's evangelical moralisation and 'New Democracy' campaign and rural analysis often led to local failures: for example, they did not succeed in abolishing the civil–religious hierarchy, the traditional *varayoq*, in Chuschi. A series of minor clashes occurred when they tried to prohibit *fiestas* and drinking, and they also failed to prohibit youth from celebrating Vida Michy (adolescent competitive games). But two factors seem to be significant in the withdrawal of peasant support: Sendero's effort to prevent markets from functioning, and the disparate attempts of terrorised peasants to find safety and peace. Peasants in Rio Pampas and Andayhualas withdrew their support from Sendero when the insurgents attempted to draw them into a wider conflict that did not address their local grievances. Many people killed by Sendero after 1982 were not perceived to be enemies of the people. The cataclysmic violence of the 1980s was so great that peasants were caught between 'the sword and the wall'. The only solution was to flee, and it is suggested that 120 000 people have fled from the violence. Perhaps this cataclysmic violence signals a *pachacutic* (a transformational world turn, or new age). One old woman in the Rio Pampas spoke of events as signalling the end of the world.[24] Clearly this prolonged terror, flight to the cities and the political lessons learnt will have created a new kind of peasant.

To conclude, the conditions in Ayacucho in general and Andahuaylas in particular in the 1970s and early 1980s were similar to those in other places where local revolutions occurred. A variety of data suggest that the economic position of the peasantry was worsening and becoming desperate. General Noel, in charge of the military zone in 1983, admitted that the military role in pacification was only 25 per cent, with regional development providing the missing 75 per cent. A drying-up of urban employment opportunities compounded the situation. The state had aroused expectations in the Peruvian Revolution a decade earlier, but by the late 1970s hopes had been dashed.

Thus, even where the peasants did not actively sympathise with Sendero, the brutalising, coercive actions of the military and class hatred of the police often influenced the situation, providing even further justification for violence. Where peasant villages became fearful of Sendero and organised their own self-defence units (*rondas campesinos*), the army gradually came to see the *rondas* as potentially as great a threat as Sendero.[25] By the late 1980s, however, this was reversed, and García began to arm *rondas*.

The chief ombudsman-cum-state attorney infuriated the government by publicly declaring in 1983 that the Sendero guerrillas were 'patriots who basically want the best for Peru'. The mysterious deaths of eight journalists following the alleged lynching of guerrillas, and the failure to prosecute anyone after a government-appointed commission investigated the atrocity discouraged investigations in the region. This and other incidents suggest that President García was increasingly having to give the military a free hand in 'pacification', and feared publication of the true facts. An especially horrific incident in 1986 brought into question García's ability to maintain respect for human rights in the civil war. When several hundred Sendero prisoners in three Lima prisons mutineered for better conditions, García sent in the military who proceeded to massacre them. In the ensuing congressional enquiry, Garciá dared not allow the armed forces to be found guilty of an unprovoked massacre, for that could precipitate a military coup. More recently, Sendero have murdered various high APRA officials and mayors, including the head of ENCI, the state food and fertiliser import agency and a close friend of García, and have even bombed the tourist train from Macchu Pichu to Cuzco, killing seven tourists. By 1992 Sendero's bombing capacity had reached almost Belfast levels, they had taken over a number of Lima shanty towns, and it was rumoured they planned to cut off Lima from external food supplies.

Yet although the capacity of Sendero to launch serious attacks in any part of the country appears as strong as ever, its prospects in the long term do not look good. Their idea of returning the peasantry to an Inca kind of economy is unrealistic, and their self-subsistence policy as well as the atrocities they have committed have provoked increasing hostility. Moreover, Sendero's isolation from the many small left-wing political parties as well as APRA has been unconstructive. The parliamentary left, which represents around 30 per cent of the electorate, has been alienated by Sendero's isolationist approach, as well as by its selective killings.

In April 1992 Fujimori instituted a bloodless coup, seizing dictatorial powers for seven months, dissolving congress and taking over the judiciary. The death of democracy brought international condemnation but Fujimori could no longer seek political compromise if he were to ensure continued military backing. The government finally had a stroke of luck in September: Abimael Guzman and several other leaders were arrested at a safe house in Lima. The chief coordinator of clandestine cells was also captured. This may well prove to be a turning-point in the civil war, though it should be noted that governments have consistently under-estimated Sendero's resilience.

In 1987, the guerrillas who showed a better tactical appreciation of the situation were those of the Movimiento Revolucionarió Tupac Amaru (MRTA), which moved out of urban areas into rural Peru. The MRTA were prepared to declare a truce in 1985 and talk to the government. Their rejection of ordinary terrorism and the use of political arguments and modern techniques of publicity have produced some interesting results. The MRTA has hijacked food trucks, distributing the food free to the people in Lima slums, and it has taken over radio stations and news agencies to issue communiqués. In the event of a military coup in the 1990s, Sendero seems likely to carry on its war against all Peru's institutions. But MRTA could become very significant if it became the guerrilla arm of a broad front which would include a radicalised left and centre-left.[26]

GUERRILLAS AND THE COCAINE TRADE

A continuing problem for small guerrilla bands fighting potentially the entire might of the country's armed forces is access to large numbers of weapons, preferably of a sophisticated kind, and especially to funds. In 1987, reports emerged of guerrilla protection of drug traffickers, and MRTA rebels began to fight with Sendero for control of *coca*-growing areas in the *selva*.

The huge drug trade that deeply involves Bolivia and Colombia is now also threatening to drown Peru in the tidal wave of cocaine that is flooding out of the country. On either side of Peru, in Bolivia and Colombia, the appalling effects of this trade can be seen. Bolivian society is said to be virtually disintegrating under the money and power of the drug traffickers. Cocaine is not only the country's biggest export, but its manufacture also generates one-third more money than all other economic activities put together (O'Shaughnessy, 1988b). Furthermore, the output of cocaine is expanding by between 30 and 50 per cent a year. On the other side of Peru, in Colombia, the 'Medellin cartel' have formed an organisation that a previous president has said is 'more powerful than the state'. Led by billionaire drug traffickers, the cartel wields great power, murdering many left-wing politicians and critics, the Minister of Justice in 1984 and Attorney-General in 1987, and a presidential candidate. A river of blood flows through Colombia, yet until the late 1980s the law could not touch most of the cartel.

Coca leaves have been chewed for comfort for thousands of years by peasants who live in the cold lands up to 4570m, and both *coca* growing and *coca* chewing are deeply rooted traditions closely associated with customary forms of reciprocity. Traditionally, *coca* was one of the major items sought in ecological interchange between people of the Andes and those of the jungle. A barter economy, of *coca* for goods, still exists today alongside trade in commodities for money (Burchard, 1974). The government has always recognised the customary role of *coca* in highland peasant culture and so has legalised and regulated trade for this traditional purpose. In recent years, however, the peasants have both been forced or have chosen to participate in *coca* growing and the cocaine trade in a greatly expanded or intensified way.

During the late 1950s and early 1960s, the government initiated a colonisation programme in the *ceja* at the base of the Andes, offering land to families from the Andes who were willing to relocate to the area. The main site was the central Huallaga zone near the town of Tingo María. Considerable effort was devoted to assisting colonists on 20ha holdings based on bananas, coffee, tea and tobacco, supplemented by subsistence crops. During the period of government investment when urban infrastructure was being improved and some cash crops fetched good prices, land use in some areas seemed to be achieving a new level of stability.[27] While *coca* was grown at that time, its price was not high, and it actually fell in 1964. Later, however, when government investment declined and forest soils had been depleted of their initial nutrients, the plantations of tea, coffee and tobacco gave much lower returns, and colonists turned to *coca* growing.[28] From the 1960s onwards, the need for *coca* increased and the growth of cocaine-producing hideouts in the forests rapidly multiplied. Here, the *coca* paste is refined into dangerous crack, or into the white powder which can be 'cut' or adulterated with other substances for final consumption.

The production of *coca* is now uncontrollable. Vast areas of largely unused land lie at the base of the Andes and much of it is ideal for *coca* production, since the bushes grow on acidic lateritic soils where few other crops would grow. No other crop offers the same profitability and ease of cultivation. *Coca* gives three times the income of any other peasant crop, so it is likely to be extremely difficult to persuade peasants not to grow it.

Along with Bolivia, Peru has become the main *coca*-producing country, often closely linked with Colombian traffickers. It was estimated in 1987 that while the legal exports of the country were valued at a little less than US$3 billion, the value of the cocaine trade was about US$1 billion,[29] and was growing rapidly. In the production, distribution and marketing of *coca* paste and cocaine, there is a clear division of labour at both local and national levels, and this has intensified as the traditional peasant trade has been infiltrated and expanded. As in most forms of social relations of production, those who contribute most in producing the commodity, the peasants, are much less rewarded than those involved in marketing. At the beginning of 1988, a kilo of cocaine could be picked up in Santa Cruz, Bolivia, for about $3500; when cut, it retailed on the streets of Manhattan for anything up to 1000 times that price (O'Shaughnessy, 1988b). The profits allow the powerful *narcos* (dealers involved in the drug trade) to buy the co-operation of any policeman, soldier, judge or politician who takes it into his head to try to oppose them. Those who choose not to be bought are either defied or killed. The next step, in accordance with their growing financial and political power, might well be to buy votes in a 'democratic election'.

Up until 1987, the Peruvian government was not too worried about the cocaine trade. However, as more of the children of affluent middle-class Peruvians in smart Lima suburbs become addicts, Peruvian concern is mounting. The governments of Andean countries have tried to encourage peasants to uproot their *coca* bushes by paying them, but the government cannot afford to pay more than growers earn from the bushes in a year or two, and few bushes have been destroyed. Fragile governments trying to grapple with their huge debt crisis are poorly equipped to tackle the cocaine trade. Poorly paid police and troops sent to search the jungle for *coca* crops and cocaine processing hideouts are not likely to be immune to the *narcos*' bribes. In 1987, more than a dozen generals in the various paramilitary forces were sacked. Knowledge of the problem is limited and legalistic, but it can be argued that as long as there is (1) a strong international demand for cocaine, (2) the farming of *coca* for traditional use is allowed, and (3) the peasants' economy in the Andes and neighbouring *selva* is tied to *coca* leaves, cocaine supply will not be eliminated (O'Shaughnessy, 1988b).

Since the great escalation in demand for cocaine in Europe and the USA is the main cause of the great expansion in the trade, it is entirely appropriate that the US and European governments should accept responsibility for mounting a major international campaign against the drug trade. These countries are now also realising that massive drug abuse is becoming one of the most serious social problems affecting the Western world. The USA has 14.5 million drug addicts out of a total of 16 million in the Americas as a whole. President Bush has been vigorous in his anti-drug campaign and the Colombian government has staunchly carried the fight to the Medellin cartel. The USA has raised its assistance to Peruvian anti-drugs and anti-guerrilla efforts from about US$1 million to $39 million in 1991, with $23.3 million for law enforcement and $52 million in economic assistance.[30] It has, however, been careful not to escalate its direct military involvement in Latin America, and Peru has resisted chemical spraying of *coca* areas. Some observers have wondered why shots have not been fired at Colombian light planes flying cocaine on three sector routes from dozens of now well-known landing strips in the Peruvian jungle. The USA has denied it is setting up five bases in the anti-drug campaign in the Upper Huallaga: only one base is to be established and American advisers are only training Peruvian forces. During 1990 business has been proceeding as usual in the Upper Huallaga whether due to protection by Sendero Luminoso, the unattractiveness of counter-insurgency opposition to chemical eradication, or greater American military involvement. Although a decision was taken early in 1990 to hit air traffic as well as laboratories, it appears the *narcos* could readily shift air strips to valleys north or south of current supply points.

No effective crop substitute has been found for *coca* bushes and no adequate agricultural solution is in sight for the Andes that might minimise ecological interdependence. The best source of income for peasants remains the underground industry and, with the great increase in unemployment, the cocaine industry is likely to remain large.

President Fujimori persists in the belief that *coca* can be readily substituted by other crops, especially tobacco, and some hope has arisen from a devastating fungus attacking *coca* bushes that locals believe followed mysterious spraying from two helicopters in February 1990. Peasants near Uchiza say 'half' the bushes are riddled with disease from leaves to roots.[31] Meanwhile changes in demand from the Western drug market, the rise of heroin and the growth of the Japanese drug market may take the heat off the anti-drug campaign in Latin America. Added to these worries is the new threat that important producing areas are coming under the control of the MRTA or Sendero Luminoso guerrillas. Since the trade has produced many multi-millionaires, the prospects of amassing enormous profits look very bright indeed. Currently, such wealth is likely to be converted into large quantities of weapons, so strengthening the guerrillas' capacity to wage war against the state.[32]

Part IV

Peasant Destinities and Outcomes

16 Agencies of Change: Dissolution of the Peasantry?

Among the agencies of change that might be expected gradually to erode the isolation of the Chilca peasantry, undermine their distinctive culture and lead ultimately to their integration into the national society, we can identify the spread of communications and roads, the impact of the press, literacy and schooling, the place of the army, the role of Cuzco and rural–urban migration. This chapter discusses the effects of these factors.

COMMUNICATIONS AND ROADS[1]

It is an ironic comment on the process of 'modernisation' that the city that was once the centre of the great Inca empire, the hub of a system of roads that stretched to Ecuador in the north and to Chile in the south, and which (even in colonial days) was an important stop on the trans-continental route to Buenos Aires, has today, along with its region, become part of an impoverished periphery.

Although Cuzco, with two airlines, has excellent daily air links with Lima, communication by road depends either on a journey of three days along a spectacular, tortuous route over many mountain passes, or a somewhat safer journey of 1600km along better roads that can sometimes be closed during the rainy season. Until 1973 there was only one stretch of paved road in the entire department: a 40km section between Cuzco and Urcos. In the late 1970s another section, destined to be used mostly by tourists, was paved in the Sacred Valley of Urubamba. During the revolutionary period the network of roads was expanded rapidly, usually with the state providing a bulldozer and driver and Indian peasants contributing unpaid labour, but the general standard and number of roads remain low. Indeed, some district capitals are not yet accessible by road, and many remote towns do not have a single locally owned motor vehicle.

Thousands of truck operators play a key role in the regional economy, plying their trade between Cuzco or other sub-regional centres and outlying small towns, *haciendas* or agricultural co-operatives. A 5-ton truck chassis is usually bought in Lima, then a wooden body fitted locally. Truck driving is the main avenue to economic success and the main form of medium-scale entrepreneurship for *cholos* in the region. Almost the entire trade of the region is carried on the ubiquitous 5-ton truck, as well as passengers visiting or returning from Cuzco who form a 'layer' on top of the sacks of potatoes. There are very few private cars, but the city has a public bus system, and taxis and buses or *colectivos* (collective taxis) also regularly travel to other areas in the Pampa de Anta.

Two railway lines provide freight and passenger service. In addition, Cuzco is linked by telephone to other large cities but not with most of the towns of the department outside the Cuzco–Puno arterial road. The postal service between Cuzco and the outside world is fast and efficient, but slow and unreliable within the department. Cuzco has a television station (as well as radio stations) but reception is limited to the urban area, and most towns have only one-way radio contact with the outside world.

PRESS

In a department in which over half of the rural population is illiterate, it is scarcely surprising that very few newspapers and other reading material (other than government notices, edicts or revolutionary posters) percolate into the countryside. In the city itself, *Time* and *Newsweek* can be seen on news stands, along with national weekly and monthly magazines and the various Lima daily newspapers. Cuzco itself has two daily newspapers, 6–8 page sheets printed on antiquated presses, with a circulation of only 1500 to 2000 each.[2] In the villages almost the only printed material to be seen are legal documents and the occasional political pamphlet.

LITERACY AND SCHOOLING

Peru has a high degree of illiteracy, even compared with most other Latin American and underdeveloped countries. In 1972, in rural areas, 33 per cent of the male population of 15 years and over was illiterate, compared with 69 per cent of the females. In total, 51 per cent of the rural population could not read or write. On the other hand, only 6 per cent of the male population and 19 per cent of the female population of these age groups was illiterate in urban areas.[3]

'Functional literacy' in 1961 was estimated at 31 per cent for Peru as a whole but only 16 per cent for Cuzco Department. However, as our data for Chilca have shown, in 1979 compared with 1964 there had been an increase in literacy and a considerable expansion in the school system, especially under the Revolutionary Government.

Although improvements have been made in the national system of education and in the curriculum, especially since 1970, Peruvian education manifests the characteristics of the old colonial, Hispanic system. Culture, the arts and literature are emphasised in a verbal education, while science, mathematics, technical education and practical skills are ignored. Although Peruvian nationalism and patriotism are stressed, there is no real recognition of the indigenous culture, which is compounded by the fact that all teachers of Quechua and Aymará Indians are effectively *mestizos*.

National figures show a net enrolment rate of 77 per cent for all age groups corresponding to primary and secondary school.[4] While attendance rates may be high in urban areas, absenteeism may reach 50 per cent or more in rural areas, especially when the need to mobilise the full household labour force is great. In 1972, one-fifth of the department's population of 713 000 was enrolled in school, whereas one-third of the population was of school age. In 1972, in the Fifth Region departments of Cuzco, Madre de Dios and Apurimac, 77 per cent of all pupils were in primary education compared with only 13 per cent in secondary education, 7 per cent in adult education and 0.5 per cent in teachers' training.[5] The figures show a very high dropout rate, with many pupils surviving only two or three of the first grades of primary school.

Cuzco's university of over 5000 students varies in quality from solid departments such as anthropology to others that offer second-rate programmes. Throughout the 1960s and 1970s the university became strongly politicised; while radical students have assisted in organising demonstrations and strikes and helped peasants and workers with organisation, the university has often been closed for many months in an academic year.

Cuzco has a number of prestigious fee-paying Catholic high schools, as well as several large free state secondary schools. Provincial capitals often (but not always) have a secondary school. While a few district capitals near a large city have secondary schools, most have only a *primaria completa* (a full 6-year primary school). Rural Indian communities have only a one- or two-teacher school, usually of poor physical quality and with few resources.

THE ARMY

Theoretically all Peruvian males are expected to serve for two years in one of the military services, but in practice many *mestizos* manage to avoid enlistment, whereas Indian peasants and other lower-class people are less fortunate. Sometimes villagers visiting the city market are impressed into the army without further ado.

The significance of the army is that, for many Indian peasants, it marks an abrupt, enforced period of cultural change. They are removed from their village to be trained in a distant, usually urban area. The process of Hispanicisation is rapid and, as the recruits adapt to the new lifestyle and institutions, their links with their birthplaces may weaken. Certainly enlistment often appears to lead to a process of social urbanisation, for many members of the armed forces become 'proto-urbanites' who later prefer to live and work in a city.

Cuzco is the major garrison town in the department, being headquarters for one of the military regions. Even before the emergency with the Sendero Luminoso guerrillas broke out in 1980, considerable numbers of troops as well as large numbers of the paramilitary Guardia Civil could be seen in the city. By the late 1980s the military presence was much greater, with the neighbouring departments of Ayacucho and Puno heavily militarised.

THE ROLE OF CUZCO

Secondary cities usually grow rapidly in developing countries. Under certain conditions they can act as catalysts in the development process, generating and strengthening development and linking it to national economic progress, and at the same time enabling a more balanced form of urbanisation to occur than the common pattern whereby a primate city dominates the country and grows at the expense of several intermediate cities. To what extent has the growth of Cuzco been a harmonious developmental process, generating economic growth in its region? Has it perhaps exploited the surrounding countryside, rather than stimulating it by spread effects?[6]

The picture is far from clear. Since the available data are fragmentary and inadequate, our findings must be tentative. Aspects of Cuzco's role seem to be generative and developmental, but in other respects the city appears to drain off resources from its hinterland. Important data are those concerning the city's rate of growth. Cuzco, which was the fourth largest city in Peru in 1940, is now the eighth largest, with a population of 182 000 in 1981. Its rate of population growth has been considerable: 344 per cent over the 40 years, or an average of 8.4 per cent a year. However, this is the slowest rate of growth for the 10 major cities and only one-quarter of the mean rate of growth of Peru's nine secondary cities (excluding the urban area of Lima-Callao). In an overall situation of strong urbanisation, this reflects the backwardness and sluggish growth of the Cuzco region and the Southern Sierra in general, in contrast to the very rapid economic growth of the northern coast.

The two factors which have had most impact on Cuzco are agriculture and tourism. Agricultural decline and decapitalisation have slowed the growth of Cuzco city and emphasised the importance of the subsistence component in peasants' livelihoods.

The expansion of the wool trade early this century benefited Sicuani and the southern portion of the department more than Cuzco itself. The degree of infrastructure created by the wool industry has been valuable for the modern development of the Cuzco region, but has not triggered off the development of any new agricultural staple. In addition, the disappointments which followed on from the agrarian reforms have led to a paralysis in agricultural growth. Thus the potential for Cuzco to become an agricultural market centre, or a centre for agricultural education and support, has not been realised.

Since the Second World War, tourism has escalated and Cuzco

has become a tourist city of both international and national significance. Without that, Cuzco is likely to have stagnated. In the last 20 years the dramatic growth of the bureaucracy and the emphasis on 'developmentalism' have also contributed to its growth.

The requirements of tourism are complementary to Cuzco's earlier functions. Its historical importance as the capital of the Inca empire and its colonial and ecclesiastical role have led to the preservation of features which interest and entice the tourist. An imposing cathedral, a spacious Plaza de Armas, ornate baroque churches, colonial architecture, Inca constructions, cobbled streets, colourfully garbed Indians, the marketplace and the *adobe* frontages of humble artisans' houses all add to the appealing pre-industrial quaintness. Superimposed on this archaic pattern are the hotels, shops and communication facilities that service a large tourist trade. There are two large tourist hotels and nearly 50 smaller ones, ranked into nine classes. The other major modern features are those that reflect the recent dominance of the middle classes: the numerous government departments, the university, the regional hospital, large high schools, the bus, truck and *colectivo* terminal, and their residential, retail and servicing sectors.

The Cuzco of the 1980s therefore presented a rather ambivalent picture. The old colonial city was still evident in the morphology and in a large market which operated daily, displaying enormous seething vitality. On Saturdays the population greatly increased as Indians flooded into the city to buy and sell, thousands of open-air vendors spilling over into the streets on all sides of the market hall. This 'bazaar economy' aspect of Cuzco, important not only to the peasantry, proletariat and middle classes but also to the overseas tourist, involves the penetration of the modern capitalist economy by peasant production and vice versa. In many ways it is symbolic of the economic and social composition of the city, straddling as it does a traditional subsistence economy based on kinship and reciprocity, and a modern urbanising economy which is both expansionist and exploitative.

Cuzco provides a habitat of changing niches that reflects the social movement which characterises its place in the centre of a district of impoverishment. The grand colonial mansions of the former elite were, by the late 1970s, empty of their former owners (who had earlier departed to Lima to pursue their more profitable interests in finance and commerce) and were mostly subdivided for rental. In the more favoured locations near the central square, tourist shops and travel agencies had taken over earlier shops. In the outer suburbs in the east, many new adobe *ranchos* (improvised shacks or houses) have been built by invading migrants (see Plate 12).

Tourist industry workers, government officials, department administrators, shopkeepers and students now comprise a large portion of the population, into the upper ranks of which were merged, during the agrarian reform, those members of the former *hacendado* class who had not left the region. A number of the archaic, parasitic functions of the old patrimonial domain still exist but small law firms, pettifogging accountants and services that preyed on the rural sector have been in decline since the arrival of the confident new bureaucrats, and a number of finance services, consulting firms and other modern services represent spin-offs from the recent government investments.

Beneath the loose collection of elite are three vaguely defined groups which comprise the great mass of the urban population: upper middle-class, a petit bourgeoisie, and proletariat and lumpen proletariat (see Table 16.1). They are predominantly *cholo* proletarians (though they include poor *mestizos*). Many retain land rights and kin links in their villages, but since they are committed to urban life they cannot be regarded as part-peasant or transitional people.[7] Many are self-employed artisans, petty traders, operators of small marginal enterprises or are engaged in a wide variety of trades, both traditional and non-traditional. Workers for larger firms or institutions enjoy moderate wages and considerable security because of trade union power. Others – waiters, errand boys, day labourers and many domestic servants – are much more exposed to abusive exploitation, relying in the main on the benevolent paternalism of their employers. In this setting, the growth of a true urban working class has been slowed. With the influx of new migrants, people are forced to seek work in a very wide range of occupations and 'ecological niches'.

While the tourist industry is impressive in its size, it is difficult to determine how many benefits are retained in the region, for in some respects it is an enclave controlled by external capitalists. Between 1968 and 1971, an annual total of 32 000 to 40 000

Table 16.1 The social strata of Cuzco city

Per cent population	*Class*	*Occupations*	*Approximate incomes*	*Ethnicity/language education*
2–3	Economic and professional elite	Larger businessmen, bank managers, old landed gentry, nouveau riche European entrepreneurs, leading political, judicial, military authorities, leaders of professions and intellectual community	High, but wide range	Exclusively Spanish, often university educated
20	Upper middle class	Salaried civil servants, middle businessmen, white collar workers, public sector (middle to high rank civil servants, technicians, secondary school teachers, army officers, engineers, many professionals, impoverished ex-*hacendados*)	Commonly US$200–$300 month	Spanish exclusively, secondary education
23	Petit bourgeoisie*	Small retail merchants, more secure artisans, clerks, typists, primary school teachers, low civil servants. Self-employed small shop keepers, petty traders, artisans. Taxi and truck drivers, carpenters, stonemasons, cobblers, mechanics, repairmen, tailors, barbers, blacksmiths, curio makers, small canteens, hole-in-wall shops	US$80–$120 month Self-employed craftsmen US$50–$60 month	Spanish, often secondary school *Mestizo* at work, speak Quechua at home
50	Proletariat	Wage workers[†] Day labourers, apprentices, waiters, errand boys, shop attendants, drivers' helpers. Domestic servants	Workers in large firms US$100–$200 month.	Spanish

			Workers in small firms about US$70 month.	Spanish
			Journeymen US$50–$75 month.	Spanish
			Shop attendants US$60–$80 month.	Spanish
			Servants US$5–$30 month plus board	May be literate, or semi-literate
3–5	Lumpen proletariat‡	Indian porters, floating unemployed or underemployed beggars, derelicts, pickpockets and petty criminals	US$0.75–$1 a day or less	Quechua, some bi-lingual, illiterate

*There is no real class barrier between the proletariat and petit bourgeoisie. The status of some members of the latter may be a little higher, but the security and incomes of some of the wage workers may be greater than some self-employed craftsmen.

†Wage workers for larger firms or institutions are protected by a well-organised trade union and minimum wage legislation; they are the elite of the proletariat with higher incomes often than members of the petit bourgeoisie.

‡Prostitutes (working-class *mestizas*) belong to this lowest class in terms of status, being treated as social outcasts. However, their average incomes would be those of the upper middle class (about US$10–$12 a night).

Sources: Van den Berghe and Primov (1977); Brisseau Louiza (1975).

foreign tourists and some 45 000 to 56 000 Peruvian visitors (not all tourists) visited Cuzco. Overseas earnings quadrupled, from US$44 million in 1970 to nearly $202 million in 1979, growing at an annual rate of 20 per cent. In 1981, 8910 jobs were generated in Cuzco from tourism.[8] Hotels and the airport are important employers, as well as restaurants and tourist agencies. There are at least 50 or 60 curio shops, many sellers of Indian weaving in open market stalls and peddlars of curios, films, chocolate and knick-knacks who congregate around main tourist hotels. Some beggars, too, specialise in spots frequented by tourists. A number of businesses, such as photo shops and taxis, derive part of their income from tourists. Local earnings are thus very substantial but, as some of the hotels and travel agencies are owned by external interests, some tourist spending leaks out of the region. On a per capitum basis, each Cuzqueño is probably US$20–35 richer through tourist spending, although the benefits are very unevenly distributed.

Tourism is an industry that is sensitive to international images of Peru. As violence escalated in the 1980s and terrorist incidents began to extend from the Sendero heartland into Cuzco, tourism plummeted. Public investment in tourism also seems to have declined. Bed occupancy fell in Cuzco from 54.9 per cent in 1980 to only 47.6 per cent in mid-1982. In 1990 it was lower still, probably only about 35 per cent.

Apart from tourism, much of the modern development in Cuzco in the 1970s occurred as a consequence of the implementation of the Revolutionary Government's agrarian reform, educational and other modernisation policies. Since these programmes were heavily bureaucratic, Cuzco benefited by a proliferation of new jobs. In the longer term, however, some of this activity has proved to be artificial urbanisation, followed by policies of drastic bureaucratic pruning and severe retrenchment enforced by the IMF and creditor banks in the 1980s.

Brisseau Louiza (1975) has shown that large-scale industry in Cuzco Department is represented by only six enterprises that employ over 50 workers and which have paid-up capital of over 500 000 *soles*. Commerce in Cuzco can be divided into three levels. Large merchants, represented by a chamber of commerce, comprised 75 members in 1971 and were more often than not non-Cuzqueños.[9] A group of medium merchants consisted of some 300 members and, at the lowest level, registered licences were held by some 2700 market sellers, taxi drivers and other self-employed operators. In the department as a whole, some 3450 enterprises existed – one for every 32 inhabitants – which indicates the keenness of competition.

Commerce in Cuzco is overwhelmingly dominated by small firms, which is indicative of the only partial and uneven penetration of modern capitalism in the city. Even more, it represents the taking over of contemporary economic activity in the city by the surrounding area.[10] In this sense it can be said that the city is continuously 'ruralised' by incoming hordes of Indian peasants and *cholos*, just as its modern sectors and institutions are at the same time, in different ways, urbanising the surrounding countryside.

It has long been argued that capital accumulation in Lima and other modern sector areas has resulted in the extraction of surplus from the Peruvian Sierra. The movement of people, enterprise, skills, goods and capital might have had negative effects on per capitum consumption or the rate of growth of the poorer region. In the same way, much lower in the urban hierarchy, Cuzco serves as a pole of accumulation and diffuser of modern lifestyles within its own region. Brisseau Louiza put forward a typology of zones in the Cuzco region, classifying them in terms of linkage with the city and the nature of the relationship. Type A consists of provinces which she calls 'dynamic' (Urubamba, Anta, Quispicanchis, Calca, Canchis, La Convención); Type B are provinces which have been exploited by Cuzco in the sense that population and resources have flowed to the city (Paruro, Acomayo, Paucartambo); and Type C are provinces which do not have a major relationship with Cuzco.

Underpayment by Cuzco merchants or truckers when dealing with Indian peasants, and many forms of primitive accumulation, unequal trade and prices serve to cream off to Cuzco part of the region's surplus. Moreover, much of the capitalism that does exist in Cuzco functions through close relations with peasant production, relying on a putting-out system to reduce costs. Tourist shops, for example, depend on cottage industries and peasant crafts including woven ponchos, *alpaca* rugs, knitted jerseys or carved wooden ornaments.

As the centre of a poor, rural periphery, however, Cuzco is itself subject to influences from Lima and Arequipa that are just as strong as those it exerts over its own provinces; serving as a halfway house in the process of capital accumulation, Cuzco passes on to Lima much of the surplus that it has gained from its region. At the same time many people and goods bypass Cuzco, moving directly to large centres elsewhere. In turn, Cuzco serves as the regional recipient of goods produced in the major cities or imported from overseas.

Despite Cuzco's steady population growth and some economic diversification, it has not itself become transformed, and neither has it possessed the capitalistic power to transform its surrounding region. Cuzco lacks the capacity to attract investment capital, skill or entrepreneurs. Too much weight, however, should not be placed on the dependency argument of Cuzco and the higher order coastal cities draining off wealth from the Southern Sierra.[11] The striking characteristic of the whole region is poverty, not wealth. It is interesting to note that the Cuzco municipality cannot raise sufficient rates from its citizens to maintain even the most basic of its services. From 1971 to 1972, less than one-fifth of its revenue was raised from the city, and the municipality was heavily dependent on the central government for the provision of subsidies. A decade later it was estimated that the central government extracted 5836 million *soles* from Cuzco, but also contributed four times this amount (20 618 million *soles*) in investment.[12]

Perhaps the most striking example of the intensity of Cuzco's influence in its region lies in the area of consumerism. The distribution of food products provides most of the trade between the city and its hinterland. Four basic foods can be termed 'urban': the consumption of refined sugar, cereal products, rice, and fats and cooking oils. In the 1960s and 1970s, the spread of these products to surrounding village stores became more marked, and the expansion of village markets and increase in number of rural stores assisted the diffusion of urban consumer preferences. One luxury urban food, noodles, has become very popular with upwardly mobile *cholos*.

RURAL–URBAN MIGRATION

Since 1950, two of the most pronounced characteristics of Peru have been the very rapid growth of the population and the inability of the economy as a whole to provide adequate employment. Attempts to modernise the economy were successful only in the industrial sector, where multinational corporations achieved a considerable penetration of the economy: the contribution of industry to GDP grew from 33 per cent in 1960 to 43 per cent in 1979.[13] The rural sector did not respond to the opportunities for modernisation; its stagnation and instability meant that it could provide few prospects for absorbing further employment.

Over this period a massive structural change was occurring, with the proportion of the total labour force employed in agriculture declining from 53 per cent in 1960 to only 38 per cent in 1979.[14] Although the industrial sector's output increased impressively, as its development was capital-intensive it created relatively few new jobs; its share of employment rose from 19 per cent in 1960 to only 20 per cent in 1979. Hence the tertiary or services sector had to absorb the great bulk of new workers entering the labour force; it grew from 28 per cent in 1960 to 42 per cent in 1979.

As these figures suggest, development in Peru over the 1960s and 1970s was highly uneven and lopsided. The modern sector of the cities surged ahead while rapid social change, unaccompanied by economic growth, took place in the countryside, dislocating populations that had formerly been relatively stable, or had engaged only in short-distance pendular migration.

The massive rural–urban population movement indicated by the changing occupational structure involved large numbers of people moving from rural areas to small towns, from towns to cities, and from cities to Lima-Callao. In general, the aspirations of peasants seem broadly to support the Todaro (1976) model of migration: migrants are aware that minimum wage levels in cities are generally much higher than minimum rural incomes and they are ready to migrate in response to differences in *expected* income. Many peasants tend to have an optimistic view of urban living, at least in comparison with the alternative of a continued rural livelihood. In the decade 1960–70, Peru experienced a veritable flood of migrants moving to towns and cities; although this slowed somewhat in the 1970s, the average annual growth rate of urban populations for 1960–80, at 4.2 per cent, put Peru into the group of 10 countries with the highest rate of urbanisation in Latin America.[15]

Many observers feel that this large-scale movement of people has merely transferred poverty, unemployment and underemployment from the country to the city; certainly it has exacerbated problems with respect to housing, water, public transportation, health and other public services in the cities (an adequate supply of these is now critical). But from the viewpoint of the migrants, there is little evidence to suggest that they regret the decision to migrate; the former peasants of the Sierra are today struggling to establish themselves in regular employment in Lima and to secure title to their impoverished *estera* (straw matting) or *adobe* houses in one of the mushrooming *pueblo jovenes* (squatter settlements) on the city's outskirts.

It has been clear for some time that, were it not for migration, Latin American cities would be growing at only half their present rate. Once urban growth has reached a significant level, as it has in Peru, we can no longer consider urbanisation as occurring in a kind of enclave. A process of 'social urbanisation' occurs (Margolies, 1979), which seems to involve the extension of urban institutions and the imposition of an urban cultural model on the countryside. This is at the same time a functional urbanisation, since it denotes the socio-economic transformation of rural areas whereby urbanisation becomes a continuous cyclical process that acts as both a cause and an effect of internal migrations.

We have seen that peasants of Chilca are usually linked in networks of family and kin that form a continuous socio-economic field stretching from Lima to a remote Andean village. Such a situation can be interpreted in the light of the transformative power of global capitalism whose influences reach into the villages. Equally it can be interpreted as showing the resourceful initiative of a scavenging peasantry who use the city and the access to new resources that it provides to improve their livelihoods. In both views there is an unbroken continuum between urban and rural poles, and we have seen that feedback influences from the city are substantial. It can be argued, too, that in more recent years expanding world capitalism has not been as dominant as it was in earlier decades in the area of production, but it has been particularly striking in areas of *consumption*. Third world central sub-systems such as Lima-Callao, and regional centres such as Cuzco, have been the recipients of consumption patterns and imported lifestyles. They, in turn, transmit these to smaller centres and rural areas, creating clienteles as they do so.

We have seen that in a poor, stagnant region like Cuzco

Department, there was an extension of marketing and the opening of many new stores in the Sicuani area in the 1960s. And again in the 1970s, at a time of pronounced recession, the extension of new consumer preferences was quite apparent, even in remote towns distant from Cuzco city. Social urbanisation seems to be a sufficiently broad and inclusive concept to help explain such a widespread phenomenon. We must indeed look beyond both the social actors, the migrants themselves, and also beyond the rural area and the metropolis. The great scale of migration has produced multifarious links between formerly discrete rural–urban poles. The context is so broad that scholars talk of the urbanisation of society itself: 'Today's peasant is tomorrow's urbanite, and rural life evolves under conditions of increasing uncertainty created by the ready availability of urban alternatives and the quantitative loss of the rural population.'[16]

17 Peru in 1990

When I returned to Peru in April 1990, I was prepared to find the country in a state of sad disarray. My dismay and shock were, however, much greater than I had imagined due to the conjunction of economic and political failure and ineptitude, social disintegration and widespread violence.

THE ECONOMY

In November 1989 *The Peru Report* noted that exports per capitum had fallen from US$150 in 1985 to US$125 in current terms in 1988. Thirty years ago exports per capitum were equivalent to US$250 in 1989 terms. The minimum legal wage was down to half what it was then and Peruvian manufacturers in 1989 were producing 37 per cent less than at the start of García's APRA government. The external debt per head had grown from US$500 in 1980 to US$800 in 1988. Total liquidity in the financial system in 1989 was less than one-third of what it was four years earlier, and bank credit had shrunk by 80 per cent. After two years of satisfactory growth, agricultural production, including livestock, fell by 3.6 per cent in real terms in 1989. Farm-gate prices for most agricultural products fell markedly, although costs of imports, such as fertilisers, rose steeply. Thus the production costs of potatoes rose by 59 per cent from September 1988 to June 1989, while real prices rose only 20 per cent.

The regression of manufacturing, many export industries and other modern sector enterprises, and the projected decline in fishing, occurred at a time of continuing rapid population growth and ongoing urbanisation. With the increasing informality of the economy, the continuing economic crisis and the incompetence and corruption of the administration, it had become impossible to tax rent and other income. Thus taxes collected, as a percentage of GDP, had plummeted from 15 per cent in 1985 to less than 4 per cent in late 1989.

The desperate, worsening economy reflects the overall weakness of capitalism in an unstable, only moderate-sized country on the periphery of the world economy, at a time of international recession and unprecedented debt crisis. It reflects, too, the effects of hyperinflation which appears likely to set a world record, and the calamitous consequences of García's failure to cut the growing fiscal deficit in 1987. By January 1990 Peru's hyperinflation had lasted longer than Germany's infamous period of hyperinflation before the rise of Hitler. By July 1990, with average monthly inflation exceeding 25 per cent, Peru had accumulated a world record million per cent inflation over the previous five years.

An authoritative source summed up the Peruvian situation in these terms: 'A cruel mixture of government corruption and incompetence has fuelled moral crisis in a society already wracked by the destructive violence of fanatical subversives. Absurd economic policies have helped discredit Peru's entire political class.'[1]

Well-known economists, such as Dornbusch and Thorp,[2] concur that García's bold, unorthodox experiment with economic heterodoxy in 1985–7 was not inherently unsound. But Dornbusch parted company with Carbonetto, García's chief economic adviser, in August 1987 when the latter refused to recognise the need to cut the fiscal deficit. At the close of 1987, however, Carbonetto silently admitted that government pruning was necessary, but García did not recognise the need until September 1988: 'one of the most disastrous delays or pieces of political cowardice in Peruvian economic history'. By November 1989 the government had only seven months'-worth of imports in reserves, and government income was barely sufficient to pay public sector wages. By April 1990 all reserves were spent and the likelihood of capital flight had become great. Under the export financing procedures of early 1990, only about US$30 million a month was passing through the Central Bank, with imports costing some US$80–90 million a month. A leading Peruvian banker predicted a situation of ships off Callao unable to unload, as had happened in late 1988.[3]

It was abundantly clear that drastic fiscal adjustment was urgent, that the government could no longer afford to subsidise so many services or costs, and that essential subsidies should be redirected from supporting rich and middle class sectors to sustaining the essential needs of the rapidly growing numbers of poor. In 1989 the highest subsidies were in electricity and telephone tariffs, and upper-class members appeared to receive a monthly state subsidy equivalent to $150, or three times the legal wage.[4]

A report by William Tyler of the World Bank on 'the terrible crisis' of Peru attempted to identify numerous erroneous policies of the APRA Government after 1985. It mentioned selective control of prices, multiple exchange rates, restrictions on imports of manufactured goods, subsidies to agriculture, subsidies to credit, negative interest rates, unilateral limitation of payment of debt servicing, fiscal stimulation towards consumerism and extension of the intervention of the state in the economy.[5]

An interesting assessment of why APRA as a government failed in this period was provided by former president Belaúnde who, by the time of the 1990 elections, had become something of a respected elder-statesman figure of the centre-right. He condemned APRA for failing to keep essential promises, like the promise to respect people's savings in dollar certificates. That failure led to capital flight and zero creditability within days of the government taking over in 1985. He also condemned the government's foreign debt stance as being 'unnecessarily aggressive'. The government lacked diplomacy and tact in a matter of grave national interest. These policies, coupled with chronic evils such as the terms of trade and other factors affecting Third World development, were the causes of the crisis.[6]

POPULATION GROWTH AND SOCIAL EFFECTS

A basic contributing cause of Peru's economic failure was, of course, that chronic affliction of many Third World countries, demographic explosion. Population in 1989 was estimated as continuing to grow at the high rate of 2.5 per cent,[7] implying a massive growth in demand for employment, housing, education, health, transport, electricity, power and numerous other services. At the same time, both the continuing impact of the communications revolution and the spread of consumerism deeper into the Andes occurred, along with the continued stagnation of peasant production and growing fear, terror and instability inspired by Sendero Luminoso. The guerillas had executed peasants in numerous incidents, including women and children. Flight from the countryside induced by terrorism thus combined with economic 'push and pull' factors which attracted migrants to Lima and other cities.

Without detailed data, it is difficult to estimate the social effects of these trends with any reliability. However, the broad impression was of a steady deterioration of modern services in Lima that had brought the city virtually to the edge of breakdown. The attractive Hispanic-colonial city of the 1960s seemed to be engulfed by huge numbers of semi-employed urban colonists. Its bus services, its electric power supply and its water supply were all in disarray. While the affluence and fashionable modernity of the rich were still highly conspicuous in some parts of Lima, the decay and stagnation of many old *barriadas* was most apparent, while the misery and stark poverty of the lowest class areas and shanty towns was evident. The director of a private medical centre warned that the city's water supply could no longer be regarded as safe without boiling, and that typhoid was rampant in several areas of the metropolis.[8]

The human dimension of Peru's descent deeper into poverty was revealed in March 1990 by the findings of the *Prisma Report*, the first reliable study into the nutritional status of 6000 shanty-town children. It showed a disturbing but unmistakable deterioration over three years in mortality and weight–height indicators for children under three. The levels were found by UNICEF staff to be amongst the lowest in the world.[9]

The report estimated that perhaps half of Peru's population of 22 million suffers from deficiencies in food, clothing, housing, health or transport. Around 2.2 million Peruvians appear to be permanent victims of 'extreme poverty' for what are called 'structural' reasons, while another 6 or 7 million people are experiencing 'critical poverty' arising from the economic crisis of 1988–90. Another social planner has noted that although Peru by 1990 was the largest food aid recipient in Latin America, receiving about 100 000 tons or US$50 million worth a year, that tonnage would have to be doubled each year for three years. The government was denounced by an APRA senator for allowing the cost of medicines to rise by 200 per cent. None of Peru's political parties had worked out a coherent poverty relief programme ahead of the election in April 1990. With the realisation that the gap had steadily widened between the minimum legal wage and what was needed to buy a basket of essential goods, several social groups emerged by March 1990 recommending a two-pronged attack on poverty: a nutrition/basic health approach mainly targeted towards pregnant and lactating mothers and children under three, combined with an investment support programme for local production projects.

TERRORISM

Peru in 1990 was clearly in the grip of passive inertia, and dominated by a mood of fatalism and despair. Although the number of hard-core Senderistas has always been small (probably only 7000 at most), they controlled one-third of the Andes. Such was their discipline, dedication and careful planning that they seemed able to carry out lightning raids to assassinate, burn or destroy targets with a large measure of success, in spite of very large military and police forces. Their declared opposition to the democratic process (since it sustained the 'old order') threatened the holding of elections. Before the November 1989 municipal elections they murdered 84 candidates and, up to mid-April 1990, 779 people (including six legislative candidates) were killed. In Ayacucho, one-third of all voters did not vote in the April 1990 elections, and 60 per cent of those who did cast blank ballots. Although the government promised round-the-clock protection to all candidates, this was difficult to provide in remote Andean regions. Guerillas threatened to kill candidates, or their families or friends. Many contenders fled to Lima and conducted their campaigns at a distance in the relative safety of the capital. However, over 80 per cent of people voted, marking a victory for democracy over terrorism.[10]

Although a pall of gloom and fear lies over Peru because of terrorism, and paralysis is widespread, there have been some favourable developments in the last three years. The military have greatly improved the behaviour of troops, brutality is now much less common and many villagers can genuinely depend on troops for a reasonable level of protection. A little confidence has returned in some parts; after being completely depopulated, some areas of Ayacucho were resettled by peasants in 1986.

The inflexible attitude of Sendero denied it support from the working masses of Peru. Thus between 1977 and 1988 nine national strikes were carried out by workers, and in the two longest (July 1977 and May 1978) millions of people from all parts of the country participated. The attitude of Sendero to the first eight varied from absolute indifference to frontal opposition; only to the ninth strike in January 1988 did they lend some partial support.[11] Moreover the increased counter-insurgency aid offered by the Bush administration seems to have been of substantial help in leading to the arrest of a considerable number of terrorists, including some leaders, with the discovery of one of their safe houses in Lima. There are no signs, however, that their campaign of violence is waning.

Until terrorism can be eliminated and the rule of law triumphs, it exacts an enormous cost on the economy in addition to inducing widespread social paralysis through fear. Thus Peru joins other Third World countries with very large military budgets. Military expenditure in Peru is about 250 per cent of its spending on education and health.

GROWTH OF THE INFORMAL SECTOR

The growing informality of the economy and the inevitable great expansion of street traders of numerous kinds can be clearly seen in Lima, even in its most opulent suburb, and also in regional cities. With the decline of the tourist industry, there appears to have been a process at work of downward social mobility, with an enormous range of street markets.

The press in Lima, especially papers representing the middle-class establishment, have featured articles with photographs of the physical expansion of *ambulantes* (migratory street traders), and have commented on the congestion and noise they cause, even at times on major roads. In this situation, municipal regulations are 'a dead letter'. On the other hand, the left-wing press regarded it as an outrage that a recently set-up squatter settlement in Lima involving 16 000 families was attacked by a powerful police force, using dogs, horses, firearms, armoured cars, tear gas and incendiary bombs. In attempting to dislodge or destroy the illegal settlement, it was alleged that the armed police seriously wounded 10 people while another 150 received minor wounds.[12]

It is clear that processes of 'urban involution' or 'tertiarisation' of the economy have occurred through the formation of a myriad number of small illegal enterprises; although these trends have been at work at least since 1950, their pace and scale have greatly increased in the 1980s. These processes appear to be similar to those which characterise many Third World countries.

Recently an exhaustive study of Lima's informal economy was carried out by Hernan De Soto's Peru research institute, which argues that the informal sector is a popular, spontaneous and creative response to the incapacity of the state to satisfy the most elemental aspirations of the poor. Not only does he document the great vitality and dynamism of the informal sector, but he also shows the inadequacy and discriminatory nature of the state in a Third World setting.

De Soto's institute investigated 'the cost of legality' and found that to gain legal recognition and to be officially registered would cost $1231, or 32 times the minimum salary. Clearly, to legalise a small industry in such conditions of costly and incompetent bureaucracy was quite outside the possibilities of a person of modest means, let alone those existing in the informal sector. Moreover, it calculated that if a group of humble families solicited the state for adjudicating land to build cheap housing, it would take on average 6 years and 11 months to complete formalities with the various ministries and municipal authorities, and cost *per person* approximately $2156, equivalent to 56 times the minimum salary at that time.[13]

A 1990 presidential candidate, the world-famous novelist, Vargas Llosa, accepted the powerful logic of De Soto, and in his essay on the informal sector, *The Silent Revolution*, sketched the image of a country in which the tragic and absurd were condoned. People were condemned to underdevelopment, to a condition in which they 'sink each day more into inefficiency and corruption'.

When poor peasants in the countryside decide to migrate, because of drought, overpopulation, falling production, fear of terrorism or because of their hopes of a better life in the city, they usually find, in conditions of urban unemployment, that the imperious legal system closes off an income. They have no other option but to invent work in some kind of informal enterprise at the margin of the law.

However, such people may be regarded as having creative and constructive responses to demoralisation. For example, De Soto's study documents the commerce, industry, housing and transport sectors. In Lima alone, informal commerce gave work to some 439 000 people. Of the 331 markets in the city, 274 were operated by the informal sector. The inhabitants of the capital depended overwhelmingly on it for transport since 95 per cent of public transport was in its hands, with over $1000 million invested in vehicles and infrastructure. Half the total population live in houses constructed by the informal sector. While the state built cheap housing of a value of $1764 million between 1960 and 1989, in the same period the informal sector built houses worth $8319 million.[14]

The positive contributions of the informal sector to the internal economy cannot be doubted, and one can only admire the vitality, resilience and ingenuity of many of the tens of thousands of street traders who attempt, and often succeed, through this other road, to gain a livelihood. As such it provides *personal* solutions to millions of struggling poor. But it is possible to exaggerate its importance in macro-economic terms. Many street traders are struggling to gain the barest of incomes, and it is not known what proportion are achieving dependable returns or providing a real exit-route to a life of modest decency. Moreover, a great deal of informal sector commerce does not create new wealth or bring in export income. Largely it merely recirculates goods already produced elsewhere. The best hope for the future is that it may become the lower circuit of a more integrated urban economy[15] that 'unwinds upwards' into the upper capitalist circuit of the modern sector.

THE AGRARIAN SITUATION, 1980–90

It is difficult to decide whether the stagnation and decline of Andean agriculture was primarily caused by macro trends affecting the Peruvian economy as a whole and that the agrarian reform was a largely irrelevant process and period in the longer term, or whether the excesses and catastrophic failures of both the Peruvian Revolution and its associated agrarian reform were perhaps of almost equal importance. Certainly both sets of factors were at work.

A main consequence of the agrarian reform was the considerable strengthening of both medium- and small-sized commercial farms, together with the agro-industrial sector. These groups surged ahead because of their strategic location in the productive process when the massive expansion of urban consumption goods became important in the 1970s and 1980s.[16] Whereas the old *hacienda* order had its power based on the ownership of large areas of land and the monopoly control over labour that this induced, from the 1960s onwards social groups which could mediate relations between the peasantry and the state – socially, culturally and economically – became dominant. The agrarian reform began to alter, bureaucratise and sometimes intensify these relationships, and those rural social groups which could mediate and often lead the new changes advanced in importance.

While almost all the coastal co-operatives were still operating in 1990, in the Sierra only a small percentage of SAIS and CAPs (10–40 per cent) still functioned. The great majority had been taken over and divided amongst invading peasant groups who were reacting to a gross lack of capitalisation in the Sierra and ongoing inequalities and injustices. There seemed in 1990 to be widespread stagnation or regression of the peasantry further into subsistence, although the further advance of migration networks of kin, proletarianisation and the search for non-agricultural sources of income also seem to have developed.

Capitalism did advance where local conditions were favourable, however, whether in the form of vigorous merchant trading or in an expansion of moderately successful small- or medium-sized farms (as on the Pampa de Anta). In such situations the gap between middle class *vecinos* and the poorer peasants would appear to have widened further. Little promising regional development occurred to ameliorate widespread poverty.

CHANGING POLITICAL ECONOMY

The irony of the Peruvian political economy is that 'the children of Velasco', as the new export groups are sometimes called, stand to inherit the fruits of victory through the 1990s, while the Peruvian economy and most of the population are doomed to increasing poverty. An international climate of monetarism illustrated by Thatcherite Britain and Pinochet's Chile created conditions favourable internationally for a model developing in Peru that concentrated wealth profoundly, and trends and policies pursued since the 1970s make this outcome even more inevitable.

Although agriculture and grazing still employed 1 240 000 people in the Andes in 1981, their importance in the Peruvian economy declined steadily from 13.8 per cent of total GDP in 1973 to only 8.1 per cent in 1983. Exports of agricultural products as a percentage of total exports had declined from 20.5 per cent in 1973 to only 6.5 per cent in 1983. Within the eight Sierra departments, agriculture and livestock were in a state of regression, their value declining from 52.7 per cent of the GDP of the region in 1971 to only 26.5 per cent in 1981.[17] At the same time food imports as a percentage of total imports in the Peruvian economy grew from 10.8 per cent in 1976 to 15.6 per cent in 1983.[18] While the economic function of the Sierra was always dominated by *desarrollo hacia afuera* (giving priority to production for the outside world), this has led merely to the constitution of enclaves mainly based on mining centres (copper, iron, lead, zinc) or hydro-electricity generation. With national functions always predominating over regional ones, the regional economy shows increasing spatial disarticulation over time. The evolving spatial structure, reflecting the dominance of the coastal natural region, has led to predominance of coastal communication systems; transverse road connections to Sierra centres and the longitudinal Sierra road are now of less importance.

Some scholars argue that this style of development, characterised by the dominance of the coastal axis and state intervention to maintain this, impeding as it does the growth of inter-sectoral demands or complementarities within the Sierra, has done little to encourage healthy development in the Sierra. Most of the growth has been focused on mineral exploitation, has led to enclave development and has been promoted mainly by foreigners.

Study of investment patterns confirms these views. While the Andes were relatively favoured in the 1970s, receiving about 42 per cent of total public investment, investment *per capitum* is generally 25 per cent below the national average. Arequipa (mainly irrigation) and Ancash absorbed about 60 per cent of Andean investment, while Apurimac and Ayacucho received only 0.5 per cent of the country's public investment. Investment was certainly localised in zones of major comparative advantage and, while it was important to promote the mining industry, these expenditures proved to have little spread effect.

Over the 20-year period of 1970–90, the dominance of policies of maintaining food security in urban centres by the provision of government subsidies has been the decisive factor in shaping the overall political economy. Lajo Lazo (1986) has shown how this policy has enabled the agro-industry in processing basic foods to increase its markets enormously, to lower the relative prices of its products and to manage its monopoly profit margins. While peasant production is often sluggish in responding to urban demand, Lajo Lazo argues convincingly that this policy is one of the substantive causes of agrarian stagnation, of the abandonment or backwardness of the Sierra and of the remaining peasant and agrarian areas of Peru.[19]

Indeed Lajo Lazo presents a powerful case that Peru has established a development model which is urban–coastal–centralist in its essential base, which leads inevitably to the growth of the informal economy of the cities, the stagnation of peasant areas and the industrial and economic crisis. Although adjustments have been made to subsidies and food import quotas, Lajo Lazo challenges the sincerity of the ministers involved. His evidence shows that the administration of prices and subsidies by government has enlarged the markets of processed food with a high imported component 'in an excessive way'. The greatest increase in production of noodles, soya oil, evaporated milk and poultry occurred in the 1970s, precisely in those years in which more subsidies were granted to imported inputs. The administration of prices and subsidies preserved the profits of the oligopolies, and over 25 years contributed to improving the relative prices of foods processed with subsidised imports and to worsen the relative prices of Peruvian foods. In the 14 years 1970–84 there was a stagnation or decline in the indices of volumes produced of cotton, potatoes, fresh milk and beef.[20]

It is clear that there is an urgent need for a redefinition of the style of agro-industrial development. There needs to be a steady change in the habits of consumption, and especially urban consumption, and in the system of relative prices in favour of national foods and internal (including peasant) production. While a minimum level of strategic foods needs to be fixed to safeguard the food security of the masses and to provide access to basic foods so that an adequate level of nutrition is guaranteed, the highly oligopolistic structure of the agro-food industry should be addressed, encouraging greater competition.

THE POLITICAL ARENA

Inevitably the effects of economic crisis, growing poverty, violence and social despair were reflected in political attitudes. In early 1990 the APRA government of Alan García was almost universally condemned or derided: the Peruvian people at large held it responsible for the nation's situation. Not only were its policies believed to be wrong, it was regarded widely as incompetent or inept and severely tainted by corruption.[21] The political mood in the country was described by Hugo Otero, García's political adviser, as one of 'profound nihilism' (a situation on which Sendero Luminoso draws heavily). He defined nihilism as the state of mind produced when you spend all your time and energy just getting something to eat. Otero believed, as events during the run-up to the elections were to confirm, that the political parties at the end of 1989 were not the expression of the people.[22]

The widespread rejection of mixed economy models, public sector enterprise and frequent government interventionism led to a considerable surge of support for right-wing, more-market, even monetarist political approaches and, when Vargas Llosa became a presidential candidate, his new party (Fredemo) capitalised on these trends and attracted support from existing right-wing parties.

In his sincerity to overhaul the Peruvian economy, Vargas proposed a radical programme of stabilisation followed by liberalisation. Strains began to appear among the loose collection of right-wing political groups that backed him, for overprotected businessmen were loath to abolish the policies that had enriched them. Some Peruvians recognised Fredemo as merely a new simplistic, though attractively packaged, right-wing approach seeking a 'nice competitive eighteenth century market place' in which Peru would discover its individual comparative advantage. The liberal model of Fredemo seemed to concentrate wealth rather than democratise it.

In February 1990 Vargas Llosa held 45 per cent of the support of the electorate, according to the polls, while his nearest rival polled a mere 14 per cent; Vargas appeared close to the 50 per cent needed in the first April vote that would make the second vote unnecessary. The spectacular rise of his popularity reflected, however, more a rejection of García's APRA government than his own substantial political strength, for political events in 1990 showed the great volatility of the electorate. The unexpected entry of a dark horse, Alberto Fujimori, into the election campaign caused a major surprise, and his independent new 'party', Cambio 90 (Change 90), immediately began to attract support. While Fujimori attracted only 3 per cent support at the beginning of March, less than three weeks later he polled 9.5 per cent.

The left-wing parties in 1990 did not present a credible alternative to Fredemo, for nobody knew where the money would come from to pay for their unrealistic programmes, and it would require almost 'a Bolshevik dictatorship' to apply their policies. Fujimori, on the other hand, did not make Vargas's mistake of alienating centrist and left-wing elements irretrievably, and ran an enormously successful campaign. A Peruvian of Japanese descent, an agronomist and ex-rector of La Molina agricultural university, Fujimori presented himself as an independent free of damaging political connections, a man with the appropriate practical, technical and administrative skills needed to implement radical and massive development initiatives. He had done post-graduate research in the USA and Germany, and in addition to his agronomic skills he spoke five languages and was also an able mathematician. His Japanese as well as his career background added to the image of a man likely to succeed in promoting national economic renovation. Moreover Fujimori showed himself to be a superb television performer. His low-key, deliberate or technical approach to many problems commanded respect, and he promised to bring honesty and a work ethic to government. His apparently centrist position (in reality Cambio 90 is a right-wing party) was one that many people could identify with, and with the widespread disillusionment with politicians it was a great asset not to be a professional politician. The upshot was an election result on 8 April 1990 that was a bombshell to some of the world's press, which had misread the volatility and complexity of Peruvian politics. Vargas Llosa won only 32 per cent of the vote while Fujimori gained 29 per cent.[23]

Fujimori, backed by a group of Protestant evangelicals and small businessmen, easily won majority support in the *barriadas*, and his message of 'Work, Honesty and Technology' also triumphed in the Andes. In the June voting the trends of April were fully confirmed: Fujimori won 56 per cent of the vote.

At the end of July 1990, when President Fujimori took office, he was faced with the fact that he would have to introduce specific measures rapidly to rescue his steadily sinking country. With the Central Bank's reserves at about minus US$400 million and inflation continuing at about 40 per cent a month, it was essential to adopt draconian measures immediately.

Thus Peru today continues its search for a viable development model which can exist between two unacceptable choices. On the one hand is oligarchy, military rule, harsh austerity and near tyranny, and on the other is weak incompetent demagogy which drives the country to bankruptcy and anarchy.

18 Chilca in 1990

Flying once more over the Andes towards Cuzco was a reminder of the precarious nature of the peasant's livelihood in this formidable mountain home. Accelerated erosion can be observed over vast areas. Top soil rarely exists, and on numerous tiny ecological niches green crops cling to the steep mountainside, perching amid the sparse, forbidding hills. The pockets of crops are linked by tortuous mule tracks with the more favoured communities lying in the valley bottoms far below.

Cuzco city repeated many of the features of Lima in 1990, swollen with ex-peasants and semi-proletarians fossicking for an existence in the greatly expanded market or on the pavements that were packed with hundreds of street traders. The old colonial city had a run-down, impoverished appearance, although many scores of new *adobe ranchos* had been improvised by invading migrants on the steep slopes at the city's outskirts. The marginality of many peoples' lives, their chronic underemployment and the great pressure on modern services characterises Cuzco in 1990. While the disjunction between rich and poor, modern and traditional is great, development and underdevelopment here are linked as twin aspects of capital accumulation.

Of course the hinterland of such a substantial city has benefited from the growth of its market and many features on the Pampa de Anta, such as thriving *pequeñas propiedades* and the rather new asphalt main road, illustrate some promising market opportunities. Izcuchaka, the regional market town, was much larger than in 1979, and was planning to construct a new, bigger marketplace. As I drove across the *pampa* towards Chilca I noticed a number of features of modernisation: a bulldozer at work and an electric fence employed for more efficient pasture rotation.

Chilca in 1990 had changed greatly.[1] The village now comprised about 2500 people, or 500 households. There were many new houses on the *pampa* side of the road on what had formerly been *hacienda* and then co-operative land, which were larger, superior dwellings compared to the average peasant house. Two or three trucks were to be seen, a new store or two and other signs of commercialism and 'mestization'. The older part of the village was more densely packed with houses, some of which had been enlarged, and with walled yards and store houses. The old centre of the village had deteriorated considerably. The church which in 1979 had needed a coat of whitewash looked almost abandoned, the plaza was no longer cared for and two or three little stores were quite dilapidated. Over all, power lines, the mark of progress, drooped from many unsightly electric power poles.

Land use on the steep slopes of *temporal* land that backed the village was also quite different. While the eucalyptus plantation had been cut down (though the trees were sprouting again from the stumps), many land owners had planted small plantations of their own or sown eucalyptus seedlings to mark land boundaries. This was clearly much more appropriate land use, giving some protection from erosion and providing a valuable resource for the future.

Many differences represented the logical culmination of longer-term processes of social change. Thus the diversion of about half of the poor eroding slopes from uneconomic short fallow cropping of barley or wheat to tree planting marks an important structural change in the evolution of land use. The installation of *agua potable* and the electrification of the village mark even more dramatic social change as a result of rising aspirations in the village and a greater role played by external agencies. Clearly the closed corporate community model, largely appropriate for describing Chilca in the early 1960s, has little relevance to this much more open community of 1990.

My return to Chilca was sad at the personal level. Several older peasants welcomed me warmly and Ricardo and Victor and their wives were astonished and delighted to see me again. My closest friend, Santiago, the *personero* who had gone to prison on three occasions in the struggle to regain the *pampa* from the *hacienda*, and his wife had both died two years earlier. Another old friend, Mariano, the father of the original innovator Justo, and Marta, the poor widow of 1979, had also died. With the continuing mobility of the peasantry many people had moved away to live in the city, while many others whom I did not know, especially young people who had been small children in 1964 and absent urban wage earners in 1979, had moved back to live in the community. Other close friends, whose daughter had been my god-daughter, and who were mainly dependent on town-based income in 1979, had shifted permanently to Cuzco, where they ran a minibus operation.

INNOVATION IN THE 1980s

While the period of Belaúnde's second administration (1980–5) was a time of tight monetary policy and reduction of subsidies to fertilisers, the extension of outside projects to Chilca brought some relief, encouraging rural development. The PRODERM project, promoted initially by the Dutch, instituted several schemes of cheap agricultural credit that lasted about 10 years. It gave credit early in the 1980s to start a dairy marketing co-operative for Chilca, based on a total of 400 cows owned by a score or two of separate households. But animal disease and variable milk supplies plagued the co-operative, and when the co-operative could not meet repayment dates on its loan it collapsed; a levy had to be placed on each household to repay the debt.

Villagers became more familiar with the role of credit and, in years when the weather was kind, larger harvests were gained from improved crop varieties. Some foreign pedigree dairy cattle were introduced and crossed with local *criollo* stock so that the quality improved. However, the severe incidence of various cattle diseases remained, and in October 1989 was so bad (in spite of superior medicines being available) that almost all cattle were slaughtered to prevent the further spread of disease. Villagers also learnt that high quality stock would rapidly deteriorate without good quality pastures. Some men, especially *agricultores* or *vecinos*, began to appreciate the good nutritional value of alfalfa, ryegrass and clover. With the help of PRODERM they began to improve their pastures.

The coincidence of the favourable balance of trade with García's new APRA government in 1985 led to a further expansion of agricultural credit. The agrarian bank offered loans at 0 per cent and later at low interest rates. Villagers resumed the widespread use of chemical fertilisers, insecticides, fungicides and animal medicines that they had been forced to give up in the late 1970s. Even where specific credit schemes collapsed, a 'phoenix effect' may have occurred, for from the ashes new ideas of innovation occasionally emerged. The educative effects of PRODERM's work seem to have been encouraging.

The community, which had discussed buying the stables from the co-operative since 1979, finally did so in 1986 with a loan from PRODERM and money from the sale of 155 cows. Some leaders thought that the large building would be useful for store feeding of cattle, fattening them for sale. However, leaders of the community admitted in hindsight that the purchase of the stables was a costly mistake. Each household fattened cattle privately for sale, rather than buying cattle and using the stables co-operatively.

The electrification of the township of Anta in 1979 had stimulated the popular demand for the spread of electric power to larger peasant villages. When staff of the regional power agency visited Chilca about 1986, people eagerly welcomed the innovation. The 7ha eucalyptus plantation was felled, paying 20 per cent of the costs of electrification, as well as contributing to paying off the loan for the stables. High voltage cables for the *pampa* were provided by French aid, and wiring and other costs were met by Finland, whose technicians supervised the installation. It appears that French and Finnish aid met the remaining costs of electrification.

All houses in the village now had electric light, some used power for cooking, a few had purchased washing machines and about 20 families had television sets. This dramatic change shows how far Chilca has moved from the traditional palaeotechnic ecotype and simple peasant economy of the early 1960s to become part of the modern world. Agricultural technological change has also modernised steadily, for the community has purchased two tractors and four sets of discs to plough the damp heavy soils of the *pampa*.

Socially and institutionally, Chilca reflects its greater openness, its greater cholofication and the acceptance of *mestizo* and cosmopolitan values and skills. Thus Honorato, the former conservative leader, said proudly that 20 per cent of Chilca people were now 'professionals'. Attitudes to schooling were interesting. With the growth of population a secondary school had been established which was regarded as a distinct asset. Seven hectares of land had been assigned to it and a portion of money from the potato harvest went to assist its funding. Some parents regarded primary school standards as very much better than in 1979, with more trust now placed in teachers. It was said that if teachers were lazy or incompetent, parents might write to the Ministry of Education and the teacher would be reprimanded. Visits of inspectors were a little more frequent. Other parents said the school was only average in quality. Others, usually more socially mobile or richer peasants, claimed the quality of schooling was still poor, noting that the teachers still lived in Cuzco and that they taught in Spanish, whereas many pupils spoke only Quechua. It was asserted that some teachers still demanded presents of eggs, chickens and the like from parents.

While many aspects of traditional peasantry remained, it is clear that the widespread uses of agricultural credit and agricultural innovations in the 1980s showed that many people had moved to an 'agricultural investment' phase, and even (as the purchase of the stables and tractors indicate) an 'investment trial' period.[2] While many of these projects might continue to fail for a decade or two, the community was now involved in raising substantial loans as a matter of course, and in projects involving planning in the community over a number of years. Clearly this marks another phase in social evolution.

THE TRIUMPH OF THE PEASANTRY

The greatest change of all, however, had led to a veritable revolution in land use. When I left Chilca in September 1979 it seemed that the beleaguered co-operative, already greatly partitioned by invading peasants, might not survive. Victor was arrested and imprisoned for a period, but in November 1979 he led the final and decisive peasant invasion. Later the co-operative was formally wound up and Ricardo showed me the title to six parcels of land totalling 666.49 ha that were passed over to Chilca. The peasantry had finally won in their eternal struggle for land.

The acquisition of large areas of *pampa* land with the collapse of the co-operative and its distribution among households led immediately to the abandonment of crop planting in the *puna*. Now families established crops on the *pampa* on the other side of the main road, and this became the main centre of their agricultural activity apart from the small *maizal parcelas* enclosed in courtyards near their houses. The *puna* was now used only for grazing in the warm wet period, for a maximum of four months.

The distribution of the new lands had acted like a magnet to many widely dispersed kinsfolk. A substantial return migration of young *cholos* occurred and the *pampa* side of the road became the location of the 'new population'. Many brought young wives from outside Chilca with them. It was suggested that they were independent and different in their style of livelihood, for they had chosen not to go back to live in their parents' homes. Return migration may have been caused also by the growing living costs and increasing unemployment in the cities, but land redistribution had now ceased and its benefits will soon be used up by the increased population.

The actual distribution of lands between families, although it had occurred a decade ago, was obviously highly controversial. Some peasants believed that the distribution was based, at least partly, on the number of children in the household. It was asserted that some households had gained only about 1ha of additional land, although 2ha may have been the minimum. Other households gained up to 5ha of additional land. Ricardo asserted that 'those who worked hardest got more', perhaps 5ha, while others got less. He had gained 4½ ha and most leaders got relatively large additional portions. Another leader asserted that if a man had good relations with one of the leaders he might get several hectares. A poor man alleged that Aurelio, the President and a former administrator of the co-operative (already one of the richest men in the community), had given help to widows in distress in return for their making their land over to him at death, a practice which was also observed in Qolquepata. The powerful people, it was said, allied with 'the good people' and not with the poor. I was unable to check the accuracy of all these allegations, but it was widely accepted that the land distribution had been carried out in an unequal way.

It had, however, benefited all families. The addition of another 2ha represented a 100 per cent increase or more for many poor families, and they recognised in a relative sense that their livelihood had been greatly improved. Now there was no shortage of land, each family could look after itself, and people said they were happy. Moreover, the old yoke of domination of the large landowner (whether *hacienda* or co-operative) had been broken: 'families are free now'.

Although this improvement in livelihood in Chilca is substantial and welcome, the parcellation of *hacienda* or co-operative lands by the surrounding peasantry does not appear to be a satisfactory long-term solution for the Andes. Like the *ejido* (land reform) movement which occurred in Mexico, a new, slightly more affluent minifundism merely replaces the old, and within another decade the advantages of greater resource availability will be mopped up by population growth. While small-scale, intensive, individualistic utilisation may be the predominant model for land use in the future, the need to achieve economies of scale (for example, in processing, transporting and marketing milk, the utilisation of tractors and expensive machinery) to gain the benefits of association, to maintain supervised credit programmes or to avoid the inevitable overgrazing of a public good such as a mountain side, requires the development of a range of voluntary co-operative institutions or regional rural development programmes. There is also a danger that the beneficiaries might become complacent rural conservatives, resisting further innovation.

REVERSION TO MIXED AGRICULTURE

The re-emergence of cropping as the principal form of land use was another surprising development. We have seen that from 1964 to 1979 peasant production became steadily more specialised, with dairy production becoming predominant. More recently, however, people began to plant potatoes and other crops on the *pampa*. This may have been induced by the distribution of the additional land and the switch from the *puna*, but the provision of 0 per cent credit in the early period of García's government, relatively high prices for a number of crops and increased local labour may have been contributing factors. Thus in 1984 and 1985 the price for *quinoa* (cropped to only a small extent in earlier years), broad beans, peas and white maize was quite good.[3] Moreover the evolution of the urban-coastal-centralist development model that Lajo Lazo has described meant that the prices of national products such as milk rose much less in the period 1985–7 (due to the importation of cheap substitutes) than the prices of crops.[4] This situation was most discouraging to Peruvian dairy producers. After four years of cropping on the *pampa*, people are still obtaining good yields unless drought or frost take their toll.

Such was the change of land use that I investigated rainfall patterns. While the changes are not statistically significant, the mean annual total of rainfall for Anta for the five years of 1985–9 was only 658.18mm, compared to 732.5mm in the five years of 1975–9 and 843mm for six years in the 1950s at nearby Chinchero.[5] More importantly, the considerable reduction in mean monthly rainfall in the two former five-year periods for the months of February, April, August, September, November and December might have been a factor. Such drier months would inhibit grass growth and make it more difficult to maintain satisfactory milk production, encouraging a switch to cropping.

Thus while culturally, institutionally and, to some extent, economically 'depeasantisation' had continued in Chilca, the 1990 pattern of land use showed some reversion to the classic peasant economy of dependence on both a number of crops and livestock. Agricultural sub-products remained important (for instance, the fodder component of maize stalks and leaves) and, while increased cropping for the market had developed, it is important to emphasise the greater diversity of land use and the important connections between the components. This tendency strengthened peasant security and the capacity to cope with risk. Moreover, even if crops were to maintain high prices, most poor or middle peasants would continue to keep a few cows and pigs for they are always a ready source of capital.

Peasant families in Chilca in 1990 could thus reproduce themselves in economic and geographical conditions of stasis rather more easily on the basis of the conjunction of more land, more labour, rather more irrigation water, cheap agricultural credit, perhaps drier soils and rather better prices for some crops compared to earlier times. The variability of their economic behaviour is largely explained by these heterogeneous complexities and inter-relationships. With greater involvement in the market, the utilisation of capitalist relations became more widespread, and non-capitalist methods of mobilising labour, such as *ayni*, less common. It is interesting to note that *ayni* was still employed on the *maizal* near the older part of the village, whereas capitalist relations were completely dominant on the *pampa*, where mechanisation and wage labour had been customary under both the *hacienda* and co-operative.

By 1990, however, the effects of hyperinflation and the economic crisis impinged directly on the community. The interest rate on agricultural credit had shot up to 40 per cent, and the price of other inputs also escalated rapidly. Many poor and middle peasants found that they were unable to pay back loans or meet interest payments. The agrarian bank had threatened to visit the village to seize cattle or household property in lieu of payment, and many peasants feared this outcome.

A crippling drought in 1990 also had the same effect, following on from a severe frost in the previous winter that had wiped out some harvests of barley, wheat and *quinoa*. It was claimed that 27 000 hectares of crops valued at over $42 million were lost through three southern departments, and 400 000 inhabitants were directly affected. Increased migration was induced, either towards the coast or the *selva*. The Government declared an emergency for 120 days and the Minister of Agriculture made an international appeal for aid.[6] The rainfall for the wet season, from November 1989 to March 1990 at Anta, dropped by 44 per cent from the mean for this period.

In Chilca a large proportion of maize and potatoes were lost, cows were producing only about a litre of milk per day and only one-third of the normal *quinoa* harvest was expected.

The effects of excessively high interest rates, input costs, frost and drought would, of course, be to encourage a retreat into subsistence, a decline in market sales and the increased use of non-capitalist relations such as *ayni*. If, however, wages and living costs in the cities improve later, relative to conditions in the countryside, greater reliance is likely to be placed again on remittances and the migration of family members to undertake wage work. The widely dispersed network of kin remains in place and there is no doubt that over time there is, as Gonzalez de Olarte (1984) has observed, a progressive separation of income from production: that is, income derived from crop and livestock production or local craft sales declines, while that deriving from external wage work, remittances and services increases proportionately.

UNITY AND ORGANISATION

Although the population of Chilca had grown by about 47 per cent (from 350 to 500 families) from 1979 to 1990, people generally declared that there was much more unity in the community now. They attributed their happiness directly to their additional land. The triumph of the peasantry was indeed two-fold: economic (gaining land) and political (their power locally was now unchallenged).

However, their perception of unity was primarily symbolic and partly superficial. It was also a perception that was not universal. When older villagers complained that disunity was now even worse, they were thinking of debates at the village assembly, the failure of people to support agreed community projects, the fact that only 40 per cent of villagers attended *faenas* to do community work, and that many absentees, fined for neglecting their communal duties, managed to avoid payment. It is apparent that differentiation of the peasantry and its variable rate of modernisation were proceeding apace, and that the community was changing fundamentally in the way it organised labour and carried out projects.

Its size had made it too large, diverse and cumbersome for some communal activities to operate efficiently and it was interesting to see that three *anexos* (hamlets) were recognised. These probably developed their own senses of community and some devolution of communal activity might well occur to them. It has been observed that collective efficiency is usually much greater in communities of less than 100 families (500–600 persons) rather than in those of 800 or 1000 families,[7] and this explains the common dismemberment or parcellation of great *comunidades* into separate *anexos* where collective management of families is both easier and more efficient.

LEADERSHIP

In 1979 three men vied for leadership in social, economic and political areas. As the community modernised and changed throughout the 1980s, different leadership roles or qualities were called for.

As I had expected, Honorato maintained the dominant role in leadership for a couple of years after 1979. But the victory of the peasantry with the collapse of the co-operative in November 1979, a struggle in which Victor had played a leading and courageous role, immediately enhanced his position and vindicated his political views. Victor was feared and hated by

Honorato, Ricardo and many of their supporters in 1976–9, for some believed the armed police might intervene brutally to support the co-operative and repress the peasants. When the victory was won, however, they paid due recognition to Victor's role and the soundness and bravery of his policies and became friendly with him.

In the early 1980s, Honorato stepped down as Justice of the Peace, although he continued to be important within the community. However, in keeping with his *vecino* non-peasant status, by 1990 he was planning to live in Cuzco and was building a house there.

Although he was a *comunero* purely through marriage, Ricardo did not need many years' residence in Chilca to demonstrate the practical usefulness of his skills. He became Justice of the Peace in 1982 and remained so through most of the decade and again in 1990. He also headed the electrification committee for a while. His entrepreneurial bent and cosmopolitan views were most valuable to the community in innumerable ways. Ricardo was one of the leader farmers in the community and the quality of his pastures on the *pampa* was relatively good. While land near his house was farmed in typical peasant fashion, he was running one of his three hectares of pasture as a trial, interplanting ryegrass with oats. Since the quality of his cattle had been improved markedly, he was acutely aware of the need for technical assistance to enable him to upgrade his pastures. He had acquired 10 imported pedigree cows with an agricultural loan.

Ricardo completely accepted the new diversity of Chilca's population and welcomed the higher education and broader experience of many of the returning migrants. He understood the forces of change at work and was not shocked at the number of absentees for *faena* work. Under his leadership more people seemed to realise that if innovations were truly desired, technical help could be hired from the cities, with the community paying for their services. He remained highly critical of some services, however. Although the Ministry of Agriculture visited frequently, 'they don't do anything'.

As Justice of the Peace, he was very conscious of family problems and disputes, and robbery which was very common in the community. The village was now large enough to need a policeman. Ricardo was highly critical of the bad administration of the current Junta Directiva, and for some general problems he favoured meetings involving several neighbouring communities. Although the community wanted to separate from the Anta district, they did not want to be isolated within the *municipio* (local administrative area). His attitude to the deterioration of the church and plaza was typically radical but sensible: the plaza was now too small and it was time to shift the church. He was satisfied that the allocation of 7ha to the new secondary school and contributions from the potato harvest should be sufficient for its operation, supplementing state funding.

Although Ricardo has been a major leader in this community and often worked tirelessly on its behalf, there is no doubt that, along with all the major leaders, he had considerably improved his personal circumstances in the process. He had gained a relatively large amount of land from the co-operative distribution and he had a large and superior new house built on the edge of the *pampa*. When we talked of the rich people of Chilca he said, 'it all depends on them'. These *vecinos* had worked hard, he believed, and so deserved their wealth and position.

Once his role was vindicated by the success of the invasion of the co-operative, Victor became a significant and widely popular figure. Throughout the last decade he had taken a keen interest in various schemes of agricultural innovation on the *pampa*. He had also planted ryegrass and other superior grasses on his own land, and experimented with medicines for his cattle. Like Ricardo, he had also benefited from various schemes of cheap rural credit and was one of the main leader farmers in the area. He had also acquired some imported Brown Swiss and Friesian cows and had crossed them with local animals. Although he currently had only 2 cows on his 6ha, his pastures and crops were in good condition. He had an unusual house, furnished with cane chairs, a small flower garden and a relatively new truck.

Victor attempted to repeat his successful milk co-operative of the 1970s by setting up other co-operatives in the region on a number of occasions. One year he ran a co-operative set up to manage the use of a tractor, lent by PRODERM, to plough the land of neighbouring communities. The scheme operated well while he was in charge but, when he had to go to Lima and a new leader took over, it collapsed. Currently he was helping the new young President of Chilca, a man who was a promising leader, to manage a co-operative involving potato planting on a few hectares contributed by surrounding communities.

In discussing the best form of rural organisation (*hacienda*, co-operative or peasant parcellation), Victor declared his preference for the third option, for each peasant family having adequate land to work separately. He believed, however, that it was desirable also to develop co-operative institutions to help peasant production (for example, for transportation or milk marketing). Bad leadership was the main problem: each leader wished to get on top, and most enterprises were riven with envy.

Victor also played a wider regional role. In 1983 he was elected president of the Peasant Federation for two years, and although he worked hard he often felt frustrated by the disorganisation of the federation. Later he was elected to an important position in the municipality. In this role he busied himself with many problems of the whole Pampa area.

Victor continued to be politically active, supporting the left-wing group Izquierda Unida (IU). As an intelligent, educated and humane man, Victor rejected the extreme policies of the Sendero Luminoso guerrillas, both for their crude, confused analysis of Peru's problems and for the terrible violence of their methods. With the demise of APRA, IU and all left-wing parties in the first vote, Victor declared that people in Chilca would cast their second vote for Fujimori.

Just before I left Victor, we discussed life in Chilca in broad terms over the last 30 years and the varying fortunes of people, ideas and institutions in this time. It is now quite clear that there will be no return to the *hacienda* system. The families of the local *hacendados*, the Luna brothers, live in Cuzco, possess no land and are no longer wealthy. As a boy Victor remembered clearly the great events of the peasant mobilisation and land occupation in La Convención and the role of Hugo Blanco, their leader. Although *vecinos* from Chilca did not want to help the La Convención peasantry, the Junta Directiva of Chilca had offered their assistance and followed the advice of the La Convención syndicate. Some years later he visited Lima as a representative of the Peasant Federation and met Hugo Blanco. He was, he declared, 'a good man, but he made mistakes too'. Victor said that Santiago, who went to prison three times in the struggle to regain the *pampa* from the *hacienda*, had been an outstanding and courageous leader in those early confrontations with the *haciendas*. Twenty years later Victor was to follow his example, going to prison himself in the course of the struggle. Santiago, an ordinary villager and middle peasant who had only died two years earlier, appeared to be achieving some local immortality already for his historic and courageous fight for the return of the lands.

Victor smiled wryly when he commented on the change in attitudes towards him after the collapse of the co-operative. The period 1976–8 had been hard, and Honorato and Ricardo and their followers had hated him in this period. When, however, on leaving prison Victor organised the final decisive invasion of the co-operative, Honorato and Ricardo declared that he was right and they became friends. Victor found this rather ironic.

19 Conclusion

The Andean closed corporate peasantry, the subject of this book, can be viewed as both a structure and a process. Thus, its members exist within a larger society defined by criteria of class and ethnicity, and at the same time they are part of a process, an historical entity with a consistency and momentum of its own.

Although the position and status of the peasantry has varied, it has always been regarded as the lowest socio-economic class, and as a great pool of labour available to be exploited, almost at will, by people with more power.

This study has focused on only one of Peru's 6000 peasant communities over a 27-year period. We have seen that some genuine development did occur, especially between 1964 and 1979, as well as pronounced social change as the corporate community opened up to external forces. Indeed the achievements of the 1970s (such as specialisation on dairying) provided lessons that sadly were not learnt for the future. In the period of 1979–1990 following the land redistribution, the community paradoxically reverted to a classic arable–livestock basis, and although household plots increased substantially in size, the gain in income would be only short-lived.

Although there is no reason to doubt that many social processes in Chilca are widely representative of most peasant communities, we must remember its distinctive features noted at the outset. Chilca has considerable potential for development, and is on a good road only 32km from a major city. Some historical factors have also been fortunate, such as accepting Peace Corps volunteers. The many peasant communities of the Sierra differ markedly in their characteristics, and of course one cannot generalise for the whole of the Andes on the basis of one case. Yet the fact that Chilca, while achieving some development as well as modernisation, attained hard-won gains which were not all sustained in the longer term emphasises the magnitude of the challenge to development among the peasantry. When we consider the wider evidence on the Sierra as a whole, a much gloomier conclusion is reached. The general pattern indeed is one of stagnation and little economic growth; a pattern of 'modernisation without development'. The achievements of Chilca show it to be the exception that proves the rule.

A MODEL OF THE PEASANTRY

We are now in a position to sketch the outlines of a model of the peasantry for the Southern Sierra. Its mobility and partial proletarianisation are distinctive features.

The very high population pressure that had developed in the Andes by the 1950s coincided with the crisis in the *hacienda* system, when the peasantry was no longer prepared to subject itself to semi-feudal production relations.[1] At about this time the barriers that for centuries had enclosed the Highland Indian within the closed system of the corporate community began to be breached more frequently, both from without and from within. Moreover, the diminution of the land base for many peasant households forced many peasants to undertake temporary wage work outside the community more and more frequently, while richer and more literate peasants also sought employment externally.

Demographic data provide the best evidence of the response of the peasantry: as many as 649 000 rural people, mostly from the Sierra, moved to urban centres in the period 1950–60 (over 13 per cent of the entire rural population).[2] Yet over the last 30 years the Andean peasantry has been maintaining itself only at a level of simple reproduction.[3] The search for sources of income outside the village was primarily to supplement village-based forms of income, and high natural population growth was moderated by the out-migration of over 1 per cent of the increase. The surveys of Figueroa and others confirm our finding of very low averages of savings and investment,[4] indicating that the peasantry as a whole is not achieving economic growth.

Therefore, although there has been a deep cultural and commercial transformation of the peasantry over the past 30 years, it has not been accompanied by a true economic revolution. A steady incorporation of peasants into the market,[5] and a great expansion of consumption that has increasingly caused traditional regions to become the tributary areas of cities, has occurred.[6] Evidence of modernisation without development is shown in expenditure and consumption data: typical peasant families spend the bulk of their income on food, non-durables, clothing, shoes and *fiestas*[7] rather than on investment and innovation expenses.

When viewed over a time span of the last 50 years, it is clear that the Andean peasantry has experienced rapid change, considerable flux and substantial reorganisation. While the most fundamental change in this whole transition process was the opening-up of the closed Andean social system and its growing receptivity to outside influences, the two most noteworthy trends were the great increase in population movement and the proletarianisation of the peasantry. Greater exposure to the outside world and to the media, improvements in schooling, and a growth of empathy are part of a broader process of social change that underlies movement from short-term circular movements of people to longer term or permanent migration to large cities.

The proletarianisation of Indian people, like that of many other Third World societies, occurred steadily after 1948, when a process of integrating the Peruvian economy into the world market occurred on a massive scale. After this date the export-led economic model was given free rein, and foreign capital and profit repatriation occurred in a virtually unrestricted way. However, dualism continued in the economic structure with two-thirds of the population existing outside the formal modern sector, and many of the rest being economically active only in marginal enterprises. While in many cases, especially in the earlier years, migration might well have been one option among several that peasants could choose (and it could be used to defend the rural base), over a period of several decades migration became the essential mechanism that created in the long term a stable, urbanised enclave of waged labour force.[8] While the internal dynamics working within the village community may have often impelled peasants to move into the external money economy only when they had to, we would argue that this impact of modernising urban-industrial society on the peasantry has been profound, changing the whole social field and increasing the trend towards proletarianisation. By 1978, Figueroa estimated wage labour comprised 19 per cent of the total income of the communities he studied, an identical figure to that of the Pampa de Anta communities. Since the peasantry of the central and northern Andes were believed to be more salaried than that of the south, Caballero estimates the overall highland average for wage income to be between 25 and 35 per cent.[9]

It is, of course, arguable that the frequent employment of short- or medium-term seasonal migration has the effect of converting the highland peasantry into a 'proletarian' society. If one adopts a Marxian approach, distinguishing the *means of production* from the *relations of production* (which refers to the division of labour, social organisation, property and power relations), there seems to be no good reason why one cannot concur with Lewellen's (1978) analysis of Aymará peasants, who have a 'peasant-like means of production' combined with 'proletarian-like relations of production'. Clearly over time large numbers of Andean peasant households are doing precisely this: the practice of traditional agriculture on tiny plots is combined with the sale of labour for wages.

Such a theoretical inconsistency in behaviour should trouble only those minds unsullied by the unexpected findings of fieldwork. In the 1980s many societies in the world appeared to combine peasant agriculture with external wage labour, and this experience serves to remind us that 'peasants' and 'proletarians' should not be regarded as absolute types that are contradictory or even contrary: they are merely social categories useful for description. Neither should we automatically assume that a peasant–proletarian mixture is invariably a transitional phase that implies inevitable movement from one pole to the other over time.

There appear to be large numbers of people who are seeking to move out of peasantry yet are not fully accommodated in stable urban–industrial employment. It is not known to what extent much of this population is 'floating' (supported by proletarian kinsfolk) or alternating between rural and urban livelihoods. Certainly, however, in such conditions any clear trend towards proletarianisation is blurred and greatly slowed down. Indeed we would stress that the evidence suggests that the 'worker–peasant' in modern Peru may often represent not a transitional type, but an ongoing type that never does become a proletarian. The *braceros* (migrant wage labourers) of Mexico, involving at least hundreds of thousands of peasants who undertake seasonal work in the USA, are one example, and Lewellen suggests that the proletarianisation process accounts for only a small percentage of the permanent migrants who leave the *altiplano* for the coast.[10]

Millions of people have been leaving their peasant villages for a period of work (or job search) in the cities and then returning, and this has been going on now for a good many years. It is, of course, true that the implications of mobility on individual, household and community betterment have often, perhaps usually, been positive, increasing incomes, widening horizons and enabling some upward social mobility to be achieved. But it is easy, from a Western perspective, to exaggerate the developmental benefits of such a proletarianisation process. Overwhelmingly such workers are merely recirculating incomes already earned and not generating new or additional earnings for Peru. Clearly the modern urban–industrial sector can absorb only a small minority of these migrants as full-time year-round workers, and while the informal sector has an enormous capacity for 'urban involution' – to swell and to provide some opportunities of employment – it too must have a ceiling. Certainly in spite of the prolonged absence of family members, family organisation appears to have been little affected by seasonal or semi-permanent migration. However, as long as the present situation persists, whether it is transitional or not, temporary migrants will remain more reliant than ever on whatever little land is left to them in the Sierra. In that sense they will continue to be at least partial peasants.

Patterns of adaptation both to the difficult and unique Andean ecosystem and to major forms of domination, labour service and clientage to their *mestizo* masters have formed the peasantry and shaped its character. Since people in the Andes will have to continue to wrest a living from the land and contend with an unfavourable or partly hostile social world at the regional, national and international levels, the 'peasantising' process will survive, at least for some decades.

Figure 19.1 presents the factors that surround the peasantry, impinge upon it and constrain it from achieving social mobility and out-migration to a less impoverished livelihood. Most basic of all, of course, are the harsh environmental factors, both organic and inorganic, and the lack of land. The barriers of class and ethnicity have always been formidable and are constantly being spelt out in an array of institutional structures, legal arrangements, numerous patron–client forms, standardised forms of behaviour and new bureaucratic or state level initiatives

Figure 19.1 A MODEL OF THE PEASANTRY

and policies. While the articulation of the countryside to the modern urban sector may vary over time, the terms of trade are rarely static, and frequently run against peasant interests, so that peasant incomes rise more slowly than those of other Andean social classes.

Our diagram thus is a Jack-in-the-Box model of peasantry, for the most innovative and enterprising peasants can hope to improve their situation only by breaking out of the confining box of limiting circumstances. Except perhaps in rare cases of altruistic individuals who become modernistic leaders, enterprising individuals cannot hope to redeem the condition of the peasantry from within. Since the various classic processes that fortify and defend the household economy, peasant community and culture oppose innovation, capital accumulation and novel forms of enterprise, the different walls of the box and its lid remain roughly closed, hemming in the peasantry. Some individuals, however, try at times to push the walls outward and over time the box becomes rather more open (for example, Chilca in 1990), and increasing numbers of individuals aspiring to become non-peasants manage to climb out of it.

Modern capitalistic organisation is not viable in many of the more remote areas of the Andes, for after production has met the costs of subsistence and of replacing capital, insufficient product is left to provide a profit. In its absence the Andean production system survives since it guarantees subsistence. Its peculiar organisational features then determine the way in which the Andean system is incorporated into the market, and market production will always remain only supplementary to the basic priority concern of subsistence production. Since productivity in the Andes remains very low relative to other regions of Peru and other countries of the world, and its isolation makes freight rates to the market very expensive, conditions are likely to continue to make it impossible for peasants to produce competitively. Thus the Andean peasant system is likely to continue as a strategy of survival.

The size of the peasantry relative to the rest of society will, however, continue to diminish, and the area of Peru occupied by the Andean system of production will also shrink, for some scope does exist for economic growth and modernisation in well favoured valleys or communities near to major markets such as Chilca. Clearly, however, efforts at modernisation involve numerous serious risks and a series of changes that lead to greater specialisation within the community and to a decline in the capacity to accept and absorb the effects of extreme natural hazards. Although in normal years modernisation might bring much needed profits, it also connotes increasing vulnerability and marginalisation. In so far as it proceeds insidiously, on an *ad hoc* basis, it gradually destroys the advantages and rationale of the traditional productive system. Incorporation of market production into the land use system will dismember the unified and complementary social system of production and land use types (of *pampa* and marginal land, *temporal* and *puna*) and destroy its whole logic of integration. Modernisation must thus be seen as a two-edged sword.

When viewed in historical perspective, the condition of the peasantry can be seen as resulting primarily not from the actions of this marginal group itself (although that does play some part) but mostly from the relationship of the peasantry with other classes of society. Since their whole history has been one of being forced off their land and on to poor or insufficient land and being chronically unable to find adequate employment, the peasantry has clearly been subjected to a process of marginalisation.

DESTRUCTION OF THE PEASANTRY

The main forces that have undermined the peasant economy in modern times are the classic conditions identified by Marx and Lenin associated with capitalist development and the differentiation of the peasantry. We showed in Chapters 6 and 8 that pronounced differentiation of the peasantry had occurred in Chilca by 1964, and this process had widened further in 1979 and even more so by 1990. The process is most revealing with respect to monetary incomes, land and livestock owned.

We cannot, of course, generalise the results of data from one community to the whole Southern Sierra. However, some conclusions can be drawn: that it is the poor peasants who are mainly employed in the local agricultural labour market, that differences in endowment and entitlement to agricultural resources influence peasant differentiation, that access to education and training is crucial in gaining access to skilled occupations and also seems to be associated with migration opportunities, and finally that rich peasants usually have more commitments to livestock and commerce than to cropping.[11]

Peasant differentiation is thus proceeding apace and is expressed partly in the decomposition of peasantry as a class and in the emergence of a new agricultural bougeoisie of which *vecinos* like Ricardo and Honorato serve as representatives. By 1990 there was even a distinctive non-peasant character to many households in Chilca, and about 20 per cent of the population had become professionals. Officially the buying and selling of land in a community is prohibited. While this is clearly observed with outsiders, we have seen that a land market does exist and that *comuneros* are permitted (or manage) to buy the land of others. In the cases of Ricardo and Honorato, several *topos* of land have been accumulated over a period of years, and several members of this agricultural bourgeoisie are assiduous in capitalising on opportunities to purchase new lands whenever possible. In spite of these trends, it is true that no dynamic land market exists in the Andes as Lenin posited in his analysis of the development of capitalism within Russian peasant society.

The data from Chilca, supported by the findings of other studies, show that change is occurring in numerous, often insignificant but incremental ways. Change is indeed seeping into the peasant community through many cracks in the old edifice. By the 1980s we could discern that a new structure, grafted uneasily on to the old, was in the process of emerging in the village. New people, non-peasants although born to peasants in the community, are now living there, and new roles are now being played in local life.

THE WAY FORWARD

In relatively favoured Andean valleys or locations like Chilca, optimists such as Figueroa (1986) argue that the situation is not hopeless if the social forms of authentic Andean production and control are utilised to improve the use of resources. Capitalist development in the Andes is limited by two factors: the lack of private profit and *campesino* resistance. We have seen, however, that peasant resistance is mobilised most strongly in the face of expropriation of land, whether by semi-feudal *haciendas* or capitalist, state-backed co-operatives; when land is regained, as at Chilca, much of the so-called 'resistance to capitalism' ceases to exist. There is no attempt to reduce peasant links with capitalist forms, and in fact the contrary applies. Moreover, over time the increased interchange of Andean communities with the market has reduced their internal interchange between vertical zones (Bradby, 1982).

Expansion of capitalism in the Andes requires both significant depopulation of the peasant population and an increase in agricultural profitability. The former demands strong capitalist development in other fields of the economy (which appeared most unlikely in 1990) to lead to a process of accumulation, the generation of surpluses, the growth of real salaries and the further proletarianisation of the peasants. In time this process would lead to the disappearance of the peasant economy in a broadly similar way to the historical experience of the Scottish highlands. Clearly this will not happen because of the debility of Sierra capitalism: 'Campesino poverty of today is partly a reflection of this underdeveloped capitalism.'[12]

The prospects, however, of raising peasant productivity and agricultural profitability are not hopeless. In micro regions of greater technical modernisation, such as Jauja, productivity of potato growing is double that of traditional regions, while *agricultores* are often 3–5 times more productive than poor peasants in the same region.[13] Often, as in the case of potato growing, new technologies are not required, but merely the development of human capacities to adopt and adapt innovations already being diffused. The instruments of policy to increase productivity are already available, and they merely have to be ordered in priority for each micro region: a policy on prices, credit, agricultural extension, marketing the availability of modern inputs, and a programme of irrigation or drainage at the micro-regional level. They do, however, have to be applied in an integrated way. If much higher incomes can be generated, regional economic growth will occur, for (unlike the rural bourgeoisie) peasants spend a high proportion of their income on regional goods and services (Figueroa, 1981). Such a trend would counter the development of enclaves that depend mainly on external demand.

In damp, flat areas, as on the *pampa* at Chilca, it might be rewarding to experiment in raised cropping beds surrounded by drainage ditches, as in the famous Tiahuanaco raised fields on the Bolivian altiplano. The water in the ditches retains heat on cold nights and evaporation leads to a fine mist that blankets the crops on the raised beds, whereas crops on conventional fields suffer heavy losses from frost. Nitrogen-fixing algae in the ditches also produce excellent organic fertiliser for the beds (Straughan, 1991).

Figueroa argues that a massive investment programme is needed to initiate a revolution in the conditions of actual production to accompany the commercial revolution that has been operating for some decades. He suggested in 1986 that peasant working capital and capital in other forms is needed in the order of US$500 million, based on the Agrarian Bank's funding of

$500 for a hectare of potatoes and reaching a million peasants. At that time, mineral profits alone generated about $700–800 million. At the most about 3 per cent of the GDP is needed, and he believed the effect would be to double the *campesino* income.

Support for such an integrated massive investment programme in the Andes came from Kervyn, who illustrated the substantial effect of a properly supervised credit programme. On one programme a loan on half a *topo* of land sown in potatoes increased net family income by 6–20 per cent. In more traditional communities, 100 *soles* lent for the first time provoked a higher average increase: of 76 *soles* in value aggregated on prepared land.[14]

As we have argued, numerous policies could, if properly devised and implemented, ameliorate the conditions under which peasants live. At the macro level some of the draconian policies of retrenchment of the late 1970s, 1980s and 1990s have been necessary, through the removal of artificial supports and subsidies, and the elimination of distortions in an attempt to make the economy as a whole more competitive. Much more needs to be done to replace the centralist-coastal-urban development model and to evolve a truly nationalist model of development. At the national level, by November 1992, Fujimori's restored popularity after the arrest of the Sendero leaders enabled him to win easily a poll for a new democratic constitutional assembly which will sideline traditional parties. He seems to be aiming for a kind of Singaporean or South Korean political system where democracy and big business will be encouraged to work together. This may greatly assist the modern sector, but he shows little sign of appreciating the special problems of the peasantry.

Fiscal transfers of productive or welfare resources to the rural sector have been minor compared to those of the urban sector. Undoubtedly the effect of strict price controls on a basic foodstuff (such as potatoes) as well as the low priority given to rural extension services, agricultural credit and rural investment especially for the domestic market, have been severe. It is clear, then, that Peru adequately demonstrates the truth of Lipton's thesis of urban bias,[15] which makes the development process needlessly slow and unfair. Although the interests of the urban masses cannot be ignored, considerable scope exists for improvements.

Greater emphasis on 'development from below' should ensure that when urban market conditions become more effective, genuine competition between middlemen or truckers is likely to lead to less unfair pricing and greater dependability in the provision of transport and other services at reasonable rates. Healthy economic growth provides the best hope, mediated through products which, like wool, meat or *alpaca* fibre, offer peasants good prices yet provide backward and forward linkages to stimulate the growth of other industries. And organic urban growth, in which cities are closely linked to the production of their hinterlands yet at the same time provide adequate services, markets and capital investment in rural areas, is very necessary. With time, it is likely that regional and district leadership by middle-class *mestizos* will become less dominated by class interests and might become more altruistic, more enlightened and based on informed judgements. We have noted that much could be achieved through the internal reorganisation of the Peruvian dairy industry, involving a fairer relationship between small peasant producers organised through co-operatives and the large multinationals. Great scope also exists for substantial improvement in breeding, pastures, lambing rates and many other agricultural innovations. But it is clear that the benefits of nearly all such policies would be experienced by only 20–30 per cent of the peasantry: that is, only the rich and progressive groups who are already closely involved in market production. By definition the great bulk of the peasantry exists largely outside, or on the extreme margin of the market economy; hence they remain largely impervious to such modern sector, market-oriented strategies. Any 'solutions' involving these people, the core peasantry, must begin with them.

In Peru, the 'journeys towards progress' have indeed been painful, difficult and tortuous. It is clear that many more journeys still have to be made.

Notes

1 Introduction: The Problem and Method

1. A major starting point in modern anthropological research on peasant society was the debate between Robert Redfield and Oscar Lewis (1951) on the character of the Mexican peasant village of Tepoztlán.
2. *Statistical Abstracts of Latin America* (*SALA*) Vol. 24 (1986): Tables 705 and 706. Peru had the fifth highest infant mortality rate of 20 Latin American countries. This did, however, improve greatly by 1980.
3. *SALA*, Vol. 24 (1986): Table 700.
4. Ibid.: Tables 820, 825. *Economic Commission for Latin America* (*ECLA*) (1978): Tables 26–28 give very similar results. However, there has been a considerable discrepancy in the results of a number of nutritional studies in the Andes. See Picón-Reátegui (1976) and Baker and Little (1976).
5. Very few monographs on peasantry consider poverty in any depth, although almost all peasant societies are poor. This would appear to result from the fact that poverty is endemic in such a society. Moreover, as so many institutions and folk ways in peasant societies have been designed over the centuries to cope with poverty, to minimise or share its effects, it may not appear to be much of a problem. I found it to be, however, a problem of overriding importance, as it was to very many informants.
6. The term is that of Sen (1982). In general in this section I draw heavily on the ideas of Sen (1981, 1982).
7. Originally, I planned a production-consumption approach along the lines I had attempted elsewhere (see Watters 1984). However, it became clear that detailed observation and daily recording of the composition of meals would be impracticable and intrude too much on household privacy. Nonetheless the household survey on production, incomes and employment, supplemented by fragmentary consumption data, seemed to give a comprehensive data base on the village economy. Some consumption data on Andean peasants are given in Figueroa (1981).
8. Notable amongst these are W. Stein (1961), Doughty (1968), Adams (1959), Orlove (1977b), Guillet (1974), Isbell (1978), Long and Roberts (1984), the Vicos studies of Cornell University, Conlin (1976), Whyte and Alberti (1976). Last but certainly not least are studies by Peruvian scholars, especially several major studies by José Maria Caballero; Figueroa (1984) and other papers; Cotlear (1989); the excellent statistical analysis of Alvarez (1984); and the very fine study by Gonzalez de Olarte (1984).
9. Exceptions to this statement are Brush (1977a), Mitchell (1977) and Freeman (1963).
10. Some brief fieldwork was also carried out in villages of the *altiplano*, Puno Department, in 1964, 1976, 1979; the tropical rainforest or *selva* in 1964 in the Tingo Maria-Pucallpa zones; and at Qolquepata and in the Paucartambo Valley, Cuzco Department.

11. I am grateful for the comments of officers of the Ministerio de Agricultura and Servicio Forestal, as well as Peace Corps volunteers, on the characteristics of various village communities. Data on file in these offices were also used. Amongst a large literature that was consulted, special mention should be made of the classic studies *Plan Regional del Sur* (1954) and Mishkin (1946).

    In almost all chapters the main data are from Chilca, but Chapter 15 draws extensively on data from Paucartambo and Chapters 13 and 14 from Qolquepata and Paucartambo, while Chapters 12 and 16 also refer to material from Qolquepata to some extent. In each case the source of the data is specified.

2 Approaches to the Peasantry

1. Wolf (1966): 2–4.
2. Wolf (1955, 1966 and 1986).
3. Redfield (1956): 144.
4. The concept of ecotype applies to a system of energy transfers from the environment to man. It involves two sets: food transfers, and devices used to harness inorganic sources of energy to the productive process. A palaeotechnic (dawn age) ecotype depends only on animal and human power, while a neotechnic ecotype relies on energy supplied by combustible fuels and skills applied by science. See Wolf (1966): Chapter 2.
5. Foster (1965).
6. Rogers (1969).
7. Kroeber (1948): 248.
8. Shanin (1973): 2.
9. Firth (1951): 136–8.
10. For example, Orlove (1977c).
11. Kleymeyer (1973).
12. Gow (1976).
13. Shanin (1973): 2.
14. See Tullis (1970), Cotler (1967–68) and Whyte and Alberti (1976)
15. This section is based mainly on Gow (1976): Chapters 8–12. See also Custred (1973), and Flores Ochoa (1977).
16. For example, Thompson (1980): 26.
17. Redfield (1956): 140.
18. Lewis (1951).
19. However, Maltby's research, especially on Hacienda Picotani, suggests that the baseless triangle model is only plausible in predominantly arable areas where *colonos* engaged in intensive cultivation might be subordinated and atomised. In areas where pastoralism is dominant and land use is extensive, *colonos* might have much greater success in opposing the absolute power of the *hacendado*. See Maltby (1980).
20. See, for example, *American Behavioural Scientist*, VIII, 7 (March 1965).
21. Gow (1976): 28–9 discussing R. Klein.
22. Brush (1977b).
23. Erasmus (1967).
24. Wolf (1966).

3 The Setting: Nation, Ecology, Region and Community

1. Isbell (1978): 22–3.
2. Kay (1983): 186.
3. Isbell (1978): 24; population data from Lovón Zavala (1986); GDP estimate from Figueroa (1986). Gonzalez de Olarte (1986) believes the GDP figure is closer to 13 per cent.
4. Thomas and Winterhalder (1976): 31–3.
5. Wright (1963).
6. Ibid.: 68.
7. Murra (1960): 395.
8. Ibid.: 393–4.
9. Orlove (1977a): 28.
10. Orlove (1977a).
11. See Isbell (1978): 51–5 for Chuschi, Ayacucho; Bonino and Italo (1973): 76 for Qollona Wasaq, Paucartambo, Cuzco; Brush (1977a): 9–10 for Uchucmarca, Cajamarca in the northern Andes; Custred (1974): 254–6 for Alccavitoria, Chumbivilcas, Cuzco; Burchard (1974): 223 for Puquio-Pampán near Huanuco in the central Andes.

    Indigenous perceptions and classification of different elements are, of course, also very important.
12. Brush (1977a): 10–16.
13. Ibid.
14. Bonino and Italo (1973): 76–7.
15. This has been generally recognised in the municipal status of the central communities and the lower order status of annexes of the smaller peripheral communities in higher or lower zones; see, for example, Bradby (1982): 111–22.
16. Webb (1975): 82–9.
17. *Plan Regional para el Desarrollo del Sur Del Peru* (*PRDSP*), 1959, vols 1, 11, 12, 13 and 26. The region termed 'Southern Peru' in this study is different from that defined as Mancha India above. For PRDSP, the region covers the Departments of Madre de Dios, Cuzco, Puno, Moquegua, Tacna, Arequipa, Apurimac and Ayacucho.
18. Ibid.: Vol. 26: 165–7.
19. These are not extraordinarily large compared to other areas of Peru or Latin America in general. Brisseau Louiza (1975): 327.
20. 'Peru Oficina Regional de Desarrollo del Sur' (1968); Van den Berghe and Primov (1977): 26.
21. Utilising the benefits of 30 years of hindsight, Wolf (1986) has reviewed the validity of his generalisations on Latin American peasantry made in the 1950s, and especially his concept of the closed corporate peasant community (Wolf 1955, 1957).
22. Theoretically, this does not of course imply an assimilationist approach that would extinguish Quechua and Aymará cultural elements in forging some new national culture, but rather a process of integration, allowing the separate cultures to co-exist.
23. Watters (1971). I also observed open and closed corporate communities

through travelling in the tropical highlands and flanking lowlands of several countries of central and South America.

24. Watters (1967).
25. For example, Cancian's (1965) correction of the functionalist emphasis on levelling mechanisms of Nash (1966). Several authors, such as Orlove (1977b, 1977c), Bradby (1982), Dow (1977) and Sanchez (1982), have shown that forms of reciprocity, often believed to strengthen social ties between roughly equal partners, in practice often lead to gains for one side at the expense of the other.
26. Davies (1974): 155. On legal changes over time, see Isbell (1978).
27. Bradby (1982): 122.

4 Historical Evolution of the Peasantry

1. Rowe (1963) II: 329.
2. Murra (1961).
3. Bernabe Cobo's *Historia del Nuevo Mundo* (1964), Vol. 2: 120, cited by Gow (1976): 79; Murra (1967): 340–1.
4. An excellent example is provided by Spalding's historical analysis of Huarochiri; Spalding (1984).
5. Murra (1967): 339–53; Dobyns and Doughty (1976): 46–58.
6. Lockhart (1969): 11.
7. Kubler (1963): 342.
8. Gow (1976): 82–4 citing E. Torres Saldamondo, *Apuntes Historicos Sobre las Encomiendas en el Peru*, Guaman Poma, Vol. 2 (1966): 143.
9. Wachtel (1977): 98.
10. Ford (1962): 33.
11. Gow (1976): 89.
12. Kubler (1963): 370; Gow (1976): 38.
13. Wachtel (1984): 240.
14. See, for example, Chevalier (1963).
15. Keith (1971): 427. His distinction is, however, too neat. It is clear that a dual economy has continued to exist on *haciendas* in some areas to the present and some have preserved aspects of a non-monetary economy (Gow, 1976: 100).
16. Cornblit (1970): 9.
17. This term has been coined by Becker (1983) to describe a type of development not uncommon in Peruvian history.
18. Dobyns and Doughty (1976): 93.

5 Modern Peru, 1895–1968

1. The 1879–80 budget was 35.2 million pesos; in 1883 it was only 1.2 million. Palmer (1980): 36–42.
2. The outstanding study on the Peruvian economy over this period is Thorp and Bertram (1978): Chapters 1–6.
3. Ibid.: Appendix 2, Table A 2.1.
4. The *enganche* system is described by Klarén (1973): 26–30 and sources.

De Wind (1979): 155–61 describes the role of *enganche* in the development of modern mining.

5. Palmer (1980): 63; see also S. Stein (1980): Chapter 3 on urbanisation and the expansion of the masses. Bourricaud (1970), Werlich (1978), Hilliker (1971), Larson and Bergman (1969), Klarén (1973), Astiz (1969) and Pike (1967) all describe the emergence and mobilisation of the middle groups and working class.
6. Thorp and Bertram (1978): 62, Tables 4.7, 4.8 and 11.1.
7. Ibid.: 115.
8. See Davies (1974): Chapter 4, and Pike (1967): Chapter 8.
9. For example, the serious rift between Haya and José Carlos Mariátegui, the acknowledged 'father of socialism' in Peru. Earlier in the 1920s they had been firm friends.
10. A particularly bloody affair occurred in 1932, when APRA planned a popular uprising at Trujillo combined with a coup led by military officers sympathetic to APRA. The uprising misfired when military elements, appalled at APRA killings, regained control of the barracks and city. Estimates of APRA casualties range from 1000 to 5000.
11. See references in note 5.
12. Bourricaud (1970): 193–4.
13. See Collier (1976), Lobo (1982), Dietz (1969) and Lloyd (1980).
14. The best studies of the Peruvian military are by Villanueva (1972, 1973). See also Astiz (1969), Fitzgerald (1976) and Stepan (1978).
15. On the 1956 political crisis, see especially Bourricaud (1970), Cotler (1983), Astiz (1969), Hilliker (1971), Pike (1967) and Werlich (1978).
16. Roëmer (1970): 45–9.
17. Ibid.
18. Thorp and Bertram (1978): 246–7.
19. Ibid.: 267–8.
20. Pike (1967): 299.
21. Werlich (1978): 284.
22. Cotler (1983): 17; Stepan (1978): 134.
23. Dobyns and Doughty (1976): 246.
24. Thorp and Bertram (1978): 292–4.
25. González Prada (1964); see also Davies (1974): 36–43.
26. Davies (1974): 123.
27. Palmer (1980): Table 5.13 provides the breakdown of voting in all Departments in presidential elections from 1931 to 1978.
28. Dobyns and Doughty (1976): 246–7.

6 Chilca in 1964

1. A total of 52 households out of 180 in the community were studied, involving interview schedules on resources, technology and land use, production, income, investment, attitudes to leadership, innovation, migration and solving problems. The *chacras* of many households were inspected and measured and aerial photographs analysed.
2. Data are the mean of 8 years' observation for nearby Cuzco. See also Freeman (1963): 23–6.

3. Freeman (1963): 54.
4. Soil samples from the three land classes were analysed for the major nutrients by the soil laboratory at the University of Florida, Gainesville.
5. Inadequate climatic data are available for Chilca, but they are likely to be closely similar to nearby Chinchero (846m annual rainfall average for 3 years, Freeman 1963: 25–8) where Freeman calculated average monthly water balance, using the Holdridge and Thornthwaite formulas and found an average of 8.5 'effectively wet months' (when the soil contains sufficient water for normal plant growth) and 3.5 effectively dry months. The period of greatest frost incidence (July–October) is also the driest time of the year, and some drought seems to occur due to an upward movement of water through the soil as a result of surface freezing.
6. Guillet (1974): 96.
7. Fragmentary evidence in local newspapers and from conversations with people suggested that the peasant rising in Cuzco Department was massive and significant. Handelman (1975): 121, states that there were over 140 land seizures in the department. See also Craig (1969), Landsberger (1969), Cotler (1969) and Hobsbawm (1969, 1974). I was unaware of the severity (indeed, ferocity) of the measures used by the authorities to repress the peasant movements. On 4 February 1964 several *haciendas* near Sicuani were invaded by nearly 8000 peasants. Police fired on the crowd, killing 19 people (mostly women) and imprisoned some 200 village and *Sindicato* leaders on charges of subversion. See Handelman (1975): 86–123.
8. All names in this work are fictitious.
9. Martinez-Alier (1974): 133–63; Gow (1976): 138–175.
10. R. Horton (1973): 272. This concept of tradition is used in our study.
11. An integral agrarian reform is an 'agronomic' as well as an 'agrarian' reform. The latter refers merely to a redistribution of land in the interests usually of social justice. An 'agronomic' or integral reform involves the integration of the necessary inputs and services designed to improve the efficiency of the farmer.
12. These and other terms referring to migration are explained in Chapter 14.
13. Gonzalez de Olarte (1984): 21.

7 Chilca, 1964–76

1. Thorp and Bertram (1978); J.M. Caballero (1974).

8 Chilca in 1979

1. The method for arriving at these figures involved checking through the area of land owned, together with that worked by means of other forms of tenure, the yields of crops gained and proportion sold from each of the three land classes, the number of livestock owned and income received for animals sold.
2. In most of the tables the answers of only 51 respondents are used, as one man (Household 9) was clearly lying with respect to his income. This household, while not included, clearly belonged in the rich category.
3. In sociological terms, not all five categories used to class households in

1978–9 could be strictly regarded as social 'groups'. It seemed useful to include two more categories than in 1964, the 'moderately rich', and the 'very poor'.

4. See Kleymeyer (1973): 107–9; also Van den Berghe and Primov (1977): 127.
5. There is a large literature adequately documenting Quechua-*mestizo* relations in Peru. See especially Fuenzalida (1969), including papers by Enrique Mayer and Fuenzalida. Two of the most valuable studies applicable to the Cuzco region are Van den Berghe and Primov (1977) and Kleymeyer (1973). See also Nuñez del Prado (1953); Bourricaud (1970); Neira (1964) and Conlin (1976); a useful discussion is contained in Webster (1970).

9 The Unequal Exchange Model of Peasantry

1. The main sources are Anuario Estadístico del Peru (1944–45, 1948–49, 1950, 1951–52, 1955, 1966); Estadística Agraria (1963–71) and Anuario Estadístico Agropecuario (1972–6). See also Maletta (1979) for 1942–77.
2. Maletta (1979): 73–4.
3. Maletta has shown that all products (apart from broad beans) showed a negative tendency. The correlation co-efficients were between 0.50 and 0.80, which implied that a decreasing tendency 'explained' between 25 and 65 per cent variation in the figures. Maletta (1979): Table 7, and pp 77–8.
4. For example, Servicio de Investigación y Promoción Agraria. Resultados de la experimentación con fertilización en el cultivo de Papas en cuatro zonas de la sierra durante el periodo 1959–1961, MS, Lima.
5. The figures for total NPK fertiliser consumption (kg/ha) at this date were: Bolivia 1.1, Colombia 38.7, Ecuador 16.3, Peru 31.8, Venezuela 39.4, Andean Group average 27.5.
6. *Sur*, 1, 8 (Nov. 1979): 1.
7. *Sur* (1978): 1.
8. 'Creditos Agricolas: Sur Importancia', Región Sur-Oriente, *Sur*, 1, 3 (June 1978): 6–8, 28.

10 The Peruvian Revolution and its Aftermath

1. Amongst the large literature on the Peruvian Revolution, the most comprehensive are Lowenthal (1975), McClintock and Lowenthal (1983), Philip (1978), Fitzgerald (1979) and Booth and Sorj (1983). Amongst the most valuable periodicals are *Marca*, *Oiga*, *Sociedad y Politica* (left-wing opposition), *Caretas*, the regime's own *Participación*, and the English language *Latin America* weekly report. *Sur* provides useful articles on the southern Sierra.
2. Fitzgerald (1979) and (1983).
3. See Stepan (1978).
4. There is a large literature on the Peruvian agrarian reform. Amongst the best are Alberts (1983), Kay (1983) and J. M. Caballero (1974). See also Bourque and Palmer (1975), Harding (1974) and (1975), Booth and Sorj (1983), especially Havens, Lastarria-Cornhiel and Otero (1983), and Petras and Havens (1981).
5. Cited in Gall (1972): 283.

6. Alberts (1983): 52.
7. This follows the classification of Havens, Lastarria-Cornhiel and Otero (1983): 25–7.
8. J. M. Caballero, 'La Reforma Agraría y Mas Alla: Del Fracaso del Modelo Agrarío del Regimen Militar' cited by Havens, Lastarria-Cornhiel and Otero (1983): 26.
9. Stepan (1978): 305–6.
10. Diebold (1961): 22. See also Harding (1974).
11. The evidence from a variety of sources is reviewed by Alberts (1983): 72–84.
12. Matos Mar and Mejía (1982): 95.
13. Alberts (1983): Table 6.11.
14. Matos Mar and Mejía (1982): 97.
15. Watters (1979): 8.
16. This useful distinction has been made by Warriner (1964).
17. Harding (1974): 17.
18. Bourque and Palmer (1975): 191–2.
19. Fitzgerald (1979).
20. Cotler (1970–71): 106–7.
21. Fitzgerald (1979).
22. Thorp (1983): 45.
23. Thorp (1983): 45; Fitzgerald (1983): 73–4. Private investment fell from 13 per cent of GDP between 1964 and 1968 to only 9 per cent between 1974 and 1976 and 8 per cent between 1977 and 1979.
24. Thorp (1983): Tables 2.8 and 2.10.
25. Thorp and Bertram (1978).
26. Thorp (1983): Table 2.7.
27. E. J. Hobsbawm, 'Peru: the "Peculiar" Revolution', *New York Review of Books*, 16 Dec. 1971, pp. 33–4, cited in Jaquette (1975): 425–6.
28. Stepan (1978): 160–5; Collier (1976): Chapter 7; Castells (1982).
29. See, in particular, Mangin (1967). Other important early work is Matos Mar (1961). See also Nelson (1969) and Cornelius (1969). Huntington (1968) argues forcefully that the second generation of settlers became radical.
30. Stepan (1978): 161.
31. SINAMOS was intended to channel popular initiatives 'in a way which is organised and not chaotic' (an official statement cited in Palmer (1980): 113). Such an organisation became almost synonymous with the tension that was generated between control from above and participation from below. Over the next 3 years, SINAMOS tried to grapple with this tension which appeared to grow over time so that the organisation eventually had a budget of over US$100 million with over 5000 employees, 13 offices and with military officers in many top positions.
32. World Bank (1981): 34–5; Eckstein (1983).
33. Albo (1979).
34. Schydlowski and Wiecht (1983).
35. *The Economist*, 26 November 1982; Robert Graham, 'Debt, paralysis and poverty in Peru', *The Dominion*, Wellington, NZ, 2 January 1985.
36. *Latin American Weekly Report* (*LAWR*), 83, 33, 26 August 1983; *The Economist*, 26 November 1983.

37. The main sources for this section are *LAWR*, *South* (1987), Bonner (1988), *The Economist*, *North American Congress on Latin America* (*NACLA*), *NACLA's Report on the Americas* (1986).
38. *LAWR*, 86, 33, 28 August 1986; *LAWR*, 86, 39, 9 October 1986; *LAWR*, 87, 02, 15 January 1987.
39. *LAWR*, 87, 02, 15 January 1987; *The Economist*, 15 July 1986.
40. *LAWR*, 87, 02, 15 January 1987; *LAWR*, 87, 36, 17 September 1987.
41. *South Survey* (1987): 46.
42. Scheetz (1983): 175. Scheetz includes as an appendix several formerly confidential IMF memoranda on stand-by arrangements for the Peruvian Governments in 1958, 1977 and 1978.

11 Agriculture, Government Policies and Food Import Dependency

1. Alberts (1983): Table 6.5.
2. This section and the following section closely follow the analysis of Alvarez (1984).
3. It needs to be borne in mind that the progress of the agrarian reform was somewhat delayed and it was only after 1972 that some of the new enterprises were set up (see Chapter 13). However, the later expropriations and redistributions of land would make very little difference to these figures.
4. The methodological problems in compiling agricultural data over the period 1950–80 mean that, as with production, data on productivity should be assessed with caution.
5. Diebold (1961): 23.
6. J. Golte, *La Racionalidad de la Organizacion Andina* Lima: Instituto de Estudios Peruanos 1980, pp. 113–14, cited in Alvarez (1984): 81–2, 101.
7. D. E. Horton (1984): 40.
8. Alvarez (1984): 85–6.
9. Ibid.: 85
10. World Bank (1981): 53; UNCTAD (1985): paras 23–6.
11. The study of 1975 cited by Alvarez (1984): 166–8.
12. UNCTAD (1985): 13.
13. World Bank (1981).
14. Alvarez (1984): 164–9 and Table 4.2.
15. Ibid.: Table 4.1.
16. Reports of 1976 and 1979 cited by Alvarez (1984): 173.
17. UNCTAD (1985): 17.
18. Ibid.: 22–4 and sources, including M. Lajo Lazo, *El Pais de la Leche Evaporado* (Lima, 1981).

12 Innovation and Leadership

1. I follow the valuable definition of the 'moral community' made by Bailey (1971): 299–321. Bailey accepts the distinction of Durkheim between 'we', the 'moral community', and 'they', the outsiders. Since the society or community is co-extensive with moral custom, interactions between people

within this moral community continuously involve judgements of what is right and wrong.

2. The Vicos studies of Cornell University pioneered research into how innovation occurs in Peruvian highland peasant communities. See, for example, 'The Vicos Case: Peasant Society in Transition', *American Behavioural Scientist*, VIII, 7 (March 1965).
3. Watters (1967). The paper of Luis Gallegos, 'La Molina que no functiona en Pilcuyo', MS, Puno, is an excellent analysis of the social implications of technological innovations in the *altiplano*.
4. Wallman (1974).

13 Agrarian Reform in the Pampa

1. Most of the following account of the implementation of the agrarian reform is based on Guillet (1974): Chapters VI–IX.
2. Guillet (1974): 233–4.
3. Ibid.: 186.
4. Watters (1976) and (1979).
5. Guillet (1979): 193, and Watters (1979).
6. Guillet (1974): 214, Guillet (1976); see also Berg (1984).
7. This section is based on various articles in *Sur*, 1978–79, including 'Anta: llego el final?' *Sur*, November 1979 and an interview with B. Kervyn, 23 May 1979. See also Hobsbawm (1974): 127.
8. *Amauta*, October 1979.

14 Migration, Empathy and Schooling

1. See Lomnitz (1977) and Young and Young (1966).
2. The polar types of 'folk society' and modern urbanisation derive mainly in social science from the folk–urban continuum concept of Robert Redfield and others of the Chicago school. However, Redfield's model was based on ideal types rather than any specific reality. The development of proto-urban values in the village such as we describe for Chilca, the persistence of rural peasant qualities in the city, and the many divergent positions and roles arising from the many ramifying branches of social networks help to explain the adaptation of migrating 'peasants' to life in large modern cities.
3. Todaro (1980): 361–402.
4. Skeldon (1985): 100–20.
5. Lerner (1958), see especially 'The Parable of the Grocer and the Chief'. Cf. Rogers (1969) on the role of communications in social change of Colombian peasants.
6. Lerner's (1958) classic parable of the striking contrast between the shy, constricted shepherd and the upstart ambitious grocer of Balgat makes the same *encogido–entrón* distinction for the Middle East.

15 Mobilisation of the Peasantry

1. For more information see Handelman (1975), Craig (1969), Tullis (1970), Neira (1964), Huizer (1972) and Blanco (1972). Since the mid-1970s many

peasant movements have been reported in the journal *Sur*.

2. See Kleymeyer's (1973) analysis of power and dependency in the southern Sierra. On power and consent in Latin America see Adams (1967, 1970), Wachtel (1977) and Godelier (1978).
3. Reviewed by Gow (1976): Chapter VI.
4. Ibid.
5. Craig (1969): 202.
6. Gow (1976): 129.
7. Alavi (1965): 241.
8. Tullis (1970): 158–9.
9. This account is based on a translation into English from the Spanish text written rather illegibly by ballpoint pen in exercise books. Gaps are left where a word could not be deciphered. Words in brackets have been added to complete, or explain, the sense of the sentence. I am grateful to Sr Domingo Cruz for allowing me to read, translate and publish this section of his diary.
10. This is clearly a reference to *enganche*, the notorious institution of debt servitude that was widely practised in the Andes in the past.
11. This apparently refers to times within the period 1948–56 when the APRA party was repressed by the right wing government of President Odría.
12. Numerous other accounts of the occupation of the *selva* confirm these allegations of cruel treatment. See, for example, Varese (1973) and Gow (1976): 146–7.
13. Bourricaud (1970): 30.
14. Similarly many urban people who take part in illegal land invasions to establish *barriadas* (shanty towns) fly Peruvian flags in an appeal for recognition of their rights and a plea not to be evicted.
15. I have used as main sources in this account *LAWR*, Berg (1986–7), Reid (1985), Bonner (1988), McClintock (1984), *NACLA* (1986), Shakespeare (1988), Degregori (1988 and 1989), Isbell (1988), and R. Gonzalez (1986).
16. Isbell (1988): 5.
17. Reid (1985): 108.
18. 'Desarrollemos la Guerra de Guerrillas', March 1982, taken from Reid (1985): 108–9.
19. See, for example, Smith's (1968) regional economic disparities based on a set of 13 socio-economic indices.
20. Reid (1985): 109–10; Berg (1986–87): 182.
21. Berg (1986–87): 173–4.
22. Ibid.: 186–9.
23. Ibid.: 189.
24. Isbell (1988): 15–16.
25. *NACLA* (1986): 41.
26. *LAWR*, 88, 01 (7 January 1988).
27. Watters (1971): 248–50.
28. Morales (1986): 149.
29. O'Shaughnessy (1988b). See also O'Shaughnessy (1988a).
30. *LAWR*, 90, 17 (10 May 1990).
31. Morales (1986): 158–9; *The Peru Report* 4 (3 March 1990), 7B–3.
32. The cavalcade of the US Secretary of State, George Shultz, was bombed by

narcos in July 1988 during a visit to La Paz; it was clearly a warning to the USA not to interfere with this trade.

16 Agencies of Change: Dissolution of the Peasantry?

1. This section is partly based on Van den Berghe and Primov (1977).
2. Van den Berghe and Primov (1977): 19.
3. UNESCO Statistical Yearbook (1982): Table 1.3.
4. UNESCO Statistical Yearbook (1982): Table 3.2.
5. Van den Berghe and Primov (1977): 78–9.
6. See Rondinelli (1983).
7. See Armstrong and McGee (1985), and Orlove (1974).
8. Van den Berghe and Primov (1977): 114; see also Lovón Zavala (1982).
9. Brisseau Louiza (1975): 570.
10. Roberts (1976) has described this process occurring in the case of Huancayo up to 1972.
11. For example, see Armstrong and McGee (1985): Chapter 6.
12. Van den Berghe and Primov (1977): 69; Pertillo (1982): 24.
13. Thorp and Bertram (1978): 270–1; Armstrong and McGee (1985): Table 4.5.
14. Ibid.: Table 4.4.
15. Armstrong and McGee (1985): Table 4.1. Amongst a large literature on urbanisation in Peru, see Vandendries (1973) and Skeldon (1977).
16. Margolies (1978): 130.

17 Peru in 1990

1. *The Peru Report* (November 1989), 2–2.
2. Ibid. (November 1989), 1–2 and 3–1; *El Comercio*, 15 April 1990.
3. *The Peru Report* (April 1990), 1–1.
4. Marañon (1989): 96; *The Peru Report* (November 1989), 2–2.
5. Cited in a letter to *El Comercio*, 1 May 1990.
6. *The Peru Report* (November 1989), 7A-2.
7. *Sur*, XIII, 131 (20 April 1990).
8. Personal communication 8 April 1990.
9. Discussed in *The Peru Report* (March 1990), 7A-1, 7A-6.
10. *The Economist*, 10 March 1990; *Newsweek*, 23 April 1990.
11. Degregori (1989): 25–6.
12. *El Comercio*, 17 April and 24 April 1990; *La República*, 22 April 1990.
13. Vargas Llosa (1986): 191–2.
14. Ibid.: 192–4.
15. See the analysis of Santos (1979) and Armstrong and McGee (1985).
16. Eguren (1989): 12.
17. Eresue (1986).
18. Lajo Lazo (1986): Tables 3 and 4.
19. Lajo Lazo (1986): 125–7.
20. Ibid. 128–40.
21. For example, the scandal over illegal importing of rice from Ecuador, using scarce overseas funds. See *El Comercio*, 14 and 26 April 1990.

22. *The Peru Report* (November 1989), 2–1.
23. *La República*, 10 April 1990; *The Independent*, London, 9 June 1990; *Newsweek*, 23 April 1990; *The Economist*, 2 June 1990.

18 Chilca in 1990

1. Fieldwork in the Chilca and Cuzco region in late April and early May 1990 was limited to a few days. Although this area was safer than the Ayacucho region, several raids and murders of foreigners had recently been carried out by Sendero Luminoso near Cuzco.
2. See Epstein's (1968) four-phase schema of economic evolution: from initial contact, to transition to agricultural investment, an investment trial period, and finally a tertiary investment period.
3. Files held in Ministerio de Agricultura, Cuzco, 1984 and 1985.
4. Lajo Lazo (1986); Marañon (1989): 97.
5. Freeman (1963): 23. Unfortunately data are missing for 1982–4 so it cannot be determined whether there is an overall trend towards a drier climate.
6. *El Comercio*, 7 April 1990; *La República*, 10 and 24 April 1990.
7. Gonzalez de Olarte (1984): 231–2.

19 Conclusion

1. This was indicated by the rise in peasant movements in late 1950s and 1960s and the decline in the number of labour rents paid to landlords. J. M. Caballero (1984): 19.
2. Barraclough and Domicke (1970): 68.
3. Output, yields, accumulated capital and incomes have stagnated or grown by only very small amounts. J. M. Caballero (1984): 19.
4. Ibid.; Figueroa (1984): 50; Proyecto Hollandais (1978): 7.
5. Monetary income averages perhaps 60–70 per cent of total income. J. M. Caballero (1984): 20.
6. I support this argument of Armstrong and McGee (1985).
7. Figueroa (1984): 50; Proyecto Hollandais (1978): Table 33.
8. Haworth (1984): 243.
9. J. M. Caballero (1984): 20.
10. Lewellen (1978): 157–8. He also cites Stavenhagen (1975).
11. Figueroa (1984) and J. M. Caballero (1984): 23–4.
12. Figueroa (1986): 345.
13. Ibid.
14. Comments of Kervyn on Figueroa in *Estrategias para el Desarrollo de la Sierra*. See also comments in this same volume by Franco and Gonzalez de Olarte. Other valuable studies are Gonzalez de Olarte *et al.*, (1987); on rural credit, see also *Ruralter*, 4, first part (1989).
15. Lipton (1977).

Glossary

adjudicacion	distribution of land to beneficiaries
adobe	sun-dried bricks
afectación	legal expropriation of the land
agricultor	farmer
agua potable	drinking water
aguacil	constable
alcalde	mayor
aldea	hamlet
allachu	narrow-bladed hoe
alpaca	kind of llama with long woolly hair
altiplano	high plateau
ambulante	migratory street trader
anexo	hamlet
aporqué	hilling up earth around stems of growing plants
Aprista	follower of the APRA Party
arrendatario	lessee of land
arribismo	the desire to move upwards and be on the top socially
arveja	green pea
ayllu	basic social unit above household, kin-based descent group
ayni	system of reciprocal labour obligations or mutual help
ayuda	request help
barbecho	preparation of the land
barriada	suburb, or slum
bofedales	moist areas
bracero	migrant wage labourer (Mexico)
cabildo	town council
cacique	boss
callotacca	parasitic snail
campesino	peasant
cañihua	ancient grain type (*Chenopodium cañihua*)
carga	a load (varies in weight according to crop)
cargo	political and/or religious office in a community
caudillo	leader
ccompis	traditional, long-storing potato
ceja de la montaña	eyebrow/edge (of the jungle)
chacra	plot of fragmented land
chaquitaclla	foot plough
chicha	maize beer
ch'inki	plants useful for grazing that are adapted to growing in moist areas subject to frequent shallow inundation
cholo	ex-peasant, intermediate between peasant and *mestizo*

chuño	freeze-dried potato
coca	plant from which cocaine is derived
cofradía	religious brotherhood
colectivo	collective taxi
colono	resident, tenant farmer or colonist on *hacienda*
comerciante	merchant
compadre	godfather, protector, benefactor, friend
compañero	companion, comrade
composición	official process of land distribution
comprador	buyer
comunero	member of the *comunidad*, family
comunidad	subdivision, community officially recognised by state
concientización	consciousness raising
convivencia	co-existence
corana	broad-bladed hoe
cordillera	mass of high mountains
corregidor	individual appointed to direct a *corregimiento*
corregimiento	institution for administering the traditional Indian population and to direct its labour resources using individuals appointed by Crown or its viceroys
corvée	forced labour on a large scale
cosecha	harvest
costa	coast
criollo	*mestizo*
curaca	headman
derechun	a gift which is part of a contractual relationship
ejido	literally, the way out, communally owned land granted under the Mexican land reform
en compañia	share farming (providing labour in return for access to land provided by landowner)
encogido	timid and withdrawn personality
encomendero	holder of *encomienda*
encomienda	grant by Spanish Crown giving rights of tribute over Indian population but not including land title; gift
enganche	forced labour, until debt paid off
entrón	aggressive, confident and extrovert personality
escribano	clerk
estera	straw used to make squatter shacks
faena	communal work task/group
feudatario	*colono* or labour service tenant on a *hacienda*
fiesta	celebration, festival, holy day
finca	farm
fundo	rural property
gamonal	master, landlord, absentee land owner, member of the landed oligarchy who is often an accumulator of land

gente decente	decent people
gerente	administrator
gringo	foreigner
guano	natural phosphate fertiliser made of bird droppings
gusanos	worms
habas	broad beans
hacendado	estate owner
hacienda	large estate
ichu	bunch grass
icosuna	wooden mallet
illa kuro	crop disease
indigenismo	indigenous nationalism
indigenista	indigenist
jalka	*suni* or *puna*; highest production zone in Andes, a zone of natural pasture
jornal	daily labour, wage for daily labour
Junta Directiva	directing board
lampa	tilling (v.), broad-bladed hoe (n.)
lanzon	narrow-bladed hoe
latifundio	large estate
laymi	rotational land use with fallow periods
limaco	a person returning home after living in Lima for a number of years
llama	South American ruminant allied to camel, but smaller, humpless and woolly-haired
maiz amarillo	yellow corn
maizal	irrigated maize land on edge of plain, privately owned
Mancha India	literally 'Indian stain'; term used for Southern Peru departments with a large Indian majority
mantaro	modern potato suitable for marketing
marca	common territory
mashua	*Tropeolum tuberosum*, Andean food staple
mawai	early potato
mayordomo	foreman
media	middle school
mestizo	a person of mixed Spanish–Indian ancestry; in Peru refers to dominant sector of population politically and economically that identifies with national culture
minifundio	system of agriculture based on a number of tiny fragmented pieces of land involving mainly subsistence level production
minifundista	peasant

minka	reciprocal community work, involving large groups of people
misti	Quechua term for *mestizo*
mita	a turn, labour service
mitimaes	forced colonisation of conquered peoples to new areas by the Inca, colonists
montaña	forest, jungle
montaña alta	high jungle
montaña baja	low jungle
moraya	freeze-dried potato
municipio	unit of local government embracing a number of villages and perhaps one or two small towns
narco	dealer involved in drug trade
oca	*Oxalis crenata* or *tuberosa*, traditional tuber grown on high *puna*
ocupante	squatter on land, often in attempting to regain land taken, sometimes illegally, by *hacendados*
olluco	*Ullucos tuberosa*, traditional tuber grown on high *puna*
oncenio	period of 11 years
otoscuro	crop disease
pachacutic	transformational world turn
pampa	poorly drained flatlands adjoining *maizal* area, communally owned, used mostly for grazing
papa blanca	white potato
parcela	piece of land
patrón	absentee owner (*hacienda*), patron
peón	worker
pequeña propiedad	small farmer
personalismo	emphasis on the personality of the leader
personero	position in the community government
Peruanos	people from Peru, citizens
picante	chilli flavouring
politico	politician, political activist
presidente	head of community government
primariá	junior school
primariá completa	complete 6-year primary school
pueblo	town, community
pueblo joven	squatter settlement or *barriada*
puna	high altitude land (above *temporal*) in cold temperatures used mainly for natural grazing or potato growing, communally owned
qochawiña	shallow man-made depressions dug to retain water at end of wet season
quebrada	gully
Quechua	Indian language; a major Indian tribe

quechua	ecological zone, from 2400m to about 3300m in Andes, which is the main cereal producing zone
quinoa	*Chenopodium quinoa*, native Andean grain
rancha	crop disease
rancho	improvised shack or house
rastrojo	harrowing
reducción	villages where Indians were forced to resettle to facilitate their social control and manipulation, providing tribute and a permanent labour force for the Crown
regidor	alderman
repartimiento	system which forced Indians to purchase inferior goods at inflated prices from *corregidor*
riego	irrigation
ronda	defence unit
roturado	ploughing and tilling
runa	human being (term used by Indians for themselves in contrast to abused term of Indio)
selva	rain forest
selva baja	low forest
Sendero Luminoso	Shining Path (guerrilla movement)
siembre	sowing
Sierra	Andes, high areas
socio	member of a co-operative
sol	unit of Peruvian currency up until 1985 when it changed to *inti* (one thousand *soles*)
suni	see *puna*
taladro	black worm
tarwi	lupin
tecnico	technician
temple	tip, gratuity; lowest production zone (*montaña* or *yunga*)
temporal	unirrigated land, depending on rainfall
teniente-gobernador	lieutenant governor
ticpa	traditional system of potato growing in Andes, with no tillage before planting
tierra caliente	tropical lands
tinterillo	literally 'ink dipper'; forger, or self-trained legal expert who exploits the ignorance of others
tiray	sectors of land, part of *laymi* system
topo	a measurement of land in Cuzco region, 80 by 40m or about one-third of a hectare
traga	sugar cane alcohol
ujana	sickle
varayoq	political and religious official of an Indian community
vecino	literally, neighbour, a higher status, richer person, as distinct from Indian *campesino*

wakcha	orphan, poor people or unlucky people
yanacona	Indian bondsman, landless labourer
yanaconate	Indian vagrant, landless labourer
yauchiy	weeding with sickle
yerbajeros	graziers, pasturers
yucca	manioc
yunga	sub-tropics, lowest production zone
yunta	plough team

References

Abbreviations to References

ECLA	*Economic Commission for Latin America*
LAWR	*Latin American Weekly Report*
NACLA	*North American Congress on Latin America*
PRDSP	*Plan Regional para el Desarrollo del Sur del Peru*
SALA	*Statistical Abstracts of Latin America*

R. N. Adams, *A Community in the Andes: Problems and Progress in Muquiyauoyo* (Seattle: University of Washington, 1959).

——, *The Second Sowing; Power and Secondary Development in Latin America* (San Francisco: Chandler, 1967).

——, *Crucifixion by Power* (Austin and London: University of Texas, 1970).

H. Alavi, 'Peasants and Revolution', *The Socialist Register* (London: Merlin Press, 1965).

G. Alberti and E. Mayer (eds), *Reciprocidad e Intercambio en los Andes Peruanos*, Peru Problema 12 (Lima: Instituto de Estudios Peruanos, 1974).

T. Alberts, *Agrarian Reform and Rural Poverty. A Case Study of Peru* (Boulder, Colorado: Westview Press, 1983).

X. Albo, 'The Future of Oppressed Languages in the Andes', in D.L. Browman and R. A. Schwarz (eds), *Peasants, Primitives and Proletariats. The Struggle for Identity in South America* (The Hague: Mouton, 1979).

E. H. Alvarez, 'Government Policies and the Persistence of Rural Poverty in Peru, 1960–1980', PhD dissertation, New York: New School for Social Research (1984).

W. Armstrong and T. G. McGee, *Theatres of Accumulation. Studies in Asian and Latin American Urbanization* (London: Methuen, 1985).

C. A. Astiz, *Pressure Groups and Power Elites in Peruvian Politics* (Ithaca and London: Cornell University Press, 1969).

F. G. Bailey, 'The Peasant View of the Bad Life', in T. Shanin (ed.), *Peasants and Peasant Societies* (Harmondsworth: Penguin, 1971): 299–321.

P. T. Baker and M. A. Little, *Man in the Andes. A Multidisciplinary Study of High-Altitude Quechua* (Stroudsburg, Penn.: Dowden, Hutchinson & Ross, 1976).

S. L. Barraclough and A. L. Domicke, 'Agrarian Structure in Seven Latin American Countries', in R. Stavenhagen (ed.), *Agrarian Problems and Peasant Movements in Latin America* (New York: Anchor Books, Doubleday & Co., 1970).

D. G. Becker, *The New Bourgeoisie and the Limits of Dependency: Mining, Class and Power in Revolutionary Peru* (Princeton University Press, 1983).

R. Berg, 'The Effects of Return Migration on a Highland Peruvian Community', PhD Dissertation in Anthropology, University of Michigan, Ann Arbor (1984).

——, 'Sendero Luminoso and the Peasantry of Andahuaylas', *Journal of*

Inter-American Studies and World Affairs, 28, 4 (Winter 1986–7): 165–196.

I. G. Bertram, 'New Thinking on the Highland Peruvian Peasantry', *Pacific Viewpoint*, 15 (1974): 89–110.

H. Blanco, *Land or Death* (New York: Pathfinder Press, 1972).

N. J. Bonino and V. Italo, 'Verticalidad Ecologia y Estructura Subyacentes en Qollona Wasaq', Thesis, Universidad Nacional de San Antonio Abad, Cuzco (1973).

R. Bonner, 'A Reporter at Large', *The New Yorker*, 4 January 1988.

D. Booth and B. Sorj, *Military Reformism and Social Classes. The Peruvian Experience, 1968–80* (London: Macmillan, 1983).

S. C. Bourque and D. S. Palmer, 'Transforming the Rural Sector: Government Policy and Peasant Response' in A.F. Lowenthal, *The Peruvian Experiment* (Princeton University Press, 1975): Chapter 5.

F. Bourricaud, *Power and Society in Contemporary Peru* (London: Faber & Faber, 1970).

B. Bradby, 'Resistance to Capitalism in the Peruvian Andes', in D. Lehmann (ed.), *Ecology and Exchange in the Andes* (Cambridge University Press, 1982).

J. Brisseau Louiza, 'Le Cusco dans sa Region: Étude de l'Aire d'Influence d'une Ville Andine', Thesis for Doctorate of Letters, University of Bourdeaux, 2 vols (1975).

S. B. Brush, *Mountain, Field, and Family: The Economy and Human Ecology of an Andean Valley* (University of Pennsylvania Press, 1977a).

——, 'The Myth of the Idle Peasant: Employment in a Subsistence Economy', in R. Halperin and J. Dow (eds), *Peasant Livelihood. Studies in Economic Anthropology and Cultural Ecology* (New York: St Martin's Press, 1977b).

S. B. Brush, H. J. Carney and Z. Huaman, 'Dynamics of Andean Potato Agriculture', *Economic Botany*, 35, 11 (1981): 70–88.

R. E. Burchard, 'Coca y Trueque de Alimentos', in Alberti and E. Giorgio y Mayer (eds), *Reciprocidad e Intercambio en los Andes Peruanos*, Peru Problema 12 (Lima: Instituto de Estudios Peruanos, 1974).

J. M. Caballero, 'Reforma y Restructuración Agraria en el Peru', MS (Wolfson College: University of Cambridge 1974).

——, *Economía Agraria de la Sierra Peruana* (Lima: Instituto de Estudios Peruanos, 1981).

——, 'Agricultura Peruano: Economia Politica y Campesinado: Balance de la Investigación Recente y Patrón de Evolución', in J. Iquiñez, *La Cuestion Rural en el Peru* (1983): 261–332.

——, 'Agriculture and the Peasantry under Industrialization Pressures: Lessons from the Peruvian Experience', *Latin American Research Review*, XIX, 2 (1984): 3–40.

M. V. Caballero, 'La Crisis de la Empresas Asociativas en el Agro Puneño', in *Peru: el Problema Agrario en Debate SEPIA* I (Lima: Universidad National de Santeris el de Huamanga, 1986).

F. Cancian, *Economics and Prestige in a Maya Community* (Stanford, CA: Stanford University Press, 1965).

M. del Carmex Portillo, *Cusco: Porvenir de una Region Propuestos para un debate* (Cusco: Centro de Estudios Rurales Andinos, 'Bartolemé de las Casas', 1982).

M. Castells, 'Squatters and Politics in Latin America: A Comparative Analysis of Urban Social Movements in Chile, Peru and Mexico', in H. Safa (ed.), *Towards a Political Economy of Urbanization in Third World Countries* (Delhi: Oxford University Press, 1982): 250–82.

A. V. Chayanov, *The Theory of Peasant Economy*, translated by D. Thorner, R. E. F. Smith and B. Kerblay (Madison, Wis: University of Wisconsin Press, 1986; first published 1925).

F. Chevalier, *Land and Society in Colonial Mexico. The Great Hacienda* (Berkeley and Los Angeles: University of California Press, 1963).

D. Collier, *Squatters and Oligarchs: Authoritarian Rule and Policy Change in Peru* (Baltimore, MD: Johns Hopkins University Press, 1976).

S. Conlin, 'Participation versus Expertise', *International Journal of Comparative Sociology*, XV, 3–4 (1974): 151–66.

——, 'By the Sweat of their Brows. Changing and Maintaining the Structure of Domination in Andean Peru', PhD Dissertation, Anthropology (University of Sussex, Brighton, 1976).

O. Cornblit, 'Society and Mass Rebellion in Eighteenth-Century Peru and Bolivia', in R. Carr (ed.), *Latin American Affairs*, St Anthony's Papers, No. 22 (Oxford University Press, 1970).

W. Cornelius, Jr, 'Urbanization as an Agent in Latin American Political Instability: The Case of Mexico', *American Political Science Review*, 63 (September 1969): 833–857.

D. Cotlear, *Desarrollo Campesino en los Andes*. Cambio Technológico y transformación social en las comunidades de la Sierra del Peru (Lima: Instituto de Estudios Peruanos, 1989).

J. Cotler, 'The Mechanics of Internal Domination and Social Change in Peru', *Studies in Comparative International Development*, 3 (1967–68): 12.

——, 'Pautas de Cambio en la Sociedad Rural', in J. Matos Mar *et al.*, *Dominación y Cambios en el Peru Rural* (Lima: Instituto de Estudios Peruanos, 1969): 69–79.

——, 'Political Crisis and Military Populism', *Studies in Comparative International Development*, 6, 5 (Spring 1970–71): 95–113.

——, 'Democracy and National Integration in Peru', in McClintock and Lowenthal (1983).

W. W. Craig, 'Peru: The Peasant Movement of La Convención', in H. A. Landsberger (ed.), *Latin American Peasant Movements* (Ithaca and London: Cornell University Press, 1969).

G. Custred, 'Symbols and Control in a High Altitude Andean Community', PhD Dissertation, University of Indiana (1973).

——, 'Llameros y Comercio Interregional', in Alberti and Mayer (1974).

T. M. Davies, *Indian Integration in Peru* (Lincoln: University of Nebraska Press, 1974).

J. H. Davis, *Choice and Change* (London: Athlone Press, 1974).

C. I. Degregori, *Sendero Luminoso: Los Hondos y Mortales Desencaentos. II Lucha Armada y Utopia Autoritar* (Lima: Institute de Estudios Peruanos, 1988).

——, 'Que Dificil es ser Dios. Ideología y Violencia Politica en Sendero Luminoso', MS (1989).

H. de Soto *et al.*, *El Otro Sendero* (Lima: Instituto Libertad y Democracia, 1988).

J. De Wind, 'From Peasants to Miners: The Background to Strikes in the Mines of Peru', in R. Cohen, P. C. W. Gutkind and P. Baker (eds), *Peasants and*

Proletarians. The Struggles of Third World Workers (London: Hutchinson, 1979).
P. B. Diebold, 'The Prospect for Agricultural Development in Peru', FAO Report to the Government of Peru, Lima (1961).
H. Dietz, 'Urban Squatter Settlements in Peru. A Case History and Analysis', *Journal of Inter-American Affairs*, 11 (1969): 353–70.
H. E. Dobyns and P. L. Doughty, *Peru – A Cultural History* (New York: Oxford University Press, 1976).
P. L. Doughty, *Huaylas. An Andean District in Search of Progress* (Ithaca: Cornell University Press, 1968).
J. Dow, 'Religion in the Organization of a Mexican Peasant Economy', in R. Halperin and J. Dow (eds), *Peasant Livelihood* (New York: St Martin's Press, 1977): 215–26.
S. Eckstein, 'Revolution and Redistribution in Latin America', in McClintock and Lowenthal (1983): Chapter 11.
F. Eguren, 'Los Nuevos Grupos Dominantes en la Agricultura Peruana', *Debate Agrarío*, 7 (July–Dec. 1989): 11–32.
T. S. Epstein, *Capitalism, Primitive and Modern* (Canberra: Australian National University, 1968).
C. Erasmus, 'Upper Limits of Peasantry and Agrarian Reform: Bolivia, Venezuela and Mexico Compared', *Ethnology*, VI, 4 (October 1967): 349–80.
——, 'Community Development and the Encogido Syndrome', *Human Organization*, 27, 1 (Spring 1968): 65–74.
M. Eresue, 'Regresión y Subordinación de la Agricultura Andina' in *Estrategias para el Desarrollo de la Sierra* (Cuzco: Universidad Nacional Agraria 'La Molina', Centro de Estudios Rurales Andinos, 'Bartolomé de las Casas', 1986).
E. E. Evans-Pritchard, 'Some Reminiscences and Reflections on Fieldwork', *Journal of the Anthropological Society of Oxford*, 4 (1973): 1–13.
A. Figueroa, 'Agricultural Price Policy and Rural Incomes in Peru', *Quarterly Review of Economics and Business*, 21, 3 (1981).
——, *Capitalist Development and the Peasant Economy in Peru* (Cambridge University Press, 1984).
——, 'Acumulación, Control de Exedentes y Desarrollo en la Sierra del Peru', in *Estrategias para el Desarrollo de la Sierra* (Cuzco: Universidad Nacional Agraria 'La Molina', Centro de Estudios Rurales Andinos 'Bartolomé de las Casas', 1986).
R. Firth, *Elements of Social Organization* (Boston, Mass.: Beacon Press, 1951).
——, *Social Change in Tikopia* (London: Allen & Unwin, 1959).
E. V. K. Fitzgerald, *The State and Economic Development – Peru since 1968*, Occasional Paper No. 49, University of Cambridge Department of Applied Economics (Cambridge University Press, 1976).
——, *The Political Economy of Peru, 1956–78. Economic Development and the Restructuring of Capital* (Cambridge University Press, 1979).
——, 'State Capitalism in Peru', in McClintock and Lowenthal (1983): Chapter 3.
J. A. Flores Ochoa (ed.), *Pastores de Puna* (Lima: Instituto de Estudios Peruanos, 1977).
T. R. Ford, *Man and Land in Peru* (Gainesville: University of Florida Press, 1962).

G. M. Foster, 'Peasant Society and the Image of Limited Good', *American Anthropologist*, 67 (1965): 293–315.
S. H. Franklin, *The European Peasantry* (London: Methuen, 1969).
P. H. Freeman, *Some Factors Affecting Land Use in Chinchero*, Inter-American Institute of Agricultural Sciences (Costa Rica: Turrialba, 1963).
F. Fuenzalida, *La Matriz Colonial de la Comunidad de Indígenas Peruanas: Una Hipótesis de Trabajo* (Lima: Instituto de Estudios Peruanos, 1969).
N. Gall, 'The Master is Dead,' *Dissent* (1971): 281–320.
M. Godelier, 'Infrastructures, Societies and History', *New Left Review*, 112 (November–December 1978): 84–96.
P. Gondard, 'Land Use in the Andean Region of Ecuador: from Inventory to Dynamic Analysis', *Land Use Systems*. Bulletin of the Working Group on the Dynamics of Land Use Systems, International Geographical Union, No. 9 (June 1987).
R. González, 'Gonzalo's Thought, Belaúnde's Answer', Report on the Americas, García's Peru, *NACLA*, XX, 3 (June 1986), 34–6.
E. Gonzalez de Olarte, *Economía de la Comunidad Campesina Analisis Economico* (Lima: Instituto de Estudios Peruanos, 1984).
——, 'Comments on Figueroa', in *Estrategias para el Desarrollo de la Sierra*, (Cuzco: Universidad Nacional Agraria 'La Molina', Centro de Estudios Rurales Andinos, 'Bartolomé de las Casas', 1986).
——, R. Hopkins, B. Kervyn, J. Alvarado and R. Barrantes, *La Lenta Modernización de la Economia Campesina* (Lima: Instituto de Estudios Peruanos, 1987).
M. González Prada, *Horas de Lucha* (Lima: Fondo de Cultura Popular, 1964).
D. D. Gow, 'The Gods and Social Change in the High Andes', PhD Dissertation, Anthropology, University of Wisconsin, Madison (1976).
F. Guaman Poma, *El Primer Nueva Coronica y Buen Gobierno*, Lima: Editorial Cultura, 3 Vols.
J. Guillén, *La Economia Agraria del Cusco 1900–1980* (Cuzco: Universidad Nacional Agraria 'La Molino' Centro de Estudios Rurales Andinos, 'Bartolemé de las Casas', 1983).
D. Guillet, 'The Dynamics of Peasant Decision-Making: Quechua Communities and the 1969 Peruvian Agrarian Reform', PhD Dissertation, Anthropology, University of Texas, Austin (1974).
——, 'Migration, Agrarian Reform and Structural Change in Rural Peru', *Human Organization*, 35, 3 (Fall 1976): 295–302.
——, *Agrarian Reform and Peasant Economy in Southern Peru* (University of Missouri, 1979).
E. E. Hagen, *On the Theory of Social Change* (London: Tavistock, 1964).
H. Handelman, *Struggle in the Andes: Peasant Political Mobilisation in Peru* (Austin: University of Texas, 1975).
C. Harding, 'Agrarian Reform and Agrarian Struggles in Peru', Working Paper, Centre of Latin American Studies, University of Cambridge (1974).
——, 'Land Reform and Social Conflict in Peru', in A. Lowenthal (ed.), *The Peruvian Experiment* (Princeton University Press, 1975): Chapter 6.
A. E. Havens, S. Lastarria-Cornhiel and G. Otero, 'Class Struggle and the Agrarian Reform Process', in Booth and Sorj (1983): Chapter 2.
N. Haworth, 'Proletarianisation in the World Order: The Peruvian Experi-

ence', in B. Manslow and H. Finch (eds), *Proletarianisation in the Third World* (London: Croom Helm, 1984): Chapter 11.

D. C. Hazen, 'The Awakening of Puno: Government Policy and the Indian Problem in Southern Peru 1900–1955', PhD Thesis, Yale University (1974).

G. Hilliker, *The Politics of Reform in Peru* (Baltimore, MD: The Johns Hopkins Press, 1971).

E. J. Hobsbawm, 'A Case of Neo-Feudalism: La Convención, Peru', *Journal of Latin American Studies*, 1 (May 1969): 31–50.

——, 'Peasant Land Occupations', *Past and Present* 62 (February 1974): 120–152.

R. Hopkins, *Desarrollo Desigual y Crisis en la Agricultura Peruana, 1944–1969* (Lima: Instituto de Estudios Peruanos, 1981).

D. E. Horton, *Social Scientists in Agricultural Research. Lessons from the Mantaro Valley Project, Peru* (Ottawa: International Development Research Centre, 1984).

R. Horton, 'Levy-Bruhl, Durkheim and the Scientific Revolution', in R. Horton and R. Finnegan (eds), *Modes of Thought. Essays on Thinking in Western and Non-Western Societies* (London: Faber & Faber, 1973).

G. Huizer, *The Revolutionary Potential of Peasants in Latin America* (Lexington, Mass.: Lexington Books, D.C. Heath, 1972).

S. P. Huntington, *Political Order in Changing Societies* (New Haven and London: Yale University Press, 1968).

B. J. Isbell, *To Defend Ourselves. Ecology and Ritual in an Andean Village* (Austin: University of Texas, 1978).

—— 'The Emerging Patterns of Peasants' Responses to Sendero Luminoso', Paper presented to Research Conference on Patterns of Social Change in the Andes (New York: NYU and Columbia University, 1988).

J. S. Jaquette, 'Belaúnde and Velasco: On the Limits of Ideological Politics' in Lowenthal (1975): Chapter 10.

C. Kay, 'The Agrarian Reform in Peru: An Assessment', in A. K. Ghose (ed.), *Agrarian Reform in Contemporary Developing Countries* (London and Canberra: Croom Helm, 1983).

R. G. Keith, 'Encomienda, Hacienda and Corregimiento in Spanish America: A Structural Analysis', *Hispanic American Historical Review*, 51, 3 (August 1971): 431–46.

B. Kervyn, 'La Economia Campesino en el Peru. Teories y Policies', in *Sepia II, Peru: el Problema Agrario en Debate* (Lima: Universidad Nacional de Santeris el de Huamanga, 1988).

—— and E. Gonzalez, *Cambio Tecnologico en Comunidades Campesinas del Peru.* Un estudio de Caso. Proyecto PROTAAL IIB, 1 vol. (San José: Instituto Ciencias Agricolas Costa Rica, 1982).

P. F. Klarén, *Modernization, Dislocation, and Aprismo* (Austin and London: University of Texas, 1973).

C. Kleymeyer, 'Social Interaction between Quechua Campesinos and Criollos', PhD Thesis, University of Wisconsin, University Microfilms (1973).

A. L. Kroeber, *Anthropology* (New York: Harcourt Brace Jovanovich, 1948).

G. Kubler, 'The Quechua in the Colonial World', in J. H. Steward (ed.), *Handbook of South American Indians*, Vol.2, The Andean Civilisations (New York: Cooper Square, 1963).

M. Lajo Lazo, *La Reforma Agroalimentaria. Antecedentes, Estrategio y Contenido*, (Cuzco: Centro de Estudios Rurales Andinos, 'Bartolomé de Las Casas', 1986).

H. A. Landsberger, *Latin American Peasant Movements* (Ithaca and London: Cornell University Press, 1969).

M. S. Larson and A. E. Bergman, *Social Stratification in Peru*, Institute of International Studies (Berkeley: University of California, 1969).

D. Lerner, *The Passing of Traditional Society: Modernizing the Middle East* (New York: Free Press, 1958).

T. Lewellen, *Peasants in Transition. The Changing Economy of the Peruvian Aymara: A General Systems Approach* (Boulder, Colorado: Westview Press, 1978).

O. Lewis, *Life in a Mexican Village: Tepoztlán Restudied* (Urbana: University of Illinois Press, 1951).

——, 'Urbanisation without Breakdown: A Case Study', *The Scientific Monthly*, 75 (1952): 31–41.

——, *Pedro Martinez. A Mexican Peasant and his Family* (New York: Random House, 1964).

——, 'The Children of Sanchez, Pedro Martinez and La Vida', *Current Anthropology*, 8 (1967): 480–500.

M. Lipton, *Why Poor People Stay Poor: A Study of Urban Bias in World Development* (London: Temple Smith, 1977).

P. C. Lloyd, *The 'Young Towns' of Lima: Aspects of Urbanization in Peru* (New York: Cambridge University Press, 1980).

S. Lobo, *A House of My Own: Social Organization in the Squatter Settlements of Lima, Peru* (Tucson: University of Arizona Press, 1982).

J. Lockhart, 'Encomienda and Hacienda: The Evolution of the Great Estate in the Spanish Indies', *Hispanic American Historical Review*, 49, 3 (August 1969): 411–29.

L. Lomnitz, *Networks and Marginality: Life in a Mexican Shantytown* (New York: Academic Press, 1977).

N. Long and B. Roberts, *Miners, Peasants and Entrepreneurs. Regional Development in the Central Highlands of Peru* (Cambridge University Press, 1984).

G. Lovón Zavala, *Mita y Realidad de Turismo en el Cusco* (Cuzco: Centro de Estudios Rurales Andinos, 'Bartolomé de las Casas', 1982).

——, 'Dinamica interna de la Sierra', in *Estrategias para el desarrollo de la Sierra* (Cuzco: Universidad Nacional Agraria 'La Molina', Centro de Estudios Rurales Andinos, 'Bartolomé de las Casas', 1986).

A. F. Lowenthal (ed.), *The Peruvian Experiment: Continuity and Change under Military Rule* (Princeton University Press, 1975).

H. Maletta, 'Campesinado, Precio y Salario', *Apuntes*, V, 9 (1979): 532–86.

L. Maltby, 'Colonos on Hacienda Picotani', in B. S. Orlove and G. Custred (eds), *Land and Power in Latin America* (New York: Holmes & Meier, 1980): Chapter 5.

W. Mangin, 'Latin American Squatter Settlements: a Problem and a Solution', *Latin American Research Review*, 2, 3 (1967): 65–98.

B. Marañon, 'Los Subsidios en el Agro 1986–87', *Debate Agrario*, 5 (1989): 85–106.

L. Margolies, 'Rural-Urban Migration and Urbanisation in Latin America', *Current Anthropology*, 19, 1 (March 1978): 130.

——, 'Introduction: The Process of Social Urbanisation in Latin America',

Urban Anthropology, 8, 3 and 4 (Winter 1979): 213–25.

J. Martinez-Alier, *Los Huachilleros del Peru: Dos Estudios de Formaciones Sociales y Agrarias* (Lima: Instituto de Estudios Peruanos, 1973).

——, 'Peru: Letters from Shepherds' Union Bulletin', *Journal of Peasant Studies* (1974).

J. Matos Mar, 'Migration and Urbanisation – the "Barriadas" of Lima: An Example of Integration into Urban Life', in P. M. Hauser (ed.), *Urbanisation in Latin America* (Paris: UNESCO, 1961): Chapter VI.

—— and J. M. Mejía, 'Casual Work, Seasonal Migration and Agrarian Reform in Peru', in P. Peek and G. Standing (eds), *State Policies and Migration* (London: Croom Helm, 1982).

C. McClintock and A. Lowenthal (eds), *The Peruvian Experiment Reconsidered* (Princeton University Press, 1983).

——, 'Why Peasants Rebel: The Case of Peru's Sendero Luminoso', *World Politics*, 37, 1 (1984): 48–84.

B. Mishkin, 'The Contemporary Quechua', in J. H. Steward (ed.), *Handbook of South American Indians*, Vol. 2 (Washington: Smithsonian Institution, 1946): 411–70.

W. P. Mitchell, 'Irrigation Farming in the Andes: Evolutionary Implications', in R. Halperin and J. Dow (eds), *Peasant Livelihood. Studies in Economic Anthropology and Cultural Ecology* (New York: St Martin's Press, 1977).

E. Morales, 'Coca and Cocaine Economy and Social Change in the Andes of Peru', *Economic Development and Cultural Change*, 35, 1 (October 1986): 143–61.

J. Murra, 'Rite and Crop in the Inca State', in S. Diamond (ed.), *Culture in History. Essays in Honor of Paul Radin* (New York: Columbia University Press, 1960).

——, 'Social Structural and Economic Themes in Andean Ethnohistory', *Anthropological Quarterly*, 34 (1961): 47–59.

——, 'Inca Political Structure', in R. Cohen and J. Middleton (eds), *Comparative Political Systems: Studies on the Politics of Pre-Industrial Societies* (New York: Natural History Press, 1967): 339–53.

——, 'El "Control Vertical" de un Maximo de Pisos Ecologicos en la Economia de las Sociedades Andinas', Universidad Hemilio Valdizon, Huanuco, Peru (1972).

NACLA, 'Report on the Americas: García's Peru. One Last Chance', XX, 3 (June 1986): 13–47.

J. Nash, 'The Social Resources of a Latin American Peasantry', *Social and Economic Studies*, 15 (1966): 353–67.

M. Nash, *Primitive and Peasant Economic Systems* (San Francisco: Chandler, 1966).

H. Neira, *Cuzco: Tierra y Muerte* (Lima: Problemas de Hoy, 1964).

J. Nelson, *Migrants, Urban Poverty and Instability in Developing Nations*, Harvard University, Occasional Papers in International Affairs No. 22 (Cambridge, Mass., 1969).

O. Nuñez del Prado, 'Problemas Anthropologicos del Area Andina (Peru-Bolivia-Ecuador)' (Cuzco: MS, Universidad San Antonio Abad de Cuzco, 1953).

B. S. Orlove, 'Urban and Rural Artisans in Southern Peru', *International Journal of Comparative Sociology*, 15, 3–4 (1974): 193–211.

——, 'Against a Definition of Peasantries: Agrarian Production in Andean

Peru', in R. Halperin and J. Dow (eds), *Peasant Livelihood* (New York: St Martin's Press, 1977a).
——, *Alpacas, Sheep and Men. The Wool Export Economy and Regional Society in Southern Peru* (New York: Academic Press, 1977b).
——, 'Inequality Among Peasants: The Forms and Uses of Reciprocal Exchange in Andean Peru', in R. Halperin and J. Dow (eds), *Peasant Livelihood* (New York: St Martin's Press, 1977c).
H. O'Shaughnessy, 'Land Sinking Under the Cocaine Wave' and 'Drug Barons Wage a Total War', *The Observer*, London, 31 January (1988a).
——, 'The Coke Connection', *The Observer*, London, 21 February (1988b).
D. S. Palmer, *Peru: The Authoritarian Tradition* (New York: Praeger, 1980).
O. Paz, *The Labyrinth of Solitude* (New York: Grove, 1961).
F. Pease, 'The Formation of Tawantinsuyu', in G. A. Collier, R. I. Rosaldo and J. D. Wirth (eds), *The Inca and Aztec States 1400–1800. Anthropology and History* (New York: Academic Press, 1982).
J. Petras and E. A. Havens, 'Peasant Behaviour and Social Change: Cooperatives and Individual Holdings', in C. S. Russell and N. K. Nicholson (eds), *Public Choice and Rural Development* (Washington D.C.: Resources for The Future, 1981).
G. D. E. Philip, *The Rise and Fall of the Peruvian Military Radicals 1968–1976* (London: The Athlone Press for the University of London, 1978).
E. Picón-Reátegui, 'Nutrition' in Baker and Little (1976): Chapter 11.
F. B. Pike, *The Modern History of Peru* (London: Weidenfeld & Nicolson, 1967).
Proyecto Hollandais, 'Plan de Desarrollo de Antapampa: Diagnostico', MS, Cuzco (1978).
R. Redfield, *The Little Community* (University of Chicago Press, 1955).
——, *Peasant Society and Culture* (University of Chicago Press, 1956).
M. Reid, *Peru. Paths to Poverty* (London: Latin American Bureau, 1985), Special Brief.
B. Roberts, 'The Social History of a Provincial Town: Huancayo 1890–1972' in R. Miller, C. T. Smith and J. Fisher (eds), *Social and Economic Change in Modern Peru* (University of Liverpool: Centre for Latin American Studies, 1976), Monograph Series No. 6.
M. Roëmer, *Fishing for Growth, Export-led Development in Peru, 1950–1967* (Cambridge, Mass.: Harvard University Press, 1970).
E. M. Rogers, *Modernization Among Peasants. The Impact of Communication* (New York: Holt, Rinehart & Winston, 1969).
D. A. Rondinelli, *Secondary Cities in Developing Countries* (London: Sage, 1983).
J. H. Rowe, 'Inca Culture at the Time of the Spanish Conquest', in J. H. Steward (ed.), *Handbook of South American Indians*, Vol. II, The Andean Civilizations (New York: Cooper Square, 1963).
R. Sanchez, 'The Andean Economic System and Capitalism', in D. Lehmann (ed.), *Ecology and Exchange in the Andes* (Cambridge University Press, 1982): Chapter 6.
M. Santos, *The Shared Space. The Two Circuits of the Urban Economy in Underdeveloped Countries* (London: Methuen, 1979).
T. E. Schutz, 'The International Monetary Fund, its Monetarist Model, and Peruvian Debt Crisis', PhD dissertation, Austin, The University of Texas (1983).

D. M. Schydlowski and J. Wiecht, 'The Anatomy of an Economic Failure', McClintock and Lowenthal (1983): Chapter 4.

A. Sen, *Poverty and Famines. An Essay on Entitlement and Deprivation* (Oxford: Clarendon Press, 1981).

——, *Poor, Relatively Speaking*. Fifteenth Geary Lecture (Dublin: The Economic and Social Research Institute, 1982).

N. Shakespeare, 'In Pursuit of Guzmán', *Granta*, Oxford (May 1988): 151–195.

T. Shanin, 'Peasantry: Delineation of a Sociological Concept and a Field of Study', *Peasant Studies Newsletter*, 2, 1 (January 1973): 1–8.

R. Skeldon, 'The Evolution of Migration Patterns during Urbanisation in Peru', *Geographical Review*, 67, 4 (1977): 394–411.

——, 'Circulation: A Transition in Mobility in Peru', in R. Prothero, R. Mansell and M. Chapman (eds), *Circulation in Third World Countries* (London: Routledge & Kegan Paul, 1985): 100–20.

C. T. Smith, 'Problems of Regional Development in Peru', *Geography*, 53 (1968): 260–81.

K. Spalding, *Huarochiri. An Andean Society under Inca and Spanish Rule* (Stanford, CA: Stanford University Press, 1984).

R. Stavenhagen (ed.), *Agrarian Problems and Peasant Movements in Latin America* (New York: Garden City, 1970).

——, *Social Classes in Agrarian Societies* (New York: Garden City, 1975).

S. Stein, *Populism in Peru. The Emergence of the Masses and the Politics of Social Control* (Madison: University of Wisconsin Press, 1980).

W. Stein, 'The Case of the Hungry Cows', *Human Organisation*, 15, 2 (Summer: 1956): 15–21.

——, *Hualcán: Life in the Highlands of Peru* (Ithaca: Cornell University Press, 1961).

A. Stepan, *The State and Society. Peru in Comparative Perspective* (Princeton University Press, 1978).

B. Straughan, 'The Secrets of Ancient Tiwanaku are Benefiting Today's Bolivia', *Smithsonian*, 22, 11 (February 1991): 39--48.

V. Thomas and B. P. Winterhalder, 'Physical and Biotic Environment of Southern Highland Peru' in Baker and Little (1976).

D. Thompson, *Change and Tradition in Rural England* (Cambridge University Press, 1980).

R. Thorp, 'The Evolution of Peru's Economy' in McLintock and Lowenthal (1983): Chapter 2.

—— and G. Bertram, *Peru 1890–1977. Growth and Policy in an Open Economy* (New York: Columbia University Press, 1978).

M. P. Todaro, 'Urban Job Expansion, Induced Migration and Rising Unemployment: A Formulation and Simplified Empirical Test for LDCs', *Journal of Development Economics* 3 (September 1976): 211–225.

——, 'Internal Migration in Developing Countries: A Survey', in R. A. Easterlin (ed.), *Population and Economic Change in Developing Countries* (University of Chicago, 1980).

J. A. Tosi, Jr., *Zonas de Vida Natural en el Peru*. Memoria Explicativa sobre el Mapa Ecologico del Peru (San José, Costa Rica: Boletin Tecnico No. 5, Instituto Interamericano de Ciencias Agricolas, 1960).

F. L. Tullis, *Lord and Peasant in Peru. A Paradigm of Political and Social Change*

(Cambridge, Mass.: Harvard University Press, 1970).
UNCTAD, *Food Processing in Peru*, UNCTAD/TT/70, United Nations (19 July 1985).
UNESCO, *Statistical Yearbook 1982* (1983).
P. L. Van den Berghe and G. P. Primov, *Inequality in the Peruvian Andes. Class and Ethnicity in Cuzco* (Columbia: University of Missouri Press, 1977).
R. Vandendries, 'Internal Migration and Economic Development in Peru', in R. E. Scott (ed.), *Latin American Modernization Problems* (Urbana: University of Illinois Press, 1973).
S. Varese, *La Sal de los Cerros* (Lima: Retablo de Papal, 1973).
M. Vargas Llosa, *The Real Life of Alejandro Mayta* (New York: Farrar, Straus & Giroux, 1986).
——, *The Silent Revolution* (Buenos Aires, 1988).
V. Villaneuva, *Cien Años de Ejercito Peruano: Frustraciones y Cambios* (Lima: Editorial Juan Mejia Boca, 1972).
——, *El CAEM y la Revolución de la Fuerza Armada* (Lima: Instituto de Estudios Peruanos, 1973).
N. Wachtel, *Vision of the Vanquished. The Spanish Conquest of Peru through Indian Eyes 1530–1570* (Hassocks, Sussex: The Harvester Press, 1977).
——, 'The Indian and the Spanish Conquest', in *The Cambridge History of Latin America*, Vol. 1 (Cambridge: Colonial Latin America, 1984): 207–48.
S. Wallman, 'Status and the Innovator', in Davis (1974).
D. Warriner, 'Land Reform and Economic Development', in C. Eicher and L. Witt (eds), *Agriculture in Economic Development* (New York: McGraw-Hill, 1964): Chapter 13.
R. F. Watters, 'Economic Backwardness in the Venezuelan Andes', *Pacific Viewpoint*, 8, 1 (May 1967): 17–67.
——, *Shifting Cultivation in Latin America*, FAO Forestry Development Paper No. 17 (Rome: FAO, 1971).
——, Report on Visit to NZ Puno Agricultural Project, Peru, 20 April–8 May, MS, Ministry of Foreign Affairs, Wellington, NZ (1976).
——, 'Report on Peru-New Zealand Puno Pasture Project, Puno, Altiplano, Peru, 1979', MS, Ministry of Foreign Affairs, Wellington, NZ (1979): 38pp.
—— with K. Banibati, *Abemama. Atoll Economy: Social Change in Kiribati and Tuvalu, No. 5* (Canberra: Development Studies Centre, Australian National University, 1984).
R. C. Webb, 'Government Policy and the Distribution of Income in Peru 1963–1973', in Lowenthal (1975): Chapter 3.
S. S. Webster, 'The Contemporary Quechua Indigenous Culture of Highland Peru: An Annotated Bibliography -II', *Behavior Science Notes*, 3 (1970): 213–70.
D. P. Werlich, *Peru: A Short History* (Carbondale and Edwardsville: Southern Illinois University Press, 1978).
W. F. Whyte and G. Alberti, *Power, Politics and Progress. Social Change in Rural Peru* (New York: Elsevier, 1976).
E. Wolf, 'Types of Latin American Peasantry: a Preliminary Discussion', *American Anthropologist*, 57, 3 (1955) Part 1: 452–71.
——, 'Closed Corporate Communities in Mesoamerica and Java', *Southwestern Journal of Anthropology*, 13, 1 (1957): 1–18.

——, *Peasants* (Englewood Cliffs, NJ: Prentice-Hall, 1966).
——, 'The Vicissitudes of the Closed Corporate Peasant Community', *American Ethnologist*, 13, 2 (May 1986): 325–9.
World Bank, *Peru. Major Development Policy Issues and Recommendations*, Country Study (Washington, DC: The World Bank, 1981).
A. C. S. Wright, 'The Soil Process and Evolution of Agriculture in Northern Chile', *Pacific Viewpoint*, 4, 1 (March 1963): 65–74.
F. Young and R. Young, 'Individual Commitment to Industrialization in Rural Mexico', *American Journal of Sociology*, LXXI, 4 (January 1966): 373–83.

Index